McGraw-Hill Publications in Psychology
CLIFFORD T. MORGAN, *Consulting Editor*

PERSONALITY MEASUREMENT

McGraw-Hill Series in Psychology

CLIFFORD T. MORGAN, *Consulting Editor*

John F. Dashiell was Consulting Editor of this series from its inception in 1931 until January 1, 1950.

PERSONALITY
MEASUREMENT

Leonard W. Ferguson

Secretary's Office, Aetna Life Insurance
Company and Affiliated Companies

1952

McGRAW-HILL BOOK COMPANY, INC.

New York   Toronto   London

PERSONALITY MEASUREMENT

II

To

PAUL R. FARNSWORTH

ACKNOWLEDGMENTS

The preparation of this book has been made possible by the generosity and courtesy of a great many firms and individuals. As the reader proceeds through the text he will find much material on which the copyright is held by individuals other than the author, or by firms other than the McGraw-Hill Publishing Company, Inc. Therefore, the author wishes to extend, and have recorded here, his thanks and appreciation for each and everyone of the permissions which has been granted.

For material appearing in Chapter 1, the author wishes to thank Dr. Maud A. Merrill and the Houghton Mifflin Company for permission to reproduce material from *Problems of Child Delinquency;* Dr. Paul R. Farnsworth, Dr. J. L. Moreno, and *Sociometry* for permission to reproduce material from "The growth of a suicidal tendency as indicated by score changes in Bernreuter's Personality Inventory"; Dr. Lewis M. Terman for permission to reproduce material from *Psychological Factors in Marital Happiness;* Dr. Clyde Kluckhohn, Dr. Dorothea Leighton, and Harvard University Press for permission to reproduce material from *The Navaho;* Dr. Alice Marriott and The University of Oklahoma Press for permission to reproduce material from *Maria; The Potter of San Ildefonso;* Dr. Ruth C. Peterson, Dr. Louis L. Thurstone, and University of Chicago Press for permission to reproduce the items from *A Scale for the Measurement of Attitude toward War;* Dr. David M. Levy, *Psychosomatic Medicine,* and Williams and Wilkins Company for permission to reproduce material from "Psychosomatic studies of some aspects of maternal behavior"; Dr. A. Davis, Dr. R. J. Havighurst, *American Sociological Review,* and the American Sociological Association for permission to reproduce material from "Social class and color differences in child rearing"; and Dr. Clyde Kluckhohn, Dr. Henry A. Murray, and Alfred A. Knopf, Inc., for permission to reproduce material from *Personality in Nature, Society and Culture.*

For material appearing in Chapters 2 and 3, the author wishes to thank Dr. Edward K. Strong, Jr. and Stanford University Press for permission to reproduce material from *Vocational Interests of Men and Women,* and from the *Manual for Vocational Interest Blank for Women;* Dr. Marion A. Bills, *Journal of Applied Psychology,* and the American Psychological Association for permission to reproduce material from "Relation of scores in Strong's interest analysis blanks to success in selling casualty insurance";

and Dr. G. Frederick Kuder and Science Research Associates for permission to reproduce material from the *Revised Manual for the Kuder Preference Record*, and from the *Examiner Manual for the Kuder Preference Record–Personal.*

For material appearing in Chapters 4 and 5, the author wishes to thank Dr. C. K. A. Wang, *Journal of Social Psychology*, and the Journal Press for permission to reproduce material from "Suggested criteria for writing attitude statements"; Dr. Louis L. Thurstone, Dr. E. J. Chave, and University of Chicago Press for permission to reproduce material from *The Measurement of Attitude;* Marion R. Ballin, Dr. Paul R. Farnsworth, *Journal of Social Psychology*, and the Journal Press for permission to reproduce material from "A graphic rating method for determining the scale values of statements in measuring social attitudes"; Dr. Paul R. Farnsworth, *Journal of Psychology*, and the Journal Press for permission to reproduce material from "Attitude scale construction and the method of equal-appearing intervals," from "Further data on the obtaining of Thurstone scale values," and from "Shifts in the values of opinion items"; Dr. Rensis Likert, Dr. Sydney Roslow, Dr. Gardner Murphy, *Journal of Social Psychology* and the Journal Press for permission to reproduce material from "A simple and reliable method of scoring the Thurstone attitude scales"; Dr. Irving Lorge, *Journal of Social Psychology*, and the Journal Press for permission to reproduce material from, "The Thurstone attitude scales: I. Reliability and consistency of rejection and acceptance"; *Journal of Psychology* and the Journal Press for permission to reproduce material from "A revision of the primary social attitude scales"; Dr. Ida B. Kelley, Dr. H. H. Remmers and the Purdue Research Foundation for permission to reproduce the items from *Kelley's Scale to Measure Attitude toward any Institution;* Dr. H. H. Remmers and the Purdue Research foundation for permission to reproduce material from *Purdue University Studies in Higher Education XXVI, XXXI and XXXIV*; *Psychometrika* and the Psychometric Corporation for permission to reproduce material from "An appraisal of the validity of the factor loadings employed in the construction of the primary social attitude scales"; Dr. Ross Stagner, Committee on the Psychology of Peace and War of the Society for the Psychological Study of Social Issues, *Journal of Social Psychology*, and the Journal Press for permission to reproduce the items from the *SPSSI Survey on Methods of Preventing War; Journal of Social Psychology* and the Journal Press for permission to reproduce material from, "The isolation and measurement of nationalism"; the *Journal of Social Psychology* and the Journal Press for permission to reproduce material from "The sociological validity of primary social attitude scale No. 1: Religionism"; Dr. Rensis Likert. *Archives of Psychology*, and the American Psychological Association for permission to reproduce material from *A Technique for the Measurement of Attitude*; Dr. Edward A. Rundquist, Dr. Raymond F. Sletto, and University of Minnesota Press for permission to reproduce material from *Personality in the Depression*; Dr. Louis L. Guttman, Dr. C. W. Churchmann, Dr. R. L. Ackoff, Dr. M. Wax, and University of Pennsylvania Press for permission to reproduce material from *Measurement of Consumer Interest*; and *Journal of Social Psychology* and the Journal Press for permission to reproduce material from "A Study of the Likert technique of attitude scale construction."

For material appearing in Chapters 6 and 7, the author wishes to thank Dr. Robert S. Woodworth and the C. H. Stoelting Company, Inc., for permission to reproduce the items from the *Woodworth Personal Data Sheet*; Dr. Donald A. Laird, *Journal of Abnormal and Social Psychology*, and the American Psychological Association for permission to reproduce material from "Detecting abnormal behavior"; Dr. Gordon W. Allport, *Journal of Abnormal Psychology*, and the American Psychological Association for permission to reproduce material from "A test for ascendance-submission"; Dr. Gordon W. Allport, Dr. Floyd H. Allport, and Houghton Mifflin Company for permission to reproduce material from the *A-S Reaction Study*; Dr. Louis L. Thurstone, Dr. Thelma Gwinn Thurstone, and University of Chicago Press for permission to reproduce selected items from *The Personality Schedule*; Dr. Louis L. Thurstone, Dr. Thelma Gwinn Thurstone, *Journal of Social Psychology*, and the Journal Press for permission to reproduce material from "A neurotic inventory"; Dr. Carney Landis, Dr. S. E. Katz, *Journal of Applied Psychology*, and the American Psychological Association for permission to reproduce material from "The validity of certain questions which purport to measure neurotic tendencies"; Dr. Robert G. Bernreuter, *Journal of Abnormal and Social Psychology*, and the American Psychological Association for permission to reproduce material from "The measurement of self-sufficiency;" Dr. Lewis M. Terman and Dr. Catherine Cox Miles for permission to reproduce material from *Sex and Personality*; Dr. Robert G. Bernreuter and Stanford University Press for permission to reproduce the definitions of the traits measured by *The Personality Inventory*; Dr. Robert G. Bernreuter, *Journal of Social Psychology*, and the Journal Press for permission to reproduce material from "The theory and construction of the Personality Inventory"; Dr. Robert G. Bernreuter and *Personnel Journal* for permission to reproduce material from "The validity of the Personality Inventory"; Dr. Floyd L. Ruch, Dr. Quinn McNemar, and Dr. Maud A. Merrill for permission to reproduce material from *Studies in Personality*; Dr. John C. Flanagan and Stanford University Press for permission to reproduce material from *Factor Analysis in the Study of Personality*; Dr. Clifford R.

Adams, Dr. William L. Lepley, and Science Research Associates for permission to reproduce the definitions of the traits measured by the *Personal Audit*; Dr. Clifford R. Adams, *Journal of Applied Psychology*, and the American Psychological Association for permission to reproduce material from "A new measure of personality"; Dr. Clifford R. Adams, Dr. William L. Lepley, and Science Research Associates for permission to reproduce material from the *Manual of Directions for Using and Interpreting the Personal Audit*; Dr. John G. Darley, Dr. Walter J. McNamara, and the Psychological Corporation for permission to reproduce material from *Manual of Directions. Minnesota Personality Scale*; Dr. John G. Darley, *Journal of Social Psychology*, and the Journal Press for permission to reproduce material from "Changes in measured attitudes and adjustments"; Dr. John G. Darley, Dr. Water J. McNamara, *Journal of Educational Psychology*, and Warwick and York for permission to reproduce material from "Factor analysis in the establishment of new personality tests"; Dr. J. P. Guilford and the Sheridan Supply Company for permission to reproduce material from *Manual of Directions (Rev. Ed.) An Inventory of Factors STDCR*, from *Manual of Directions and Norms. The Guilford-Martin Inventory of Factors GAMIN*, and from *Manual of Directions and Norms. The Guilford-Martin Personnel Inventory*; Dr. J. P. Guilford, Dr. Ruth B. Guilford, *Journal of Abnormal and Social Psychology*, and the American Psychological Association for permission to reproduce material from "An analysis of the factors in a typical test of introversion—extroversion," from "Personality factors D, R, T, and A," and from "Personality factors N and G D"; Dr. J. P. Guilford, Dr. Ruth B. Guilford, *Journal of Psychology*, and the Journal Press for permission to reproduce material from "Personality factors S, E, and M, and their measurement"; Dr. Gordon W. Allport, Dr. P. E. Vernon, *Journal of Abnormal and Social Psychology*, and the American Psychological Association for permission to reproduce material from "A test for personal values"; Dr. Gordon W. Allport, Dr. P. E. Vernon, and Houghton Mifflin Company for permission to reproduce material from *Study of Values*; Dr. P. L. Whitely, *Journal of Abnormal and Social Psychology*, and the American Psychological Association for permission to reproduce material from "A study of the Allport-Vernon test for personal values"; Dr. Gordon W. Allport, Dr. P. E. Vernon, Dr. Gardner Lindzey, and Houghton Mifflin Company for permission to reproduce material from *Study of Values (Rev. Ed.) Manual of Directions*; Dr. Hadley Cantril, Dr. Gordon W. Allport, *Journal of Abnormal and Social Psychology*, and the American Psychological Association for permission to reproduce material from "Recent applications of the Study of Values"; *Psychological Record* and the Principia Press for permission to reproduce material from "The evaluative attitudes of Jonathan

Swift"; Dr. Lloyd G. Humphreys, Frances W. Strong, *Journal of Educational Psychology*, and Warwick and York for permission to reproduce material from "A factorial analysis of interests and values"; Dr. Elizabeth Duffy, Dr. William J. E. Crissy, *Journal of Abnormal and Social Psychology*, and the American Psychological Association for permission to reproduce material from, "Evaluative attitudes as related to vocational interests and academic achievement"; and Dr. T. R. Sarbin, Dr. Ralph R. Berdie, *Journal of Applied Psychology*, and the American Psychological Association for permission to reproduce material from the "Relation of measured interests to the Allport-Vernon Study of Values."

For material appearing in Chapters 8 and 9, the author wishes to thank Dr. Hugh M. Bell and Stanford University Press for permission to reproduce material from *The Theory and Practice of Personal Counseling;* Dr. S. R. Hathaway, *Journal of Psychology*, and the Journal Press for permission to reproduce material from "A multiphasic personality schedule. I. Construction of the Schedule," from "A multiphasic personality Schedule: II. A differential study of hypochondriasis," and from "A multiphasic personality schedule: III. The measurement of symptomatic depression"; Dr. S. R. Hathaway, *Journal of Applied Psychology*, and the American Psychological Association for permission to reproduce material from "A multiphasic personality schedule: IV. Psychasthenia," and from "The MMPI: V. Hysteria, hypomania, and psychopatic deviate"; Dr. S. R. Hathaway, the Psychological Corporation, and University of Minnesota Press for permission to reproduce material from *Manual for the Minnesota Multiphasic Personality Inventory;* Dr. S. R. Hathaway, the Psychological Corporation, and University of Minnesota Press for permission to reproduce material from *Supplementary Manual for the Minnesota Multiphasic Personality Inventory;* Dr. Ernest W. Burgess, Dr. Leonard S. Cottrell, Jr., and Prentice-Hall, Inc., for permission to reproduce material from *Predicting Success or Failure in Marriage;* Dr. Lewis M. Terman for permission to reproduce material from *Psychological Factors in Marital Happiness;* Dr. Albert K. Kurtz, Dr. Rains Wallace, Jr., and the Life Insurance Agency Management Association for permission to reproduce material from *How Well Does the Aptitude Index Work?;* and Dr. Walter C. Shipley, Dr. Clarence L. Graham, Dr. Charles W. Bray, and Princeton University Press for permission to reproduce material from *Psychology and Military Efficiency.*

For material appearing in Chapters 10 and 11, the author wishes to thank the Allison Division of General Motors, the Chase Brass & Copper Company, the Graybar Electric Company, the John Hancock Mutual Life Insurance Company, the J. L. Hudson Company, the London Life Insurance Company, the McKesson & Robbins Company, the National City

Bank and Trust Company, the Pure Oil Company, and the Union Central Life Insurance Company for permission to indicate the nature of the items included in their respective merit rating scales; Mr. William R. Crooks and the Life Office Management Association for permission to reproduce material from *Life Office Job Evaluation Plans-Progress Report;* Metropolitan Life Insurance Company for permission to reproduce material from *Agents' Experimental Performance Ratings;* Rinehart & Company for permission to reproduce material from *Assessment of Men;* Dr. Carney Landis and Paul B. Hoeber, Inc., for permission to reproduce material from *Sex in Development;* Dr. Margaret Mead for permission to reproduce material from *Cooperation and Competition among Primitive Peoples;* Dr. Edward A. Rundquist and *Personnel Psychology* for permission to reproduce material from "Forced choice—The new Army rating"; the Clerical Salary Study Committee of the Life Office Management Association and *Personnel Psychology* for permission to reproduce material from "The L.O.M.A. Merit Rating Scales"; and the Metropolitan Life Insurance Company, *Personnel,* and the American Management Association for permission to reproduce material from "The Development of a method of appraisal."

For material appearing in Chapters 12 and 13, the author wishes to thank Dr. Bruno Klopfer, Dr. D. McG. Kelley, and the World Book Company for permission to reproduce material from *Rorschach Technique;* Dr. Maud A. Merrill and Houghton Mifflin Company for permission to reproduce material from *Problems of Child Delinquency;* Dr. J. E. Bell and Longmans, Green & Co., Inc., for permission to reproduce material from *Projective Techniques;* Dr. Marguerite R. Hertz, *Journal of Applied Psychology* and the American Psychological Association for permission to reproduce material from "The reliability of the Rorschach ink-blot tests"; Dr. Ruth L. Munroe, *Applied Psychology Monographs,* and the American Psychological Association for permission to reproduce material from "Prediction of adjustment and academic performance of college students by a modification of the Rorschach method"; Dr. Gardner Murphy and Harper & Brothers for permission to reproduce material from *Personality;* Dr. H. J. Eysenck, Dr. Molly Harrower-Erickson, and Routledge and Kegan Paul, Ltd., for permission to reproduce material from *Dimensions of Personality;* Dr. Albert K. Kurtz and *Personnel Psychology* for permission to reproduce material from "A research test of the Rorschach test"; and Dr. Henry A. Murray and the Harvard University Press for permission to reproduce material from the *Thematic Apperception Test Manual.*

For material appearing in Chapters 14 and 15 the author wishes to thank Dr. Roger G. Barker, Dr. Tamara Dembo, and the *University of Iowa Studies in Child Welfare* for permission to reproduce material from *Frustration and Regression: An Experiment with Young Children;* Rinehart &

Company, Inc., for permission to reproduce material from *Assessment of Men;* Dr. H. J. Eysenck and Routledge and Kegan Paul, Ltd., for permission to reproduce material from *Dimensions of Personality;* and Dr. Roger G. Barker, Dr. L. P. Herrington, Dr. Robert R. Sears, Dr. Quinn McNemar, and Dr. Maud A. Merrill for permission to reproduce material from *Studies in Personality*.

In addition to these copyright acknowledgments the author would like to thank Dr. Paul R. Farnsworth for reading the text in its entirety, Dr. Edward K. Strong, Jr., for reading Chapters 2 and 3, and Dr. Lewis M. Terman for reading Chapters 1 to 9. The author, and the text, benefited a great deal from the suggestions which these three were kind enough to make.

My former secretary, Miss Ann M. Briggs, must be given credit for the many weary hours she spent in preparing the manuscript for the printer. Her pleasant and cheerful disposition from the beginning, to well beyond the end, of this *dreary* task made my part of the job a most enjoyable one.

And finally, but by no means least, I must acknowledge the patience and understanding on the part of my wife, Edith P. Ferguson. Her contribution was that of relieving me of many of the household responsibilities that are a husband's normal and expected lot. She complained not at all about any of those long evenings she spent alone while I was ensconced in my room writing, or was away from home altogether, poring over some dusty tome in the general reading room of the New York Public Library.

LEONARD W. FERGUSON

HARTFORD, CONN.
April, 1952

CONTENTS

CONTENTS

I

FUNDAMENTAL CONCEPTS

An abiding faith in the importance of understanding the principles which govern human behavior underlies all psychological investigation and study. The study of personality, like the study of any other psychological discipline, is pursued with the thought that it will ultimately lead to the greater understanding of the forces that control human behavior.

In this textbook we shall attempt to gain insight into the meaning of personality and to gain an appreciation of the value of personality as an explanatory principle in human behavior. We shall do this by making a detailed study of the major methods used in the measurement of personality. If we can accept Lord Kelvin's dictum: that whatever exists can be measured, and if we can find a successful "measurer" of personality, we shall then surely know what personality is.

OBJECTIVES OF PERSONALITY MEASUREMENT

There are three objectives to be gained by the measurement of personality. They are the better understanding of individual behavior, the better understanding of group behavior, and the better understanding of the interactions between individual and group behavior. Traditionally, the first of these objectives belongs to psychology, the second to sociology, and the third to that hybrid discipline, social psychology. We shall not concern ourselves with this tripartite division, however, as it adds nothing of significance for our purposes. We shall be concerned in this volume with all useful methods of personality measurement; and unless it is necessary for our better understanding of them, we shall not concern ourselves with their academic origins.

1

Individual Behavior. Our first objective is that of understanding individual behavior. By this statement we mean to imply that we should like to be able to describe, predict, and control the behavior of individuals. We should like to be able to tell what personality characteristics an individual possesses, to tell what types of behavior these personality characteristics imply, and, in part at least, to have some measure of control over the occurrence or nonoccurrence of this implied behavior.

Let us understand at once that the control of human behavior, in the sense herein intended, implies in no way the type of control involved in autocracy, despotism, or statism. It can at times mean police control but most frequently means control in the sense of our having some knowledge of possible outcomes. An example of the type of control intended can be seen in the field of astronomy. The astronomer in no way forces an eclipse to occur or prevents one from occurring. But he alters his own behavior in accord with his knowledge concerning the time and place of the event in question. In brief, the astronomer can describe an eclipse, he can understand the meaning of an eclipse, he can predict its occurrence, and he can, in the light of this knowledge, exercise a type of control that enables him to make use of such an event when it occurs.

It is in a similar sense that control should be understood in regard to human behavior. Certainly no psychologist—to the author's knowledge—wishes to emulate Hitler in controlling the actions of other individuals. The psychologist is interested, however, in control in the sense of being able to take proper action in the light of the behavior of other individuals.

Criminal Tendency. An illuminating example showing wherein knowledge of personality can be useful in describing, understanding, predicting, and controlling individual human behavior is given by Dr. Maud A. Merrill in her readable volume *Problems of Child Delinquency*. One of her case histories describes in careful detail the development of a criminal career. It is as follows:

Age 8 years, 3 months. (First contact with probation office.) Jerry and his brother, Al, broke a window and entered a store where they stole marbles. They were apprehended by the police, taken to the detention home, and locked up overnight before being returned to their home.

Age 8 years, 9 months. (First clinic contact.) Jerry and his brother got books from the public library on a library card bearing their father's name, tore identifying marks from the books and then sold them to buy candy. They were taken by the welfare officer to the probation office where they were talked to and then sent home. A plan was outlined at this time by which the boys were to be given small jobs like weeding gardens, so they could earn money for candy and amusements.

Age 9 years, 3 months. Jerry and his brother stole two bicycles from a military academy. They were turned over to the city welfare officer and no report of the theft was made to the probation office.

Age 9 years, 4 months. (First juvenile court contact, Judge A presiding.) Jerry and his brother broke into an oil station and stole four dollars from the cash register. They were certified to the juvenile court, made wards, and released to go home under a suspended threat of placement at St. G's (Catholic) boarding school.

Age 9 years, 5 months. (First twenty-four-hour school.) Jerry and another boy stole two bicycles, whereupon Jerry was placed, by the juvenile court, at St. G's parochial school. Jerry remained at St. G's ten months and then returned home.

Age 10 years, 7 months. (Training school.) Jerry again in company with his brother, Al, stole two bicycles from the same military academy which was the scene of their former exploit. Jerry was committed to W. State Training School, his brother released to go home. He remained at the institution nine months and sixteen days and returned to his own home.

Age 12 years, 6 months. (Recommitted as parole violator.) Jerry and his brother broke into a sporting goods store and stole ten dollars from the cash register. Jerry, on parole to the training school, was returned to the institution and Al was also sent to the same training school. This time Jerry remained at the institution another nine months before he was released.

Age 14 years, 8 months. Jerry and his brother broke into a store and stole candy and gum. They were certified to the juvenile court and the parole officer from W. notified, but instead of returning the boys to the institution the parole officer released them to their home.

Age 15 years, 7 months. (Again committed as parole violator.) Jerry and his brother were apprehended after stealing many valuable articles such as a camera, case of surgical instruments, etc., from parked cars. At this time, the boys confessed to burglarizing two oil stations on the two previous nights. Jerry was returned to W., Al released to his home on probation (by Judge B). This time Jerry was released from W. after nine months and then returned home.

Age 16 years, 7 months. (State Reformatory.) Jerry, unaccompanied by a companion, entered a dwelling and stole money and jewelry. He was committed by the juvenile court to the P. state reformatory where he served an eighteen-months' sentence before he was released to return to his own home.

Age 19 years, 9 months. (State prison.) Jerry stole an automobile, was charged with grand theft, tried by jury in superior court and acquitted. On his way home after the trial he stole another car. But this time he was promptly found guilty and sentenced to state's prison.

Dr. Merrill's analysis of this case makes it clear that Jerry's behavior can, in large part, be explained and understood in terms of his personality characteristics. Jerry was 8 years old when first brought to the clinic. It was immediately apparent to the counselor that his actions represented an attempt to satisfy the common childhood cravings for playthings and sweets. These needs were not satisfied at home because of the poor economic circumstances of his family. His mother being dead, he received little supervision, and an older sister, who might have given proper guidance, was too busy combining her school- and housework.

Jerry's appearance was disarming and likable. Therefore, his teachers readily excused his misdemeanors. A similar situation prevailed at home. The adult members of his family accepted his behavior, rationalized it, and were more than willing to make excuses for his conduct. Throughout his childhood, Jerry had an ability to "smile his way out of situations." As time went on, he became more and more adept in this technique. The attitudes of the adults with whom he came in contact made his actions socially acceptable.

Had there been early in Jerry's life a proper understanding of his personality and an adequate prognosis of the types of behavior into which they might later, as they did in fact, lead, it might have been possible for the training officers to have exerted a greater degree of control over Jerry's behavior. And if this had been the case, it is entirely possible that one less criminal career might now be on record.

Mental Maladjustment. A second example showing wherein greater knowledge of personality might have resulted in beneficial control is given by Farnsworth and Ferguson. They describe the case of a suicide involving marked and measurable changes in personality.

B, a college student, was, along with other members of his freshman class, asked to take the Bernreuter Personality Inventory (to be described in Chap. 7). One year later, when a sophomore, B, along with many of his sophomore classmates, took the Bernreuter test a second time and shortly thereafter committed suicide. On the first testing, when B was a freshman, he received scores commonly interpreted as indicating above-average degrees of self-sufficiency and self-confidence, an average degree of emotional stability, and a below-average degree of sociability. He was neither extrovert nor introvert, being best described as an ambivert, and was neither dominant nor submissive in face-to-face situations. He differed from the typical member of his freshman class by being somewhat more self-sufficient, more nonsocial, and in possessing more than an average degree of self-confidence.

When tested as a sophomore, B secured scores which are commonly interpreted to mean serious emotional instability, lack of self-confidence, a low degree of sociability, marked submissiveness, and decided introversion. Scores on self-sufficiency showed no change. The authors state:

> Originally, B denied . . . that he had ever crossed the street to avoid meeting some person; that he had been troubled with shyness; that he frequently felt grouchy; that he experienced many pleasant or unpleasant moods or periods of loneliness even in the company of other people; that he found it difficult to speak in public; that he lacked self-confidence; that he allowed particularly useless or bothersome thoughts to come into his mind; that his mind often wandered so badly that he lost track of what he was doing; that his feelings alternated between happiness and sadness without apparent reason; that he felt that marriage was essential to his present or future happiness; or that he was usually considered to be indifferent to the opposite sex. On the retest he admitted all of these things. Originally he professed to believe that he made new friends easily, but on the retest blank he asserted he found this difficult.

The numerical results of both the first and second testings, and the differences between them, are set forth in Table 1. The greatest

TABLE 1. *Scores Made by Student B on the Bernreuter Personality Inventory**

Bernreuter scale	Percentile ranks		
	First test	Second test	Change in rank
B1–N (neuroticism)...............	50	83	33
B2–S (self-sufficiency).............	85	87	2
B3–I (introversion)...............	43	78	35
B4–D (dominance)................	55	25	−30
F1–C (self-confidence)............	33	77	44
F2–S (sociability).................	88	98	10

* From Farnsworth, P. R., and Ferguson, L. W. The growth of a suicidal tendency as indicated by score changes in Bernreuter's Personality Inventory. *Sociometry*, 1938, **1**, 339–341.

change is in self-confidence, which changes from the 33d percentile on the first test to the 77th percentile on the second test. The next greatest change comes in the increasing degree of introversion (35 percentile points) or neuroticism (33 percentile points); and the third change, one of 30 percentile points, comes in the lower degree of dominance in face-to-face situations. These changes are decidedly atypical when viewed against the background of changes for most of B's classmates. The average intercorrelation between the scores on the first and second tests approximates .70; and only two of B's classmates, who scored as he did on the first test, exhibited similar changes. And in both of these instances, the changes that did occur were not of the same magnitude as those for B.

It appears from these data that personality changes may have played an important part in B's decision to commit suicide. Therefore, had appropriate information been in the hands of a counselor, it is possible that effective preventive steps might have been taken. In this case, there is a strong suggestion that one testing of personality may not always be sufficient for a complete understanding of individual behavior. The changes which took place in B over a year's period of time seem to constitute significant data. The authors conclude, "From these data one could not have foretold the subsequent tragedy; yet it would seem rather obvious that B needed counseling and perhaps psychiatric attention. . . . The retest procedure gives a dynamic picture which can never be attained by a single test."

Marital Happiness. A third example of the way in which knowledge gained from the measurement of personality may contribute to the understanding of individual behavior is given in Terman's study of *Psychological Factors in Marital Happiness*. One of the goals in this study was to determine the relative importance of personality, background, and sex-adjustment factors in marital happiness. Personality factors were assessed primarily by means of the Bernreuter Personality Inventory and the Strong Vocational Interest Test. Along with background and sex-adjustment factors, personality factors were found to be important determiners of marital happiness. Some of the pertinent correlations which Terman reports are presented in Table 2. In view of these correlations there need be no question that the understanding of personality can lead to the better prediction and control of the behavior to be expected in marriage.

Let us consider again what the psychologist means by the control of human behavior. It is important that we clearly understand this concept, or the example just given will have no point. Many critics of Terman's and other investigators' studies of marital happiness contend that it is foolish to think that two people in love would submit themselves to a premarital happiness test and would dissolve their intended partnership if the scores secured were not entirely satisfactory. *Granted!* But the critic who stops here has an entirely inadequate concept of our ideas concerning the control of behavior. In the instance under consideration, control is exercised in our possession of the knowledge of factors which may detract from an optimum state of marital happiness. For example, one of Dr. Terman's findings was that differences in mental ability, particularly

TABLE 2. *Marital Happiness in Relation to Personality, Background, and Sex Adjustment**

Factor	Husband	Wife
Personality..............	.47	.46
Background.............	.35	.29
Sex adjustment..........	.49	.49
Total.................	.59	.57

* From Terman, L. M. *Psychological Factors in Marital Happiness*. New York: McGraw-Hill Book Company, Inc., 1938.

when the wife was the superior partner, frequently proved a handicap in the achievement of an optimum degree of marital happiness. Now if both partners can be made aware of this possibility, this factor can be controlled. The partners can take steps, not to remove the mental inequality, but to see that this factor does not prevent their achieving marital happiness. Briefly, the mentally superior partner will have to give up any expectation of equal participation by the inferior spouse in many intellectual pursuits. Likewise, the mentally inferior partner will have to give up any expectation of attempting to be an equal of the superior spouse in many intellectual pursuits. Knowledge of the inequality and of the fact that it sometimes creates trouble provides the basis for making suitable adjustments therefor.

It is sometimes the case that religious differences make for unhappiness in marriage. This does not mean that two individuals of differing religious faiths should not marry each other. But it does mean that they should be aware of the possible effects of such differences in their religious views, so that effective countermeasures can be taken. Just as the astronomer does, *we can adjust ourselves and our behavior to anticipated outcomes* and can exert control in making suitable adaptations to the phenomena or behavior in question.

Vocational Success. Our fourth and last example showing that knowledge of personality is an important factor in the better understanding of individual behavior lies in the field of vocational selection. It has for many years been suspected, and for a smaller number of years been definitely established, that personality factors loom large in the success of life insurance salesmen. Drs. Albert K. Kurtz and Arthur W. Kornhauser, among others, have shown, through the validation of a test known as the Aptitude Index, that a knowledge of the personality of a prospective life insurance salesman enables an employer to make a reasonably accurate estimate of an applicant's chances for success in the life insurance business. By and large, applicants who secure above-average scores on the Aptitude Index tend to produce an above-average volume of business. And applicants who secure below-average scores on the Aptitude Index tend to produce a below-average volume of business. One set of data illustrating this point is given in Table 3.

TABLE 3. *Aptitude Index Scores and Volume of Life Insurance Sold*

Score on Test	Average Yearly Sales
Above average	$69,000
Average	53,000
Below average	42,000

These data indicate that a proper understanding of personality, as measured by the Aptitude Index, can lead to an effective degree of control in the selection of applicants for employment in the life insurance business. Similar examples in other lines of business might also be given, but they would be largely repetitious and would not contribute further to our discussion.

We have described four ways in which an understanding of personality can lead to the more accurate description and prediction and to the more effective control of individual human behavior. These are in the early diagnosis of incipient criminal tendency, in the detection and prevention of serious mental maladjustment, in the discovery of factors related to marital happiness, and in the prediction of vocational success. In each of these areas, and in many others that we have not listed, the psychologist is interested in making accurate predictions of certain future events. In this endeavor he finds that an understanding of personality can be of material aid.

Group Behavior. Our second objective is to describe, understand, predict, and control the behavior of groups of individuals. We should like to know the predominant personality characteristics of the Chinese, the Russians, the African Hottentot, the lower class, the college graduate, the adolescent in our society, the adolescent in other societies, the parent, the child, the employer, the employee, and so on. We should like to be able to say what types of group behavior and attitudes these predominating personality characteristics imply. And we should like to be able to exert some control, as we have twice defined it, over anticipated behavioral outcomes.

There are to be found many examples of attempts to influence the behavior of groups of individuals. Not all these attempts have been based upon adequate knowledge of the personality characteristics involved, however, and were destined, therefore, for failure.

Historically, we could cite numerous instances of one nationality group trying to influence other nationality groups, frequently with disastrous results, World War II and its aftermath being our most recent example. Various church groups have sent missionaries throughout the world to convert the heathen. One of the most interesting recent accounts of such a venture is that given by E. Lucas Bridges in his volume *Uttermost Part of the Earth*. In this informative volume, Bridges describes how his father, William Bridges, an Englishman, set out to convert the Indians of Tierra del Fuego: the Ona, Aush, Yahgans, etc., to many of the ways of European civilization.

Destruction of Morale. While a detailed examination of any one or more of the foregoing attempts to exert influence would prove highly interesting, it will prove more profitable for us to examine an attempt that was based upon a more adequate knowledge of the psychological factors involved. During World War II there was set up in the Office of War Information a Foreign Morale Analysis Division. One of the major duties of this Division was to make an analysis of the status of Japanese morale, both military and civilian, and to suggest ways in which this morale could be affected—adversely for the Japanese, favorably for the Allies. The manner in which this work was conducted and a brief account of the results are given by Leighton in his book *Human Relations in a Changing World*.

When the Foreign Morale Analysis Division first tackled the problem which Leighton describes, Japanese military morale was exceedingly high, and there was no outward reason to believe that civilian morale was not equal thereto. Allied policymakers wished information which would show them why this morale had such strength, whether it had flaws, what changes (if any) could be expected, and what could be done to influence it in a direction favorable to the Allied cause.

To seek the answers to these questions the Foreign Morale Analysis Division developed a systematic method of examining and classifying all available intelligence data. Primary sources available for examination were captured diaries, letters and official documents, reports from neutral observers, Japanese newspapers and periodicals, radio broadcasts, and prisoner-of-war interrogation reports. Data from these sources were subjected to continuous analysis in accord with a specific and predetermined frame of reference. This frame of reference was designed to make possible the integration of the data received, so that they could be made useful as a basis for the formulation of methods which the Allies might employ to damage or to affect adversely Japanese civilian and military morale.

The frame of reference within, and according to, which the Foreign Morale Analysis Division proceeded to make its analyses is set forth by Leighton in a series of 14 theoretical conceptions. In these conceptions an attempt was made to set up a series of assumptions of universal validity, that is, a set of assumptions that would possess validity regardless of the particular group of individuals whose behavior was to be studied or influenced.

The procedure followed by the Foreign Morale Analysis Division was to gather information from the sources cited; to analyze these data in the light of their relevance, according to the basic assumptions; to prepare reports showing how the analyzed information suggested particular courses of action; and to show in what ways these courses of action would lower Japanese morale. Subsequently the Division made several follow-up studies to see if the desired results had been achieved. In this way, it was possible to evaluate the correctness of some of the original analyses and the wisdom of following the particular courses of action which had been suggested.

Enhancement of Morale. A long-range project having as its goal the enhancement of morale and the preservation of a group of individuals, rather than their destruction and disintegration, is to be found in the work of the U.S. Office of Indian Affairs. The administration of this bureau has not always been lily-white, but in its more recent years it has made serious and conscientious attempts to influence to their own advantage such Indian groups as the Navaho, the Hopi, the Aleuts, and the Eskimo. Without destroying the long-standing values in the cultures concerned, the Office of Indian Affairs is making serious effort to see that these and other Indian groups adapt themselves to such modes of the white man's way of living as will ensure their economic and cultural survival. This requires real, earnest, and thorough knowledge of many characteristics—including personality characteristics—of the Indian groups concerned.

We may cite as an outstanding example, in this connection, the work described by Kluckhohn and Leighton in their volumes *Children of the People* and *The Navaho*. The former treats primarily of the individual and of the formation of his personality, while the latter is devoted chiefly to the situational and cultural aspects of Navaho life. In these volumes, Kluckhohn and Leighton sought "to investigate, analyze, and compare the development of personality in five Indian tribes in the context of their total environment—sociocultural, geographical, and historical—for implications in regard to Indian Service Administration." Kluckhohn and Leighton observe:

The Navaho way of life may be learned only by knowing individual Navahos; conversely, Navaho personality may be fully understood only insofar as it is seen in relation to this lifeway and to the other factors in the environment in the widest sense. Understanding of Navaho culture is dependent upon acquaintance with personal figures, but equally these personal figures get their definition and organization as individuals when the student is in a position to contrast each one with the generalized background provided by the culture of The People.

We cannot review here all of the significant problems discussed by Kluckhohn and Leighton. They cover much of Navaho history, analyze their language structure, review their relations with the white man, discuss economic factors in their gaining a livelihood, discuss their personal and social habits, and finally suggest a line of conduct for the Office of Indian Affairs. For our purposes it will be sufficient if we take note of a comparison of the marriage patterns of the white person and the Navaho. The contrast in these two patterns will point up the difficult problem facing any white man who, with his background, sets out to understand the attitudes and behavior of the Navaho. Kluckhohn and Leighton state:

1. For whites, marriage is an arrangement, economic and otherwise, between two individuals. The two spouses and the children, if any, are the ones primarily involved in any question of inheritance.

For the Navaho, marriage is an arrangement between two families much more than it is between two individuals.

2. For whites, a man's recognized children, legitimate or illegitimate, have a claim upon his property.

For the Navaho, sexual rights are property rights. Therefore, if a man has children from a woman without undertaking during his lifetime the economic responsibilities which are normally a part of Navaho marrige, the children—however much he admitted to biological fatherhood—were not really his: "He just stole them."

3. For whites, inheritance is normally from the father or from both sides of the family.

For the Navaho, inheritance is normally from the mother, the mother's brother, or other relatives of the mother; from the father's side of the family little or nothing has traditionally been expected.

4. For whites, as long as a wife or children survive, no other relatives are concerned in the inheritance, unless there was a will to that effect.

For the Navaho, while children today, in most areas, expect to inherit something from their father, they do not expect to receive his whole estate or to divide it with their mother only. Sons and daughters have different expectations.

5. For whites, all types of property are inherited in roughly the same way.

For the Navaho, different rules apply to different types of property. Range land is hardly heritable property at all; farm land normally stays with the family which has been cultivating it; livestock usually goes back, for the most part, to the father's sisters and maternal nephews; jewelry and other personal property tend to be divided among the children and other relatives; ceremonial equipment may go to a son who is a practitioner or to a clansman of the deceased.

In these two patterns we see five important ways in which Navahos and whites differ from each other, and this in only one segment of the entire cultural complexes of the two peoples. Certainly we need not emphasize the obvious point that the understanding of Navaho personality is essential to the adequate description, perdiction, and control of Navaho behavior.

Individual and Group Interaction. Our third objective in wanting to measure or evaluate personality is our wish to be able to describe, understand, predict, and control the interactions between individual behavior and group behavior. How does the behavior of an individual affect that of the group? And how does group behavior affect that of the individual?

Effect of Group on Individual. Data illustrating the effect of the group upon individual behavior are provided by Kinsey, Pomeroy, and Martin in their much publicized volume *Sexual Behavior in the Human Male.* Kinsey, Pomeroy, and Martin show, among other things, that contact with animals as a male sexual outlet varies in frequency according to educational level. In a group of boys with rural backgrounds, Kinsey, Pomeroy, and Martin found those reporting the greatest frequency of contact with animals were boys who had completed 13 or more grades of school. The group reporting the next most frequent contact with animals were boys who had completed from 9 to 12 grades, and the group reporting the least frequent contact with animals were boys who had completed 8 grades of school or less. The striking feature in this trend is that it becomes apparent, prior to the time it would be supposed, that much conscious thought could have been given to the amount of schooling to be obtained. There must be at work here some differential selective factor that tends to segregate as one group both boys who will obtain the greatest amount of schooling and boys who will also have the greatest frequency of contact with animals. It does not appear unreasonable to assume that this subtle influence stems from the characteristics of the group in which the individual maintains, or attempts to maintain, his chief childhood status.

Effect of Individual on Group. Examples showing the influence of the personality of one individual upon the characteristics of a group are far less numerous than those showing the effect of a group upon an individual. When they do occur, they are apt to be more striking, however, as indeed they must be in order to receive any notice. One of the most unfortunate examples of recent date is to be found in the person of Adolf Hitler and in his influence upon several generations of German youth. A much more pleasant example may be found in Maria, the famous potter of San Ildefonso. Almost singlehandedly, Maria changed for the better a very large segment of the cultural complex of her now famous Pueblo.

Before we can describe how Maria exerted her influence, we must understand, as narrated by many authors, that the early Pueblo Indians in the American Southwest earned their livelihood primarily in an agricultural rather than in a hunting economy. Such an economy provides, as we well know, certain off seasons of leisure time. The Pueblo Indians made use of this leisure time to develop a highly complex and most interesting civilization. If we can take note of just one aspect of this civilization—the art of pottery making—and briefly sketch its history, we will have the background for Marriott's account of the story of Maria.

Archeologists, in general, divide the cultural history of the Pueblos into seven great periods. The first of these is considered to extend from A.D. 100 to 500, the second from 500 to 700, the third from 700 to 900, the fourth from 900 to 1050, the fifth from 1050 to 1300, the sixth from 1300 to 1700, and the seventh from 1700 to the present. In the very first of these periods, the Basket Maker period, pottery making was unknown. In the second period, the Pueblos invented or were told how to make very simple unfired pottery. From this simple beginning, through each succeeding period up to the fifth (the Classic period) the Pueblos increased both their technical and artistic skill in the art of pottery making. After this there began a decline, first in the loss of artistic skill and later in the loss of technical skill as well. When the Spaniards, under Coronado, invaded the Southwest in 1540, they initiated so many changes in Pueblo culture that ultimately the art of pottery making was lost completely.

San Ildefonso, the particular village with which we are concerned, was founded, according to Martin, Quimby and Collier (see their book *Indians before Columbus*), about 1700, at the beginning of the period known as Pueblo V, the period of domination by Europeans. By 1915 San Ildefonso, because of Spanish, Mexican, and American domination, was an impoverished group with little reason for optimism regarding its future. Then Maria, by rediscovering the ancient art of pottery making and by her skill therein, was able to bring about a revivalistic movement of such proportions as to play an economically important part in the life of her people.

Maria was born in 1881, or thereabouts, and when 14 or 15 years of age, she began to take a serious interest in pottery making. Receiving encouragement from a group of archaeologists and help from her artistically capable husband, Maria was able to master the old craft of pottery making. Finding her pottery salable on the white market, she was able to find a solution to her own economic problems and then finally to those of her entire village.

For some years prior to the advent of Maria's pottery making, the population of the San Ildefonso Pueblo had declined from approximately 150 to about 80. When Maria found the way out, the population began to increase and now numbers, according to Marriott, more than 200.

Maria, a single person, and a woman of character, it might be added, had a marked and clear-cut effect upon, and changed by a considerable extent, the culture of her Pueblo village. She saved herself, her family, and undoubtedly her entire people from a short road to oblivion. To understand and appreciate fully the part that Maria's personality played in this transformation of a cultural complex one must read in full Alice Marriott's account of *Maria, the Potter of San Ildefonso*. This book is a must for anyone interested in the effects which the personality of one individual can have upon the characteristics and way of life of a cultural group.

ASSUMED NATURE OF PERSONALITY ORGANIZATION

There have been many discussions designed to settle an old argument as to whether personality traits are general or specific in nature. At one extreme we have Hartshorne and May, with their pioneering studies in character, arguing that most personality traits are specific to the stimulating situation. At the other extreme we have Gordon W. Allport arguing that in spite of great evidence of apparent specificity, there is an underlying generality in at least a great many personality traits.

In personality research, just as in all other research, our conclusions are inextricably interwoven with the methods of study we employ. Consciously or unconsciously one research worker will find generality and another will find specificity, because of the research technique each has used. Let us carefully examine this specificity-generality continuum and see if we can get a clear view of some of the difficulties that seem to be involved.

We may as well anticipate our results and state at the outset that the generality or specificity of a personality trait depends almost entirely upon the definition which the research worker formulates and very little upon the data which he collects. To illustrate let us briefly review one of the techniques used in measuring attitudes: the equal-appearing-interval method developed by Thurstone. In this technique the principal measuring rod (as we shall explain in Chap. 4) consists of a series of simple declaratory statements. Each of these statements is taken to be indicative of some specified degree of favorableness or unfavorableness in attitude toward some designated object. An example of such a scale is given in Table 4. On this scale, a

TABLE 4. *Statements in Form A of the Peterson-Thurstone Scale for the Measurement of Attitude toward War**

1. Under some conditions, war is necessary to maintain justice.
2. The benefits of war rarely pay for its losses even for the victor.
3. War brings out the best qualities in men.
4. There is no conceivable justification for war.
5. War has some benefits; but it's a big price to pay for them.
6. War is often the only means of preserving national honor.
7. War is a ghastly mess.
8. I never think about war and it doesn't interest me.
9. War is a futile struggle resulting in self-destruction.
10. The desirable results of war have not received the attention they deserve.
11. Pacifists have the right attitude, but some pacifists go too far.
12. The evils of war are greater than any possible benefits.
13. Although war is terrible it has some value.
14. International disputes should be settled without war.
15. War is glorious.
16. Defensive war is justified but other wars are not.
17. War breeds disrespect for human life.
18. There can be no progress without war.
19. It is good judgment to sacrifice certain rights in order to prevent war.
20. War is the only way to right tremendous wrongs.

*From Peterson, R. C. *A Scale for the Measurement of Attitude toward War*. Chicago: University of Chicago Press, 1930.

person's attitude toward war is indicated by a summation of numerical values associated with his answers to the statements with which he indicates some degree of agreement. Now how general or how specific is his attitude toward war? Let us assume it to be properly represented by position C in Fig. 1. Let us now look for attitudes toward war that are more specific or more general than that indicated by position C. If there are attitudes toward war more specific than those represented by position C, they will exhibit a lower degree of intercorrelation among themselves than will those scaled at position C. We find this lower degree of intercorrelation and greater specificity in our subject's answer to any one of the

20 items in the war attitude scale. Each of these items taps a more specific attitude toward war than any measure based upon several of them jointly considered. Let us indicate the degree of specificity-generality involved at point B on our continuum.

It should already be obvious that we cannot peg "attitude toward war" at some one point on a specificity-generality continuum. If our primary interest is in an item response, we shall surely find that "attitude toward war" is a more specific personality trait, *i.e.*, the various measures thereof will exhibit a lower degree of intercorrelation, than if we interest ourselves in any summary score based upon several of the item responses.

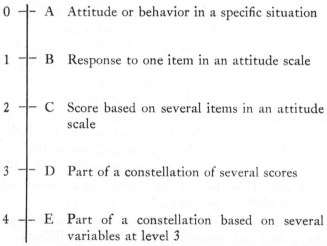

0 ┼ A Attitude or behavior in a specific situation

1 ┼ B Response to one item in an attitude scale

2 ┼ C Score based on several items in an attitude scale

3 ┼ D Part of a constellation of several scores

4 ┼ E Part of a constellation based on several variables at level 3

FIG. 1. The specificity-generality continuum for attitude toward war.

Can we find greater specificity than that implied in an item response? Most assuredly! To give an answer to any one of the items in the war attitude scale, our subject must think of specific instances in his own past behavior that would lead him to agree with the statement and of other instances that would lead him to disagree. As soon as he has thought of several such situations, both pro and con (point A on our continuum), he may find that these separate experiences are not in complete accord. And, in general, these separate experiences will exhibit a degree of intercorrelation even lower than that among the item responses we have already discussed. This forces our subject into a certain degree of generality which he must abstract from his specific experiences in order to respond, as we have asked him to respond, to the items (point B) in our war attitude scale.

Let us return to point C in Fig. 1 and see if we can find greater generality. If there are attitudes toward war more general than those represented by position C, they will exhibit higher intercorrelations among themselves than will those scaled at position C. Attitude toward war, as measured by the total score on an attitude scale, has been found to correlate with attitudes toward capital punishment and the treatment of criminals (see Chap. 4). The cluster formed by these three attitude variables can be considered under the more general heading of *humanitarianism*, and this can be represented at point D on our specificity-generality continuum.

If we can group together under a generalized frame of reference, such as radicalism-conservatism, several of the attitude clusters characteristic of point D on our continuum, we can arrive at point E. Here we find still higher intercorrelations among our separate measures and therefore even greater generality. An example would be a person who secures conservative scores on the three attitude variables, religionism, humanitarianism, and nationalism, described in Chap. 4. These variables form a meaningful cluster because an individual is apt to be forced into adopting a conservative or a radical position with respect to each one of them.

Let us now summarize the various specificity-generality levels we have distinguished and arrange them in order as follows:

Level 0. This is a behavioral response, overt or covert, made in a specific situation. It is unique to the time, place, and individual who made it. It is, for this very reason, usually devoid of scientific value or at least is ordinarily not tapped by the psychological measuring techniques in current use.

Level 1. This is the response made to a single item in a test such as that included in a Thurstone attitude scale. The response involves some generality because the answer must depend upon several specific instances such as those described at Level 0. In terms of the analyses permitted by most of the current psychological measuring techniques this is just about as specific and unique (although it is neither) a response as is sought or desired.

Level 2. Any summary of the responses to several of the items in a psychological test, such as a summary of the responses to the items in a Thurstone attitude scale, characterizes this level of specificity-generality. The *response* is an abstraction and is twice removed from the uniqueness and specificity of a single personal event such as that characterizing Level 0. It will be consistent with psychological terminology if we label our result at this level a *trait* score. It will be seen, therefore, that traits cannot be specific. We have eliminated this possibility by definition.

Level 3. The response derived from a grouping or constellation of several traits, such as those which define the attitude variables religionism, humanitarianism, and nationalism, characterizes this level of our specificity-generality continuum.

Level 4. Popular and even some scientific discussion (see Stagner) still continues to group under general titles such as radicalism-conservatism or introversion-extroversion, various syndromes or clusters defined as characterizing Level 3. Thus a person who assumes a conservative attitude in one area (say, religion) may also assume a conservative attitude in a second albeit independent area (say, humanitarianism).

We may profitably conclude our discussion on specificity-generality by pointing out that as soon as the psychologist becomes interested in any phenomenon he, like any other scientist, begins to abstract that which is common to a number of observed situations. This forces him to consider generalities and not unique occurrences. It is up to the psychologist to determine, however, as to how far toward the generality end of the continuum he wishes to proceed. He can work effectively at any of the levels we have described.

DETERMINANTS OF PERSONALITY STRUCTURE

In order that we may accomplish the objectives set forth in a preceding section, we must discover the relations obtaining between what we can call predictors and what we can call predictands. From our study of elementary chemistry, we should all be familiar with Boyle's law. If a chemist knows the pressure exerted on a gas and holds temperature constant, he can predict its volume. The known pressure is our *predictor* and the unknown volume is our *predictand*.

The predictor is what we have to start with or what we know. The predictand is what we do not have immediately given or what we do not know. Something about it is to be predicted from something else, our predictor.

It is our hope in the study of personality that our various methods of measurement will fall primarily into the class of predictors. From the knowledge or facts we gain from a personality test we hope to be able to make some prediction about behavior: either future behavior or at least behavior that is not immediately available for present observation. It is not necessary, however, that we attempt to use our measures of personality as predictors only. We may wish to consider other items as our predictors and see if from them we can estimate an individual's responses on a personality test. It is important that we understand this dual usage, for it is possible that in some situations we may decide that a particular method of personality measurement is satisfactory as a predictor but not as a predictand, or vice versa. It is our hope, however, that ultimately, methods of personality measurement can be made equally satisfactory for both purposes.

We will now find it helpful to discuss several studies which illustrate the utility of four predictors of personality. In addition these studies will show that a knowledge of personality is of material importance in helping us attain our three afore-mentioned objectives: the description, the prediction, and the control of individual behavior, group behavior, and their mutually interdependent relations.

Constitutional Determinants. In "Psychosomatic Studies of Some Aspects of Maternal Behavior" Levy presents data to show that maternal feelings are related to duration of menstrual flow, and possibly to diameter of areola, but not to a number of other variables such as body weight, height, shoulder or hip width, and gross size of breast. Levy's data show that we can distinguish between women who are apt to develop a high degree of maternal feeling and women not apt to do so, and we can do this by reference, primarily, to duration of menstrual flow and, secondarily, by reference to areolar diameter.

To establish these facts Levy interviewed 72 mothers and classified them on degree of maternal feeling. This did not prove to be an easy task, but Levy states that all cases rated as "high maternal" and all cases rated as "low maternal" are reasonably clear-cut. An example of a case included in each of these categories, as well as one included in a midgroup, is given below:

High Maternal. Mother of four children. As a young child her favorite game was taking care of dolls, dressing them, putting them to bed. She played with dolls until age 14 or 15. She used to make visits among her mother's friends to take care of their babies. When she thought of being a mother, she hoped to have six children, and have them as soon as possible. When she saw a pretty baby on the street, she had a strong urge to take it in her arms and hug it. She was a "baby-carriage peeker" before, and after, marriage. In her relations with men she was always maternal; much more, she said, than they liked. Having had four children she is now pregnant with her fifth. She had a nurse for her first child and was miserable, she said, because she couldn't take full care of it. She hated the hospital rule of not having the baby in her room. She had a copious supply of milk. Her husband stated that she really spoiled the children; that every so often she fought against this tendency and became severe, to protect them from her spoiling. But the children "see through it."

Midgroup. Mother of one child. She played with dolls probably to age five or six. She was not especially interested in maternal play in childhood. For a period of two years, age twelve and thirteen, she used to look after some neighbor's children because she liked to. She never anticipated the number of her children or had fantasies of being a mother. When she saw a pretty baby on the street, she was interested but had no urge to hold it, or have one of her own. After marriage, however, she became pregnant very soon and willingly. She voluntarily took sole care of her child and is evidently an affectionate mother. Her pregnancy was very difficult and she was warned by her physician against further impregnation.

Low Maternal. Mother of two children. She never played any maternal games in childhood, nor played a maternal role to another child. She had very little interest in dolls and stopped playing with them when about age six. When she saw a pretty baby on the street she was not at all interested. As an adolescent, she never in-dulged in the phantasy of being a mother and having children. She was ambitious to get married but never thought about having children. As a mother she felt quite incompetent. She took her children off the breast after two weeks, because she didn't like it; she felt like a cow, she said. She still hates the physical care of children, though she is a dutiful mother and rather affectionate. She never was maternal toward men. Her interests have always been feminine, and she has been quite popular with men.

Levy found no correlation, either in his main group of 72 mothers or in subsequent groups of women, between ratings of maternal behavior and size of nipple, height, weight, hip width, and age at first mensis. He did find a striking correlation of .58, however, between maternal behavior and length of menstrual flow. Women whose menstrual flow lasts six or more days tend, in general, to be high in maternal feeling, while women whose menstrual flow lasts four days or less tend to be low in maternal feeling.

Correlations with areolar diameter, though positive, are not so high. Those reported are .23 and .33. Being based upon approximately 200 cases, however, they can be considered significant.

While it is known that duration of menstrual flow is not determined entirely by constitutional factors, it would be difficult to conclude that areolar diameter had anything but a constitutional, at least a somatic, basis. Therefore we may consider Levy's study as illustrating that a personality trait can have in part at least a constitutional or somatic basis.

Group Determinants. Our next example shows how personality traits may have their origin in social custom, habit, or attitude. Davis and Havighurst have presented data showing that both social class and color are closely related to certain practices of child rearing. In their study, Davis and Havighurst interviewed 200 mothers representing two class and two color groups: middle and lower class, and white and Negro. There were 50 mothers in each group, and all were resident in Chicago. Davis and Havighurst's chief conclusions are summarized by Kluckhohn and Murray as follows:

1. There are significant differences in child-rearing practices between the middle and lower social classes in a large city. The same type of differences exist between middle and lower-class Negroes as between middle and lower-class whites.
2. Middle-class parents are more rigorous than lower-class parents in their training of children for feeding and cleanliness habits. They also expect their children to take responsibility for themselves earlier than lower-class parents do. Middle-class parents place their children under a stricter regimen, with more frustration of their impulses, than do lower-class parents.
3. In addition to these social-class differences, there are some differences between Negroes and whites in their child-rearing practices. Negroes are more permissive than whites in the feeding and weaning of their children, but they are much more rigorous than whites in toilet training.

We learn, then, that there are differences in child training due to color and social class. Knowing the color and social class and treating these as our predictors, we can make certain inferences about the type of child training (our predictand). Let us hasten to add with regard to the color differences that we have in no way proved that there are *racial* differences. Race is a biological concept, and it is pretty generally agreed among scientists that there are no entirely satisfactory and clear-cut biological standards by which membership in a race can be determined. The differences under consideration have not been proved to have biological origins and therefore cannot be said to have racial significance.

Role Determinants. Under ordinary circumstances a girl expects to model her behavior, as have other girls before her, upon that of adult women, and a boy expects to model his behavior, as have other boys before him, upon that of adult men. Sometimes, however, the maturing boy or girl will reject all attempts to achieve what would appear to be his or her proper adult sex role, and will attempt to achieve status by assuming some of the characteristics, habits, and attitudes of the opposite sex. What can cause a boy to reject the masculine role and to assume a feminine role? And what can cause a girl to reject the feminine role and to assume a masculine role?

In a study conducted by the author it was found that harsh or irrational childhood discipline, rejection by parents, and other parental behavior not condoned as leading to good mental hygiene apparently can cause some boys to reject the masculine role and to assume the feminine role, and can cause some girls to reject the feminine role and to assume the masculine role. Kind, rational, but firm childhood discipline and the sort of discipline condoned as leading to good mental hygiene are apparently conducive to boys accepting their intended masculine sex role and to girls accepting their intended feminine adult sex role. Thus, "proper" childhood discipline can lead a child to accept his or her normal adult sex role, and "improper" childhood discipline can lead a child to reject his or her normal adult sex role. The assumption of the opposing sex role can be viewed as an attempt upon the part of the person concerned to achieve a status which apparently is otherwise going to be denied.

Situational Determinants. As our last example of the relation between a personality predictor and a personality predictand we may cite a study conducted by J. McV. Hunt when he was on the staff of St. Elizabeths Hospital in Washington, D.C. Through one of the patients at the hospital, Hunt was able to trace the histories of a group of childhood playmates who, in one setting, were placed in a situation that required them (to achieve status) to participate in a number of sexual perversions and, at the same time, to participate in a series of intensely religious revival meetings. Participation in the revival meetings gave the boys a set of values completely incompatible with their sexual indulgences and produced in them a serious conflict situation. It is our purpose, as it was Hunt's, to note the effect of this conflict upon resultant personality development.

In collecting his material, Hunt secured data on 15 boys. He secured data as to which of these boys participated in neighborhood athletics, in the perversions, in the revivals, and in the use of alcoholic beverages. Hunt found that all except two of seven boys who participated in *both* the sex perversions and in the revival meetings were committed to St. Elizabeths Hospital. Four boys who participated in the perversions but not seriously in the revivals were not committed to the hospital, nor were four other boys, three of whom participated in neither the perversions nor the revivals and one of whom participated only in the revivals.

Hunt found that the ages of commitment to St. Elizabeths extended over a fairly wide range. This led him to postulate a continuum of *frustration tolerance;* that is, to some boys their conflict became a real and earnest threat early in life and caused early mental breakdown and commitment. To others, the conflict did not become serious, or if serious, did not become a threat until after the lapse of a number of years. Finally it came, but only when their higher resistance thresholds had been reached.

We have now examined four predictors or determinants of personality: constitutional, social, role, and situational. These constitute only four examples, however, and cannot in any sense be considered as exhaustive of the type of predictor or determinant needing investigation. Nevertheless, the student should have gained from these examples some insight into the importance of personality in the description, understanding, prediction, and control of human behavior.

GUIDING PRINCIPLES FOR RESEARCH AND STUDY

The guiding principles for research and study in the field of personality measurement are no different from those which obtain for research and study in any other field of psychological investigation. These are basically three in number: a firm adherence to the principles of experimental psychology, a firm adherence to the principles of sound statistical analysis, and an adequate emphasis upon the theoretical framework within which any set of data is to find its meaning. Let us briefly consider each of these principles.

Adherence to the Principles of Experimental Psychology. Too many investigators in the field of personality measurement contend or imply by their actions that the principles of sound experimental psychology need not be applied in the field of personality measurement. This is, indeed, a most unfortunate circumstance. Nothing can delay progress quite so much as failure to abide by certain basic, elementary, and simple rules of experimental procedure.

One of the most basic and fundamental rules in experimental psychology, as indeed it is in all science, is that we control all variables known or thought to have significance for the problem at hand. We can then permit alterations in one of the variables (the one we select for our predictor) and see what changes it causes in one or more of the remaining variables (our predictands).

As a chemist or physicist interested in determining anew the relations expressed in Boyle's law we must control pressure, volume, and temperature. We hold temperature constant, allow pressure to vary, and see what changes this causes in volume. If we are interested in verifying Charles's law: that pressure varies with temperature, we hold pressure constant, allow temperature to vary, and see what changes this produces in volume. If in attempting to verify Boyle's law, we neglect to hold temperature constant; or if in attempting to verify Charles's law, we neglect to hold pressure constant, we would never, as physicists or chemists, be able to discover the fundamental relations involved in the famous formula $PV = kMT$.

In the fields of experimental psychology and personality measurement it is much more difficult to control the significant variables than it is in traditional physics. This does not mean, however, that we can disregard such control. As difficult as it may be, we must in some manner exert this control or forever flounder in superstition and error.

If this admonition be interpreted to mean that the psychologist interested in the field of personality measurement must ape in complete detail the procedures of the brass-instrument psychologist, the reader has seriously missed the author's point. Experimental control does not need to imply brass-instrument or laboratory psychology. It implies nothing more than a careful consideration and control of all factors which may affect an investigator's conclusions. To illustrate we may point out that the psychologist interested in determining sex differences on some personality test should assure himself:

1. That the items on the test adequately tap the personality functions to be studied
2. That the men and women tested constitute representative or random samples of all men and women
3. That sufficient cases are studied to rule out chance variation as a principal component in the explanation of results
4. That factors such as age are held fixed or constant or are taken appropriately into account so as not to obscure the significance of the results
5. That the men and women tested have had equal opportunity to learn the personality habits or characteristics under study and have been equally motivated to reveal them in the testing situation designed by the investigator

Adequate attention to points such as these constitutes the type of control possible and necessary in the field of personality measurement. Many investigators secure and publish data with too little thought having been given beforehand to the control of factors such as we have just discussed. Once in a while an investigator may be lucky and will secure significant data even though no conscious thought was given to such control. This represents a rare and infrequent occurrence, however, and the practice of ignoring such control is not to be recommended.

Adherence to the Principles of Sound Statistical Analysis. The basic principle to be followed in this connection is to be sure of the soundness and adequacy of the original experimental design. Data collected through sloppy experimental procedures cannot be saved by any legerdemain of statistical analysis. Valid experimental data can be invalidated, however, by inadequate or unsound statistical methods.

Having once decided upon a sound experimental approach, it is well to consider the alternative types of statistical analysis that can be employed. Frequently it will happen that several experimental procedures, equally sound from the standpoint of control, may differ considerably in merit in terms of the type of statistical analysis that can be used in connection therewith. We can illustrate this by an example in the field of learning. Suppose it is the purpose of an experimenter to determine which method of classroom instruction, A or B, is the better. He can proceed experimentally in two ways: he can equate two groups of subjects and can teach one group by method A and the other group by method B, or he can equate two learning skills and can teach both skills to the same group of subjects, one by method A and the other by method B. In the first procedure the basic formula to determine the significance of the difference in the results produced by the two methods is

$$CR = \frac{\text{difference}}{\sqrt{\sigma_A{}^2 + \sigma_B{}^2}}$$

This gives the standard error of a difference between two uncorrelated samples or, in this instance, between two different subject populations. If our investigator chose to follow the second of our two experimental procedures he would find his major basic formula to be

$$CR = \frac{\text{difference}}{\sqrt{\sigma_A{}^2 + \sigma_B{}^2 - 2r\sigma_A\sigma_B}}$$

This formula differs from the first by taking into account any correlation that may exist between the two samples to be compared. The formula shows that the higher this correlation the less the value of the standard error. Thus a given difference may be found to possess differing degrees of significance depending upon the composition of the basic experimental groups. If the two groups to be compared consist of the selfsame subjects, there is obviously a correlational factor to be considered. And when this correlational factor is considered, it leads to greater precision in defining any difference that may be obtained.

Emphasis upon Theoretical Framework. Some investigators feel that the collection or discovery of a new fact, if it can be established as such, is a sufficient goal for research. Other investigators feel that facts as such are not worth the time, money, and effort needed to establish them unless they can be integrated into some theoretical or conceptual scheme. Perhaps we can reach a compromise between these two points of view and allow that each side of the argument has merit. It would seem, however, that future advancement in the field of personality measurement will require much theory formulation. This theory formulation can then be followed by the gathering of facts to verify or disprove the theories that may be involved. Should isolated facts be discovered they should, of course, be recorded, but it would seem that most research workers would find their work more interesting and, indeed, more profitable if they first developed theoretical guideposts to steer them along their various ways. It is frequently said that a theory is no good unless there are facts to support it. This may well be true, but let us also heed the warning given by Sir Arthur Eddington: that facts are no good either, unless they are supported by an adequate theory.

2

INTERESTS: AN EMPIRICAL APPROACH

In this and in the following chapter, we shall be concerned with techniques for the measurement of interests. In this chapter we propose to discuss an empirical approach to the problem, and in the next chapter, a rational approach. The latter approach was used by Dr. G. Frederic Kuder in the development of his Preference Records; while the empirical approach, the subject of our present chapter, was used by Dr. Edward K. Strong, Jr., in the development of his Vocational Interest Tests.

The chief purpose of the Strong Vocational Interest Tests is to show a person the extent to which his interests correspond to those of successful men or women in a variety of occupations. In addition, they can show the extent to which a person's interests correspond to those characteristic of men in contrast with those characteristic of women (masculinity-femininity). The men's blank can also show the extent to which a person's interests correspond to those of 25-year-old men in contrast with those of 15-year-old boys (interest maturity), and the extent to which they correspond to those of professional and businessmen in contrast with those of unskilled workmen (occupational level).

Each of the two tests consists of a total of 400 items. In terms of their content, those in the blank for men can be classified as in Table 5. In most of these parts the subject is asked to draw a circle around one of three letters: L, I, or D, to indicate whether he likes, is indifferent to, or dislikes the occupation, school subject, amusement, activity, or kind of person in question. In Part VI, however, in indicating preference among activities, the subject is asked (in each of 4 groups of 10 activities) to check the 3 he likes best, the 3 he likes least, and to check the 4 remaining as neutral. In Part VII, the section requiring a comparison between activity items, *e.g.*, between streetcar conductor and streetcar motorman, the subject must indicate whether he prefers one of these two activities in contrast to the other or whether he likes them equally well. And, finally, in

TABLE 5. *Type of Item in the Strong Vocational Interest Test for Men**

Item	Number of Items
Occupations	100
School subjects	36
Amusements	49
Activities	48
Kinds of people	47
Order of preference for activities	40
Comparison between two items	40
Present abilities	40
Total	400

* From Strong, E. K., Jr. *Vocational Interests of Men and Women.* Stanford University, Calif.: Stanford University Press, 1943.

indicating his present abilities (Part VIII) the subject is asked to indicate whether each one of 40 statements about abilities characterizes him, does not characterize him, or whether he cannot decide.

PURPOSES OF TEST

The scores on the Strong Vocational Interest Test can be put to a variety of uses. Four of the most important are educational guidance, vocational guidance, vocational selection, and research.

Educational Guidance. The beginning college student who is undecided about what course of study to follow may find that the scores on the Strong Vocational Interest Test will give him valuable help. If his scores indicate that he has interests like those of successful lawyers, he can consider this as a suggestion to take one or two courses in prelegal subjects to see how well he likes them. If the student has already thought of this course of action, he can consider the scores on the Strong Vocational Interest Test as confirmatory evidence that he is pursuing a proper line of endeavor.

Two courses of action are always possible: one in line with that suggested by test scores and one contrary thereto. A person should not follow scores on the Vocational Interest Test blindly, but he should have good reasons for choosing any alternate course of action. A person should not fear acting in a manner contraindicated by test scores, but if he does, he must have cogent reasons for so doing.

Vocational Guidance. We can echo here what we have just said in our discussion on educational guidance. It is sometimes, and not infrequently, the case that a student will near the end of his collegiate career without being entirely certain as to which specific vocation he wishes to enter. Reference to the scores on the Vocational Interest Test, along with other considerations, may help him reach a decision. Here, as in the case of educational guidance, two courses of action are possible. The student may choose to follow the indications of the test, or he may choose to ignore them. It would seem proper, however, for a student seriously to consider entering any occupation in which he receives a high score; and he should seriously consider *not* entering any occupation in which he receives a low score. If he decides *not to enter* an occupation in which he receives a high score or *to enter* an occupation in which he receives a low score, he should have good and cogent reasons therefor.

What the student gets from the Strong Vocational Interest Test is an indication of whether or not his own interests, his own likes and dislikes, his own preferences and aversions correspond to or do not correspond to those of successful men or women in the occupations designated. For example, it tells the student whether his interests are similar to, or dissimilar to, those of successful lawyers; similar to, or dissimilar to, those of successful psychologists; similar to, or dissimilar to, those of successful engineers; similar to, or dissimilar to, those of successful bankers; and so on. Strong's basic theory, well substantiated by the empirical facts which he has assiduously collected for more than twenty-five years, is that when other factors such as ability are equal, a person will be much happier and presumably more successful in an occupation in which he finds a large number of men with interests similar to his own. This does not mean, of course, that a person cannot be successful in an occupation if his interests are dissimilar to those of men already engaged in it. But it does seem logical to expect that he will be less happy in such an occupation than in one having men in it with interests corresponding to his own.

It should be clearly understood that the Strong Vocational Interest Test gives no indication of ability. This must be discovered through intelligence or aptitude tests, or in other ways, if such tests are not available. If the Strong Vocational Interest Test indicates that a student has interests like those of successful engineers, but a mathematical aptitude test shows lack of facility in mathematics, the student should probably steer clear of the field of engineering.

However, if a student has the necessary aptitude and the requisite degree of intelligence to enter, let us say, either engineering or law, and the Strong Vocational Interest Test yields a high interest score in engineering but a low score in law, the student should carefully consider going into engineering before deciding definitely against it, and should carefully consider *not* going into law if, prior to the test, he had some intention of entering this profession.

A point that must be clearly understood in interpreting a score on the Strong Vocational Interest Test is that it does not indicate interest *in* an occupation. This may be a technicality, but a high score on the law scale does not indicate an interest *in* law. It merely shows that the subject's interests, whatever they may be, correspond to those possessed by the majority of successful lawyers. Fortunately there seems to be a positive correlation between having interests like those of successful practitioners in an occupation and having an interest in the activities involved in the occupation. Nevertheless, the distinction is an important one and should not be glossed over in interpreting a score.

Vocational Selection. Strong developed his Vocational Interest Test primarily as a means of helping college students decide upon appropriate courses of study and suitable vocations. If the test does this, and we know that it does, it would also seem reasonable that it should be of assistance to employers seeking applicants in those occupations for which the test can be scored. If the test helps a college student to decide that chemistry is the line of work he should follow, it would seem that an employer of chemists could profitably use the test as an aid in selecting applicants for employment.

While this sounds reasonable, and in fact the test can be used in this way, it is necessary for us to be on guard with respect to certain possible flaws in the logic involved. When an employer selects an applicant for employment, he is interested in selecting a person that he thinks is going to be successful. To do this he needs some method of distinguishing applicants who will later become successful from applicants who will later become unsuccessful. This is a different problem, and may have a different answer, from that involved in deciding whether a person's interests are like chemists as a group in contrast to those of men engaged in other occupational pursuits.

Strong has discussed this problem in detail and points out that the differences between a successful and an unsuccessful chemist may not, and need not, in fact, correspond to the differences between all chemists (successful and unsuccessful) and other occupational groups (including successes and failures). In the field of life insurance there is an overlap, however, between the kinds of things that differentiate most life insurance salesmen from men-in-general, and successful life insurance salesmen from unsuccessful life insurance salesmen. This fact has made the Vocational Interest Test an exceedingly useful instrument as an aid in the selection of life insurance salesmen.

When the Vocational Interest Test is used for educational or vocational guidance, the norms which Strong has supplied should be used. When the test is used in vocational selection, however, new validation data must be obtained, and new norms must be prepared. These are necessary to show whether or not the test will be useful for the purpose intended. It is quite possible, and it has been repeatedly demonstrated, that a test can be valid for the selection of employees in one company but invalid for selection in another company. In this respect, the Strong Vocational Interest Test is no different from any other. It must be validated anew for each situation in which it is intended to be used. The test possesses an advantage, however, that no other selection test possesses. It not only can be made to yield a new scale for the specific occupation in question but also yields information on the previously developed occupational scales as well. Frequently a pattern of interests tells much more about an applicant than does the score on any particular scale, even though this scale is the one most pertinent to the position in question.

Research. The Strong Vocational Interest Test has proved a most useful instrument in research on the structure of that segment of personality covered by the concept *interest*. Strong himself has done a monumental job for more than twenty-five years, but many other investigators have made good use of his test also. In most of the remaining sections of this chapter we shall have occasion to report or comment upon elements of personality structure which would not now be known or which would be known less well, were it not for the research made possible by the Strong Vocational Interest Test. To give a few examples:

1. We now know a good deal about how interests change with age and what significance these changes have in vocational guidance.

2. We now know a good deal about how the interests of various occupational groups compare with each other. This provides us with added insight useful in vocational guidance.

3. We now know that higher and lower occupational groups differ in terms of their interests. Thus, through interests, we can tell something not only about the direction in which a person can appropriately bend his efforts but also something about the job level he should strive to attain.

4. We now know something about the extent to which certain interests are related to certain personality traits, to intelligence, to various aptitudes, and so forth, and we find that interests constitute a definite and measurable segment of personality, not adequately covered by other types of personality tests.

DEVELOPMENT OF OCCUPATIONAL SCALES

We have referred to Dr. Strong's approach as an empirical one. By this we mean that every method of scoring which Dr. Strong has devised has been based directly upon demonstrated differences among contrasting criterion groups. Strong and other members of the now famous Carnegie group (including, among others, Miner, Ream, Freyd, and Moore) started research which later led to the Vocational Interest Test, with one basic theory: that occupational groups can, in terms of their interests, in terms of their likes and dislikes, and in terms of their preferences and aversions, be distinguished from one another; that is, that the members of one occupational group (say, chemists) will have a different set of likes and dislikes from those of the members of another occupational group (say, lawyers). To check this theory, Strong has compared the interests of various professional groups, not directly with each other, but with what he calls men-in-general. For example, he has compared the interests of lawyers with those of men-in-general, and he has compared the interests of chemists with those of men-in-general. He finds not only that lawyers and chemists differ from men-in-general but also that they differ from men-in-general in different ways. Therefore, they are different from each other.

The procedures which Strong has used in the development of each of his occupational scales are as follows:

1. Representatives of an occupational group complete the blanks.
2. The number of men who answer L, I, and D to each item is determined.
3. These numbers are translated into percentages.

TABLE 6. *Determination of the Scoring Weights for the First 10 Items of the Engineering Interest Scale**

First 10 items	Percentage of men-in-general			Percentage of engineers			Difference in percentages			Scoring weights		
	L	I	D	L	I	D	L	I	D	L	I	D
Actor (not movie)..	21	32	47	9	31	60	−12	− 1	13	−1	0	1
Advertiser.........	33	38	29	14	37	49	−19	− 1	20	−2	0	2
Architect..........	37	40	23	58	32	10	21	− 8	−13	2	−1	−1
Army officer........	22	29	49	31	33	36	9	4	−13	1	0	−1
Artist.............	24	40	36	28	39	33	4	− 1	− 3	0	0	0
Astronomer........	26	44	30	38	44	18	12	0	−12	1	0	−1
Athletic director....	26	41	33	15	51	34	−11	10	1	−1	1	0
Auctioneer.........	8	27	65	1	16	83	− 7	−11	18	−1	−1	2
Author of novel....	32	38	30	22	44	34	−10	6	4	−1	1	0
Author of technical book............	31	41	28	59	32	9	28	− 9	−19	3	−1	−2

* From Strong, E. K., Jr. *Vocational Interests of Men and Women.* Stanford University, Calif.: Stanford University Press, 1943.

TABLE 7. *Scores Obtained by One Subject on Six Scales of the Vocational Interest Test**

Item	Response	Engineer	Lawyer	Life insurance salesman	Minister	Y.M.C.A. secretary	Accountant
Actor (not movie)......	D	1	−1	−1	−2	−1	−1
Advertiser.............	D	2	1	−1	0	−2	−1
Architect..............	D	−1	1	1	0	0	0
Army officer...........	I	0	0	0	−1	0	0
Artist.................	I	0	0	−1	1	1	0
Astronomer............	L	1	0	0	2	0	0
Athletic director........	I	1	0	0	1	0	0
Auctioneer.............	I	−1	−1	0	0	0	0
Author of novel........	I	1	0	0	0	0	0
Author of technical book	L	3	0	−1	−1	−1	1
Total 10 items........	....	7	0	−3	0	−3	−1
Total 400 items......	....	182	23	−115	−91	−134	−33

* From Strong, E. K., Jr. *Vocational Interests of Men and Women.* Stanford University, Calif.: Stanford University Press, 1943.

TABLE 8. *Norms for the Architect Scale**

Architect			Percentile ranks		
Raw score	Standard score	Rating	241 architects	306 Stanford freshmen	285 Stanford seniors
220	69	A	99		
210	67	A	98		
200	65	A	97		
190	63	A	92		
180	61	A	87		
170	59	A	80		
160	57	A	75		99
150	55	A	65	99	99
140	53	A	60	99	99
130	51	A	51	98	98
120	49	A	41	98	98
110	47	A	34	97	96
100	45	A	30	95	93
90	43	B+	25	93	91
80	41	B+	20	90	87
70	39	B+	15	86	83
60	37	B	12	83	80
50	35	B	7	77	76
40	33	B−	6	73	70
30	31	B−	5	67	65
20	29	B−	3	60	59
10	27	C+	2	55	53
0	25	C+	1	50	46
−10	23	C	1	44	40
−20	21	C	1	36	35
−30	19	C	1	31	29
−40	17	C	..	25	23
−50	15	C	..	20	18
−60	13	C	..	15	13
−70	11	C	..	13	9
−80	9	C	..	10	7
−90	7	C	..	7	4
−100	5	C	..	5	2
−110	3	C	..	3	1
−120	1	C	..	2	1
−130	−1	C	..	2	1
−140	−3	C	..	1	
−150	−5	C	..	1	
−160	−7	C	..	1	

* From Strong, E. K., Jr. *Vocational Interests of Men and Women.* Stanford University, Calif.: Stanford University Press, 1943.

4. These percentages are compared with the corresponding percentages for men-in-general.

5. By means of an appropriate formula or chart, item weights reflecting the magnitude of the differences between the percentages for the occupational group in question and the men-in-general group are assigned.

Table 6 gives the results of the preceding steps for the engineering scale for the first 10 items of the test. It shows the percentage distribution of answers for engineers and for men-in-general, the differences between these percentages, and the scoring weights assigned. Having determined the scoring weights, the score for an individual is obtained by summing (algebraically) the scoring values associated with the responses he checks. An illustration of the scoring process and of the results is given in Table 7.

The Strong Vocational Interest Test for Men can be scored for 42 occupations, and that for women can be scored for 24. For each of these occupations, Strong provides raw scores, standard scores, letter grades, and percentile norms. An example is given in Table 8. The means and standard deviations of the raw-score distributions differ, of course, from one scale to another. The means and standard deviations of the standard-score distributions are identical, however, for all scales. These are 50 and 10, respectively. Letter grades, also, are the same for all scales, being assigned, as they are, upon the basis of standard scores in accord with the schedule in Table 9.

TABLE 9. *Schedule of Letter Grades and Standard-score Equivalents**

Letter grade	Standard score	Percentage of cases
A	45 and up	70.2
B+	40–44	11.9
B	35–39	9.6
B−	30–34	4.8
C+	25–29	2.5
C	24 and below	1.0
Total..........	....	100.0

* From Strong, E. K., Jr. *Vocational Interests of Men and Women.* Stanford University, Calif.: Stanford University Press, 1943.

The data in Table 9 show that 70 per cent of the members of each occupational group secure a grade of A on the scale for their own occupation, that 29 per cent receive grades of B+, B, B−, and

C+, and that only 1 per cent receives a grade of C. Therefore, when an individual secures a grade of A, that is, a standard score of 45 or higher it means that his interests correspond to those of at least 70 per cent of the members of that professional group. If he gets a score of B, his interests correspond, at best, to no more than those of 29 or 30 per cent of the members of the professional group in question. And, finally, if he gets a score of C the chances are pretty good that his own interests do not correspond to more than 1 per cent of those of the members of that professional group. For all practical purposes, they just do not correspond.

CRITERION GROUPS

To appreciate fully the value of the scores provided by the Strong Vocational Interest Tests, we should take careful note of the character of the criterion groups which Dr. Strong has used.

Occupational Criterion Groups. We have already indicated that representatives of different occupational groups were in turn, and one by one, compared with a men- (or women-) in-general group. In the case of each occupational group, the individuals were successful practitioners in their particular line of work. Criteria of success were generally some years of experience in the business, an average annual income in excess of $2,500 (these were prewar standards), recognition in terms of membership in an appropriate national society, certification by a state licensing board, or a listing in a Who's Who of the profession concerned. The average number of subjects in each of the men's criterion groups is 321, but this varies from a minimum of 113 to a maximum of 1,048. The average number of cases in the women's criterion groups is 366, but this also varies from a minimum of 162 to a maximum of 1,256. Tables 10 and 11 show the total number of subjects used in deriving the scales, the number of subjects used in deriving norms, the average age of the subjects, and the average school grade completed by the members of each criterion group.

Men-in-general Group. In the course of his research, Strong has used several different men-in-general groups. The one used in the derivation of the scales currently available for men consists of 4,746 men representing 106 groups of professional and businessmen earning $2,500 or more per year (prewar standards). Each of these 106 groups

TABLE 10. *Number of Cases, Average Age, and Average Educational Status of Men in Occupational Criterion Groups**

Occupation	Standardization group	Norm group	Age	Education
Accountant	338	345	37.4	12.3
Advertising man	230	168	37.6	14.0
Architect	244	241	42.8	14.4
Artist	278	231	42.7	11.9
Author-journalist	250	249	45.0	14.3
Aviator	510	510		
Banker	250	247	45.5	12.2
Carpenter	185	181	43.2	12.2
Certified public accountant	423	354	37.3	14.3
Certified public accountant, senior	611	...	37.7	14.4
Chemist	293	297	35.2	16.8
City school superintendent	190	190	46.5	16.9
Coast guard	256	256		
Dentist	249	239	42.4	14.9
Engineer	513	513	43.9	15.4
Farmer	245	241	37.6	14.6
Forest service	410	405	38.5	14.2
Lawyer	324	251	39.2	17.0
Life insurance salesman	596	315	39.9	13.6
Mathematician	181	181	46.1	18.8
Mathematics-science teacher	228	237	33.6	16.4
Minister	255	250	42.6	18.2
Mortician	360	...	44.7	13.0
Musician	250	250	32.6	12.4
Office worker	326	317	33.2	11.5
Osteopath	585	585	37.9	
Personnel manager	147	146	41.0	14.7
Pharmacist	315	...	41.2	
Physician	432	337	40.9	18.5
Policeman	259	254	34.8	10.4
President of manufacturing concern	172	169	48.0	13.1
Printer	258	279	35.5	10.8
Production manager	218	216	42.8	13.3
Psychologist	1048	...	44.0	
Public administrator	515	515		
Purchasing agent	221	219	39.8	11.8
Real estate salesman	246	243	40.1	12.1
Sales manager	223	228	42.2	13.0
Social science teacher	224	217	33.7	16.4
Veterinarian	310	...	44.4	
Y.M.C.A. physical director	220	215	31.4	14.0
Y.M.C.A. secretary	113	113	42.0	14.4
Mean	321	276	40.1	14.2

* From Strong, E. K., Jr. *Vocational Interests of Men and Women.* Stanford University, Calif.: Stanford University Press, 1943.

is represented in the men-in-general group in the same proportion that it was represented in the United States census.

Strong had available differing numbers of test blanks for each of the 106 occupational groups. Therefore, since the occupations were to be weighted in proportion to their relative numbers in the census

TABLE 11. *Number of Cases, Average Age, and Average Educational Status of Women in Occupational Criterion Groups**

Occupation	Number	Age	Education
Artist..	402	43.4	14.3
Author..	402	39.9	14.8
Buyer..	204	34.4	12.4
Dentist..	195	40.0	16.0
Dietitian..	416	34.0	16.2
Housewife..	1256	38.2	12.5
Laboratory technician................................	356	33.5	15.1
Lawyer..	373	38.0	16.1
Librarian..	425	44.0	16.1
Life insurance saleswoman...........................	205	46.0	13.5
Nurse..	396	34.0	13.2
Occupational therapist..............................	162	34.1	14.5
Office worker...	226	33.6	12.3
Physician...	400	41.0	19.0
Psychologist..	380	37.4	18.4
Social worker...	432	38.0	16.3
Steonographer-secretary..............................	298	29.3	12.5
Teacher of elementary school.........................	238	36.0	15.9
Teacher of English in high school.....................	293	41.0	16.6
Teacher of home economics...........................	420	35.6	16.5
Teacher of mathematics and physical science in high school	467	39.0	16.7
Teacher of physical education in high school............	250	33.4	16.5
Teacher of social science in high school................	396	35.0	16.6
Y.W.C.A. secretary...................................	202	45.2	15.5
Mean..	366	37.7	15.3

* From Strong, E. K., Jr. *Manual for Vocational Interest Blank for Women.* Stanford University, Calif.: Stanford University Press, 1947.

population, Strong averaged the responses for all men in a given occupation before combining them with those in the other groups. For example, 114 architects completed the blanks, but according to quota only one architect needed to be included in the men-in-general group. Therefore, to get the responses of the typical architect, Strong computed the average percentages for all 114 blanks. These averages were taken as the responses of the one architect to be included in the men-in-general group. The quota for teacher was 6. The number of blanks available was 282. Therefore, the averages were based upon the 282 cases, and these averages were multiplied by 6 to give them their proportionate quota weight in the men-in-general group. All of Strong's currently published scales, unless otherwise specified, make use of this men-in-general group as a basic point of reference.

When Strong first developed his interest test, he used as a men-in-general group all men for whom he happened to have records available. But when revising his test in 1938, he decided to secure a men-in-general group truly representative according to the United States census. Strong secured such a group, used it in revising the occupational scales, and found such remarkably high intercorrelations among them that they appeared to be practically useless. This proved, at the time, a most disturbing finding, but later it became apparent to Strong that a men-in-general group according to the census represents a group much lower in the occupational hierarchy than the original men-in-general group composed, as it was, of business and professional men. These groups of business and professional men can be differentiated from one another when compared among themselves. But they have much in common when contrasted with a group far removed from them in the occupational hierarchy.

To illustrate this problem a little more concretely, we may cite the experience we all feel in viewing for the first time the members of a foreign nationality group. To most Occidentals, all Chinese look pretty much alike, and they do, when contrasted with Occidentals. But Chinese do differ from each other if we compare them, not with Occidentals, but with each other. Thus, if we are interested in proving how much Chinese look alike we should choose a point of reference far removed from the central tendency of the group. We do this by choosing Occidentals as our point of reference. But, if we want to prove how different Chinese are from one another, we choose a point of reference representing the central tendency of the group, namely, the Chinese themselves.

Strong's original men-in-general group constituted a much more appropriate point of reference than did the one prepared according to the United States census. When Strong had solved this problem, he prepared the more adequate professional men-in-general group already described.

NONOCCUPATIONAL SCALES

We have already indicated that in addition to the occupational scores, the Strong Vocational Interest Test yields scores for interest maturity, masculinity-femininity, and occupational level.

Interest Maturity. This scale gives an indication of the extent to which a person's interests are like those of 25-year-old men in contrast with those of 15-year-old boys. It was developed to show how interests, in a quantitative sense, can change with age, and to aid in the classification of occupations in such a way as to show whether a high or low degree of interest maturity is appropriate for entry therein.

If we are to use expressed interests as one of the bases for educational and vocational guidance, it is important that we know something about how interests change with age. Is there perhaps no change with age? Is there a consistent increase (or decrease) in liking or disliking certain items? Is there at one time an increase (or decrease) and at another time a decrease (or increase) in liking or disliking certain items? And, whatever the answers, what significance do they have for vocational and educational guidance?

Strong reports that "liking for approximately two-fifths of the items in the Vocational Interest Test increases or decreases in a straight line from 15 to 55 years of age; liking for two-fifths of the items increases (or decreases) from 15 to 25 years of age and then decreases (or increases) from 25 to 55 years; and liking for the remaining items differ with different groups of men." Anticipating just a little, the interest-maturity scale shows that interests, on a quantitative basis, tend to change in a consistent direction over the age period 15 to 25 and that most of the change which is to occur over the age span 15 to 55 takes place by age 25. Therefore, it is possible to use the interest-maturity score to show how mature or how immature a person's interests may be. The interests of a person with a high score on the interest-maturity scale are subject to relatively little future change. Therefore, his expressed interests provide a much more stable and adequate basis for guidance than do the expressed interests of someone with a low score on the interest-maturity scale.

We can use the interest-maturity score in two ways: to tell how near a person's interests are to maturity and to tell, in connection with his occupational scores, which occupations he should and should not consider. A typical 15-year-old boy will secure a fairly low score on the interest-maturity scale. It can be expected, therefore, that his interests will be subject to considerable future change. Therefore, not much reliance, for vocational guidance purposes, should be placed upon his pattern of interests. A 15-year-old boy who secures a high score on the interest-maturity scale has already acquired a mature interest pattern, and this pattern can be used, with some degree of confidence, as a basis for vocational guidance.

During the course of his research on interest maturity Strong has developed three interest-maturity scales: the first contrasts the interests of 15-year-old boys and 55-year-old men; a second contrasts the interests of 25-year-old men and 55-year-old men; and a third contrasts the interests of 15-year-old boys and 25-year-old men. Strong finds the intercorrelations among these scales to be as follows:

1. (15–25) vs. (15–55).......... .74
2. (15–25) vs. (25–55).......... −.41
3. (25–55) vs. (15–55).......... −.03

These correlations show that most of the change in interest between ages 15 and 55 takes place between ages 15 and 25; and that the direction of the change which takes place between ages 25 and 55 tends to be opposite that which takes place between ages 15 and 25. Since vocational guidance, if it is to serve its primary purpose, must be given much nearer the age of 15 than 25, the changes which may take place over this ten-year period of time are much more important than the changes which take place thereafter. Therefore, the most useful of the three scales, and the only one now published, is that contrasting the interests of 15-year-old boys and 25-year-old men. The 15-year-old group consists of 472 boys fairly representative of the California high-school population of 1933, and the 25-year-old group consists of 215 men representing the occupational pattern in the United States census.

Masculinity-Femininity. This scale shows the extent to which a person's interests correspond to those of men in contrast with those of women. Strong has found it helpful to consider the score on this scale along with a person's occupational scores to show whether he should consider entering an occupation characterized by more masculine interests (say, engineering) or an occupation characterized by more feminine interests (say, journalism).

Altogether, Strong has developed seven masculinity-femininity scales. One of these, the one used chiefly in connection with the women's interest blank, is based upon a comparison of men's and women's answers to the 263 items common to the original women's blank and the revised men's blank, and need not be discussed further. The other six scales, all developed in connection with the men's interest blank, contrast the responses of various groups of men and women on all 400 items of the form. In these six scales the groups of subjects represented are 114 high-school boys and 114 high-school girls, 154 college men and 154 college women, and 335 adult men and 335 adult women. Strong developed separate scales for each of these groups as well as three scales based upon all groups. These latter three scales differ from each other only in the range of item weights represented: (1) ± 15; (2) ± 3; and (3) ± 4.

To develop these scales Strong followed the item-weighting procedure described on page 37. In this instance, there had to be computed the percentage of men and the percentage of women who responded L, I, and D to each item, the differences between these percentages, and the item weights. These procedures were repeated, of course, for each of the seven scales. In developing the scales based upon all subjects, the percentages for the high-school group, college group, and adult group were averaged. This gave each group equal weight in contributing to the composite or average scales.

The intercorrelations among the various M-F scales are not perfect, but they are high. The high-school and adult scales correlate .90; the high-school and college scales correlate .81; and the college and adult scales correlate .74. Strong reports that all three scales correlate .90 or over with the average scale having item weights ± 15 (high-school scale, .96; college scale, .92; and adult scale, .92). For most purposes we shall not need to concern ourselves with the minute differences among these scales and, for this reason, it is only necessary to score the test upon the scale most recently developed, namely, the total scale with item weights ranging between $+4$ and -4. For this scale the reader may find it helpful to have available the data presented in Table 12. It shows the standard-score means and the distribution standard deviations of high school, college, and adult groups. The differences between the mean scores of men and women are obviously large and the critical ratios given in column 6 demonstrate that they are of non-chance significance.

TABLE 12. *Means and Standard Deviations for Men and Women on the Masculinity-Femininity Scale**

Group	N	Men		Women		Critical ratio
		Mean	SD	Mean	SD	
High school..........	129	52.3	8.2	30.1	7.9	18.7
College..............	143	49.5	10.8	26.6	7.6	15.9
Adult...............	100	47.7	10.2	26.8	7.9	17.3
Total............	372	50.0	10.0	27.9	7.9	31.2

* From Strong, E. K., Jr. *Vocational Interests of Men and Women*. Stanford University, Calif.: Stanford University Press, 1943.

Strong has determined the relation between masculinity-femininity and occupational interests in three ways: in terms of mean M-F scores for different occupational groups, in terms of the correlations between M-F scores and occupational scores, and in terms of the critical ratios of the sex differences in mean occupational scores for contrasting groups of men and women. The results of these three methods (each method being applied to a different set of data) are given in Table 13. The rank-order correlation among the classifications is exceedingly high, averaging .90 for all combinations among the three methods of classification. We may cite as examples of masculine occupations engineer, farmer, purchasing agent, chemist, and dentist. All these are included in the one-third most masculine groups in all three classifications. Occupations consistently classified in the one-third most feminine groups on all three bases are musician, artist, advertising man, journalist, minister, and life insurance salesman. Occupations consistently classified as neutral (neither masculine nor feminine) are physician, psychologist, mathematician, Y.M.C.A. physical director, realtor, certified public accountant, and architect.

The masculinity-femininity score can be used in conjunction with the occupational scores to help a person decide upon the suitability of a given occupation. A person who gets a high score as lawyer can have added confidence that this is the right occupation if he also gets a feminine score on the M-F scale; and a person who gets a high score as an engineer can have greater confidence that this is the right occupation for him if he also gets a high masculine score on the M-F scale.

In using the M-F scale it is important to know whether the scores on it vary with, or are independent of, age. Strong finds only a slight

TABLE 13. *Classification of Occupations According to Masculinity-Femininity**

Critical ratio basis		Mean score basis		Correlation basis	
Engineer	8.8	Engineer	53	Farmer	.68
Farmer	7.0	Chemist	50	Engineer	.64
Purchasing agent	6.4	Teacher of mathematics		Purchasing agent	.46
Chemist	6.3	and physical science	50	Chemist	.44
Accountant	4.5	Farmer	50	Physicist	.32
Physicist	3.8	Purchasing agent	49	Accountant	.32
Dentist	2.1	Dentist	48	Office man	.16
Personnel manager	1.8	Personnel manager	47	Dentist	.14
Physician	0.8	Office man	46	Mathematician	.11
Office man	0.5	Certified public account-		Y.M.C.A. physical direc-	
Psychologist	0.4	ant	46	tor	−.03
Mathematician	0.3	Accountant	46	Physician	−.06
Y.M.C.A. physical direc-		Psychologist	45	Personnel manager	−.06
tor	−0.4	Mathematician	45	Architect	−.11
Realtor	−1.2	Realtor	45	Psychologist	−.14
Y.M.C.A. secretary	−1.9	Y.M.C.A. physical direc-		Realtor	−.28
Teacher	−1.9	tor	45	Certified public account-	
Certified public account-		Physician	44	ant	−.29
ant	−1.9	Lawyer	43	Y.M.C.A. secretary	−.34
Architect	−2.0	City school superintend-		Teacher	−.40
Lawyer	−2.3	ent	43	Musician	−.41
City school superintend-		Architect	43	Artist	−.44
ent	−2.7	Teacher of social science	42	Life insurance salesman	−.49
Life insurance salesman	−3.4	Life insurance salesman	42	City school superintend-	
Minister	−4.3	Musician	40	ent	−.51
Journalist	−4.4	Y.M.C.A. secretary	40	Minister	−.56
Advertising man	−5.1	Advertising man	40	Lawyer	−.62
Artist	−5.4	Minister	37	Journalist	−.66
Musician	−5.6	Artist	37	Advertising man	−.74
		Journalist	36		

* From Strong, E. K., Jr. *Vocational Interests of Men and Women.* Stanford University, Calif.: Stanford University Press, 1943.

relation to age, but the older a person gets the more feminine his interests tend to become. This is true of both men and women. There is always a large gap between men and women of comparable ages, but at the older ages the differences tend to be less than at the earlier ages.

Occupational Level. This scale gives an indication of the extent to which a person's interests are like those of professional men in contrast with those of unskilled workers. It was constructed by contrasting the responses of a group of 4,746 professional and businessmen with those of a group of 258 unskilled workers. Therefore, if a person secures a high score on the occupational-level scale, he should consider some activity at the business or professional level. If he secures a low score he should consider seriously such occupations as policeman, carpenter, printer, etc., *i.e.*, those at the skilled, semiskilled, or unskilled level.

The occupational-level scale can also be used as an aid in deciding whether or not the score on any given occupational scale is appropriate. For example, if a person gets a high score as lawyer and a high score on the occupational-level scale, he can have more confidence in the score as lawyer than if he had received a low score on the occupational-level scale. Also, if a person receives a high score as carpenter and a low score on occupational level, he can be more certain that this occupation is appropriate than if he had secured a high score on occupational level.

INTERCORRELATIONS AMONG SCALES

It will have occurred to the reader that occupational groups such as physicists and chemists will have many more interests in common than, let us say, artists and certified public accountants. Therefore, we are led to ask whether it is possible to make any meaningful classifications of the occupations for which scales have been developed. If so, the results can be telescoped into useful patterns. In other words, in interpreting the results on the Strong Vocational Interest Test, must we concern ourselves with each and every one of the occupational scores and with the three special scales, interest maturity, masculinity-femininity, and occupational level? Or is there some useful, economic, and meaningful method of grouping the scores to reduce the number of apparently separate and discrete score entities?

Strong has experimented with three methods of classification: upon the basis of the three special scales, upon the basis of factor analysis, and upon the basis of a trial-and-error empirical grouping based upon the scale intercorrelations. The last two methods give

TABLE 14. *Occupational Interest in Relation to Interest Maturity, Masculinity-Femininity, Occupational Level, and Intelligence**

Group no.	Occupation	Standard scores			Correlations			
		Interest maturity	Masculinity-femininity	Occupa-tional level	Interest maturity	Masculinity-femininity	Occupa-tional level	Intelligence
1	Artist	46.2	33.0	58.9	−.53	−.44	.18	.18
	Psychologist	51.6	47.9	60.9	−.14	−.14	−.14	.38
	Architect	50.7	43.8	61.0	−.46	−.11	−.03	.23
	Physician	49.7	46.4	61.3	−.51	−.06	.03	.24
	Dentist	51.8	53.2	57.7	−.39	.14	−.24	.07
2	Mathematician	49.4	47.8	61.5	−.47	.11	−.13	.35
	Physicist	47.8	55.7	61.0	−.51	.32	−.17	.34
	Engineer	51.6	61.9	61.4	−.44	.64	−.20	.28
	Chemist	50.6	57.1	60.0	−.38	.44	−.28	.35
3	Production manager	53.0	59.1	60.2	.01	.79	−.23	.04
4	Aviator	50.7	58.2	54.3	−.26	.76	−.59	.22
	Farmer	50.2	51.2	55.7	−.29	.68	−.62	.06
	Carpenter	51.3	58.6	48.5	−.14	.63	−.72	−.02
	Printer	53.4	47.3	51.5	.03	.37	−.82	.12
	Mathematics science teacher	55.1	50.3	55.0	.30	.49	−.72	.08
	Policeman	53.8	51.2	50.0	.27	.57	−.77	−.13
	Forest service	52.5	52.2	56.4	.08	.59	−.62	−.03
5	Y.M.C.A. physical director	56.2	47.1	55.8	.67	−.03	−.49	−.18
	Personnel manager	56.5	50.7	61.4	.75	−.06	−.10	−.02
	Y.M.C.A. secretary	58.7	40.0	59.4	.84	−.34	−.18	−.18
	Social science teacher	57.0	42.9	56.1	.75	−.40	−.21	−.21
	City school superintendent	56.5	44.6	63.4	.63	−.51	.10	−.06

TABLE 14. *Occupational Interest in Relation to Interest Maturity, Masculinity-Femininity, Occupational Level, and Intelligence*[*]
(Continued)

Group no.	Occupation	Standard scores			Correlations			
		Interest maturity	Masculinity-femininity	Occupational level	Interest maturity	Masculinity-femininity	Occupational level	Intelligence
6	Minister	57.3	35.1	58.8	.54	−.56	−.14	.02
7	Musician	52.8	40.6	53.8	.04	−.41	−.42	.02
8	Certified public accountant	53.9	46.4	63.4	.09	−.29	.43	.22
9	Accountant	55.4	50.1	59.5	.52	.32	−.26	−.10
	Office worker	54.6	52.0	57.0	.61	.16	−.33	−.25
	Purchasing agent	53.9	55.6	60.0	.03	.46	.01	−.21
	Banker	53.4	49.2	58.1	.17	−.01	.05	−.33
10	Sales manager	54.3	51.8	63.3	.21	−.31	.42	−.23
	Real estate salesman	51.9	47.3	60.4	−.02	−.28	.41	−.22
	Life insurance salesman	53.8	42.4	62.3	.27	−.49	.47	−.26
11	Advertising man	52.8	39.0	63.8	−.08	−.74	.52	.01
	Lawyer	52.4	47.0	64.4	−.15	−.62	.60	.13
	Author-journalist	47.5	31.8	63.0	−.45	−.66	.46	.18
	President of manufacturing concern	52.8	51.7	63.4	−.32	.03	.63	−.03

* From Strong, E. K., Jr. *Vocational Interests of Men and Women.* Stanford University, Calif.: Stanford University Press, 1943.

essentially similar results, but Strong has found it helpful to consider the results of both methods in relation to each other. Table 14 shows the results of these classifications and the correlations of the occupational scales with intelligence and with the three special scales, interest maturity, masculinity-femininity, and occupational level. This table is useful in showing that scores on occupations such as artist, psychologist, architect, physician, and dentist tend to be highly related to each other. Therefore, if a student is interested in dentistry, let us say, and if he gets high scores in other occupations in Group 1, as well as a high score in dentistry itself, he can have additional confidence in his intended choice of a vocation. However, if he secures high scores, not on the scales in the same group but, let us say, on the scales in Group 8, purchasing agent, office worker, accountant, and banker, these will call into question the advisability of his going into dentistry.

GROUP SCALES

To facilitate economy in scoring and to provide a broader basis of occupational classification, Strong has developed six group scales. These were constructed by averaging the responses of two or more closely related occupational groups and by contrasting the composite results with the men-in-general group. The group scales now available are as follows:

Group I. Artist, psychologist, architect, physician, dentist
Group II. Engineer, chemist
Group V. Y.M.C.A. physical director, personnel manager, Y.M.C.A. secretary, social-science high-school teacher, city school superintendent, minister
Group VIII. Accountant, office worker, purchasing agent, banker
Group IX. Sales manager, realtor, life insurance salesman
Group X. Advertising man, lawyer, author-journalist

We can use these group scales, if we are interested in determining whether a student should consider preparing in some general direction when he is not yet ready to direct his efforts toward a specific occupation. Thus we can direct him toward scientific or technical work (Group I or II), toward work with people (Group V), toward office and clerical work (Group VIII), toward sales work (Group IX), or toward work involving an interest in language (Group X).

PERMANENCE OF INTERESTS

One of the important considerations in the use of an interest test for educational or vocational guidance is the permanence of the psychological variables measured by the test. If interests fluctuate widely from one period of time to another, there would be little likelihood that we could use interests at one time as a proper guide for those at another time. Strong has devoted considerable attention, therefore, to a study of the permanence of the interests measured by the Vocational Interest Test. He has measured this permanence of interests in four ways: in terms of the correlation between two series of scores, the correlation between two profiles, the comparison of mean scores, and the comparison of ratings before and after specified periods of time. We shall discuss briefly the results secured from each of these methods, although it is obvious that they are not independent of one another.

Correlational Data. For 29 occupational scales Strong finds an average correlation of .80 for a group of college freshmen tested one year after they first took the test, an average correlation of .79 three years later, and an average correlation of .56 nine years later. For a group of college seniors, Strong finds an average correlation of .75 with scores five years later and an average correlation of .71 with scores ten years later. Except for the correlation of .56 for the college freshmen, these all seem like highly respectable indications of permanence of interests. In extenuation of the correlation of .56, we might point out that this could reflect the initial younger age of this group upon its first testing. Interests do tend to change with age, and the younger the person upon the first test, the greater the likelihood of change thereafter. College seniors are much nearer 25, the age after which no appreciable change, or at least relatively little change, in interests will take place.

Profile Data. In this instance, for each of 50 individuals in three groups of subjects (freshmen, seniors, and graduate students), Strong computed the correlations between 34 scores on an original test with those secured on retests five, ten, and twenty-two years later. Thus each correlation to be mentioned represents profile consistency over each of the periods of time in question. The median correlations which Strong reports are .84 for a five-year interval,

.82 for a ten-year interval, and .76 for a twenty-two-year interval. We can certainly agree "that the chances are very good that those who had interests most similar to engineers, lawyers, or ministers while in college will have similar scores twenty years later."

Mean-score Data. Strong gives data for 18 occupational scales for 168 college seniors tested in 1927, 1932, and 1937. He finds only seven statistically significant changes from 1927 to 1932 and two such changes from 1932 to 1937. Between 1927 and 1937 he finds eight statistically significant changes. In most of the comparisons the mean scores increased but only by a very slight amount. Strong concludes that if changes due to increasing interest maturity could be subtracted from the mean-score changes, there would be very little change left to be accounted for. The average score of 95 seniors before and after entering an occupation and remaining in it for ten years changed only from 46.2 to 46.9. It is evident that in terms of mean scores interests may be considered fairly stable and permanent.

Rating Data. The extent to which a person taking the Vocational Interest Test at one time may expect, upon a second testing, to get the same rating or a rating one or two steps removed from the original rating is set forth in Table 15. Strong concludes, "Even

TABLE 15. *Comparison of College Seniors on Two Different Testings**

Group	Time interval, years	Received identical ratings	Received identical ratings or ratings one step removed	Received identical ratings or ratings one or two steps removed
High school juniors..................	6	40.5%	72.8%	88.5%
College freshmen....................	1	52.0	86.2	95.9
College seniors......................	5	45.9	77.5	93.2
College seniors......................	10	40.7	72.1	91.4
College seniors, 5 years later..........	5	48.3	82.0	95.6

* From Strong, E. K., Jr. *Vocational Interests of Men and Women.* Stanford University, Calif.: Stanford University Press, 1943.

after ten years, it appears there is only one chance in one hundred with college seniors that an A or C diagnosis is incorrect, that is, an A becomes a C or vice-versa."

PREDICTION OF SUCCESS

We can now turn our attention to the extent to which the Vocational Interest Test is useful in differentiating superior and inferior students, and superior and inferior members of various occupational groups.

Academic Success. We have available for the study of this problem scales designed to differentiate between occupations, between courses of study, and between superior and inferior students.

Occupational Scales. The occupational scales yield very low correlations with academic achievement. The highest correlation which Strong reports is one of .34 between the engineering scale and grades in engineering. The Vocational Interest Test does poorly, therefore, what an intelligence test or scholastic aptitude test can do much better. Strong reports a study by Segel, however, in which Segel correlated the occupational scales with " (*a*) the differences between grades in two school subjects and (*b*) the differences between achievement scores in two educational subjects." In this study, Segel found a correlation of .61 between the engineering scale and the differences in grades for mathematics and science-history. He found a correlation of .57 with the differences in scores between a mathematics and a history–social-science test. These are higher than those found to obtain between the engineering scale and grades or test scores. Strong's explanation is that the difference in achievement in two school subjects represents the residue to be explained after the ability or intelligence factor is eliminated from consideration. In other words, ability is required for achievement in any school subject. But the procedure of subtracting the grade in one subject from that in another cancels ability as a factor. Therefore, it is reasonable to suppose that the difference in grades is due to something other than ability, and part of this other factor could easily be a person's interests.

Scales Differentiating Courses of Study. We can summarize the work in this area by quoting Strong directly:

. . . it is possible to differentiate students in terms of major courses of study on the basis of interests in the same way that men are differentiated with respect to occupations. So far this has not been done in a thorough going manner nor with as high a degree of differentiation. Three explanations may be advanced: First, scales have not been based in most cases on large enough samples. Second, the criteria are not as good as with occupational scales. . . . Third, the interests of students are less stable than the interests of adults who are well established in their occupation.

Superior and Inferior Students. The most significant study in this area is that centering around the work of Young and Estabrooks and their studiousness scale. They constructed this scale by proceeding through the following steps:

1. They computed the correlation between intelligence and grades.

2. Upon the basis of the regression equation which they obtained, they made predictions from intelligence as to what grades 588 students, individually, should obtain.

3. They subtracted the predicted grade from the obtained grade to get a residual score. This they interpreted as a measure of studiousness.

4. They selected as two criterion groups the 100 students with the highest studiousness scores and the 100 students with the lowest studiousness scores.

5. They determined the percentage of each of these groups that gave the alternative answers L, I, and D to each item, and from the differences obtained they constructed their studiousness scale.

This scale was found to correlate approximately .33 with college grades at Colgate University. For the same students, intelligence-test scores correlated .45 with grades. Using both intelligence and the studiousness scale a multiple R, predicting grades, of .56 was obtained. At the University of Florida, Mosier was able to verify these results for liberal-arts students but not for technical or business students. At the University of Minnesota, Williamson, who made still another check of the results, found that the studiousness scale correlated .20 with grades for liberal-arts students. This did not turn out to be a very useful relationship, however. When combined with the predictions made from the American Council on Education Psychological Examination, the multiple correlation predicting grades was found to be .48, an increase of only .03 over what the ACE alone was capable of doing.

Vocational Success. This problem can be attacked by using the occupational scales or by developing new scales designed to differentiate between superior and inferior members of a specific occupation. We shall review the evidence available from both these lines of study.

Occupational Scales. Strong presents more complete data for the life insurance scale than for any other. Table 16 shows the relation between the scores on the life insurance scale and the average annual production of 211 life insurance agents. This table shows, among other trends, that 56 per cent of those with A ratings, but only 6 per cent of those with C ratings, achieved an average annual production of $150,000 or more. Another way of seeing the relationship is to note that 52 per cent of those receiving C ratings produced less

TABLE 16. *Scores on the Life Insurance Scale and Average Annual Production of Life Insurance**

Production	N	Percentage receiving rating				
		C	B−	B	B+	A
$400,000 and up..............	6	0	0	5	4	3
$200,000 to $399,000..........	47	0	17	0	20	31
150,000 to 199,000..........	37	6	17	9	13	22
100,000 to 149,000..........	31	18	17	14	7	19
50,000 to 99,000..........	52	24	17	45	34	16
0 to 49,000..........	38	52	32	27	22	9
Total number..............	211	17	6	22	45	121

* From Strong, E. K., Jr. *Vocational Interests of Men and Women.* Stanford University, Calif.: Stanford University Press, 1943.

than $50,000 per year, that 24 per cent produced from $50,000 to $99,000 per year, that 18 per cent produced $100,000 to $149,000 per year, and, as we noted above, that only 6 per cent produced $150,000 or more per year. The reader can examine other columns or rows of the table for additional confirmation of the relationship between the test scores and production. We can summarize the over-all relationship by noting that it results in a Pearsonian coefficient of .37. This correlation is not considered high by many academicians, but it is significant and indicative of a useful degree of relationship between the test scores and production in the life insurance business.

Another set of data is provided by Dr. Marion A. Bills. She found a decided relationship between success in selling casualty insurance and the scores on the life insurance and real estate interest scales. Her data are presented in Table 17. Reading across the top row of the table, we find a steady decline, as we go from high to low interest scores, in the percentage of cases rated by their managers as "outstanding successes." Conversely, as we proceed along the bottom row of the table, from high to low interest scores, we find a steady increase in the percentage of cases rated "failures" by their managers. The over-all relationship is expressed in a coefficient of only .25 but again this represents a significant relationship. There certainly is little question that in the fields of life and casualty insurance there

TABLE 17. *Scores on the Life Insurance and Realtor Scales and the Production of Casualty Insurance**

Ratings	Percentage of cases who received designated ratings				
	... +6	+4 +5	+3 −2	−3 −5	−6
Outstanding success...............	25	16	11	8	4
Success.........................	53	56	47	39	20
Failure.........................	22	28	42	53	76
Total number	139	130	193	71	55

* From Bills, M. A. Relation of scores in Strong's interest analysis blanks to success in selling casualty insurance. *J. Appl. Psychol.*, 1938, **22**, 97–104.

is a useful relationship between the scores on the life insurance interest scale and success in selling. This shows, as we remarked a few pages earlier, that the differences between life insurance salesmen and men-in-general are related positively to the differences which distinguish the successful from the unsuccessful life insurance salesman.

TABLE 18. *Occupational Interest Scores in Relation to Supervisors' Ratings**

Scale	r
Chemist..........................	.341
Engineer..........................	.307
Certified public accountant..........	.253
Teacher..........................	.139
Personnel manager.................	.134
Accountant.......................	.034
Lawyer..........................	.009
Life insurance salesman.............	− .308

* From Strong, E. K., Jr. *Vocational Interests of Men and Women*. Stanford University, Calif.: Stanford University Press, 1943.

There have been reported entirely too few studies on the relationship of the occupational interest scores to success in fields other than life insurance. One such study, however, resulted in the correlations reported in Table 18. These show the relationships for 59 foremen between their scores on ratings by their supervisors and their own scores on several of the occupational scales. Since these foremen were employed in chemical and engineering plants, the correlations seem appropriate.

Superior and Inferior Members of an Occupation. Strong reports only one study in this connection. It consisted in an attempt to differentiate successful from unsuccessful aviators. Strong used as his successful aviators 101 Army, 71 Navy, and 215 transport pilots and 125 Civilian Aeronautics Authority instructors, and contrasted these with 173 "failures." These "failures" consisted "of 65 naval trainees and 32 Civilian Aeronautics Authority trainees who failed their preliminary course and 76 men rated the 'poorest in my section.'" The results achieved with this scale, as well as with the aviation interest scale itself, proved ineffective in differentiating successful from unsuccessful aviators. Here we find a different result, then, than we did in the case of life and casualty insurance salesmen. This illustrates the danger of attempting to generalize the results which may be secured for one scale to those which may be expected for any of the others.

RELIABILITY, OBJECTIVITY, AND VALIDITY

Having now described the methods Strong used in the development of the Vocational Interest Test, having mentioned something about the nature of each scale, and having given some indication of the uses to which these scales may be put, we must now inquire into the data pertinent to a determination of their reliability, objectivity, and validity. These data will show how effectively the Vocational Interest Test measures the area of personality it was designed to explore.

Reliability. Table 19 shows the Spearman-Brown coefficients which Strong has reported. This table gives data for 35 of the men's occupational scales and for 18 of the women's occupational scales. It gives data for 6 of the group scales and for the nonoccupational scales: interest maturity, masculinity-femininity, and occupational level. The coefficients for men are based upon the records of 285 Stanford seniors, and the coefficients for women are based upon the records of 500 married women. None of these cases was included in the original criterion groups. The lowest of the coefficients reported is that of .73 for certified public accountant, and the next two lowest

TABLE 19. *Reliability Coefficients for the Scales on the Vocational Interest Test**

Men's Scales: *r*

Artist.................................... .92
Psychologist............................. .88
Architect................................ .90
Physician................................ .89
Dentist.................................. .84
Mathematician........................... .92
Engineer................................ .94
Chemist................................. .91
Production manager...................... .85
Aviator.................................. .90
Farmer.................................. .88
Carpenter............................... .90
Printer.................................. .80
Mathematics-science teacher .... .88
Policeman............................... .83
Forest Service........................... .88
Y.M.C.A. physical director............... .84
Personnel manager....................... .82
Y.M.C.A. secretary...................... .90
Social science teacher.................... .88
City school superintendent............... .84
Minister................................ .90
Musician................................ .87
Certified public accountant............... .73
Accountant.............................. .84
Office worker............................ .88
Purchasing agent........................ .85
Banker.................................. .83
Sales manager........................... .90
Realtor................................. .90
Life insurance salesman.................. .93
Advertising man......................... .91
Lawyer.................................. .88
Author-journalist........................ .94
President of manufacturing concern........ .82

Women's Scales:

Artist................................... .93
Author.................................. .94
Dentist................................. .78
Office worker............................ .92
Housewife............................... .90
Lawyer.................................. .81
Librarian................................ .87
Life insurance saleswoman................ .74
Nurse.................................. .87
Physician................................ .87
Social worker............................ .83

TABLE 19. *Reliability Coefficients for the Scales on the Vocational Interest Test**

(Continued)

Women's Scales:	r
Stenographer-secretary	.85
Teacher of English	.82
Teacher of mathematics-physical science	.84
Teacher of social science	.86
Y.W.C.A. secretary	.88
Physical education teacher	.86
Elementary school teacher	.90
Nonoccupational Scales:	
Interest maturity	.93
Occupational level	.88
Masculinity-femininity (men)	.93
Masculinity-femininity (women)	.74
Group Scales:	
I. Physician	.94
II. Chemist	.94
V. Y.M.C.A. secretary	.90
VIII. Accountant	.85
IX. Life insurance	.94
X. Lawyer	.93

* From Strong, E. K., Jr. *Vocational Interests of Men and Women.* Stanford University, Calif.: Stanford University Press, 1943.

are for life insurance saleswoman and the women's masculinity-femininity scale. Both of these coefficients are .74. The highest reliability reported is .94. This obtains for the author scale on the women's blank, for the engineering and author-journalist scale on the men's blank, and for the chemist-engineering scale and selling scale on the group keys. Of the 64 coefficients 26 are .90 or over.

Objectivity. This term has usually been taken as referring to the degree to which a test score may be in error because of variations introduced by the person scoring the test. Using the term in this traditional sense, we may say that the Vocational Interest Test is completely objective. There is a fixed and set series of weights to be used in scoring, and there is no possibility that variation in results can be introduced by the test scorer. (We are ruling out, of course, purely mechanical errors, as we are assuming that adequate provision will be made for checking the numerical accuracy of all test results.) There may be minor variations induced by a test examiner, depending upon the tone he sets in giving instructions for taking the test. If he implies by his actions that the test results are to be treated lightly, chances are that the subject will not give the same care in answering, as otherwise might be the case.

The situation under, and the purpose for, which the test is given would also seem to be a source of uncontrollable variation. A college student who really believes that the test will help him make a wise choice of a future career will undoubtedly exert more care in giving his answers than will another student not so convinced. And both of these students, having nothing to gain and much to lose by dishonesty, may give a different set of answers than will the applicant who feels that the showing he makes on the test will have some bearing upon his being considered favorably for employment.

In this latter case, we must recognize three possible sets of conditions under which the test may be taken: honestly, dishonestly at a conscious level, and dishonestly at a subconscious level. Test scores secured under one of these conditions may show little relation to those secured under either of the other two conditions. We can certainly venture the assertion that test scores are most useful, not only to a potential employer, but also to an applicant himself, if he gives an honest set of answers.

In the employment situation we must recognize, however, that an applicant may put down consciously or unconsciously the answers which he feels will get him the job, rather than those which may more accurately describe him. A number of investigators have found that it is easy, when one is so inclined, to fake the answers on the Vocational Interest Test. Strong, himself, asked 22 engineering students and 13 business-school students to secure scores as high as possible on the engineering interest scale. The engineers, even though their original scores on engineering were high, increased their average score on the scale by 142 raw-score points. The business-school students, whose scores on the engineering interest scale were low, raised their average score by 392 raw-score points.

Steinmetz asked 46 students to secure high scores on the teacher-administrator scale and found a mean raw-score increase over their original scores of 247 points. This deliberate fudging also caused large changes on the scales for Y.M.C.A. secretary, minister, personnel manager, and certified public accountant. At the same time, it caused a marked decrease in scores for realtor, artist, and farmer. There is certainly no question that test scores can be deliberately falsified. The only safeguard is to "sell" a person on the value to himself of giving honest answers and of thus getting a report of real value.

Validity. We now come to the most important of the three basic requirements for any psychological measuring instrument. Does the Strong Vocational Interest Test give results which can be taken as valid? There is to this question, as much as we might like it, no straightforward and simple answer. We cannot say that the test is valid or is not valid without specifically defining the purpose to be served or the specific scale in question. Let us review the scales we have discussed and see what problems are involved in determining their respective validities.

First, let us consider the occupational scales. Their primary purpose is to differentiate designated groups of business or professional men (or women) from men- (or women-) in-general. They will be valid, therefore, if they do this job well but not valid if they do this job poorly. Since we have 39 such scales on the men's blank and 18 on the women's blank, we at once find that we have not one, but 54 validities to consider.

Next, we have the group scales. These scales are supposed to distinguish certain general groupings of occupations (not specific occupations) from men- (or women-) in-general. The validity question is analogous to that for each of the specific occupational scales but is, nevertheless, a different one. And since there are 6 group scales, we now find a total of 60 validities that need to be considered.

Third, we have the nonoccupational scales, interest maturity, masculinity-femininity, and occupational level—three more scales and three more validity problems. Does the masculinity-femininity scale distinguish between the interests of men and those of women? Does the occupational-level scale distinguish between those high and low in the occupational hierarchy? Does the interest-maturity scale differentiate between the interests of older and younger men?

A fourth type of scale is that designed to differentiate among students engaged in different courses of study, a fifth (not reported on in this text) is that designed to differentiate between superior and inferior students in specific subjects, and a sixth type is designed to differentiate between superior and inferior members of designated occupational groups.

Altogether there must be well over 150 different validities to be considered in relation to the purposes of the Strong Vocational

Interest Test. We cannot say, therefore, that the test as a whole is valid or is not valid. It is valid for some purposes to a high degree, for other purposes to a moderate degree, and for other purposes it possesses no validity whatsoever.

Occupational Scales. These scales are valid, we said above, if they can be shown to differentiate the members of different occupational groups from each other. If they did not, the test could obviously not be used as a basis for guiding a person toward one occupation or line of study rather than toward another. It would be impossible for us to review here the data for all scales, but it will be most instructive if we follow Strong's discussion on the differentiation of artists and accountants. Strong finds that accountants secure a mean score of 17 on the artist scale and that artists secure a mean score of 11 on the accountant scale. Immediately, we see that these scales are different. Table 20 shows the mean scores of 19 occupational groups on the artist scale, and Table 21 shows the mean

TABLE 20. *Differentiation of Artists from 19 Other Occupational Groups by Use of the Artist Scale**

Occupation	Mean	Critical ratio	Percentage overlapping
Artist..........................	52		
Physician.........................	33	12.8	37
Mathematician....................	33	13.3	35
Musician........................	33	11.9	40
Advertiser.......................	30	14.1	32
Chemist.........................	29	15.8	26
Printer..........................	26	18.2	20
Minister.........................	26	18.1	20
Lawyer..........................	26	18.9	19
Farmer..........................	24	20.1	15
Carpenter.......................	24	21.1	13
President of manufacturing concern...	22	20.1	15
Certified public accountant..........	22	21.7	13
Life insurance salesman.............	22	22.8	11
City school superintendent..........	20	23.4	10
Production manager................	20	24.1	9
Policeman.......................	19	23.6	10
Personnel manager.................	19	23.9	10
Banker..........................	17	24.8	8
Accountant......................	17	25.8	7

* From Strong, E. K., Jr. *Vocational Interests of Men and Women.* Stanford University, Calif.: Stanford University Press, 1943.

TABLE 21. *Differentiation of Accountants from 19 Other Occupational Groups by Use of the Accountant Scale**

Occupation	Mean	Critical ratio	Percentage overlapping
Accountant........................	49		
Certified public accountant..........	43	4.7	74
Banker............................	39	7.0	62
Personnel manager.................	36	9.5	50
Production manager................	35	10.2	47
Policeman.........................	34	10.4	47
Carpenter.........................	33	11.2	43
Printer............................	32	12.6	37
President of manufacturing concern...	31	12.1	39
City school superintendent..........	30	14.1	32
Chemist...........................	29	13.5	34
Mathematician.....................	28	16.1	27
Musician..........................	26	15.2	27
Farmer............................	26	16.6	26
Lawyer............................	26	16.3	26
Advertiser.........................	25	16.3	27
Life insurance salesman.............	25	15.7	27
Minister...........................	20	21.3	14
Physician..........................	19	22.9	11
Artist.............................	11	28.4	6

* From Strong, E. K., Jr. *Vocational Interests of Men and Women*. Stanford University, Calif.: Stanford University Press, 1943.

scores of these same occupational groups on the accountant scale. In each of these tables, column 3 shows the percentage of overlapping between the distribution of scores for artists or accountants, as the case may be, and those for the other occupational groups. As used by Strong, percentage of overlapping means "the percentage of scores made by one group which could be matched with scores in the other group." In both tables there can be seen a steady reduction in percentage overlapping as one proceeds from the top to bottom row of the table.

We have no way of knowing, apart from the data secured by means of the Strong Vocational Interest Test, what the "true" overlap between the scores for artists and accountants may be. But the fact that there can be as little overlap as 7 per cent (between artists and accountants) or 4 per cent (between nurses and life insurance saleswomen) would seem to validate the assumption that the members of different occupational groups can be differentiated from one another. The Strong Vocational Interest Test can be considered a valid test in that it reveals these differences.

Not all scales show so little overlapping as the artist and accountant scales or as the nurse and life insurance saleswoman scales. The musician and artist scales, for example, overlap to the extent of 40 per cent, and the accountant and banker scales overlap to the extent of 62 per cent. It seems reasonable that musicians and artists should overlap more than accountants and artists. And it seems reasonable that accountants and bankers should overlap to a greater extent than accountants and artists. But whether the true overlaps are 40 and 62 per cent or whether they should be reversed, there is no way of telling.

Group Scales. Data relative to the validity of group scales are presented in Table 22. This table shows the percentage of each occupa-

TABLE 22. *The Validity of Group Scales**

Scale	%	Scale	%
Group scale I:		Group scale VIII:	
Artist	92	Accountant	70
Architect	72	Office worker	65
Psychologist	74	Purchasing agent	65
Dentist	49	Banker	74
Physician	62	Average	68
Average	70	Group scale IX:	
Group scale II:		Sales manager	66
Engineer	62	Life insurance salesman	81
Chemist	78	Realtor	67
Mathematician	72	Average	71
Physicist	97	Group scale X:	
Average	77	Advertiser	69
Group scale V:		Lawyer	56
Y.M.C.A. physical director	75	Journalist	83
Personnel manager	48	Average	69
Y.M.C.A. secretary	87		
Social science teacher	73		
City school superintendent	66		
Minister	92		
Average	72		

* From Strong, E. K., Jr. *Vocational Interests of Men and Women.* Stanford University, Calif.: Stanford University Press, 1943.

tional group that gets a score of A on the group scale. We know from our previous discussion that approximately 70 per cent of each criterion group of subjects secure a letter rating of A, that is, a standard score of 45 or more, on their own occupational scale. Therefore, we can determine the validity of a group scale for any occupational group by noting what percentage of its members secures a rating of A on the group scale designed to represent them. With this thought in mind we can see that Group Scale I possesses its greatest validity for architects and psychologists and its least validity for artists and dentists. Similarly, Group Scale V is seen to be more valid for Y.M.C.A. physical directors and social-science teachers than it is for ministers and personnel managers. We must conclude that the group scales vary in validity, depending upon the particular occupations involved.

Nonoccupational Scales. In this instance we can almost say that the scales are valid by definition. Strong defined carefully that which was to be measured: interest maturity, masculinity-femininity, and occupational level, and described in detail how he selected the criterion groups involved. Since we have gone over this material, it seems unnecessary to review it here. The only additional thought of value in connection with our current discussion on validity is that the scales can be considered valid when the scores are interpreted with due regard for the manner in which the criterion groups were selected and the scales constructed. Whenever in doubt as to the true meaning of the scores on one of these special scales, the reader should refer to our earlier discussion or, better yet, to Strong's own explanation in Chaps. 10 to 12 of his book *Vocational Interests of Men and Women.*

It will not be worth our while to review the evidence for the remaining types of scales, for it is scattered and incomplete. Of necessity, the value of this evidence varies with the specific scales, with the investigator, with the purpose to be served, and so forth. Also, our primary purpose in this chapter is to understand the methods which Strong himself has used in his research on the Vocational Interest Test, and we have covered most of these in our previous discussion.

SCORE INTERPRETATION

In concluding this chapter on the Strong Vocational Interest Test, it will be well for us to consider again the meaning to be attached to the various scores that can be secured. In most test-score interpretation it is customary for us to consider extreme test-score deviates as the atypical members of some defined group. Thus we commonly think of an I.Q. of 200 or of 50 as representing the near extremes of the distribution of intelligence of a normal population and as being far removed from the typical or average member having an I.Q. of 100. In the case of the occupational scores on the Strong Vocational Interest Test, this customary interpretation cannot be applied. In this instance, the higher the score on an occupational scale, the more typically like that group do we consider the individual in question. This phenomenon comes about because of the method by which a Strong occupational scale is constructed. To construct the scale for artist, Strong contrasted the responses given by 241 artists with those of 4,746 men-in-general. Upon the basis of the differences obtained, a scoring scale was constructed. And this scoring scale was constructed upon the basis of the hypothesis that items showing large differences should be weighted more heavily than items showing small differences. Therefore, when a subject answers an item in the same way as artists, he receives a high score on this item. If he answers an item in the same way as men-in-general, he receives a low score on this item. Therefore, if a subject answers many items in the same way as artists, he receives a high score on the artist scale. This high score indicates that he has the same interests as artists, and if this is the case, it means he is like the typical artist. On the other hand, if the subject answers more items like men-in-general, he receives a low score as artist. The lower this score, the more he is like men-in-general. Thus an extremely high score indicates that our subject is like the typical artist, while an extremely low score indicates that our subject is like the typical man-in-general.

3

INTERESTS: A RATIONAL APPROACH

We learned in the last chapter that the development of a scale on the Strong Vocational Interest Test can be a time-consuming and painstaking task. It has taken Dr. Strong over twenty-five years to develop his 60 plus scales, and these cover only a few of the many thousands of existing occupations. To extend Dr. Strong's procedures to cover all occupations would seem to constitute an almost endless and, perhaps, a thankless task. Yet if guidance by means of tests is a legitimate endeavor, why should we deny this service to those who may wish to consider entering any of the many occupations for which the Strong Vocational Interest Test cannot be scored?

This was one of the considerations, among others, that led Dr. G. Frederic Kuder to a new approach and to the ultimate development of his Preference Records. In these Preference Records, as we shall see in detail later, an attempt is made to provide scores on a number of "basic" preferences having, it is supposed, differential degrees of significance for a variety of occupations. When the scores in these areas are obtained, the subject or his counselor, or both together, are supposed to be able to use them in deciding upon occupations suitable for serious consideration. The timesaving feature, in contrast to Strong's approach, lies in the supposition that the preferences measured by the Kuder Preference Records are relatively independent and that, in differently weighted combinations, they can be applied to almost any occupation.

In the Strong Vocational Interest Test, it is possible for two scales to be highly interrelated. For example, scores on the physicist scale correlate .91 with those on the mathematician scale. Therefore, if one of these scores is known, not too much additional information can be gained from a knowledge of the other. This does not hold, of course, for all scales. Scores for certified public accountants and artists, for example, correlate not at all ($r = .00$). Therefore, knowledge of both of these scores tells us much more about a person's interests than does knowledge of either one alone. Our chief point in bringing this up is to demonstrate that in Strong's approach to interest measurement there can be no forehand knowledge (there can be speculation, of course) as to how any proposed scale will correlate with scales previously developed. If a new scale should correlate highly with one already developed, as indeed one for physicist did correlate with one for chemist ($r = .93$), there is too little gain in knowledge to compensate for the time and effort involved in its original development and in its later scoring. Therefore, if we could assure ourselves ahead of time that each new scale to be developed would not correlate with any preexisting scale, we could feel that we would not need to run the risk of duplicating results already obtainable.

This gives us the background for Kuder's approach. He wanted scales which would not correlate with each other. Therefore he developed his scales by methods which would assure their maximal independence. It is for this reason that we call Kuder's approach a rational one. He started out, not with Strong's purpose of establishing empirical differences among occupational groups, but with the avowed intention of constructing uncorrelated scales. This is clearly a rational as opposed to an empirical objective. Kuder developed his scales without reference to what they might actually measure in terms of vocational significance. This problem was to be attacked later.

THE PREFERENCE RECORD—VOCATIONAL

The Kuder Preference Record—Vocational (1946 revision) consists of 160 triadic groups of items. In each of these triads the subject is asked to indicate which of the three activities he likes best and to indicate which of the three activities he likes least. These instructions make it possible for the subject to show which of the three activities is preferred to two of the other activities, which of the three activities is preferred to only one of the other activities, and which of the three activities is not preferred to either one or both of the other two activities.

An example of the type of item in the Preference Record is as follows:

a. Visit an art gallery
b. Browse in a library
c. Visit a museum

A subject can check any one of the three activities, *a*, *b*, or *c*, as most preferred and any one of the three activities as least preferred. This leads to six possible preference orders of the three activities. These are *a, b, c; a, c, b; b, a, c; b, c, a; c, a, b;* or *c, b, a.* In other words, there are two ways in which activity *a* can be indicated as first choice; there are two ways in which activity *b* can be indicated as first choice; and there are two ways in which activity *c* can be indicated as first choice. Accompanying each of these are two correlative ways in which an activity can be placed in second position and two correlative ways in which an activity can be placed in third position. Kuder assigns a weight of 2 for an activity preferred to two other activities, a weight of 1 for an activity preferred to only one other activity, and a weight of 0 to an activity preferred to neither of the other two activities in the triad. The total score on a scale is obtained by a simple addition of these item weights.

The Kuder Preference Record—Vocational yields 10 different scores. These indicate preferences for activities described as mechanical, computational, scientific, persuasive, artistic, literary, musical, social service, clerical, and outdoor. The score on each scale is supposed to indicate the degree of a subject's preference for the type of activity involved in the designated area. Raw scores are interpreted in terms of their percentile ranks, separate norms being available for high-school students and for adults. Kuder suggests that an individual should seriously consider entering any occupation involving the type of activity indicated by a scale on which he receives a percentile rank of 75 or over and that he should seriously consider staying out of any occupation involving the activity indicated by a scale on which he receives a percentile rank of 25 or less.

To aid a person in making an appropriate choice of occupation Kuder gives a list of occupations which are suitable for consideration by those with specified scores on the Preference Record. Kuder states that a few of the suggestions made are based on research data, but the vast majority are based on nothing more than Kuder's judgment as to what occupations should be considered. We have nothing against Kuder's judgment, but we must point out that judgment was involved. This is a definite weakness of the guidance

available on the strength of the scores on the Kuder Preference
Record in contrast with that available upon the basis of the scores
provided by the Strong Vocational Interest Test. In the latter, all
scales are based upon empirically demonstrated differences among
occupational groups and not upon anyone's subjective judgment
as to whether two occupational groups may or may not be different.

Development of the Scales. Kuder's first step in the development of his Preference Record—Vocational was to prepare a list of
200 activities. These activities were those which, on an a priori
basis, appeared to be useful indicators of interest preference. Kuder
arranged these items into 40 groups of five activities each and took
care to have as many different types of activity as possible represented in each group. He gave this form of the test to 500 Ohio State
University students (1934–35) and asked them to rank, in order of
preference, the activities in each of the 40 groups.

In this preliminary edition a number of activities appeared to be
classifiable as mechanical in nature, and another group appeared to
be classifiable as literary in nature. Using these items, and on an
a priori basis, item weights were assigned to indicate a liking for
mechanical activity in preference to other types of activity and a
liking for literary activity in preference to other types of activity.
The items in the literary scale were found to produce total scores
possessing a split-half reliability of .85, so it appeared that they
measured something (presumably, preference for literary activity)
in a reasonably consistent manner. This fact led Kuder to choose
this scale as the anchoring post for the development of a second scale.

The next step in this further development was that of computing
the correlations between the responses of each of the original 200
items and the total score on the literary scale. Items found to have
low correlations with the literary preference score were selected for
further study. Examination of the content of these items revealed
a sizable number which Kuder thought to be indicative of a preference for experimental (or, later, scientific) activity. Therefore, a
core of these items was selected and weighted to constitute a new
scale. When scored, this scale produced a split-half reliability of .65.

The next thing which Kuder did was to correlate all 200 items with
this experimental scale, and all items that were found to correlate
significantly with it were incorporated therein. But if any item added
to the experimental scale correlated in a significant positive direction

with the literary scale, it was balanced by another item which correlated in a significant negative direction. In this way, the correlation between the literary and experimental scales was kept near zero.

Kuder now examined the items not included in either the literary or experimental scales and selected, from these remaining items, those which seemed to indicate preference for artistic activity. Item correlations with this scale were determined, and items found to correlate with it were added thereto. In adding these items Kuder attempted to balance as nearly as possible their correlations with the literary and experimental scales. His goal was to use in the artistic scale only those items which correlated zero with both the literary and experimental scales, but since not every item met this criterion, items were balanced against each other so that the total score on the artistic scale would correlate as little as possible with the total scores on the literary and experimental scales.

The fourth scale Kuder developed was designed to measure "social prestige." The procedures followed were the same as those described in connection with the previous scales, but, in this case, the problem was much more complex. Items had to show no correlation with the literary, experimental, and artistic scales. Upon the completion of the prestige scale the remaining items did not seem to lend themselves to meaningful classification, so, from this initial set of items, no further scales were constructed.

Kuder now collected additional items and administered these, together with all previous items, to new groups of students. The correlation of each item with each of the existing scales was ascertained, and many of the items, because of these correlations, were found suitable for inclusion in the previously developed scales. There remained many items, however, which could not be added to previously existing scales, so these were examined for content with a view toward using them as the building blocks for additional scales.

Kuder tried to develop scales for athletics, religion, finance, politics, and annoyances. For various reasons, however, none of these scales proved satisfactory. One of the stumbling blocks encountered in the attempt to develop these additional scales was the fact that no scale beyond the first three—literary, experimental, and artistic—could be developed without showing a marked correlation with the social prestige scale. Therefore, Kuder dropped the prestige scale and divided many of its items between two other scales now proposed. This made it possible for Kuder to continue until seven scales had been constructed. These seven scales are literary, experimental, artistic, computational, persuasive, musical, and social service.

Kuder now published the test as Form A and, in this form, it was used extensively by personnel and guidance workers. Later, as a result of various criticisms, suggestions, and further study, Kuder felt it would be desirable to add scales for mechanical and clerical activities. But Kuder developed these scales only in terms of a criterion of internal consistency and did not concern himself with how the items in them correlated with the total scores on the other seven scales.

Intercorrelations among Scales. The seven scales originally prepared have, as they should, fairly low intercorrelations. The highest correlation Kuder reports is that between the persuasive and scientific scales. This averages −.38 for six groups of subjects. Most of the other intercorrelations are very near zero, as the data presented in Table 23 demonstrate.

TABLE 23. *Intercorrelations among the Scales on the Kuder Preference Record—Vocational**

Scale	Computational	Scientific	Persuasive	Artistic	Literary	Musical	Social	Clerical
Mechanical	−.038	.352	−.219	.145	−.384	−.288	−.205	−.225
Computational		.198	−.169	−.252	−.095	−.162	−.116	.464
Scientific			−.377	−.110	−.182	−.283	−.075	−.227
Persuasive				−.157	.137	−.001	−.023	.104
Artistic					−.180	.036	−.278	−.272
Literary						.093	−.131	−.143
Musical							−.106	−.027
Social								−.222

* Adapted from Kuder, G. F. *Revised Manual for the Kuder Preference Record*. Chicago: Science Research Associates, 1946.

Validity and Reliability. The reliabilities reported by Kuder are given in Table 24. They range from .80 to .98 and have a median value of .91. The groups upon which these values are based vary in size from 41 to 300 and include eighth graders, high-school and college students, and adults.

We may conclude, then, that Kuder has been reasonably successful in reaching his main objective: that of getting reliable measures of nearly independent variables. Now if these scales cover interests in an adequate fashion, they should make for great economy in giving a person some idea of the scope and direction of his interests. It must be clearly understood, however, that on any Kuder scale, a score represents the extent to which a certain group of activities (the nature of which was subjectively determined) is preferred to several other types of activity. And whether any given score is to be considered high or low can be determined only in

TABLE 24. *Reliabilities of the Scales on the Kuder Preference Record—Vocational**

Group	Number	Mechanical	Computational	Scientific	Persuasive	Artistic	Literary	Musical	Social	Clerical
Graduate students....	41	.97	.98	.95	.97	.96	.95	.95	.93	.98
College students......	166	.94	.90	.93	.93	.91	.90	.90	.91	.89
College students......	101	.91	.88	.88	.94	.90	.92	.85	.90	.86
College students......	50	.85	.87	.91	.81	.95	.84	.96	.92	.95
High school seniors...	125	.93	.90	.90	.82	.91	.91	.90	.87	.87
High school seniors...	125	.89	.83	.89	.80	.92	.91	.91	.93	.90
8th grade students....	100	.96	.86	.92	.84	.92	.86	.93	.91	.89
Men in occupations...	300	.95	.91	.89	.89	.90	.93	.94	.93	.88

* From Kuder, G. F. *Revised Manual for the Kuder Preference Record*. Chicago: Science Research Associates, 1946.

terms of its percentile position with reference to the scores made by the high-school students or adults in the basic normative groups. A score is not high or low, as in the Strong Vocational Interest Test, with reference to any specific occupation.

But if the scores on the Kuder Preference Record are to be used in guidance work, and they are, we must learn whether or not they are useful in distinguishing occupational groups from each other. Kuder's data on this point are not so extensive as those provided by Strong, but he does show, in many instances, that the members of different occupations do in fact secure distinguishing Preference Record scores. Tables 25 and 26 show the mean Preference Record— Vocational scores secured by the members of various occupational groups. Kuder presents data for other occupations also, but we have included in these tables only those means based upon 50 or more cases.

Kuder presents data for 15 occupational groups which appear (except for the smaller and less carefully selected populations) to be

TABLE 25. *Mean Preference Record Scores for Men**

Group	Number	Mechanical	Computational	Scientific	Persuasive	Artistic	Literary	Musical	Social	Clerical
Base group...........	2,667	79	35	64	74	46	48	17	74	52
High school boys.....	1,858	78	35	68	67	48	47	18	62	54
Accountants.........	117	68	50	61	74	41	54	18	69	62
Authors.............	50	48	27	52	82	42	76	22	73	48
Mechanical engineers..	60	94	37	74	74	48	45	16	65	44
Drug store managers..	130	72	36	72	84	44	44	16	71	50
Secondary school teachers...........	120	65	36	63	69	41	53	17	85	51
Meteorologists.......	185	84	36	77	63	45	54	17	66	46
Personnel managers...	67	67	33	60	85	40	53	17	83	49
Physical education instructors........	60	67	30	64	68	40	49	17	96	40
Weather observers....	99	82	40	77	59	45	52	18	66	52
Retail managers......	82	72	36	60	85	43	45	16	74	55
Sales managers.......	89	73	31	60	95	42	51	18	71	47
Securities salesmen....	59	66	33	55	103	43	47	19	80	50
Salesmen to consumers	130	73	32	62	95	42	47	16	72	50
Manufacturing foremen..............	69	93	38	71	68	48	42	14	72	51
Steel manufacturing foremen..........	54	94	38	70	69	50	41	13	70	51

* From Kuder, G. F. *Revised Manual for the Kuder Preference Record*. Chicago: Science Research Associates, 1946.

TABLE 26. *Mean Preference Record Scores for Women**

Group	Number	Mechanical	Computational	Scientific	Persuasive	Artistic	Literary	Musical	Social	Clerical
Base group...........	1,429	53	32	55	62	53	53	21	81	62
High school girls......	2,005	50	29	53	66	52	49	24	79	63
High school English teachers...........	69	42	28	46	58	55	71	25	78	56
High school home economics teachers.....	94	57	30	56	58	58	51	20	81	53
Occupational therapists..............	70	73	26	55	51	68	49	24	86	44
Trained nurses.......	183	54	29	60	53	54	50	22	93	50
Bookkeepers.........	59	45	38	53	62	51	53	23	82	65
Office clerks..........	78	54	35	54	62	54	48	22	81	69
Stenographer-typists..	168	51	30	55	58	52	50	23	78	69

* From Kuder, G. F. *Revised Manual for the Kuder Preference Record*. Chicago: Science Research Associates, 1946.

similar to the standardization groups used by Strong. It should be instructive and profitable for us to compare the classifications of these 15 occupational groups as given by the Kuder and Strong inventories. Table 27 shows the 15 occupations, their mean scores on

TABLE 27. *Comparison of Scores on the Kuder Preference Record and the Strong Vocational Interest Test**

Occupation	Kuder				Strong			
	Scientific		Persuasive		Chemist		Life insurance scale	
	Mean	Rank	Mean	Rank	r	Rank	r	Rank
Accountant....................	61	7	74	8	−.16	9	−.02	10
Author.......................	52	14	82	4	.06	6	.11	7
Aviator.......................	79	2	64	13	.71	2	−.69	14
Chemist......................	86	1	63	14	.....	1	−.84	15
School administrator..........	62	6	74	8	−.42	12	.36	5
Lawyer.......................	58	12	79	5	−.31	10.5	.47	3
Life insurance salesman........	57	13	91	2	−.84	15	.....	1
High school mathematics teacher	77	3	57	15	.56	3	−.64	13
Clergyman....................	60	9	66	12	−.10	7	.09	8.5
Musician......................	51	15	71	10	.23	5	−.23	11
Personnel manager.............	60	9	85	3	−.31	10.5	.31	6
Production manager............	67	4	78	6	.40	4	−.38	12
Sales manager.................	60	9	95	1	−.74	14	.82	2
Social science teacher..........	59	11	74	8	−.59	13	.44	4
Physical education instructor....	64	5	68	11	−.11	8	.09	8.5

* Adapted from Strong, E. K., Jr. *Vocational Interests of Men and Women.* Stanford University, Calif.: Stanford University Press, 1943; and from Kuder, G. F. *Revised Manual for the Kuder Preference Record.* Chicago: Science Research Associates, 1946.

the Kuder persuasive and scientific scales, and their correlations with the chemist and life insurance scales on Strong's test. A careful study of this table reveals the following relationships:

1. Ranks based on the Kuder science scale and on the Strong chemist scale are highly and positively correlated.
2. Ranks based on the Kuder persuasive scale and on the Strong life insurance scale are highly and positively correlated.
3. Ranks based on the Kuder science scale and on the persuasive scale are highly and negatively correlated.
4. Ranks based on the Strong chemist scale and on the life insurance scale are highly and negatively correlated.

5. Ranks based on the Kuder science scale and on the Strong life insurance scale are highly and negatively correlated.

6. Ranks based on the Kuder persuasive scale and on the Strong chemist scale are highly and negatively correlated.

These results show, it must be admitted, a striking resemblance. This appears truly remarkable in view of the markedly different approaches used by Strong and Kuder in the development of their inventories. The similarity of results, in view of these extremely divergent approaches, shows the rankings to possess a considerable degree of substantial or psychological validity. They demonstrate that important practical results can be reached through a theoretical or rational approach, as well as through an empirical one. We must point out in this connection, however, that results on the Kuder Preference Record and on the Strong Vocational Interest Test do not agree in all particulars as well as they do in our illustration. And when they differ, it would seem the safer course to assume that Strong's data possess the greater validity.

Short Form. We have up to this point been discussing only one of three Kuder Preference Records. It is available in two formats (Forms BB and BM) for hand or machine scoring. A shorter form consisting of 120 groups of activities rather than of 160 groups of activities, as in the longer form, is known as the short form (BI). Kuder developed this form by selecting the "better" groups (triads) of items from the longer form. It is to be used, says Kuder, in those situations in which time cannot be made available for the longer

TABLE 28. *Reliabilities of the Scales on the Short Form of the Kuder Preference Record— Vocational and Their Correlations with the Scales on the Long Form**

Group	Me-chan-ical	Com-puta-tional	Scien-tific	Per-sua-sive	Artis-tic	Liter-ary	Musi-cal	Social	Cler-ical
Intercorrelations:									
Men (N = 100)	.98	.97	.97	.96	.94	.96	.97	.97	.98
Women (N = 100)	.96	.97	.95	.96	.95	.93	.97	.96	.98
Reliabilities:									
Men (N = 100)	.94	.86	.90	.91	.90	.90	.88	.88	.85
Women (N = 100)	.88	.88	.87	.86	.87	.90	.88	.90	.90

* From Kuder, G. F. *Revised Manual for the Kuder Preference Record.* Chicago: Science Research Associates, 1946.

form. The reliabilities of the scales on the short form and their correlations with the scores on the long form are given in Table 28.

THE PREFERENCE RECORD—PERSONAL

The third Kuder Preference Record is known as the Kuder Preference Record—Personal. It yields scores on five types of activities not heretofore discussed: sociable, practical, theoretical, agreeable, and dominant. Kuder's definition of each of these scales is as follows:

Sociable. This scale measures expressed preferences for personal activities of a sociable nature. A preference for taking the lead and being in the center of activities involving people.

Practical. This scale measures expressed preference for personal activities of a practical nature. A preference for dealing with practical problems and everyday affairs rather than interest in imaginary or glamorous activities.

Theoretical. This scale measures expressed preference for personal activities of a theoretical nature. A preference for thinking, philosophizing, and speculating.

Agreeable. This scale measures expressed preference for personal activities of an agreeable nature. A preference for pleasant and smooth relations which are free from conflict.

Dominant. This scale measures expressed preference for personal activities of a dominant nature. A preference for activities involving the use of authority and power.

The principles followed in the construction of the Kuder Preference Record—Personal were much the same as those used in the development of the Kuder Preference Record—Vocational. Therefore, they need not be reviewed in any great detail. Kuder's aim was to devise scales measuring factors not already covered by the vocational inventory and, of course, which did not intercorrelate among themselves.

The preliminary form of the personal inventory included almost 900 groups of activities in triads. Seven tentative scales were developed. Then the item correlations with these scales, as well as with those on the vocational inventory, were obtained. Following procedures we have already described, items were added to the various scales in such a way as to augment reliability and to minimize intercorrelations. New items were then assembled, the scales were further augmented, and eventually two of the proposed seven scales were dropped. This left the five scales on which the inventory can now be scored. One of the scales has a reliability of .84, two have reliabilities of .85, and two have reliabilities of .86. These are all lower than for the vocational inventory. The intercorrelations among the scales are shown in Table 29.

TABLE 29. *Intercorrelations among the Scales on the Kuder Preference Record— Personal**

Scale	Sociable	Practical	Theoretical	Agreeable
Practical..............	−.26			
Theoretical............	.17	−.03		
Agreeable.............	−.06	.21	.24	
Dominant.............	.32	−.22	.25	−.21

* From Kuder, G. F. *Examiner Manual for the Kuder Preference Record—Personal*. Chicago: Science Research Associates, 1948.

RATIONAL VS. EMPIRICAL APPROACH

Throughout this chapter we have made many references to Kuder's approach as a rational one and to Strong's approach as an empirical one. In concluding this chapter, we should like to bring this difference into even sharper focus, because the differences in the procedures followed by Strong and Kuder have not received the attention they deserve. Too many personnel psychologists, vocational counselors, and guidance workers assume that an interest test is an interest test is an interest test, and let it go at that. We cannot urge too strongly that a thorough understanding of the different procedures followed by Strong and Kuder is fundamental to giving proper guidance and counsel in the field of interest measurement.

To repeat, Strong's approach can be called empirical. Not that theory is not involved, but Strong started out to secure data which would show that different occupational groups could be differentiated in terms of the interests of successful men in each of several occupations. The development of each scale followed an empirical finding that one occupational group could be differentiated from another or from a men-in-general group. If the empirical finding showed that a given occupational group could not be differentiated from any other occupational group or from a men-in-general group, no scale was developed. Obviously, it would serve no purpose.

Kuder's approach can be called rational. Not that empiricism is not involved, but Kuder started out to secure scales which would have no correlation with each other. He wanted to differentiate people from one another but upon a basis that one method of classification would yield results entirely independent of those yielded by a second method of classification. Kuder felt that the empirical application of his scales should follow their rational development. Strong felt that the scales should be developed originally in an empirical manner.

Kuder felt that the rational development of scales would lead to considerable economy in the description of the interests a person might possess. Thus if several independent variables can be demonstrated to offer a fairly complete picture of the interests which a person is likely to possess, it does not seem unreasonable to suppose that such a scale should be found useful whenever a measure of interests is desired. Theoretically, there is some limit to the number of scales which Kuder might find it useful to develop. This number is reached as soon as it is discovered that an additional scale adds no information independent of the preceding scales.

In Strong's approach there is no limit to the number of scales which might be developed. Theoretically, there could be a scale for each occupational group now in existence. Thus the number of scales might be twenty or thirty thousand. This, of course, is carrying things to an extreme. Certain occupations are so much alike that it is pointless to have a separate scale for each of them. There is no definite and clear-cut way of finding this out, however, until separate scales for the two groups have been developed. Thus Strong's approach leaves open the possibility that much labor may be expended in developing a new scale only to find that it already duplicates closely a previously existing scale. The only preventive to this is, of course, the investigator's own good judgment, and, unfortunately, we know this cannot always be relied upon.

Another way in which the Strong and Kuder inventories differ from each other is in the groups for which they were designed. Strong's inventory was designed primarily to serve the needs of the college student looking toward a professional career. It was designed to help such a student, in the light of his interests, focus his attention on an occupation or upon a group of closely related occupations which would be appropriate for him to consider. Other things such as ability being equal, Strong theorized that a person would find himself happier and more successful in an occupation where he would find men with interests similar to his own. He would not definitely be a failure, but presumably less happy and less successful if he were to enter an occupation which attracted, for the most part, men with interests largely different from his own.

Kuder's Preference Records are designed, primarily, for the high-school student, for the younger student, and for the student who is not yet ready to pinpoint his efforts in preparation for a specific occupation. It is also designed with the thought that it should be useful to a broader class of students than those who are slated only for a job in one of the professions. Kuder's Preference Records are geared to lead the student to a consideration of a broad or general field, such as the physical sciences, without concern as to whether the ultimate career is to be in physics, chemistry, or engineering. Or it will lead him to consider literary activity without regard as to whether the ultimate career is to be in teaching English, in being a playwright, or in becoming poet laureate.

As a general field usually has to be selected much earlier than a final field of specialization, it would seem that an appropriate joint use of Kuder's and Strong's interest inventories, at younger and older ages, might well be considered as part of any complete vocational guidance program.

4

ATTITUDES: AN A PRIORI APPROACH

We learned in the last two chapters that the concept *interest* covers such things as our likes and dislikes, our preferences, and our aversions. In contrast, the concept *attitude*, with which we are to deal in this and in the next chapter, covers our beliefs. We believe something is right or that something is wrong. We favor this and object to that. We accept this position and reject that position. This believing or disbelieving, this favoring or not favoring, this accepting or rejecting, constitute expressions of attitude.

To illustrate concretely the difference between an interest and an attitude, let us consider the statement "I like bananas." Are we to consider this statement expressive of an attitude toward bananas or expressive of an interest in bananas? Ordinarily, we would classify this statement as an expression of interest, not as an expression of attitude. We do this because there is implied in this statement no acceptance or denial of any belief about bananas. The statement "I like bananas" implies nothing at all as to whether I think it is a good or a bad thing for me to do so. The statement "Bananas are good for children" we would classify as an expression of attitude. It clearly implies a certain belief about bananas, namely, that they are good for children.

Our interest in bananas and our attitude toward bananas are two independent concepts. We can believe that bananas are good for children (attitude), but still not like them (interest). We can believe that bananas are not good for children (attitude), but we can, nevertheless, like them (interest). We can believe that bananas are good for children (attitude), and can also like them (interest). And last of all, we can believe that bananas are bad for children (attitude), and we can also dislike them (interest). We may summarize our discussion by saying that an interest is an expression of feeling, whereas an attitude is an expression of belief.

In the field of attitudes, as in the field of interests, there are two principal measuring techniques to be discussed. These are Thurstone's method of equal-appearing intervals and Likert's method of summated ratings. We have selected these methods for discussion, not only because they are the two principal methods in the field, but also because they illustrate two diametrically opposite approaches to the central problem involved.

This central problem is the scaling of test items. In Thurstone's method, the method of equal-appearing intervals, the scaling of test items takes place before the collection of attitude data. For this reason we call it an a priori approach. In Likert's method, the method of summated ratings, the scaling of test items takes place after the collection of attitude data. It is, in fact, dependent upon them. For this reason we call it an a posteriori approach. We shall discuss this latter approach in Chap. 5. The remainder of this chapter will be given over to a discussion of the method of equal-appearing intervals.

The first complete description of the method of equal-appearing intervals as applied to the measurement of attitudes appeared in a monograph published in 1929. This monograph, "The Measurement of Attitude," represented the joint efforts of Professors L. L. Thurstone and E. J. Chave of the University of Chicago. In this mono-

TABLE 30. *Equal-appearing-interval Attitude Scales*
Edited by Professor L. L. Thurstone

Attitude toward the Bible	Attitude toward God (influence on conduct)
Attitude toward birth control	Attitude toward honesty in public office
Attitude toward capital punishment	Attitude toward immigration
Attitude toward censorship	Attitude toward the law
Attitude toward the Chinese	Attitude toward the League of Nations
Attitude toward the church	Attitude toward the Monroe Doctrine
Attitude toward communism	Attitude toward the Negro
Attitude toward the Constitution	Attitude toward patriotism
Attitude toward divorce	Attitude toward preparedness
Attitude toward the economic position of	Attitude toward prohibition
women	Attitude toward public office
Attitude toward evolution	Attitude toward public ownership
Attitude toward foreign missions	Attitude toward the social position of women
Attitude toward free trade	Attitude toward Sunday observance
Attitude toward freedom of speech	Attitude toward the treatment of criminals
Attitude toward German war guilt	Attitude toward unions
Attitude toward the Germans	Attitude toward war
Attitude toward God (belief in the reality of)	

graph, Thurstone and Chave illustrate the method of equal-appearing intervals as they applied it in developing a scale to measure attitude toward the church. Following the publication of this monograph, Thurstone or his students, or both together, developed the scales listed in Table 30.

Many investigators have followed Thurstone's lead and have developed their own equal-appearing-interval attitude scales. Not all these scales have been published, however, so it is difficult to estimate their total number. But they certainly must exceed 300.

DEVELOPMENTAL STEPS

The basic premises in the method of equal-appearing intervals are that a series of statements can be made to serve as the markers on a yardstick for the measurement of attitudes; that each of these statements will represent a specified degree of acceptance or rejection of a belief; and that these specified degrees of acceptance or rejection will be equally spaced throughout the entire range of the attitude continuum. The theory is that, if a person will indicate which of the statements he will accept and which he will reject, we can locate him at a definite position on the attitude continuum. Our problems in scale construction are to select an appropriate series of statements and to determine what positions on the attitude continuum each of our statements represents. These problems are solved by Thurstone and Chave in seven major steps. These steps are:

1. The collection of a preliminary list of statements
2. The evaluation of these statements
3. The determination of scale values
4. The selection of a final list of statements
5. The elimination of ambiguous statements
6. The elimination of irrelevant statements
7. The collection of normative data

In the following paragraphs we shall add the details which will illustrate the purpose to be served by each of these steps, and we shall discuss some of the problems which each of these steps involves.

Collection of Statements. Statements can be made up by the investigator, they can be suggested by colleagues, they can be clipped from magazines and newspapers, and so forth. In all cases, they should represent the entire attitude continuum: from complete acceptance of a belief to its complete rejection.

We cannot say in advance how many statements should be collected, but 200 or 300 will not be too many. Thurstone and Chave, in their study, however, used only 130. At the other extreme, Ferguson (in a study we shall describe in Chap. 13) reports using more than 600. The number of statements will vary with the needs to be met and with the insight of the investigator.

After statements have been collected, they must be edited. Many statements, upon close scrutiny, will not seem so pertinent as they once did. And, in the hustle and bustle of collecting them, careless phraseology may have been employed. Editing will usually reveal a number of double-barreled and ambiguous statements. Duplication of content will be found, and many of the statements will be seen to be more effective if reworded.

Thurstone and Chave present a number of useful rules to follow in this editing process, but a more complete set has been presented by one of Thurstone's students, C. K. A. Wang. Close adherence to these rules will help materially in the preparation of significant and adequate sets of stimulus statements. The more important of Wang's rules are as follows:

1. Each statement must be debatable. That is, it must reflect opinion, not fact.
2. Each statement should be relevant to the attitude variable under consideration.
3. Each statement should be subject to just one interpretation.
4. Each statement should be simple, not compound.
5. Each statement should be short.
6. Each statement should be complete in denoting a definite attitude toward a specific issue.
7. Each statement should contain one complete thought.
8. Each statement should be clear-cut and direct.
9. Each statement should be stated in the active, not in the passive voice.
10. Each statement should contain the term of issue as its subject.

Evaluation of Statements. After a sufficient number of statements have been collected and edited, we are faced with the task of their evaluation. We must determine what position on the attitude continuum each of the statements will represent. We do this by asking judges to sort the statements into various categories.

Directions to Judges. Thurstone and Chave mimeographed their statements on small slips of paper. Each statement was put on a separate slip. Then these slips were handed to a number of judges who were instructed as follows:

1. The 130 slips contain statements regarding the value of the church. These have been made by various persons, students, and others.

2. As a first step in the making of a scale that may be used in a test of opinions relating to the church and religion we want a number of persons to sort these slips into eleven piles.

3. You are given eleven slips with letters on them: A, B, C, D, E, F, G, H, I, J, K. Please arrange these before you in regular order. On slip A put those statements which you believe express the highest *appreciation* of the value of the church. On slip K put those slips which express the strongest *depreciation* of the church. On the rest of the slips arrange statements in accordance with the degree of appreciation or depreciation expressed in them.

4. This means that when you are through sorting you will have eleven piles arranged in order of value-estimate from A, the highest, to K, the lowest.

5. Do not try to get the same number in each pile. They are not evenly distributed.

6. The numbers on the slips are code numbers and have nothing to do with the arrangement in piles.

7. You will find it easier to sort them if you look over a number of the slips, chosen at random, before you begin to sort.

8. It will probably take you about forty-five minutes to sort them. . . .

Since Thurstone and Chave's pioneering study, a number of variations in instructions have been tried. Among the more important of these variations we may list those described by Seashore and Hevner, by Farnsworth, and by Ferguson.

The principal change suggested by Seashore and Hevner is to mimeograph the statements as a list, together with a series of letters or numbers in front of each statement. This avoids the necessity of separate slips and of their sorting into different piles. Judges indicate their evaluations by drawing circles around letters or numbers. Seashore and Hevner report that results are the same as those secured by Thurstone and Chave but that these results are secured with a considerable saving in time.

We are describing the steps in what is known as the equal-appearing-interval method of attitude measurement. This designation conforms to historical usage, but Farnsworth has raised a question as to whether raters operate, when rating statements, within the framework implied in the strict psychophysical sense of the term *equal-appearing intervals*. Farnsworth wonders whether a judge considers position 7, for example, as equidistant between positions 6 and 8. Perhaps, says Farnsworth, some judges consider position 7 a little closer to position 8, and some judges consider it a little closer to position 6.

To check on this theory, Farnsworth asked a group of judges to evaluate the statements in Form A of Peterson's scale for the measurement of attitude toward war and to do this in accord with the Thurstone-Chave directions. When the judges had completed this task, Farnsworth asked them to indicate whether position E had been considered to be exactly halfway between positions D and F or whether it had been considered as more militaristic than D but not at a point exactly halfway between D and F. Of the judges who replied 63.5 per cent answered in the affirmative to the second alternative. They did not consider position E as exactly halfway between positions D and F.

In further exploration of the judgmental processes involved, Farnsworth asked another group of judges to indicate on a line with a neutrality point indicated, the positions of extreme pacifism and extreme militarism. Farnsworth argued that, if the equal-appearing-interval process were operating, the mean distance of the point representing extreme pacifism should be just as far from the neutrality point as the mean distance of the point representing extreme militarism. Farnsworth's judges did not place the extreme points at equal distances from the point of neutrality, so he concluded that they were not operating within the framework implied by the concept *equal-appearing intervals*.

In view of these results, Farnsworth has suggested two graphic line approaches which avoid the use of the equal-appearing-interval concept. The results obtained with these approaches are much the same as those secured either by the Thurstone and Chave or by the Seashore and Hevner methods.

One of Farnsworth's graphic line approaches involves the following set of instructions:

You are to read the statements carefully and decide how pacifistic or militaristic they are. Note that the extreme left of the rating line is the pacifistic end and the extreme right the militaristic. Item number 21 is already rated for you, i.e., its placement on the line represents the judgment of many previous raters. It was regarded as completely pacifistic in character. Rate the other 20 items similarly. Put dots on the line at the points which you feel best express the degree of pacifism-militarism of the item. Place the number of the items over the dots. More than one item may be placed on the same point on the line.

The material for Farnsworth's second graphic line procedure consists of a sheet with 18 vertical lines exactly 11 centimeters long and numbered 2 to 19. "These lines are bounded by two horizontal lines numbered 20 (top) and 1 (bottom)." The directions presented to a judge are as follows:

You are to estimate the degree of pacifism or militarism of 18 statements (numbered 2 through 19) relative to the pacifism-militarism of two sample statements. Consider the top horizontal line to represent the value of a very militaristic sample, and the baseline that of a very pacifistic sample. For example, if a certain statement seems midway in value between the pacifistic and militaristic samples check its rating line at the midpoint; if it seems closer in value to one of the samples than to the other put a check mark closer to the appropriate sample. None of the statements will be as pacifistic as the pacifistic sample (statement 1) nor as militaristic as the militaristic sample (statement 20). Each statement has its particular line on which its value is to be estimated.

As we said before, Farnsworth's procedures avoid the use of the equal-appearing-interval concept, yet they give results closely allied to the Thurstone and Chave, and to the Seashore and Hevner techniques.

Ferguson has used various sets of instructions. Some of these have been in strict conformity with the Thurstone and Chave procedure, and others have not. Among the latter we can mention two for our present consideration. Both of these were used in the development of employee merit-rating scales. The first set was used in the development of a series of clerical merit-rating scales, and the second set was used in the development of an evaluation form for assistant managerial personnel. Ferguson has reported no comparison of the results secured by these directions with those obtained by a strict adherence to the Thurstone and Chave sorting procedure. But judging from the results reported by Seashore and Hevner, and by Farnsworth, it does not seem rash for us to assume that they would be much the same.

Number of Statements for Each Scale Position. Thurstone and Chave made no attempt to control the number of statements which a judge could place in each pile. But they proceeded to disregard the ratings of any judge who placed 30 or more statements, out of 130, in one pile. They did this on the assumption that a judge who placed this many statements in one pile lacked the ability, or at least did not take the trouble, to make an adequate number of discriminations among the statements to be evaluated.

Ferguson, as we can see from the two sets of directions just mentioned, has secured evaluations with and without control of the number of statements to be given any one evaluation. These contrasting approaches appear to produce no difference, however, in the distribution of statements throughout the intervals of the scale. All distributions show a marked tendency for judges to interpret a statement as favoring either the acceptable (or positive) or the unacceptable (or negative) portions of the continuum, as well as a resistance to judging a statement as having neutral significance.

Number of Intervals. Thurstone and Chave, and all of Thurstone's collaborators and students, have divided their attitude continuua into 11 intervals. Ferguson has used 9 and 7 intervals. Orear and Waldenfels have used 5. The number of intervals to be considered appropriate depends upon the attitude variable which is to be measured and upon the preferences of the investigator. Anyone having occasion to construct an equal-appearing-interval scale will find it helpful, however, to consult Symond's data on the reliabilities of scales with different numbers of step intervals. These data can be found in Chap. III of Symond's text *Diagnosing Personality and Conduct*.

Source and Number of Judges. College students, because of their accessibility to college professors and their willingness and eagerness to participate in such studies, more frequently than other groups are asked to serve as judges. This is not a necessity, however, as Rice at one time implied. Other groups have been used. Selover, and Waters at the Prudential Insurance Company of America, Kingsbury at the Continental Illinois National Bank and Trust Company, Jurgensen at the Kimberly-Clark Company, Gibbons at the Owens-Illinois Glass Company, Knauft at the Federal Bake Shops, and Ferguson at the Metropolitan Life Insurance Company are among those who have used nonstudent groups for statement evaluation.

Thurstone and Chave used 300 judges in their study. Reliable evaluations can be secured, however, with as few as 25 judges. Therefore, in most situations, a compromise between this number and the 300 suggested by Thurstone and Chave would seem to be in order. The author has used 25, 50, 75, 100, 125, 150, and 200 judges.

The only advantage which appears to accrue from the use of the larger groups is the additional sales appeal to potential users of the completed scales. We need not be arbitrary, but the occasions will be rare when more than, let us say, 50 judges will be needed.

Determination of Scale Values. Our next steps are to determine for each statement its median evaluation and its ambiguity. To determine these values we first count the number of times a statement is allocated to each scale position. This gives us a simple frequency distribution. Second, we convert this simple frequency distribution into a cumulative frequency distribution. And, third, we convert this cumulative frequency distribution into a cumulative percentage distribution.

What we need next are three percentile points: Q_1, Q_2, and Q_3. These are the 25th, 50th, and 75th percentile points, respectively. These can be computed arithmetically from our cumulative percentage distribution or graphically. The 50th percentile of our distribution constitutes the median value of our statement. The 75th and 25th percentiles are used in determining its ambiguity. This is found by the formula: $(Q_3 - Q_1)/2$. Thus our index of ambiguity is one-half the difference between the 75th and 25th percentiles. It is, in fact, nothing more than the well-known quartile deviation. Statements which are ambiguous are assigned a large variety of ratings and have large quartile deviations. Statements with precise and definite meanings are assigned a small variety of ratings and have relatively small quartile deviations.

In the section on evaluation of statements, we discussed several factors which could have some effect upon the results of the process of statement evaluation. We discussed variations in the instructions, the number of preliminary statements to be collected, the number of intervals on the continuum, and the number of judges to be used. These factors are basic and fundamental, because some decision must be made on each one before any of our statements can be evaluated. We now find it necessary to discuss a number of additional factors which can affect the statement evaluation process. These factors are as follows:

1. Errors in judgment
2. Errors due to position or number preference
3. The personal attitudes of the judges
4. The cultural context in which the scale is constructed

5. The relevance of the attitude variable as a personal issue to the rater

6. The status of the raters in relation to that of the persons whose attitudes are to be measured

Errors in Judgment. In making his ratings, it is possible that a judge will mistakenly place a statement in position 7, when he should have placed it in position 6 or 8. This may be due to carelessness or due to an erroneous evaluation. There is no absolute safeguard against this type of error. Therefore, judges should be carefully instructed and should be given ample time to make their evaluations. Of course, the evaluation procedure is to some extent self-correcting for errors of this type, because of its requirement that more than one judge submit evaluations. The errors made by one judge will be counterbalanced by the errors made by another judge, and this mutual cancellation of errors will leave some residue of truth in the mean or median evaluations.

It is not ordinarily done, but one way to introduce a greater degree of precision in the evaluations is to convert the ratings supplied by each judge into standard scores before averaging them with those given by other judges. The increased degree of precision, as measured by reduction in the size of the standard deviations of the final scale values, is demonstrated in the data given in Table 31.

TABLE 31. *Variability Data for Statements in an Equal-appearing-interval Scale*

Scale value	Standard deviations				Percentage of reduction in standard deviations	
	Based on raw scores		Based on standard scores			
	Set A	Set B	Set A	Set B	Set A	Set B
9	1.79	1.60	.71	.63	60.3	60.6
8	1.47	1.49	.54	.51	63.3	65.8
7	1.24	1.55	.47	.43	62.1	72.3
6	1.53	1.78	.41	.31	73.2	82.6
5	2.33	2.51	.34	.26	85.4	89.6
4	1.84	1.70	.31	.23	83.2	86.5
3	1.21	1.23	.32 .	.34	73.6	72.4
2	1.45	1.43	.44	.48	69.7	66.4
1	1.58	1.61	.56	.56	64.6	65.2

Perhaps this degree of increased precision cannot always be expected, but there seems to be no reason to doubt that some increase in precision can always be attained.

Position or Number Preference. We present some data in Table 32 to show that judges can have position or number preferences. In the study which led to the collection of these data, there was no reason

TABLE 32. *Distributions of Ratings Secured in Evaluating Statements for an Equal-appearing-interval Scale*

Scale value	Obtained percentage		Expected percentage
	Set A	Set B	
9	6.00	5.62	4.00
8	8.45	8.46	7.00
7	12.34	13.49	12.00
6	11.85	12.05	17.00
5	16.09	15.78	20.00
4	12.64	11.50	17.00
3	14.19	13.97	12.00
2	10.60	11.04	7.00
1	7.84	8.09	4.00
Total..........	100.00	100.00	100.00

for a greater number of statements to have been assigned to position 3 rather than to position 4 or to position 7 rather than to position 6. The greater number of ratings in positions 3 and 7, as compared with those in positions 4 and 6, represents nothing more than a number or position preference.

It can be said, of course, that judges may lack sufficient insight to make the fine discriminations required. This may well be true, but if so, this fact allows position or number preference to have its effect. If judges could be more discriminating, their evaluations would not be subject to the errors caused by position or number preference.

Personal Attitudes of the Judges. It does not seem unreasonable from a common-sense standpoint to suppose that the attitude of a rater should have some effect upon his evaluations of a set of statements. However, Thurstone and Chave, in their original monograph, took the position that these evaluations would prove to be independent of the attitude of the raters. Four studies have now proved this to be the case.

The first of these four studies was conducted by H. C. Beyle. He asked two groups of subjects, differentiated in their attitudes toward Alfred E. Smith, to evaluate statements intended for use in a scale to measure attitudes toward Alfred E. Smith during the 1928 presidential election campaign. He found no appreciable difference in the scale values assigned by these two groups of judges.

Hinckley was the second investigator to study the problem. Hinckley asked a group of Negro students and two groups of white students to evaluate 114 statements from which a scale for measuring attitude toward the Negro was to be constructed. One of the white groups consisted of Southern students openly antagonistic toward Negroes, and the other consisted of Northern students professing to have attitudes favorable to Negroes. Hinckley used the responses of these three groups separately and constructed three scales. These three scales proved to be identical in content, and only one statement was found *not* to occupy the same relative position in all three scales.

Ferguson asked groups of R.O.T.C. students and other Stanford University students, and groups of Epworth Leaguers (now known as the Methodist Youth Fellowship) in Berkeley and San Jose, California, to take Form A of Peterson's scale for the measurement of attitude toward war and then to evaluate, by means of the paired-comparisons method (see Chap. 12) the relative values of the statements in Form B of this same scale. On the basis of their answers to Form A, Ferguson divided his subjects into three groups differing significantly in their attitude toward war. Then, separately for each of these groups, he determined the mean scale values assigned to the statements in Form B of the Peterson scale. He found that the scale values assigned by these three groups correlated .96 or higher with each other and .97 with those published by Peterson.

Finally, at Columbia University, Pintner and Forlano asked 411 students to take Form A of the Thiele and Thurstone scale for the measurement of attitude toward patriotism and to evaluate, by the method of equal-appearing intervals, the statements in Form B of this same scale. Upon the basis of their answers to the statements in Form A, Pintner and Forlano divided their students into three groups differing significantly in their expressions of patriotic attitude. These three groups consisted of the upper 27 per cent, the middle 46 per cent, and the lower 27 per cent. Pintner and Forlano found correlations of .98 and over among the scale values assigned by these three groups of judges.

Except for a complicating factor discussed in the next section, we can say that these four studies effectively dispose of the question involved. We can conclude that Thurstone and Chave's assumption is correct. The attitude of a rater has no effect upon, and is not related to, his evaluations of the statements for an equal-appearing-interval attitude scale.

Cultural Context. Farnsworth, in discussing the results of the foregoing studies, raises a question as to whether scale values secured at different time periods will be affected by changing cultural influence. To answer this question he asked a group of Stanford University students to give their opinions on the values of the items in Form A of Peterson's scale for the measurement of attitude toward war. He did this in 1940–41 and then compared the evaluations he secured with those secured by Peterson in 1930–31. Farnsworth found a high degree of correlation (.97) between the new and the old series of scale values. But he also found a sizable difference in mean scores from the use of these two series of values. This led Farnsworth to suggest that over the decade 1930–31 to 1940–41 the significance of the items in Peterson's scale was affected by cultural change.

If Farnsworth had been content with the computation of the intercorrelation between the two series of scale values, it is very likely that he would have come to the conclusion that cultural change is of no importance insofar as its effect upon the scale values of the statements in an equal-appearing-interval attitude scale is concerned. Farnsworth was able to detect the effects he suspected only by a comparison of mean scores.

This result brings into some question the adequacy of the conclusion reached, albeit independently, by Beyle, by Hinckley, by Ferguson, and by Pintner and Forlano. None of these investigators reported mean-score differences. They confined themselves to the computation and to the consideration of the intercorrelations among different series of scale values. It is possible, therefore, that their conclusion would stand in need of some modification were mean-score comparisons, as suggested by Farnsworth's study, to be effected.

Personal Issue. In the Hinckley study discussed in the section on the personal attitudes of the judges, both Negro and white students evaluated statements in a scale proposed to measure attitude toward the Negro. In addition to differing attitudes, it is possible that ego involvement, particularly on the part of the Negro subjects, may have been a factor in determining the ratings assigned. However, the negative results secured by Hinckley would seem to indicate that neither the difference in attitudes nor the difference in ego involvement caused any material change in the relative scale values assigned.

Status of Raters. Another factor that may affect statement evaluation is group status. In a study by Ferguson, three groups, managers, assistant managers, and agents, evaluated statements from which an assistant managerial evaluation form was to be constructed. It was found that the judges from all three groups rated or evaluated the statements in approximately the same way. Thus, the ego-involved assistant manager group, the superior status group (managers), and the inferior status group (agents) all rated the statements in the same way. Therefore, in the Thurstone equal-appearing-interval procedure we can disregard group status as a factor in statement evaluation.

Selection of Final Statements. When mean or median scale values have been determined, we shall find it advisable to arrange our statements in the order of their mean or median values. The beginning of such a list for Thurstone and Chave's scale for the measurement of attitude toward the church is given in Table 33.

TABLE 33. *Several of the Statements Designed by Thurstone and Chave to Measure Attitude toward the Church**

Statement number	Scale value	Q value	Statement
65	11.0	1.4	I think the church is a parasite on society.
18	10.8	1.8	I am an atheist and have no use for the church.
72	10.7	1.7	I think the organized church is an enemy of science and truth.
96	10.5	1.9	I regard the church as a static, crystallized institution, and as such it is unwholesome and detrimental to society and the individual.
25	10.5	1.6	I believe the churches are doing far more harm than good.
108	10.5	1.6	I believe the church is full of hypocrites and have no use for it.
41	10.5	1.0	I think the country would be better off if the churches were closed and ministers set to some useful work.
48	10.4	1.4	The church represents shallowness, hypocrisy and prejudice.

* Adapted from Thurstone, L. L., and Chave, E. J. *The Measurement of Attitude.* Chicago: University of Chicago Press, 1929.

Our task is to choose some small number of these statements to represent each position along the attitude continuum.

The total number of statements to be selected must be determined in an arbitrary manner. Thurstone and his collaborators have generally tended to use 20 statements. The author has used 20, 26, 52, and 78 statements. Uhrbrock has used 50 statements, and other investigators have used still other numbers. In making a decision on this point, we must keep in mind the fact that the total number of statements we select will determine for us the number of statements that we can have to represent each interval on the continuum. If we choose a total of 33 statements for a continuum divided into 11 intervals, we can have each of these intervals represented three times. If we choose 22 statements, we can have each interval represented only twice. Another factor to keep in mind is the effect of the length of any psychological test upon the reliability of the scores which it yields. In general, and within certain limits, the longer our test, the more reliable the scores based on it.

Thurstone and Chave decided that they wanted 45 statements in their scale for the measurement of attitude toward the church. Therefore, each of their 11 intervals could be represented about 4 times. Actually, 2 of their intervals have 3 statement representatives, 1 has 5, and 1 has 6. This leaves 7 intervals that are represented by 4 statements each. The statements which Thurstone and Chave selected to represent the interval 10.0 to 11.0 were numbers (see Table 33) 65, 72, 96, 41, and 48. Their median values are 11.0, 10.7, 10.5, 10.5, and 10.4. These values average 10.6, so, collectively, they can be considered adequate representatives of the interval with which we are concerned.

In the process of selecting our final list of statements, it is generally desirable to give thought to the preparation of at least two alternative forms of our scale. An easy way to do this would be to arrange them in order according to scale value, number them, and then assign all odd-numbered statements to Form A and all even-numbered statements to Form B. This procedure would not be entirely satisfactory, however. It would result in the allocation of the higher valued statement in each odd-even pair of statements to one form and in the allocation of the lower valued statement in each odd-even pair of statements to the alternate form. Thurstone and Chave solved this problem by assigning the higher valued statement in their first pair of statements to Form A and the lower valued statement to Form B. Then, in their second pair of statements they assigned the higher valued statement to Form B and the lower valued statement to Form A. Alternating in this way, they avoided the possibility that all of the higher valued statements would be assigned to one form and all the lower valued statements to the other form.

Ambiguous Statements. Our measure of statement ambiguity is the quartile deviation of the distribution of ratings given to each statement. We have already indicated its method of computation. Obviously we want statements with precise and clear-cut meanings. This is not an all-or-none proposition, however, so we must have some standard by which we can select the less ambiguous statements in contrast with the more ambiguous ones. Therefore, if we have 6 statements available and need to use only 3 of them, we should choose the 3 statements with the lowest degree of ambiguity. We do this by choosing the 3 statements with the smallest quartile deviations. Table 33 shows the quartile deviations for 8 of the Thurstone-Chave statements concerning attitude toward the church. We find from these data that the average quartile deviation for the statements retained is 1.48, while that of the 3 statements not retained is 1.67. Thurstone and Chave tended to select the less ambiguous statements, yet one of the statements retained has a large quartile deviation. This illustrates that other factors besides degree of ambiguity are also taken into account.

The number of statements scaled at the various intervals of our continuum will undoubtedly be found to vary. For some intervals there will be an overabundance of statements, for some there will be a bare sufficiency, and for some, perhaps, not really enough. Therefore, the same standard of ambiguity cannot, in all probability, be applied throughout all intervals of the attitude continuum.

Irrelevant Statements. We are now ready to give our scale an experimental trial. We must select an appropriate group of subjects and ask them to indicate the statements with which they agree and the statements with which they disagree. When we get these data, we compute what Thurstone and Chave call the criterion of statement irrelevance. This criterion of irrelevance is an index which shows the degree to which each statement in our scale gives results consistent with the other statements. The theory is that, if statements A and B are scaled at similar positions on our continuum, the same proportion of subjects (and in fact the same individuals) that endorse statement A also ought to endorse statement B. Contrariwise, if statements C and D represent widely divergent scale positions, the individuals who endorse statement C should not endorse statement D, and vice versa. We compute the criterion of irrelevance, for statement A, in accord with the formula C/B. In this formula, C represents the number of subjects who endorse both statements A and B, and B represents the number of subjects who endorse statement B only.

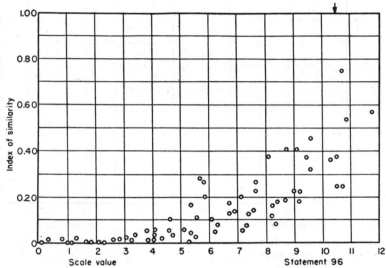

FIG. 2. Irrelevancy values for a statement which passes the irrelevancy test. (From Thurstone, L. L., and Chave, E. J. *The Measurement of Attitude.* Chicago: University of Chicago Press, 1929.)

If all subjects who endorse statement A also endorse statement B, our index will be unity. If none of the individuals who endorse statement A endorse statement B, our index will be 0.

It is necessary to compute our criterion of irrelevance $N(N-1)$ times. In a 20-item scale we have 20×19 (or 380) criterion values to compute. We need to compute it 19 times for statement 1, 19 times for statement 2, 19 times for statement 3, and so on. When we have made these computations, we prepare a series of graphs such as those shown in Figs. 2 and 3. By inspecting these graphs we can determine which of the items, if any, do not meet our criterion, and we shall eliminate these items from our scale.

Figure 2 shows the plot for a statement which has a scale value of 10.5 and which passes the irrelevancy test. It passes the test because items having similar scale values are endorsed, in the main, by the same subjects. It is not endorsed by subjects who endorse statements with markedly different scale values.

Figure 3 shows the plot for a statement which has a scale value of 4.1 and which does not pass our criterion. It does not pass, because

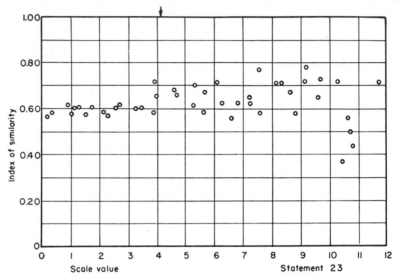

Fig. 3. Irrelevancy values for a statement which fails the irrelevancy test. (From Thurstone, L. L., and Chave, E. J. *The Measurement of Attitude*. Chicago: University of Chicago Press, 1929.)

the numerical value of the index remains fairly constant, and this is true regardless of the scale value of the item being compared with the one whose irrelevancy is at stake. The graph shows that subjects endorsing the statement in question are no more likely to endorse other statements closely allied in scale value than they are to statements far removed in scale value. We conclude the item to be irrelevant and shall eliminate it from our scale.

In their monograph, Thurstone and Chave express some dissatisfaction with this criterion of irrelevance and state that a better one should be developed. Guttman, among others, has accepted this challenge and has described for this purpose what he calls a technique of scalability. We shall not discuss this technique here, however, as it can better be described in connection with Likert's method of attitude-scale construction (see Chap. 5).

In the meantime, we can point to one other technique of determining item irrelevancy. This is factor analysis. We can show by this technique the extent to which the various items in our scale contribute to some one major factor underlying item intercorrelations. Statements that do not contribute significantly to such a factor can be considered irrelevant and can be eliminated from our scale.

Collection of Norms. There is nothing in this operation unique to the Thurstone method of equal-appearing intervals. The only requirement is that we secure distributions of scores for the groups we consider most adequate as standardization groups. For their scale measuring attitude toward the church, Thurstone and Chave secured distributions for 16 groups of subjects. Most of these were student groups at the University of Chicago. The groups represented were freshmen, sophomores, juniors, seniors, graduate students, divinity students, and members of the Chicago forum. The remaining groups, consisting of a reclassification of the subjects in the groups already mentioned (and not mutually exclusive), are Catholics, Protestants, and Jews; churchgoers and nonchurchgoers; and active and inactive church members. Tables 34 and 35 (in which low scores

TABLE 34. *Attitude toward the Church According to Religious Preference**

Attitude score	Catholic		Protestant		Jewish	
	N	%	N	%	N	%
1.0–1.9	28	38.8	37	8.0	2	1.1
2.0–2.9	19	26.3	149	32.1	17	9.7
3.0–3.9	13	18.1	92	19.9	22	12.5
4.0–4.9	3	4.2	58	12.5	31	17.6
5.0–5.9	3	4.2	47	10.2	34	19.4
6.0–6.9	3	4.2	44	9.5	33	18.7
7.0–7.9	2	2.8	25	5.4	24	13.7
8.0–8.9	..	.....	10	2.2	9	5.1
9.0–9.9	1	1.4	1	0.2	4	2.3
Total..........	72	100.0	163	100.0	176	100.0
Mean..........	2.90		3.97		5.44	

* From Thurstone, L. L., and Chave, E. J. *The Measurement of Attitude.* Chicago: University of Chicago Press, 1929.

indicate attitudes favorable to the church) show the distributions of scores for certain of these groups of subjects and illustrate the types of normative data Thurstone and Chave provided.

TABLE 35. *Attitude toward the Church According to Membership and Attendance**

Attitude score	Active church members				Church attendance			
	Yes		No		Yes		No	
	N	%	N	%	N	%	N	%
1.0– 1.9	106	18.2	13	1.7	119	17.6	6	0.9
2.0– 2.9	245	42.3	81	10.4	282	41.6	40	5.8
3.0– 3.9	114	19.6	106	13.6	155	22.9	75	10.8
4.0– 4.9	54	9.3	106	13.6	66	9.7	98	14.2
5.0– 5.9	33	5.7	108	13.8	30	4.4	120	17.3
6.0– 6.9	20	3.4	139	17.7	15	2.2	148	21.3
7.0– 7.9	7	1.2	116	14.8	7	1.0	100	14.5
8.0– 8.9	2	0.3	84	10.8	4	0.6	81	11.7
9.0– 9.9	...	.....	26	3.3	...	.....	22	3.2
10.0–10.9	...	.....	2	0.3	...	.....	2	0.3
Total.........	581	100.0	781	100.0	678	100.0	692	100.0
Mean.........	3.09		5.66		3.06		5.93	

* From Thurstone, L. L., and Chave, E. J. *The Measurement of Attitude*. Chicago: University of Chicago Press, 1929.

Our scale is now complete and ready for use. The steps we have been through are as follows:

1. We collected a long list of statements.
2. We had a number of judges evaluate these statements.
3. We determined their scale values.
4. We eliminated the more ambiguous statements.
5. We eliminated irrelevant statements.
6. We selected a final list of statements.
7. We prepared tables of norms.

Our two remaining tasks are to determine reliability and validity.

RELIABILITY AND VALIDITY

We can determine reliability in either one of two ways: by the usual split-half technique or, and this is more usual, by determining the correlation between the alternate forms of our scales. Thurstone has claimed that the reliabilities of all scales under his editorship are in excess of .80, but other investigators have sometimes found lower reliabilities. Table 36 contains a sampling of the coefficients reported by Likert, Roslow, and Murphy, by Lorge, and by Ferguson.

TABLE 36. *Reliability Coefficients for Thurstone Attitude Scales**

Attitude scale	Low	High
Likert, Roslow, and Murphy		
Attitude toward birth control	.62	.93
Attitude toward the Chinese	.57	.86
Attitude toward communism	.66	.93
Attitude toward evolution	.67	.86
Attitude toward the Germans	.42	.59
Attitude toward God		
Belief in the reality of	.79	.93
Influence on conduct	.84	.92
Attitude toward the Negro	.57	.73
Attitude toward war		
Droba's scale	.71	.83
Peterson's scale	.70	.86
Lorge		
Attitude toward the Bible	.52	.83
Attitude toward birth control	.68	.84
Attitude toward capital punishment	.59	.88
Attitude toward censorship	.65	.82
Attitude toward the Chinese	.39	.67
Attitude toward the Constitution	.76	.84
Attitude toward communism	.81	.95
Attitude toward evolution	.71	.92
Attitude toward the Germans	.51	.58
Attitude toward God (belief in reality of)	.81	.91
Attitude toward the Negro	.47	.77
Attitude toward patriotism	.69	.83
Attitude toward Sunday observance	.73	.83
Attitude toward the treatment of criminals	.69	.76
Attitude toward war (Peterson)	.44	.84
Ferguson		
Attitude toward birth control	.72	.84
Attitude toward capital punishment	.79	.88
Attitude toward censorship	.72	.84
Attitude toward communism	.78	.88
Attitude toward evolution	.82	.90
Attitude toward God (belief in reality of)	.85	.92
Attitude toward law	.47	.64
Attitude toward the treatment of criminals	.57	.73
Attitude toward war	.62	.77

* From Ferguson, L. W. A revision of the primary social attitude scales. *J. Psychol.*, 1944, **17**, 229–241. From Likert, R., Roslow, S., and Murphy, G. A simple and reliable method of scoring the Thurstone attitude scales. *J. soc. Psychol.*, 1934, **5**, 228–238. From Lorge, I. The Thurstone attitude scales: I. Reliability and consistency of rejection and acceptance. *J. soc. Psychol.*, 1939, **10**, 187–198.

Thurstone and Chave discuss the validity of their scale to measure attitude toward the church in terms of its correlation with self-ratings, in terms of its differentiation of religious groups, and in terms of its differentiation of active church members from inactive church members. They point out that scores on the attitude scale correlate .67 with self-ratings, that Catholics secure more favorable scores than Jews, and that active church members attain more favorable scores than inactive church members.

Ida B. Kelley, working with Remmers, determined the validity of the scale to measure attitude toward Sunday observance by comparing the scores of Seventh-Day Adventists with other denominational groups. Stouffer and Hattie N. Smith have made comparisons between attitude scores and case-history studies, while other investigators have relied upon the correlations with other scales designed to measure the same or similar attitudes.

EXTENSIONS OF THURSTONE'S TECHNIQUE

Attitude scales developed in accord with the Thurstone equal-appearing-interval procedure have been put to many uses. There are more than 500 references to them in the literature in which they have played an important part. In these studies, Thurstone-type attitude scales have been used to determine the effects of movies on attitudes toward crime and toward nationality groups. They have been used to determine the effects of social-science courses upon student attitudes. They have been used in studies designed to determine the origin of attitudes. They have been used to determine the relative effectiveness of written and oral propaganda. They have been used to determine the effect of college attendance upon attitudes. They have been used to determine important attitude intercorrelations. They have been used to determine the degree of employee morale. And, finally, they have been used as a basis for various systems of employee appraisal. We could give many more illustrations, but these will suffice to show the great productivity of the Thurstone attitude-measuring technique. It would be interesting for us to review many of these applications. But since most of them involve no advance in the technique of measurement, they fall outside the intended scope of this volume.

There have been two major attempts to extend the usefulness of the Thurstone technique. These attempts have been made by Remmers and by Ferguson. Both of these investigators have tried to generalize the technique but in markedly different ways.

Remmers. This investigator has generalized the Thurstone technique by preparing a type of scale that can be used to measure attitudes toward a great many objects of some designated class of objects. For example, he had Ida B. Kelley develop a scale to measure attitude toward any social institution. This scale must be completed separately for each social institution toward which we wish to know a person's attitude, but the same statements are used regardless of the institution involved.

A strict application of the Thurstone approach requires the development of a scale for each attitudinal object in which we are interested. If we are interested in attitudes toward communism and in attitudes toward war, we need to develop one scale to measure attitude toward communism and another scale to measure attitude toward war. Remmers has attempted to short-cut this process by developing one general scale by means of which we can measure attitude toward communism, attitude toward war, and, in fact, attitude toward any social institution. A copy of one form of this scale is shown in Table 37. Subsequent to the development of this first scale, Remmers and his collaborators developed the additional scales listed in Table 38.

In each instance, the name of the school subject, homemaking activity, or poem must be indicated. But the same statements are used for any member of the appropriate attitudinal group.

The problems involved in the development of a Remmers-type attitude scale are, for the most part, the same as those involved in developing a Thurstone-type scale. One new problem arises, however. This revolves around the extent to which one series of statements can be made applicable to all of the objects in one attitudinal class. For example, can one set of statements be used in measuring attitudes toward marriage and attitudes toward our penal system, both of which are social institutions? We have cited an extreme example for the sake of pointing up the problem, and in this case, the answer is probably "No." Remmers's own data, however, are conflicting. When Kelley's scale was used to measure attitudes toward communism and Sunday observance, correlations of .98 and .83 with the corresponding Thurstone scales were obtained. When it was used to measure attitude toward war, a correlation of $-.15$ was obtained.

TABLE 37. *Statements in Form A of Kelley's Scale to Measure Attitude toward Any Institution**

1. Is perfect in every way.
2. Is the most admirable of institutions.
3. Is necessary to the very existence of civilization.
4. Is the most beloved of institutions.
5. Represents the best thought in modern life.
6. Grew up in answer to a felt need and is serving that need perfectly.
7. Exerts a strong influence for good government and right living.
8. Has more pleasant things connected with it than any other institution.
9. Is a strong influence for right living.
10. Gives real help in meeting moral problems.
11. Gives real help in meeting social problems.
12. Is valuable in creating ideals.
13. Is necessary to the very existence of society.
14. Encourages social improvement.
15. Serves society, as a whole, well.
16. Aids the individual in wise use of leisure time.
17. Is necessary to society as organized.
18. Adjusts itself to changing conditions.
19. Is improving with the years.
20. Does more good than harm.
21. Will not harm anybody.
22. Inspires no definite likes or dislikes.
23. Is necessary only until a better can be found.
24. Is too liberal in its policies.
25. Is too conservative for a changing civilization.
26. Does not consider individual differences.
27. Is losing ground as education advances.
28. Gives too little service.
29. Represents outgrown beliefs.
30. Gives no opportunity for self-expression.
31. Promotes false beliefs and much wishful thinking.
32. Is too selfish to benefit society.
33. Does more harm than good.
34. Is cordially hated by the majority for its smugness and snobbishness.
35. Satisfies only the most stupid with its services.
36. Is hopelessly out of date.
37. No one any longer has faith in this institution.
38. Is entirely unnecessary.
39. Is detrimental to society and the individual.
40. The world would be better off without this institution.
41. Is in a hopeless condition.
42. Will destroy civilization if it is not radically changed.
43. Never was any good.
44. Benefits no one.
45. Has positively no value.

*From Remmers, H. H. (Ed.) *Studies in Higher Education XXVI. Studies in Attitudes.* Lafayette, Ind.: Purdue University, 1934.

TABLE 38. *Equal-appearing-interval Attitude Scales*
Edited by Professor H. H. Remmers

Attitude toward any disciplinary procedure
Attitude toward any group
Attitude toward any home making activity
Attitude toward any play
Attitude toward any poem
Attitude toward any practice
Attitude toward any proposed social action
Attitude toward any proposed social activity
Attitude toward any school subject
Attitude toward any teacher
Attitude toward training
Attitude toward any vocation

Remmers attributes this low correlation, however, to the low degree of reliability of the Thurstone scale. When Grices' scale to measure attitude toward any group was used to measure attitude toward the Negro and toward the Chinese correlations of .98 and .77 with the corresponding Thurstone scales were obtained. Finally F. D. Miller constructed a Thurstone-type scale to measure attitude toward teaching and found that the scores on it correlated only .58 with the scores on attitude toward teaching when measured by H. E. Miller's scale to measure attitude toward any vocation. These varying results suggest that generalized scales must be used with caution. Some will give the same results as the corresponding Thurstone scales, and some will not.

Table 39 presents a summary of the reliability data which Remmers reports for his generalized scales. The lowest coefficient is .47, the highest is .98, and the average is .75.

Remmers and his collaborators have made extensive use of these generalized scales to ascertain some of the determinants of our social attitudes. For example, they have attempted to determine how children's attitudes toward law are influenced by their participation in self-government, how the study of school subjects can affect attitudes toward divorce, social insurance, capital punishment, and labor unions, how propaganda can affect attitudes toward the Negro, and how lecture material can affect attitudes toward extra-national political organization.

Ferguson. This investigator's attempt to generalize the Thurstone technique proceeds along lines quite different from those used by

TABLE 39. *Reliability Data for Remmers's Generalized Attitude Scales**

Scale	N	r_{AB}
Attitude toward any group:		
Chinese	217	.77
Negro	217	.84
Attitude toward any home-making activity:		
Caring for children	320	.90
Meal preparation	320	.88
Attitude toward any institution:		
Communism	83	.89
Divorce	117	.81
Labor unions	92	.76
Marriage	127	.71
Sunday observance	222	.98
War	80	.77
Attitude toward any play:		
Brief Moment	230	.75
Lucky Break	123	.76
Reaching for the Moon	84	.65
Tune In	100	.79
What about Betty	65	.61
Attitude toward any practice:		
Capital punishment	60	.86
Attending movies	40	.68
Attitude toward any proposed social action:		
Abolition of compulsory military training in college	78	.91
Abolition of township trustees in Indiana	78	.81
Compulsory sex education for adults	40	.70
Divorce	102	.81
Social insurance	100	.75
Old age pensions	78	.78
Outlawing communism	78	.73
Attitude toward any school subject:		
Biology	269	.81
Chemistry	771	.70
English	705	.68
Mathematics	579	.74
Attitude toward training	223	.60
Attitude toward any teacher	875	.71
Attitude toward any vocation:		
Beauty parlor operator	293	.76
Carpenter	261	.47
Doctor	620	.66
Engineering	132	.84
Farmer	292	.70
Father's vocation	255	.77
High school teaching	428	.84
Homemaker	301	.67
Ministry	308	.76
Salesgirl	294	.72
Teacher	318	.59
Unskilled laborer	266	.57

* Adapted from Remmers, H. H. (Ed.) *Studies in Higher Education XXVI, XXXI, and XXXIV*. Lafayette, Ind.: Purdue University, 1934, 1936, 1938.

Remmers. He started with ten Thurstone-edited scales, computed their intercorrelations, subjected these intercorrelations to several centroid factor analyses, and, upon the basis of these analyses, developed three new scales to do the work of the original ten. The steps in Ferguson's line of attack were as follows:

1. The original scales were selected.
2. Subjects were secured.
3. The scales were scored.
4. Intercorrelations among the scales were computed.
5. These intercorrelations were subjected to several centroid factor analyses, and three factors were extracted.
6. Scores on each of these factors were determined.
7. Criterion groups scoring high and low on each factor were selected.
8. The percentages of the criterion groups agreeing and disagreeing with each item were determined.
9. Items for the new scales were selected.
10. Scoring weights for these items were assigned.
11. Scores on the new scales were computed.
12. Norms were prepared.

In the following paragraphs we shall review each of these steps. This should enable any reader, who wishes, to repeat the studies involved or to apply the same methods in the development of additional generalized scales.

Selection of Attitude Variables. In pursuing this approach, the scales to be used will depend upon the nature of the problem to be investigated, upon the insight and hunches of the investigator, and upon the availability of scales from which a choice can be made. We can set forth no general rules to be followed, for the particular demands of each investigation will dictate the choices to be made. In the present instance the scales used were among those used by Thelma Gwinn Thurstone and by H. B. Carlson in two earlier factor-analysis studies. Ferguson wanted to see if certain of the suggestions made by these investigators could be clarified and extended. The scales he used are listed in Table 40.

Selection of Subjects. Choice of the subjects to be tested will depend upon the purpose and scope of the investigation to be conducted, upon their accessibility to an investigator, upon the cost involved, and upon any special characteristics that may be desired. The subjects used in the present instance were students at Stanford University and at the University of Connecticut. Certain collateral studies were based upon students from these and from 16 other colleges and universities. In the major parts of the investigation the data for the Stanford and Connecticut groups were separately analyzed, were found to yield comparable results, and were then

TABLE 40. *Equal-appearing-interval Scales Used in the Derivation of the Primary Attitude Scales*

Attitude toward evolution
Attitude toward birth control
Attitude toward God
Attitude toward capital punishment
Attitude toward the treatment of criminals
Attitude toward war
Attitude toward censorship
Attitude toward communism
Attitude toward law
Attitude toward patriotism

combined. Most of the results which we shall report are based upon the combined sets of data. Occasionally, however, it will be necessary for us to make separate reference to the Stanford and Connecticut groups.

Scoring the Attitude Scales. We know from our earlier discussion on the subject that the score on a Thurstone-type attitude scale consists of the mean or median value of the statements with which a subject indicates agreement. Statements with which he indicates disagreement are disregarded in scoring. Each of the scales included in Ferguson's study contained 20 statements. And since he used a total of 20 scales (two forms for each attitude variable), each subject had to respond to a total of 400 statements. On each scale, Ferguson took as a subject's score the mean value of the statements he endorsed.

Computation of Intercorrelations. In most instances the type of correlation to be computed to show the relation between the scores on two Thurstone attitude scales will be r, the Pearsonian coefficient of linear correlation. To provide the necessary degree of accuracy in factor analysis, these correlations must be carried to a minimum of three decimal places, sometimes to a minimum of four. In the present instance three decimals were considered sufficient. It is necessary for our purposes here, however, to report the results only to the second decimal, and they are so reported in Table 41.

TABLE 41. *Intercorrelations among 10 Thurstone Attitude Scales**

(N = 643 or 462)

Scale	Form	War		Patriotism†		God		Treatment of criminals		Capital punishment		Censorship†		Evolution		Birth control		Law†		Communism†
		A	B	A	B	A	B	A	B	A	B	A	B	A	B	A	B	A	B	A
War	B	.62																		
	A																			
Patriotism†	B	.18	.21	.60																
	A	.11	.19																	
God	B	-.06	.06	.24	.24	.85														
	A	.00	.08	.23	.26															
Treatment of criminals	B	.21	.17	.25	.25	.10	.12	.57												
	A	.22	.18	.23	.24	.07	.07													
Capital punishment	B	.19	.15	.16	.16	.01	.00	.44	.46	.79										
	A	.16	.11	.19	.19	.02	.03	.47	.46											
Censorship†	B	.00	.02	.22	.19	.28	.28	.10	.12	.06	.11	.72								
	A	.02	.04	.20	.18	.23	.27	.10	.04	.03	.08									
Evolution	B	-.07	-.12	-.17	-.20	-.44	-.48	-.07	-.04	.06	.06	-.19	-.21	.82						
	A	-.06	.10	-.17	-.20	-.46	-.50	-.09	-.08	.03	.05	-.25	-.26							
Birth control	B	-.14	-.18	-.07	-.10	-.23	-.24	-.04	-.06	-.04	-.03	-.09	-.09	.38	.41	.72				
	A	-.09	-.14	-.09	-.11	-.23	-.25	-.06	-.04	-.02	-.02	-.18	-.18	.38	.40					
Law†	B	.04	.06	.30	.28	.26	.25	.18	.15	.10	.18	.34	.33	-.14	-.15	-.02	-.02	.47		
	A	-.02	.06	.19	.19	.19	.18	.16	.18	.07	.17	.29	.32	-.07	-.07	.04	-.01			
Communism†	B	-.06	-.03	-.32	-.28	-.22	-.22	-.25	-.27	-.19	-.19	-.25	-.25	.23	.20	.08	.10	-.27	-.23	.78
	A	-.12	-.09	-.37	-.29	-.27	-.28	-.27	-.24	-.26	-.25	-.27	-.28	.25	.24	.10	.13	-.30	-.27	

* From Ferguson, L. W. A revision of the primary social attitude scales. *J. Psychol.*, 1944, **17**, 229–241.

† Correlations for the variables marked with dagger are based upon 462 cases.

We have already indicated that the scales used in this study were available in two alternate forms. This leads to four coefficients showing the relationship between each pair of attitude variables. For example, we have the correlation between Form A of the first variable and Form A of the second variable; we have the correlation between Form A of the first variable and Form B of the second variable; we have the correlation between Form B of the first variable and Form A of the second variable; and, finally, we have the correlation between Form B of the first variable and Form B of the second variable. Table 41 shows a remarkable similarity among the four coefficients in each such set. For example, the coefficients expressing the relationship between attitude toward censorship and attitude toward patriotism are .18, .19, .20, and .22. In Table 41 there are only six sets of coefficients in which the individual coefficients differ by more than .05 from the set average.

TABLE 42. *Summary of Factor Loadings**

Attitude scale		Factor I		Factor II		Factor III		Mean loadings
		1 & 2	1 & 3	1 & 2	2 & 3	1 & 3	2 & 3	
God	A	− .66	− .66					− .66
	B	− .70	− .70					− .70
Evolution	A	.76	.76					.76
	B	.80	.80					.80
Birth control	A	.57	.57					.57
	B	.57	.57					.57
War	A			− .47	− .46			− .46
	B			− .41	− .43			− .42
Treatment of criminals	A			− .56	− .56			− .56
	B			− .63	− .61			− .62
Capital punishment	A			− .71	− .65			− .68
	B			− .69	− .64			− .66
Patriotism	A					.55	.49	.52
	B					.50	.44	.47
Censorship	A					.58	.58	.58
	B					.59	.59	.59
Law	A					.57	.55	.56
	B					.49	.52	.50
Communism	A					− .60	− .60	− .60
	B					− .67	− .68	− .68

* From Ferguson, L. W. A revision of the primary social attitude scales. *J. Psychol.*, 1944, **17**, 229–241.

Factor Analyses. There are several methods of factor analysis. Among the most important are Burt's summation method, Hotelling's principal component method, and Thurstone's centroid method. For most problems Thurstone's method will be found the easiest to apply and the easiest to understand. It gives an idea of the smallest number of factors we need to postulate to account for the intercorrelations which we subject to analysis. In the present instance, using Thurstone's method, three factors were found to be sufficient to explain the intercorrelations. The results are given in Table 42 and in Fig. 4.

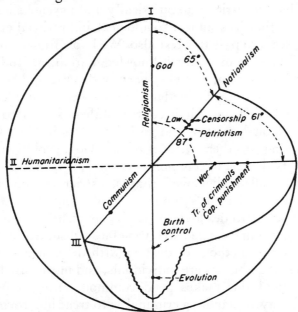

Fig. 4. Factor structure of the primary social attitudes—religionism, humanitarianism, and nationalism, principle projections only. (The angular separations are 87 degrees between Factors I and II, 65 degrees between Factors I and III, and 61 degrees between Factors II and III. The sum of the two latter angular separations need not equal the first as the diagram might seem to suggest.)

In Fig. 4 Factors I and II can be said to be orthogonal, that is, unrelated to each other, but Factors II and III exhibit a substantial relationship. Nevertheless, these last two factors are clearly distinct, and can be treated operationally as different variables.

One of the characteristics of a statistically and psychologically significant factor is that its factor loadings remain invariant in different test batteries. Table 42 shows that the factor loadings under consideration possess this characteristic of invariance, so we can conclude that our factors possess at least one of the characteristics prerequisite to their being considered statistically and psychologically significant.

A second characteristic of a statistically and psychologically significant factor is that it appears in the same form in data based upon different subject populations. Our factors meet this test also. They were isolated independently from data for two subject populations: Stanford students in 1937 and Connecticut students in 1941. The results secured from these analyses are almost identical.

A third characteristic of a statistically and psychologically significant factor is that it is subject to a logical and rational explanation. Our factors seem to pass this test also. We know from common-sense observation and from general knowledge that attitudes toward birth control, evolution, and God vary in definite and specific ways in relation to each other. Fundamentalists believe in God and disbelieve in evolution and birth control. Liberals tend to believe in evolution and birth control and to believe less in God. Our factor analysis, linking together attitudes toward God, evolution, and birth control, meets the test of common sense and appears to be a measure of what can be called religionism, that is, a strict devotion to religion.

Let us now consider our second factor. We find attitudes favoring war linked with attitudes favoring capital punishment and the harsh treatment of criminals. The three variables subsumed by this factor have reference to methods of dealing with delinquents. In two instances, these delinquents are individuals, and in the other, a nation. Apparently (and this makes good common sense), a person who believes the way to handle a criminal is to treat him roughly and to make an example of him applies this same kind of remedy to the settlement of international disputes. Conversely, a person who believes in a more humane type of treatment for an individual offender also believes in the same type of treatment for the national deviate. This factor, therefore, can be called humanitarianism.

Finally, let us consider Factor III. Here we have subsumed the more specific attitudes toward patriotism, law, censorship, and communism. It certainly accords with common-sense observation that the patriotic person is an upholder of the law and of the practice of censorship and is opposed to communism. In accord with our present-day cultural beliefs, we can call this factor nationalism.

We must consider ourselves fortunate in finding such easily interpretable factors. In many studies we would not achieve such a happy result. Many studies will end right at this point, therefore, because no logical, rational, or common-sense explanations of the factors will be forthcoming. This is one of the occupational hazards of factor-analysis research.

Determination of Factor Scores. We assume, at this point, that all necessary axis rotations have been completed. This being the case, we compute, from these rotated factor loadings, factor scores for each individual in our subject population. A convenient method of doing this is suggested by Godfrey Thomson in his book *The Factorial Analysis of Human Ability*. These calculations give weights of 0 to any scales not related to the primary axis, and varying weights, as they should, to the scales related to the primary axis. They also yield estimates of the validity with which factor scores can be predicted from the scores on the subsumed scales. Based upon the 185 Stanford University cases originally processed, the validities of the factor scores were found to be as follows:

Factor I............ .91
Factor II.......... .92
Factor III......... .90

In determining the validities of factor scores, we must be on guard against arriving at spuriously high estimates. The formula suggested by Thomson is such that validity increases as we increase the number of tests in our battery. Theoretically, we could secure perfect validity if we used a sufficient number of tests. Now have we, in the present instance, secured spuriously high estimates of validity by using alternate forms of the same tests in our factor teams? When we try to predict the validity of scores for Factors I and II, should we consider that we have six tests or only three? In Factor I we actually have two forms of a scale measuring attitude toward God, two forms of a scale measuring attitude toward evolution, and two forms of a scale measuring attitude toward birth control. Fundamentally, we have only three attitude variables, so our question is whether or not we should derive the validity estimates from three tests rather than from six tests? And, if this is the case, should we compute these validities from the factor loadings we have already presented? Or should they be based on factor loadings derived from new matrices of the intercorrelations among three tests rather than among six tests? This same reasoning holds for Factors II and III, but in the last instance we must remember that the choice will be between four and eight tests rather than between three and six tests.

To answer the questions we have just raised, the original matrices were subdivided so that the correlations based on Forms A of all scales and those based on Forms B of all scales could be separately analyzed. We find the same pattern, almost the same factor loadings, and the same communalities in these new analyses as we found in the original analyses based upon the larger matrices. The mean difference between factor loadings determined from the two sets of reduced matrices is only .06. That between the new loadings and those derived from the original larger matrices is only .03. The average difference in communality coefficients between the reduced and the original matrices is .04. We can conclude that the inclusion of alternate test forms inflated neither the original factor loadings nor the communalities.

The reliabilities of our factor-score estimates vary between .91 and .96. These estimates were derived from the correlations between the factor scores obtained from Forms A of our attitude scales and those derived from Forms B of our scales, when both were included in the same matrix. After these correlations were obtained, they were entered in the Spearman-Brown Prophecy Formula to give us our final estimates.

Selection of Criterion Groups. When factor scores have become available, we can select our criterion groups. We need two groups for each factor variable: one with high factor scores and one with low factor scores. The proportion of the total subject population to be included in each criterion group can be set at the upper and lower thirds, the upper and lower 25 per cent, the upper and lower 27 per cent, or at any other desired figure. In the present case, Ferguson followed Truman L. Kelley's recommendation to use the upper and lower 27 per cent. Ferguson did this because of Kelley's contention that the use of the upper and lower 27 per cent offers the best compromise between the two variables which can affect the reliability of our results. These two variables are the number of cases and the scalar distance between the two groups. These variables are inversely related. As we increase the number of cases, the scalar distance contracts. And as we increase the scalar distance, the number of cases diminishes. Kelley suggests that the point of maximum reliability is achieved when we dichotomize at 27 per cent.

Item Analysis. By item analysis we mean, of course, any of the many processes by which we can find which items differentiate and which items do not differentiate between our contrasting criterion groups. If we decide to use the upper and lower thirds of our subject population as criterion groups, we can compute for these groups the critical ratios of the differences between the percentages agreeing with each of our attitude statements. If we decide to use the upper and lower 25 per cent of our subject population as criterion groups, we can use Guilford's *abac* (see page 297 of his text *Fundamental Statistics in Psychology and Education*) for determining item significance. In the study under review, Ferguson chose to use the upper and lower 27 per cent of the subject population as criterion groups. This made it possible for him to use Flanagan's item-weighting chart to determine the correlation of each item with the factor scores. To use Flanagan's chart we compute for each criterion group the percentage agreeing with each of our attitude statements. We enter these percentages in Flanagan's chart and read off the correlation of the item response with the factor variable.

We have already indicated that the number of items to be included in a scale must be decided in an arbitrary manner. In the original editions of the primary social attitude scales, Ferguson used 38 items for Factors I and II and 64 items (32 items in each of two alternate forms) for Factor III. In the revised editions Ferguson used a uniform number of 25 items in each form of each scale. In selecting these items, he excluded from consideration items endorsed by more than 90 per cent of the subjects or by less than 10 per cent of the subjects in either of the two criterion groups. Of the items remaining, those with the highest correlations with the factor scores were retained to comprise the final scales.

Assignment of Item Weights. Following our selection of items, we are faced with the problem of assigning numerical scoring weights. We can base these weights upon our a priori judgment, upon any of the numerous item-analysis charts or *abacs*, or upon biserial correlations showing how each item correlates with the factor involved. In the present instance, weights were based on the correlations derived from Flanagan's chart. The correlation for each item was rounded to the nearest one-digit number, the decimal was disregarded, and the result became the scoring weight.

The proper procedure to follow will depend upon the setting of a study, its purposes, goals, and so forth. A useful rule to keep in mind, however, is that of separating the item-weighting process from the process involved in determining item significance. If we do not separate these two processes, we are likely to fall into the error of assigning differential weights upon some nonrelevant basis.

We suggest avoiding the use of critical ratios, a frequently used criterion, as the basis for item weighting. In the first place, a critical ratio indicates nothing more than the probability that any difference at hand can be ascribed to non-chance rather than to chance factors. It does not indicate an amount, or degree, or a magnitude of relationship. A second reason for avoiding the use of critical ratios as a basis for item weighting is that its value is so dependent upon the number of cases. It is true that the more cases available, the greater the confidence we can have in our results. But this greater confidence does not mean that the relationship under consideration has increased in magnitude. We must be careful, therefore, not to let an increase in the number of cases, and its consequent augmentation of a critical ratio, deceive us into believing that a greater relationship is indicated and that a higher scoring weight is required. This leads us to the conclusion that we should use as a basis for item weighting some statistic, the numerical magnitude of which is not affected by the number of cases we need in our criterion groups.

Determination of General Attitude Scores. Our next step is to arrive at attitude scores derived from the items we have selected for our scales. This can be a simple process, and, in the present instance, involves nothing more than an algebraic summation of the numerical weights associated with the statements which each subject endorses. We have six scores to derive for each subject. These are his scores on Forms A and B of each of our three attitude variables.

Preparation of Norms. Our preparation of norms can proceed in the same way as for any other psychological measuring device. The steps in this process are the giving of the completed scales to a standardization group, the preparation of raw-score and standard-score distributions, and the tabulation of percentile norms.

Reliability. The reliabilities of the scores on the scales we have just discussed are presented in Table 43. The values for the com-

TABLE 43. *Reliability Data for the Primary Attitude Scales**

Factor I: Religionism.................... .95
 Form A.......................... .90
 Form B.......................... .90
Factor II: Humanitarianism........... .92
 Form A.......................... .85
 Form B.......................... .85
Factor III: Nationalism.............. .88
 Form A.......................... .78
 Form B.......................... .78

* From Ferguson, L. W. A revision of the primary social attitude scales. *J. Psychol.*, 1944, 17, 229–241.

posite scores were determined by correlating the scores on Form A with those on Form B and by entering the result in the Spearman-Brown Prophecy Formula. The reliabilities for the alternate forms were determined by correlating the scores on the alternate forms with each other.

Validity. Our usual definition of a valid test is that it is a test which measures that which it is supposed to measure. In the case of the general attitude scales we have just discussed, they are supposed to measure the factors which we isolated in our factor analyses. Our scales will be valid scales if they correlate highly with our factor scores. And we find that they do. Scores on primary attitude scale I correlate .92 with scores on Factor I. Scores on primary attitude scale II correlate .92 with scores on Factor II. And scores on primary attitude scale III correlate .90 with scores on Factor III.

These validity coefficients are fine, as far as they go. They show that we can take a set of 25 or 50 statements and manipulate them together in some way to give us a score that is much the same as we get when we manipulate these same items some other way. Actually, these validity coefficients *beg* the real question. This question is, "How valid are our scales in measuring the real attitudes of people?" Does primary attitude scale I accurately measure religious attitudes? Does primary attitude scale II accurately measure humanitarian (or aggressive) attitudes? And does primary attitude scale III accurately measure nationalistic attitudes? Two attempts have been made to answer these questions. One attempt has reference to the religionism scale, and the other has reference to the nationalism scale. The less complex of these two attempts is that relating to the nationalism scale, so we shall discuss it first.

This study consisted in a straightforward attempt to relate the

TABLE 44. *Mean Nationalism Scores for Students Giving Nationalistic and Internationalistic Answers to the Items in the SPSSI Survey on Methods of Preventing War**

Mean nation-alism scores					We, the people of the United States, in order to preserve peace should:
Yes	No				
35	14	Yes†	?	No	1. Build up our military strength, on land and sea and in the air, so that no nation or combination of nations would dare to attack us.
30	40	Yes	?	*No*	2. Join with other peace-loving nations in economic and other non-military measures to prevent further attacks by any country.
30	34	Yes	?	*No*	3. Stop giving military protection to our citizens, or their trade or their property, in other parts of the world.
40	28	*Yes*	?	No	4. Establish higher protective tariffs, so as to build up American industry to a point of self-sufficiency where it will be independent of the entanglements resulting from foreign trade.
39	32	Yes	?	No	5. Educate the American people to realize that strong labor unions are a great bulwark against war and fascist tendencies in the United States.
14	34	Yes	?	*No*	6. Reduce our naval and air strength until it is only strong enough to defend our own shores and Hawaii— not the Philippines, nor our trade and investments in the Far East.
38	16	*Yes*	?	No	7. Educate American children in the fundamentals of patriotism, making sure they realize that America has always stood for peace and justice among the nations.
25	40	Yes	?	*No*	8. Take the lead in reducing tariffs, with reciprocal trade treaties wherever possible, so as to lower the economic barriers which now separate nation from nation.
37	12	*Yes*	?	No	9. Oppose socialism, communism and other alien philosophies which threaten to make America more like the war-making European dictatorships.
34	21	*Yes*	?	No	10. Make it perfectly clear that America is ready to defend herself—that anyone who attacks our honor or our vital interests must count on fighting it to a finish.
29	41	Yes	?	*No*	11. Educate children to be international-minded—to support any movement which contributes to the welfare of the world as a whole, regardless of special national interests.
24	35	Yes	?	No	12. Establish social ownership of industry, in order to eliminate the autocratic power of the big business men who now profit from war, or from the policies which lead to war.

TABLE 44. *Mean Nationalism Scores for Students Giving Nationalistic and Internationalistic Answers to the Items in the SPSSI Survey on Methods of Preventing War* (Continued)*

Mean nationalism scores		We, the people of the United States, in order to preserve peace should:			
Yes	No				
26	36	Yes	?	*No*†	13. Help establish a "United States of the World" in which America would be about as independent as the state of Illinois is now in the U.S.A.
34	28	Yes	?	No	14. Keep out of alliances now but support a League of Nations, with strong armed forces of its own, as soon as there is any prospect of establishing it on a world-wide basis.
35	23	*Yes*	?	No	15. Permanently keep away from entangling alliances which might limit our national freedom of action or involve us in the quarrels of other nations.

* Data from Ferguson, L. W. The isolation and measurement of nationalism. *J. soc. Psychol.*, 1942, **16**, 215–228.

† Nationalistic answer is italicized.

scores on the nationalism scale to a second "recognized" measure of nationalistic attitudes. This second measure is contained in the "Survey of Opinion on Methods of Preventing War," a survey prepared by the Committee on War and Peace of the Society for the Psychological Study of Social Issues (SPSSI). The items in the SPSSI survey cover attitudes toward patriotism and internationalism, national honor and anti-imperialism, tariffs, militarism, socialism and communism, and international relations. The statements were not originally presented as a scale, but the SPSSI Committee has indicated which answers it considers nationalistic and which answers it considers internationalistic. We have in this survey a consensus of expert psychological opinion as to what nationalistic and internationalistic attitudes are supposed to be.

A group of 158 students at the University of Connecticut were asked to take both the SPSSI survey and the nationalism scale. On each question in the SPSSI survey these 158 students were divided into those who gave the nationalistic answers and those who gave the internationalistic answers. Then for each of these groups mean scores on nationalism were determined. The results are given in Table 44. Without exception the group giving the nationalistic answers on the SPSSI survey receives a higher mean score on nationalism than does the group giving the internationalistic answer.

The second study on validation concerns the scores on the religionism scale. This study represents a considerably more complex approach than the one we have just considered, so our discussion will have to be more detailed. The basic principle, however, is simple enough. This was to secure groups of subjects whose attitudes could be known without reference to their scores on the religionism, humanitarianism, and nationalism scales; then to compare these groups on the attitude scales and see if they could be differentiated from one another.

The groups selected for study were 46 Catholics, 91 Protestants, and 33 Jews. The subjects in each of these groups expressed a definite preference for, or claimed membership in, one or the other of these religious faiths. Therefore, if the subjects can be considered typical representatives of their respective faiths, we can say that certain of their religious attitudes are known. It should follow that any scale purporting to be a measure of religious attitudes should reveal important differences among these three groups. If the religionism scale is valid to any substantial degree, it should yield larger differences than should the scales on humanitarianism and nationalism. And we should find the most pronounced differences between Catholics and Jews. Our data, as we shall see, fulfill these two expectations completely.

The first step in this validation study consisted of the construction of nine ideological scoring keys. These keys, three for each primary attitude variable, were based upon the differences in responses between Catholics and Jews, between Catholics and Protestants, and between Protestants and Jews.

Diagnostic items were found by dividing criterion group differences by 10 and by taking as the scoring weights the unit figures which most nearly approximated these quotients. For the Catholic-Jewish continuum, item 1 of the religionism scale was assigned a weight of −1 (67 per cent, the figure for Catholics, minus 76 per cent, the figure for Jews, equals −9. When this is divided by 10, it gives −.9 which is very nearly −1.). When item weights had been determined, they were used in scoring the attitudes of 100 subjects not included in the criterion groups. We secured a Catholic-Jewish score, a Catholic-Protestant score, and a Protestant-Jewish score. The reliabilities of these scores are reported in Table 45. The reli-

TABLE 45. *Reliabilities of the "Religious" Scores**

Scale	I	II	III	Average
Catholic-Jewish continuum............	.867	.775	.708	.78
Catholic-Protestant continuum........	.796	.805	.608	.74
Protestant-Jewish continuum..........	.883	.410	.346	.55
Average....................	.85	.66	.55	.69

* From Ferguson, L. W. The sociological validity of primary social attitude scale No. I: Religionism. *J. soc. Psychol.*, 1946, **23**, 197–204.

abilities of the scores based upon the items in the religionism scale are higher than those of the scores based upon the items in the humanitarianism and nationalism scales. Also, Catholic-Jewish scores are more reliable than Catholic-Protestant scores or Protestant-Jewish scores. The average of the reliabilities for religionism is .85. The average for humanitarianism is .66, and the average for nationalism is .55.

The three sets of Catholic-Jewish scores possess an average reliability of .78; the three sets of Catholic-Protestant scores possess an average reliability of .74; and the three sets of Protestant-Jewish scores possess an average reliability of .55. Three of the coefficients presented in Table 45 are so low that little confidence can be placed in the accuracy of individual scores. But the items on the religionism scale yield scores of high reliability.

Correlations among the Catholic-Protestant, Catholic-Jewish, and Protestant-Jewish scores are presented in Table 46. These correla-

TABLE 46. *Correlations among the "Religious" Scores**

Scales intercorrelated	I	II	III	Average
Catholic-Jewish scores vs. Catholic-Protestant scores.....	.970	.828	− .830	.88
Catholic-Jewish scores vs. Protestant-Jewish scores.......	.952	.679	.551	.73
Catholic-Protestant scores vs. Protestant-Jewish scores....	.873	.203	− .055	.38
Average....................................	.93	.60	.38	.65

* From Ferguson, L. W. The sociological validity of primary social attitude scale No. I: Religionism. *J. soc. Psychol.*, 1946, **23**, 197–204.

tions decrease from an average of .93 for religionism to .60 for humanitarianism and to .38 for nationalism. On religionism Catholics secure the highest scores and Jews the lowest. The linear arrangement is Catholics → Protestants → Jews.

The reverse arrangement holds true for scores on the humanitarianism scale. Jews secure higher humanitarian scores than Protestants, and Protestants secure higher humanitarian scores than Catholics.

Scores based on the nationalism scale yield the same arrangement as those based on the religionism scale. Catholics secure the highest scores, and Jews secure the lowest. The linear arrangement is Catholics → Protestants → Jews.

How do the sets of ideological difference scores compare with the original general attitude scores? The various sets of religious ideological difference scores correlate highly with scores on religionism, their average correlation being .93. They do not correlate so well with the other scales, however. The average correlation drops to .76 for humanitarianism and to .67 for nationalism. These correlations are sufficiently large, however, to suggest that ideological differences other than those of a strictly religious nature serve to differentiate religious groups from each other. Among other things, the data indicate that Jews are more humanitarian than Protestants, that Protestants are more humanitarian than Catholics, that Protestants are more nationalistic than Catholics, and that Catholics are more nationalistic than Jews.

The point of paramount importance in this study is the high correlation between the ideological difference scores and scores on religionism. The item weights for the two scoring systems were derived independently, in markedly different ways, and for different subject populations. Therefore, the correlation between them is authentic and psychologically significant. And this significance is augmented by the fact that the ideological scales based upon the items in the humanitarianism and nationalism scales are not highly related to those based upon the items in the religionism scale.

Our concern in this chapter has been to outline the steps in the development of the Thurstone equal-appearing-interval technique of attitude-scale construction, to discuss some of the problems encountered in the application of this technique, and to show two ways in which attempts have been made to seek greater generality in its usage. We shall now leave the Thurstone technique of equal-appearing intervals and shall turn our attention in the next chapter to a markedly different approach to the problems involved in attitude measurement.

5

ATTITUDES: AN A POSTERIORI APPROACH

We are to examine in this chapter a second major technique for the measurement of attitudes. This is the method of summated ratings, developed by Rensis Likert. In the last chapter we called this method an a posteriori approach, because, in contrast to the Thurstone technique of equal-appearing intervals, scale values are determined after, rather than before, the collection of attitude data.

Likert first described the method of summated ratings in a monograph published in 1932. In this monograph, "A Technique for the Measurement of Attitudes," Likert describes the development of scales to measure attitudes toward internationalism, imperialism, and the Negro. The first two of these scales are now out of date, but the third scale, attitude toward the Negro, can still be used.

A second major report on the use of the method of summated ratings is contained in the monograph "Personality in the Depression." This monograph was prepared by Rundquist and Sletto and was published in 1936. In this monograph Rundquist and Sletto show how they applied Likert's technique in the development of scales to measure general morale, inferiority, family relations, respect for law, economic conservatism, and attitude toward the value of education. A description of the methods used in the development of these scales will serve two purposes. It will illustrate, better than some of Likert's own data, the method of summated ratings. And it will put us in a position to understand the development of one of the personality inventories that we plan to discuss in Chap. 7.

The basic assumptions in the method of summated ratings are that each statement in our scale covers the entire attitude continuum; that specific points on this scale can be indicated by alternative responses to each statement; that the points to be represented by the alternative responses can be determined from a knowledge of the percentage of subjects who give each of these responses; and that an individual's attitude can be determined from a summation of his responses to all statements in the scale. This final score is to be viewed as a kind of average estimate which we get from the application of a number of different yardsticks (the different statements), each one of which extends the whole length of the attitude continuum. This is in marked contrast to the Thurstone concept that each statement in an equal-appearing-interval scale represents only a specific part of the attitude continuum.

DEVELOPMENTAL STEPS

The preparation of an attitude scale in accord with the Likert technique proceeds through the following steps:

1. A list of statements is collected.
2. These statements are edited.
3. The edited statements, constituting the attitude scale, are given to the individuals whose attitudes are to be measured.
4. The number and percentage of subjects giving the alternative responses to each statement are determined.
5. Scoring weights for the alternative responses to each statement are determined.
6. The scale is scored.
7. Item-consistency data are secured.
8. Inconsistent items, if any, are eliminated.
9. The revised scale is rescored.
10. Norms are prepared.

We shall discuss each of these steps in some detail. In connection with each one we shall outline the problems involved and shall explain various solutions which are available.

Collection of Statements. These statements may be made up by the investigator, they may be taken from preexisting scales, they may be culled from newspapers and periodicals, or they may be selected from comments and talks of appropriate authorities. Each statement should be one to which individuals having different attitudes will, if given a chance, respond differently. Therefore, we must avoid statements of fact, ambiguous statements, double-barreled statements, statements having several parts, and statements reflecting more than one attitude variable.

Editing of Statements. Our statements must be edited to ensure a terminology consistent with the purposes to be served by the completed scale and to assure their appropriateness for the alternative responses we decide to allow. These alternative responses can be: "Yes," " ?," "No"; "strongly approve," "approve," "undecided," "disapprove," "strongly disapprove"; or "strongly agree," "agree," "undecided," "disagree," "strongly disagree." Of course, other wordings and other numbers of alternatives are possible. We have given here those used by Likert, and by Rundquist and Sletto.

When our list of statements is complete, we must give it a preliminary tryout. This will elicit comments and queries about ambiguities and obscurities that we had not previously detected and will enable us to make the necessary corrections before we prepare the final form of our scale. In the Likert-type attitude scale the editing of statements is a much more important step than it is in a Thurstone-type scale. The reason for this is that there is no such objective check upon ambiguity in the Likert method as there is in the Thurstone procedure. Therefore, there is more opportunity for an ambiguous statement to remain undetected in a Likert-type scale than there is in a Thurstone-type scale. This being the case, we must exercise all the care we can during the editing process.

There is no set number of statements to be collected, nor any fixed number of statements to be included, in a Likert-type attitude scale. Likert used 24 statements in his internationalism scale, 12 items in his imperialism scale, and 15 items in his Negro scale. Rundquist and Sletto used a uniform number of 22 statements in each of their six scales. This number can vary with the investigator and with his ability to prepare useful and significant statements.

Preliminary Tryout. Likert's scale for measuring attitude toward the Negro is presented in Table 47, and one of the six scales prepared by Rundquist and Sletto is given in Table 48. When these scales were first used, the statements were not segregated, however, as they are in these tables. Likert's statements on the Negro were included in an omnibus "Survey" along with his other statements on imperialism and internationalism, and the statements in Rundquist and Sletto's scales were also "scrambled." No one scale stood out as a separate unit.

The desirability of isolating statements or of including them unidentified among statements pertaining to other attitude variables depends, to a large extent, upon the purposes of the investigator

Table 47. *Statements in Likert's Scale Measuring Attitude toward the Negro*[*]

1. Would most negroes, if not held in their place, become officious, overbearing, and disagreeable?[†]

2. If you went into a cafeteria in a northern city, sat down, and then realized you were at the table with a negro, would you leave the table?

3. Would you shake hands with a negro?

4. Do you disapprove of the use of the term "nigger"?

5. If you heard of a negro who had bought a home or a farm would you be glad?

6. In a community in which the negroes outnumber the whites, under what circumstances is the lynching of a negro justifiable?

   a. Never.

   b. In very exceptional cases where a specially brutal crime against a white person calls for swift punishment.

   c. As punishment for any brutal crime against a white person.

   d. As punishment for any gross offense (felony or extreme insolence) committed against a white person.

   e. As punishment for any act of insolence against a white person.

7. How far in our educational system (aside from trade education) should the most intelligent negroes be allowed to go?

   a. Grade school.

   b. Junior high school.

   c. High school.

   d. College.

   e. Graduate and professional school.

8. In a community where the negroes outnumber the whites, a negro who is insolent to a white man should be:

   a. Excused or ignored.

   b. Reprimanded.

   c. Fined and jailed.

   d. Not only fined and jailed, but also given corporal punishment (whipping, etc.).

   e. Lynched.

9. All negroes belong in one class and should be treated in about the same way.[‡]

10. Negro homes should be segregated from those of white people.

11. Where there is segregation, the negro section should have the same equipment in paving, water, and electric light facilities as are found in the white districts.

12. If the same preparation is required, the negro teacher should receive the same salary as the white.

13. Practically all American hotels should refuse to admit negroes.

14. No negro should be deprived of the franchise except for reasons which would also disfranchise a white man.

15. In a community of 1,000 whites and 50 negroes, a drunken negro shoots and kills an officer who is trying to arrest him. THE WHITE POPULATION IMMEDIATELY DRIVE ALL THE NEGROES OUT OF TOWN.

[*] From Likert, R. A technique for the measurement of attitude. *Arch. Psychol.*, 1932, No. 140.

[†] Items 1 to 5 to be answered: Yes, ?, No.

[‡] Items 9 to 15 to be answered: strongly approve, approve, undecided disapprove, strongly disapprove.

TABLE 48. *Statements in the Rundquist-Sletto Morale Scale**

1. The future is too uncertain for a person to plan on marrying.
2. It is difficult to think clearly these days.
3. The future looks very black.
4. Life is just one worry after another.
5. Most people can be trusted.
6. Times are getting better.
7. It does not take long to get over feeling gloomy.
8. The day is not long enough to do one's work well and have any time for fun.
9. No one cares much what happens to you.
10. Any man with ability and willingness to work hard has a good chance of being successful.
11. It is great to be living in these exciting times.
12. These days one is inclined to give up hope of amounting to something.
13. There is little chance for advancement in industry and business unless a man has unfair pull.
14. The young man of today can expect much of the future.
15. This generation will probably never see such hard times again.
16. Real friends are as easy to find as ever.
17. Life is just a series of disappointments.
18. One seldom worries so much as to become very miserable.
19. A man does not have to pretend he is smarter than he really is to "get by."
20. Success is more dependent on luck than on real ability.
21. A person can plan his future so that everything will come out all right in the long run.
22. There is really no point in living.

* From Rundquist, E. A., and Sletto, R. F. *Personality in the Depression.* Minneapolis, Minn.: University of Minnesota Press, 1936.

and upon the need which exists for the utilization of one scale separately from the others with which it can be combined. Neither in Likert's study nor in Rundquist and Sletto's was there any need to have the statements of the different scales isolated from each other. It was advantageous, therefore, for these investigators to include their statements in lengthy omnibus lists. In this way some of the halo that might have accrued to statements in isolation may be assumed to have been effectively curtailed.

Number and Percentage of Subjects Giving Alternate Responses. The procedure we must follow here is illustrated in Table 49. This table shows the number and percentage of subjects giving each of the alternative responses to the statement "Most people can be trusted," one of the items in the Rundquist-Sletto morale scale. The figures in column 1 show that 22 subjects strongly agree with this statement; that 200 subjects agree with this statement; that 79 subjects are undecided; that 144 subjects disagree with this statement; and that 55 subjects strongly disagree with this state-

TABLE 49. *Number and Percentage of Subjects Giving Different Answers to the Item "Most people can be trusted"**

Response	Number	Percentage
Strongly agree.............	22	4.40
Agree.....................	200	40.00
Undecided................	79	15.80
Disagree..................	144	28.80
Strongly disagree..........	55	11.00
Total..................	500	100.00

* From Rundquist, E. A., and Sletto, R. F. *Personality in the Depression.* Minneapolis, Minn.: University of Minnesota Press, 1936.

ment. In column 2 these figures have been converted into percentages. It is necessary for us to obtain similar data for every statement in our scale.

Determination of Scoring Weights. We can determine scoring values in any one of three different ways. Two of these ways were suggested by Likert. The third was suggested by Rundquist and Sletto. We can use an arbitrary weighting method, a standard-score weighting method, or a sigma-deviate weighting method. The last of these methods is the only one which meets the theoretical preconceptions of the Likert technique, so we shall describe it first.

Sigma-deviate Weighting Method. Likert assumes, as does any investigator who uses the sigma-deviate scoring method, that attitudes are distributed normally. If an investigator were omniscient, he could word his statements and their alternate responses in such a way that only normal distributions would be obtained. The distributions we shall obtain will depart from this ideal because our statements are faulty, because the alternative responses are not psychologically equidistant from each other, or because modal responses depart from intended points of neutrality.

Our fundamental problem is that of determining the position on the attitude continuum that each alternative response can be said to represent. And because the distributions for the different statements in our scale will differ from each other, we have to determine these values for each statement. Likert does not explain as clearly as he might the method by which these scale positions are determined. Guilford has come to our rescue, however, and in his text *Fundamental Statistics in Psychology and Education* has given a complete explanation of the manner in which these scale positions can be determined. We shall follow closely Guilford's explanation, but we shall use Likert's data so we can compare our results with those which Likert presents.

TABLE 50. *Calculations Involved in the Sigma-deviate Weighting Method**

Response	Proportion of subjects giving each answer	Proportion of subjects giving less favorable answers	Proportion of subjects giving equally favorable or less favorable answers	Ordinate corresponding to proportion in column 2	Ordinate corresponding to proportion in column 3	Difference between ordinates in columns 4 and 5	Sigma deviate value for response	Final scale value
	(1)	(2)	(3)	(4)	(5)	(6)	(7)	(8)
Strongly approve.......	.13	.87	1.00	.211	.000	.211	1.63	34
Approve..............	.43	.44	.87	.394	.211	.183	.43	22
Undecided............	.21	.23	.44	.304	.394	−.090	−.43	13
Disapprove...........	.13	.10	.23	.176	.304	−.128	−.99	8
Strongly disapprove.....	.10	.00	.10	.000	.176	−.176	−1.76	0

* Data from Likert, R. A technique for the measurement of attitude. *Arch. Psychol.*, 1932, No. 140.

Column 1 of Table 50 shows the proportion of subjects who give each one of the alternate answers to one of the statements in Likert's scale on internationalism. We begin with these proportions, and, using them as a basis for our calculations, we proceed as follows.

In column 2 we list opposite each indicated degree of agreement the proportion of cases giving answers indicating a lesser degree of agreement. We write the proportion .00 opposite "strongly disapprove," because there is no response indicating less agreement. We write the proportion .10 opposite "disapprove," because this proportion of subjects answered "strongly disapprove," and this response indicates less agreement than the response "disapprove."

In column 3 we list opposite each indicated degree of agreement the proportion of cases indicating the same or a lesser degree of agreement. We write the proportion .10 opposite "strongly disapprove," because this proportion of subjects indicate this degree of agreement (*i.e.*, "strongly disapprove") or a lesser degree of agreement. We write the proportion .23 opposite "disapprove," because this proportion of subjects indicate this degree of agreement (*i.e.,* "disapprove") or a lesser degree of agreement (*i.e.,* "strongly disapprove"). The proportion to be entered opposite "strongly approve" will always be 1.00, because all subjects will indicate a complete or a lesser degree of agreement with a statement.

Our next step is to determine the value of the ordinates corresponding to the proportions we have entered in columns 2 and 3. We determine these values by looking them up in any one of the numerous tables giving the ordinates corresponding to the proportions of the area under a normal distribution curve. We list these ordinates in columns 4 and 5. We subtract the entries in column 5 from the corresponding entries in column 4 and enter the differences in column 6.

Last, we divide the differences in column 6 by the percentages in column 1. The quotients we list in column 7. These values correspond to those given by Likert in his monograph. They show the position of each alternate response on the underlying attitude continuum. Our purpose in getting these values is that we want to use them as our scoring weights. But now that we have them, we can see that they would prove most inconvenient. Who wants to work with decimals and with minus numbers in scoring?

We can easily eliminate the negative numbers. All we need to do is add a constant of 1.76 to each of the values entered in column 7. This makes all entries 0 or positive. And we can eliminate the decimals by multiplying each of these figures by 10 and by rounding the result to the nearest whole number. These operations give us the values in column 8. These values preserve the essential relationships we sought to obtain and are obviously much more convenient for scoring.

We have illustrated the method of deriving scoring weights for just one statement. We must remember that we have to repeat the process for all statements in our scale. We have to derive the value of the constant only once, however. We can make it equal in absolute value to the largest negative sigma deviate. It should not be computed separately for each item, for if we did, we would destroy its relative position on the underlying attitude continuum.

Arbitrary Weighting Method. Likert noted, after the computation of a number of sigma-deviate values, that they did not differ very much from the relations involved in the simple series of arbitrary weights 1, 2, 3, 4, 5. He suggests, therefore, that these values can be assigned as scoring weights for the alternate responses to each statement. Strangely enough, Likert found that scores resulting from these weights correlate .99 with scores based upon the sigma-deviate method.

Standard-score Weighting Method. Rundquist and Sletto describe a third way in which item-scoring weights can be derived. They suggest that scoring values can be based upon the extent to which response values in the arbitrary scoring system deviate, in standard-score units, from the mean rating on the item. This procedure requires the assignment of an arbitrary system of weights, *e.g.*, 1 to 5; a count of the number of times each alternate response is given; the determination of the mean rating assigned; the calculation of the standard deviation of the distribution of ratings around this mean value; and the determination, in sigma-score units, of the difference between the response values 1, 2, 3, 4, and 5 and the mean rating. These differences, or some linear function of them, become our scoring weights. The calculations involved in this procedure are illustrated in Table 51.

TABLE 51. *Calculations Involved in the Standard-score Weighting Method**

Response	x	f	fx	fx^2	$\dfrac{x-m}{\sigma}$	$\left(\dfrac{x-m}{\sigma}\right)+c$
Strongly approve...............	5	13	65	325	1.41	3.44
Approve......................	4	43	172	688	.55	2.58
Undecided....................	3	21	63	189	− .31	1.72
Disapprove...................	2	13	26	52	−1.17	.86
Strongly disapprove...........	1	10	10	10	−2.03	0.00
Parameters.................	Mean = 3.36.			Standard deviation = 1.16		

* From Rundquist, E. A., and Sletto, R. F. *Personality in the Depression.* Minneapolis, Minn.: University of Minnesota Press, 1936.

Unfortunately, this procedure accomplishes nothing beyond that which the original system of arbitrary weights cannot itself accomplish. The standard scores derived are simple, direct, and perfect linear transformations of the original arbitrary weights. Therefore, if an arbitrary system of weights is to be used, there is no point in transforming them into standard scores. We may as well save ourselves the computational labor and use the arbitrary scores directly.

Scoring of Scale. We use as our scoring weights those derived by any one of the three methods we have just described. To get an attitude score for one subject, we add together the numerical values associated with his responses.

We have already indicated that the sigma-deviate method of weighting is the only method which meets the theoretical preconceptions involved in the method of summated ratings. It is the only method which meets these preconceptions, because it is the only method which utilizes the responses of the subjects as a basis for the determination of the scoring weights. Therefore, if we use the arbitrary weighting method or the standard-score method, we are not, in reality, making use of the method of summated ratings.

Item Analysis. We can secure item-consistency data in several ways. We can compare the mean item scores of high- and low-scoring subjects or compute the correlation between each item and total scores, or we can go through either one of these processes with subjects scoring high and low upon the basis of an independent criterion. If we choose to compute the correlation between each item and total scores, we can use tetrachoric, biserial, contingency, or Pearsonian coefficients.

If we wish to compute tetrachoric correlations, we divide our cases into above-average and below-average groups, and, at the same time, into "favorable" answer and "unfavorable" answer groups. When we have done this, we convert our figures into percentages, and, utilizing the Chesire, Thurstone, and Saffir Computing Diagrams, we determine the value of our coefficient.

If we wish to compute a biserial coefficient, we divide our subjects into "favorable" and "unfavorable" answer groups and, at the same time, into 10 or 15 groups upon the basis of their total scores. We compute the standard deviation of the distribution of total scores; the mean score for those who answered favorably and the mean score for those who answered unfavorably; the percentage of cases who answered favorably and the percentage of cases who answered unfavorably; and the value of the ordinate at the point of the curve dividing the unfavorable and favorable answer groups. We enter these values in the biserial formula to get our coefficient.

If we compute a Pearsonian coefficient, we can have only five divisions on the "response" axis, but we may have any number we wish on the "total score" axis. Usually, however, it is pointless for us to have more divisions on this axis than we can have on the "response" axis.

To compute a contingency coefficient, we arrange the data in the same manner as we would to compute a tetrachoric coefficient. Then we calculate the number of cases which we can expect, by chance, to enter each cell of our diagram. We compare these expected percentages with those we obtain and from this comparison compute our coefficient of contingency. It shows us the extent to which we must allow chance as a causative agent in producing our results.

The factors determining which of the foregoing coefficients we should use are the assumptions we wish to make, the number of cases in our subject groups, and our own preferences regarding the computational details involved.

A second method of securing item-consistency data is that of comparing the average scores of the highest and lowest scoring subjects. This is the method used by Likert in his original study and also by Rundquist and Sletto in theirs. We can select for this purpose, as we indicated in the last chapter, the top and bottom 25 per cent or any other convenient proportion. Likert used the upper and lower 10 per cent in his study, and Rundquist and Sletto used the upper and lower 25 per cent in theirs.

When we have decided upon the proportion of cases to assign to our high- and low-scoring groups, we can proceed with our comparisons. Rundquist and Sletto illustrate the procedure with a set of data for 184 subjects. First they used the Likert arbitrary weighting system in scoring. Then for each of their six scales they selected the 46 highest scoring subjects (the top 25 per cent) and the 46 lowest scoring subjects (the bottom 25 per cent) as criterion groups. They computed, for each of these groups, the numerical values of their mean responses to each statement. These calculations are illustrated in Table 52. The difference between the mean response for the high-scoring group and the mean response for the low-scoring group is used as a measure of item consistency. This difference Rundquist and Sletto call the item scale value difference.

Inconsistent Statements. When our indices of item consistency have been computed, we review them for the purpose of detecting items giving results inconsistent with total scores on our test. All inconsistent items, regardless of what other merits they possess, are discarded.

Both the correlational method and the item scale value difference method of item analysis enable us to detect and to eliminate items which do not give results consistent with total scores. Yet, as we have described them, they are both open to question. One question

TABLE 52. *Calculations Involved in Computing an Item Scale Value Difference for the Item "No one cares much what happens to you"**

Response	Weight	Lowest 25 per cent		Highest 25 per cent	
		f	fw	f	fw
Strongly agree..................	1	2	2	0	
Agree...........................	2	14	28	3	6
Undecided......................	3	1	3	3	9
Disagree.......................	4	1	4	8	32
Strongly disagree...............	5	0	..	4	20
Total........................	..	18	37	18	67
Mean.........................	..	2.056		3.722	
Scale value difference...........	..	3.722 − 2.056 = 1.666			

* From Rundquist, E. A., and Sletto, R. F. *Personality in the Depression*. Minneapolis, Minn.: University of Minnesota Press, 1936.

is raised by the fact that all items in our analyses have themselves contributed to the total scores. Therefore any correlation we compute or any item scale value difference we determine is bound to be spuriously high. We could, however, get around this difficulty by eliminating each item's contribution to the total score before computing our correlations.

A second question relates to the possible instability of our indices of item consistency for different groups of subjects. Rundquist and Sletto report two interesting findings in this connection. The first is to the effect that the average item scale value difference for the items in their scales remained at approximately the same level for 10 different groups of subjects. The second shows that the rank order of the individual items as determined from their consistency values changed materially among these same groups. These findings are difficult to interpret clearly, however, because of the spurious factor we have already mentioned.

Irrelevant Statements. Inconsistent items are not the only type of item we want eliminated from our completed scales. We also want to eliminate items that are irrelevant to the continuum which we are interested in measuring. In the Likert technique the only index we can use for this purpose is our index of item consistency. To what extent does this index enable us to eliminate irrelevant as well as inconsistent statements? To answer this question Rundquist and Sletto computed for the statements in their morale scale their scale-value differences in all other scales. Later they did this separately, and in turn, for all other scales. They found that items discriminate best in their own scales and less well in other scales. Rundquist and Sletto took this result to mean that most of the items were placed by them in the scale for which they were most highly relevant. We must demur. When the scale-value differences were computed for the economic conservatism scale, these selfsame items were instrumental in the segregation of the criterion groups. These items were not involved, however, in the segregation of the criterion groups on the other scales. If they had been, the results might well have been different.

In our discussion of the Thurstone technique of equal-appearing intervals, we mentioned, just briefly, Guttman's attempt to devise a method of measuring item irrelevancy. We can now describe Guttman's technique, for it is based directly upon several of the concepts involved in Likert's method of summated ratings. We can best explain Guttman's technique by working through a hypothetical problem. Let us suppose that we have tested 100 subjects and have found that their answers on one of our Likert-type statements are distributed as follows:

Strongly agree	20%
Agree	20
Undecided	20
Disagree	20
Strongly disagree	20
	100%

Now if the item on which we obtained this distribution is a perfect measure of the attitude, we should find that the 20 subjects who gave the answer "strongly agree" should have the highest total scores on our scale. The 20 subjects who gave the answer "agree" should have the next highest total scores, and so on. Thus, knowing total scores, we should be able to make a perfect prediction of item responses. Or, knowing item responses, we should be able to say which of our subjects secured the 20 highest scores, which of our subjects secured the 20 next highest scores, and so on down the line.

To dispel the idea that equal numbers of alternative responses are necessary, let us look at a second distribution.

Strongly agree.............	10%
Agree....................	20
Undecided...............	40
Disagree.................	20
Strongly disagree..........	10
	100%

If the item which elicited this distribution is a perfect measure of the attitude, we should find that the 10 subjects giving the answer "strongly agree" should have the 10 highest total scores. And the 20 subjects who answer "agree" should have the 20 next-highest total scores, and so on.

Now let us consider both of our items together. The 10 subjects with the highest total scores should be those who respond "strongly agree" to both items. The 10 subjects with the 10 next highest scores should be those who respond "strongly agree" to item 1 and "agree" to item 2. The 10 subjects with the 10 next highest scores should be those who respond "agree" to both items. Pursuing this line of reasoning for all combinations of responses, we find these combinations related to total scores as in Table 53.

TABLE 53. *Theoretical Joint Distribution of Two Item Responses*

Rank on total scores	Response to item 1	Response to item 2
1– 10	Strongly agree	Strongly agree
11– 20	Strongly agree	Agree
21– 30	Agree	Agree
31– 40	Agree	Undecided
41– 60	Undecided	Undecided
61– 70	Disagree	Undecided
71– 80	Disagree	Disagree
81– 90	Strongly disagree	Disagree
91–100	Strongly disagree	Strongly disagree

Guttman says that if we can achieve results like these (within reasonable limits, of course), the universe of content is scalable. In other words, all items are relevant to the attitude variable in question. When such results are not achieved, Guttman says the universe of content is not scalable. In other words, many of the individual items are irrelevant to the attitude variable in question.

Another way of putting Guttman's results is to say that if there is perfect correlation between each item and total scores, the universe of content is scalable. Therefore it appears that Guttman has done little more than to set up a rather elaborate set of procedures to determine the correlation between an item and the total score to which it contributes. This result can be obtained just as well by the computation of a biserial, tetrachoric, contingency, or Pearsonian coefficient.

If Guttman's criterion of scalability can be met, why is more than one item needed in a scale? We conjecture that Guttman's answer to this question might be something like this: first, to counteract random error and second, because one item gives, let us say, only 5 discriminations. A second item with its 5 responses gives, in combination with the first item, a possible total of 25 discriminations. It will do this, however, only when the cumulative percentages for the two items do not agree with each other. When these percentages agree for every response, the second item adds no information over and above that yielded by the first. We would merely have succeeded in asking the same question in two different, but equally successful, ways.

A questionable assumption in the Guttman technique is that a universe of content must be considered unscalable if it is found that total scores cannot be predicted almost perfectly from item responses. This assumption is questionable, because the technique involves no check upon the wisdom with which the items in the scale were originally selected. This need not overly concern us as far as the Thurstone-type scale is concerned, but when Guttman's technique is applied to a Likert-type scale, we shall find no other check upon the value of the items. One investigator may just happen to have selected a set of items that will meet Guttman's criterion, but another investigator, in attempting to cover the same area, may have been less fortunate in his selection and may have used a group of items which does not meet Guttman's criterion. This latter set of items can be considered unsatisfactory, but to conclude that the universe of content is not scalable seems unwarranted.

Rundquist and Sletto were careful to include in their scales equal numbers of positive and negative statements. Positive statements are those phrased so that agreement with them indicates a favorable attitude on the underlying continuum. Negative statements are those phrased so that agreement with them indicates an unfavorable attitude on the underlying continuum. Our discussion on item relevance suggests that we ought to inquire as to whether we get different or the same results from these two types of item.

Rundquist and Sletto report that subjects tend to disagree with negative items to a greater extent than they tend to agree with positive items. Rundquist and Sletto also report that negative statements yield distributions more heavily weighted at the favorable end of the scales (hence, the means are lower); that responses to negative statements tend to be more internally consistent and therefore tend to yield larger standard deviations; that negative statements tend to yield more consistent responses from test to retest; and that positive and negative statements correlate low within a single scale but correlate equally well with total scores.

Rundquist and Sletto suggest that the difference between the scores on positive and negative statements might be found useful as a measure of adjustment. They predicate this on the hypothesis that negative statements may create tension or conflict. If this is true, the greater the discrepancy between the scores on positive and negative statements, the greater the conflict or tension created and the greater the maladjustment. Rundquist and Sletto explored this possibility to some extent, but they had no satisfactory criterion of maladjustment. It is to be hoped that this interesting lead can someday be put to further test.

Norms. When all inconsistent and irrelevant items have been eliminated, the items remaining in the scale are rescored. Then norms are prepared. Norms for Likert-type attitude scales can be prepared in the same way as those for most other psychological scales. They can also be prepared, however, in a manner suggested by Guttman. This method enables us to determine the degree to which any given attitude departs from a psychologically and rationally determined point of neutrality.

To determine this point of neutrality it is necessary for us to distinguish between an attitude per se and its intensity. For example, A has a very favorable attitude toward war and feels intensely that he is right. B, on the other hand, has a very unfavorable attitude toward war and feels intensely that he is right. A and B differ in the content of their attitudes or in their positions on the attitude continuum, but they occupy the same position on an intensity continuum. Guttman suggests that this nonlinear relationship between an attitude and its intensity be used as a basis for determining the point of neutrality on the total score continuum. This point is to be found, says Guttman, where intensity has its lowest mean value.

Fold-over Technique. Guttman describes two methods of determining intensity values. One is called the *fold-over technique*, and the other is called the *two-part technique*. In the first, the fold-over technique, Guttman assumes that the point of neutrality for each statement is located at the response called "undecided" and that there are equal increases in intensity in both directions from this neutral point. When five responses are involved, the "undecided" position is assigned a value of 0, the responses "agree" and "disagree" are assigned a value of 1, and the responses "strongly agree" and "strongly disagree" are assigned a value of 2. Total intensity scores for all subjects are obtained by addition. When these scores have been obtained, a scatter plot showing their relation to the attitude scores is prepared. An example of such a scatter plot is shown in Table 54. We compute the mean intensity value for each vertical array of attitude scores and take as our point of neutrality the attitude score associated with the lowest intensity level. In our illustration this value turns out to be 4.

Two-part Technique. This requires that responses for intensity be secured separately from those for attitude content. This procedure has two advantages. It makes certain that intensity responses are independent of (this does not mean unrelated to) the content responses, and it avoids the assumption of the fold-over technique that the responses "strongly agree" and "strongly disagree" are equidistant from the point of neutrality. In the two-part technique the actual distances can be determined through Likert's sigma-deviate method of scoring. When these scoring values have been determined, total intensity scores can be secured, and the remainder of the procedure follows as before. When we have determined our point of

TABLE 54. *The Relation between Attitude Content and Intensity**

Intensity	Content							Total
	0–2	3–5	6–8	9–10	11	12–13	14	
14	..	..	..	..	..	..	1	1
13	..	..	..	..	..	..	..	0
12	1	..	..	..	..	..	..	1
11	..	..	..	1	..	2	1	4
10	..	..	..	..	1	2	..	3
9	4	1	1	..	1	1	..	8
8	2	1	1	2	..	..	..	6
7	1	1	4	2	4	1	..	13
6	..	1	3	4	2	..	..	10
5	..	1	..	..	..	..	..	1
4	..	1	..	..	1	..	..	2
3	..	1	..	..	..	..	..	1
Total	8	7	9	9	9	6	2	50

* From Churchman, C. W., Ackoff, R. L., and Wax, M. (Eds.) *Measurement of Consumer Interest*. Philadelphia: University of Pennsylvania Press, 1947.

neutrality, we can determine how favorable or how unfavorable any given attitude is to be considered by noting how far, and in what direction, it departs from this point of neutrality.

ADVANTAGES OF THE METHOD OF SUMMATED RATINGS

The advantages which Likert claims for the method of summated ratings, in contrast with the Thurstone method of equal-appearing intervals, are that the scale is easier to construct, that no preliminary judging group is necessary, that greater reliability is secured, that the scoring system can be better adapted to groups whose attitudes are to be measured, and that it does not require certain of the assumptions inherent in the Thurstone technique. Let us review these claims and see to what extent they can be substantiated.

Simplified Scale Construction. The ease with which a scale can be constructed depends upon the insight of the investigator in selecting useful and significant statements. It also depends upon the number of statements to be collected, the number of statements to be included in the completed scale, and upon the number of subjects whose records are to be included in the scale-standardization process. And when the method is applied strictly, the items must be rescaled for every group whose attitudes are to be measured. In view of these facts it is difficult to see how the construction of a Likert-type attitude scale can be, except by chance, much less laborious than the construction of a Thurstone-type attitude scale. Perhaps we should not attempt to settle here the issue which Likert has raised, but we can certainly conclude that there is some question about the claim which he makes.

Eliminates Judging Group. The second advantage which Likert claims for his technique is that it does away with the need for a preliminary judging group. The purpose of the judging group is to ensure the selection of statements scaled at equal intervals throughout the attitude continuum. Therefore if Likert's technique eliminates the need for a judging group, we should find items selected according to the Likert technique fairly evenly spaced throughout the attitude continuum. Is this result obtained? There have been two attempts to answer this question: that by Ferguson and that by Edwards and Kenney.

Ferguson asked 100 University of Connecticut students to rate the statements in Rundquist and Sletto's Survey of Opinions by the Seashore-Hevner method. Following Thurstone and Chave's methods, equal-appearing-interval scale values of these items were computed. The results are given in Fig. 5. It is obvious that the statements in most of the scales represent only the very favorable or the very unfavorable portions of the continuum. In spite of the care exercised by Rundquist and Sletto in the construction of their survey, they achieved little success in securing statements representing all degrees of attitude along each continuum. In view of these results we venture the opinion that Likert's technique does not do away with the need for a preliminary group of judges.

Edwards and Kenney have criticized this conclusion by pointing out that it is based upon a Thurstone-type rescaling of items which were designed originally for a Likert-type scale. Therefore they started with Thurstone and Chave's original list of the 130 items used to construct their scale measuring attitude toward the church and put them through both the Thurstone and Likert procedures. The subjects were 80 students at the University of Maryland.

Edwards and Kenney selected two sets of 20 items to constitute two alternate forms of their Thurstone-type scale and one set of 25 items to constitute their Likert-type scale. Only five items were found to be common to the two scales. Edwards and Kenney then computed the correlations between the scores secured from the Likert-type and Thurstone-type scales and reported coefficients of .79 and .92. They seized upon the latter correlation as demonstrating "the fact that *it is possible* to construct scales by the two methods which will yield comparable scores." But their coefficient of .79 demonstrates that it is also possible to construct scales by the two methods which will not yield completely comparable scores. We are left with our original conclusion that the Likert method of attitude-scale construction does not obviate the need for a group of preliminary judges.

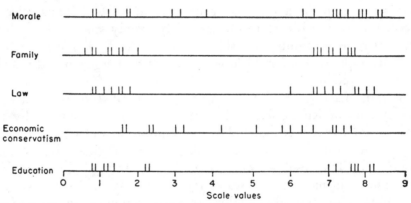

Fig. 5. Distributions of the scale values for the statements in the Minnesota Survey of Opinions. (From Ferguson, L. W. A study of the Likert technique of attitude-scale construction. *J. soc. Psychol.*, 1941, **31**, 51–57.)

Greater Reliability. The third proposed advantage of the Likert technique is that it produces scales of greater reliability than the Thurstone technique. Likert offers in favor of this claim an attained reliability of .88 for his 24-item internationalism scale as compared with reliabilities of .78 and .74 for the 22-item Droba scale for the measurement of attitude toward war. Likert makes much of the fact that to attain a reliability of .88 with the Droba scale, it would be necessary to use both forms of the scale, or a total of 44 items.

In discussing reliability, let us keep clearly in mind the fact that in the typical Thurstone technique all we ask of a subject is that he respond with a check mark ($\checkmark$) if he agrees with a statement or with a cross (x) if he disagrees. In the typical Likert technique we ask our subject to check one of five alternate answers. Therefore it is not quite fair to say that a 20-item Thurstone scale is the same length as a 20-item Likert scale. In the latter there are 100 possible responses, and in the former there are only 40. In our example the Likert scale is really two and one-half times longer than the Thurstone scale.

Likert realized the nature of this inequality. Therefore he revised the Droba scale so it could be used with his five-choice alternate answers. However, to do this he found it necessary to eliminate four statements from each form of the scale as being unamenable to his method of answering. This left 18 items in each form of the scale. On this revision Likert secured a reliability of .88 for each of these forms. This reliability is equal to that reported by Likert for his 24-item internationalism scale. So, using data which Likert himself provides, we can conclude that the Thurstone and Likert methods yield reliabilities of comparable magnitude.

Scoring Adapted to Group. The fourth advantage which Likert claims for his technique is that the scoring can be better adapted to the particular group whose attitudes are to be measured. In other words we can change the scoring values for each new group whose attitudes we wish to measure. It is difficult to see how this change, if indeed it is to be effected, can be an advantage. In the first place, it makes it impossible for us to compare the groups with each other, because the units of measurement will be different. And in the second place, it requires the labor of recalculating the scale values for each group whose attitudes are to be measured.

Likert might at this point argue that his demonstration that an arbitrary scoring system gives the same results as the sigma-deviate scoring technique makes this recalculation of weights unnecessary. But if Likert is to offer this argument, he must give up the claim that his technique makes it possible for us to readapt the scoring values for each group. If it is unnecessary to make this adaptation—and if the arbitrary scoring system works it *is* unnecessary—the alleged advantage fails to materialize.

Fewer Assumptions. Finally, Likert states that his technique does not require some of the questionable assumptions of the Thurstone technique. He mentions chiefly the assumption that the attitudes of a rater have no effect upon his evaluation of the statements. We have already presented evidence indicating that this assumption is a legitimate one and need no longer be held in question.

The Likert technique, when strictly applied, involves the assumption that attitudes are normally distributed. In the Thurstone method of attitude-scale construction this assumption is not necessary.

We must conclude that most of the advantages claimed for the Likert technique either do not exist or, if they do, must be so seriously qualified that it is difficult to see in what way the method is to be preferred to the Thurstone technique.

6

PERSONALITY: UNIDIMENSIONAL

APPROACHES

There are a large number of psychological tests which are supposed to measure "personality." It is unfortunate that we cannot think of more discrete and descriptive titles for some of these tests, because some are quite limited in scope and do not cover all that is usually implied in the general concept *personality*. Another unfortunate consequence of our inadequate nomenclature is that we talk, for example, of interest tests, of attitude tests, and of personality tests. This makes it look as if attitude and interest tests were not personality tests. About all we can do to clear up the confusion is to remember that we use the term *personality test* in two senses: in a general way to cover all tests discussed in this volume and in a more specific way to connote those tests not given any subclassification, such as interest or attitude test.

In this chapter and in Chap. 7, we propose to discuss several approaches to the construction of personality tests, using this term in its more restricted meaning. We shall divide these tests into two categories: one will include unidimensional approaches, and the other will include multidimensional approaches. Unidimensional approaches are those in which one trait is defined or in which only one test score is secured. The trait involved may be narrow in scope or fairly broad, but whatever its nature, it is considered as a unitary function. Multidimensional approaches are those leading to several scores from the same set of items. These several scores may purport to cover the whole of personality or only a small segment of it. In either event different dimensions are covered, and the methods involved in developing such tests frequently are different from those used in the unidimensional approaches.

In this chapter we shall discuss six unidimensional approaches to the measurement of personality. Five of the tests to be represented in our discussion have more historical than current interest, but it is important that we understand the methods used in their development. It is important that we understand these methods, because, for one reason, the tests constructed by these methods form the bases upon which Bernreuter constructed his widely used Personality Inventory. We shall discuss this inventory in our chapter on multidimensional approaches, but we would not be able to understand its value and its limitations without the material we are to present in this chapter.

The tests which, historically, paved the way for the Bernreuter Personality Inventory are the Woodworth Personal Data Sheet, the Thurstones' Personality Schedule, the Bernreuter Self-sufficiency Test, Laird's Colgate Mental Hygiene Test, and the Allports' Ascendance-Submission Reaction Study.

The sixth test we plan to discuss in this chapter is the Terman-Miles Masculinity-Femininity Test. The development of this test follows a different tradition from that characterizing the other tests we have mentioned and will constitute an enlightening contrast to them.

WOODWORTH'S PERSONAL DATA SHEET

This test can be called the grandfather of practically all present-day personality tests. It has many direct descendants and has inspired the development of many other tests, even though not contributing directly to their content. Woodworth devised the test in 1917 as a tool for eliminating emotionally unstable soldiers as unfit for duty in the United States Army. It consists of 116 questions to which a subject must answer "Yes" or "No."

Woodworth himself apparently never published more than the sketchiest of notes, if any, concerning the test, so we shall rely upon House's account for details of its development. According to House, the development of the test proceeded through five stages. First, Woodworth made a list of approximately 200 questions which he thought to be symptomatic of psychoneurotic or at least of emotionally unstable tendencies. These questions were culled from pertinent comment and from textbook descriptions. Second, Woodworth gave this list of questions to a small group of students at

Columbia University and asked them to indicate their answers to the questions. Third, he reviewed the answers given by these Columbia students and decided to eliminate any item to which more than 25 per cent of them gave the "psychoneurotic" answer. The reason for this was Woodworth's assumption that if so large a proportion of a supposedly normal group of subjects could give the "psychoneurotic" answer, the question could not be considered symptomatic of mental maladjustment. These eliminations reduced the list to a total of 179 questions. Fourth, this revised list of questions was given to 1,000 unselected normal draftees (1917) and, says House, to "a small selected group of declared psychoneurotic soldiers." Fifth, the criteria for the elimination of statements were reapplied to these data, and, as a result, the list was reduced to its final total of 116 questions. Because of its historical importance, we give this list of questions in Table 55. On this list it was thought that psychoneurotics would average some 30 or 40 "psychoneurotic" answers, whereas normals would average only 10.

The Woodworth Personal Data Sheet has been subjected to numerous revisions. Many of these will be of no concern to us here,

TABLE 55. *Questions in Woodworth's Personal Data Sheet**

---

1. Do you usually feel well and strong?
2. Do you usually sleep well?
3. Are you often frightened in the middle of the night?
4. Are you troubled with dreams about your work?
5. Do you have nightmares?
6. Do you have too many sexual dreams?
7. Do you ever walk in your sleep?
8. Do you have the sensation of falling when going to sleep?
9. Does your heart ever thump in your ears so that you cannot sleep?
10. Do ideas run through your head so that you cannot sleep?
11. Do you feel well rested in the morning?
12. Do your eyes often pain you?
13. Do things ever seem to swim or get misty before your eyes?
14. Do you often have the feeling of suffocating?
15. Do you have continual itchings in the face?
16. Are you bothered much by blushing?
17. Are you bothered by fluttering of the heart?
18. Do you feel tired most of the time?
19. Have you ever had fits of dizziness?
20. Do you have queer, unpleasant feelings in any part of the body?
21. Do you ever feel an awful pressure in or about the head?
22. Do you often have bad pains in any part of the body?

TABLE 55. *Questions in Woodworth's Personal Data Sheet* (Continued)

23. Do you have a great many bad headaches?
24. Is your head apt to ache on one side?
25. Have you *ever* fainted away?
26. Have you *often* fainted away?
27. Have you ever been blind, half-blind, deaf or dumb for a time?
28. Have you ever had an arm or leg paralyzed?
29. Have you ever lost your memory for a time?
30. Did you have a happy childhood?
31. Were you happy when 14 to 18 years old?
32. Were you considered a bad boy?
33. As a child did you like to play alone better than to play with other children?
34. Did the other children let you play with them?
35. Were you shy with other boys?
36. Did you ever run away from home?
37. Did you ever have a strong desire to run away from home?
38. Has your family always treated you right?
39. Did the teachers in school generally treat you right?
40. Have your employers generally treated you right?
41. Do you know of any body who is trying to do you harm?
42. Do people find fault with you more than you deserve?
43. Do you make friends easily?
44. Did you ever make love to a girl?
45. Do you get used to new places quickly?
46. Do you find your way about easily?
47. Does liquor make you quarrelsome?
48. Do you think drinking has hurt you?
49. Do you think tobacco has hurt you?
50. Do you think you have hurt yourself by going too much with women?
51. Have you hurt yourself by masturbation (self-abuse)?
52. Did you ever think you had lost your manhood?
53. Have you ever had any great mental shock?
54. Have you ever seen a vision?
55. Did you ever have the habit of taking any form of "dope?"
56. Do you have trouble in walking in the dark?
57. Have you ever felt as if someone was hypnotizing you and making you act against your will?
58. Are you ever bothered by the feeling that people are reading your thoughts?
59. Do you ever have a queer feeling as if you were not your old self?
60. Are you ever bothered by a feeling that things are not real?
61. Are you troubled with the idea that people are watching you on the street?
62. Are you troubled with the fear of being crushed in a crowd?
63. Does it make you uneasy to cross a bridge over a river?
64. Does it make you uneasy to go into a tunnel or a subway?
65. Does it make you uneasy to have to cross a wide street or open square?
66. Does it make you uneasy to sit in a small room with the door shut?
67. Do you usually know just what you want to do next?
68. Do you worry too much about little things?
69. Do you think you worry too much when you have an unfinished job on your hands?

TABLE 55. *Questions in Woodworth's Personal Data Sheet* * *(Continued)*

70. Do you think you have too much trouble in making up your mind?
71. Can you do good work while people are looking on?
72. Do you get rattled easily?
73. Can you sit still without fidgeting?
74. Does your mind wander badly so that you lose track of what you are doing?
75. Does some particular useless thought keep coming into your mind to bother you?
76. Can you do the little chores of the day without worrying over them?
77. Do you feel you must do a thing over several times before you can drop it?
78. Are you afraid of responsibility?
79. Do you feel like jumping off when you are on a high place?
80. At night are you troubled with the idea that somebody is following you?
81. Do you find it difficult to pass urine in the presence of others?
82. Do you have a great fear of fire?
83. Do you ever feel a strong desire to go out and set fire to something?
84. Do you ever feel a strong desire to steal things?
85. Did you ever have the habit of biting your fingernails?
86. Did you ever have the habit of stuttering?
87. Did you ever have the habit of twitching your face, neck or shoulders?
88. Did you ever have the habit of wetting the bed?
89. Are you troubled with shyness?
90. Have you a good appetite?
91. Is it easy to make you laugh?
92. Is it easy to get you angry?
93. Is it easy to get you cross or grouchy?
94. Do you get tired of people quickly?
95. Do you get tired of amusements quickly?
96. Do you get tired of work quickly?
97. Do your interests change frequently?
98. Do your feelings keep changing from happy to sad to happy without any reason?
99. Do you feel sad or low-spirited most of the time?
100. Did you ever have a strong desire to commit suicide?
101. Did you ever have heart disease?
102. Did you ever have St. Vitus's dance?
103. Did you ever have convulsions?
104. Did you ever have anemia badly?
105. Did you ever have dyspepsia?
106. Did you ever have asthma or hay fever?
107. Did you ever have a nervous breakdown?
108. Have you ever been afraid of going insane?
109. Has any of your family been insane, epileptic or feeble-minded?
110. Has any of your family committed suicide?
111. Has any of your family had a drug habit?
112. Has any of your family been a drunkard?
113. Can you stand pain quietly?
114. Can you stand the sight of blood?
115. Can you stand disgusting smells?
116. Do you like out-door life?

* From Woodworth, R. S. Personal Data Sheet. Chicago: C. H. Stoelting Co., 1918.

however, as they involve no change in the logic or technique of test construction. Among the revisions in this category, we may list those by Johnson in 1920, by Mathews in 1923, by Cady in 1923, by House in 1927, and by Papurt in 1930.

The revisions in which we shall interest ourselves in this text are those which involve an important change in the logic or methodology or which have led to the development of later tests. Among the revisions in this category we may list those by Laird (the Colgate Mental Hygiene Inventory), by Gordon W. Allport and Floyd H. Allport (the Ascendance-Submission Reaction Study), and by Louis L. Thurstone and Thelma Gwinn Thurstone (the Personality Schedule). All of these revisions we shall discuss in this chapter. Two later tests owing their existence to the Woodworth Personal Data Sheet are the Bernreuter Personality Inventory (which we shall discuss in Chap. 7) and the Bell Adjustment Inventory (which we shall discuss in Chap. 8).

THE COLGATE MENTAL HYGIENE TEST

Our second example of a unidimensional approach to the measurement of personality is that contained in the Colgate Mental Hygiene Test. This test was developed by Donald A. Laird and was published in 1925. Laird's purposes were to get "a fairly reliable, objective and valid method of spotting persons in need of mental hygiene," and "to provide an instrument which would give a fairly precise quantitative measure of the degree and kind of deviation" from a normal group.

The test consists of two separate schedules. The first of these, the B1 schedule (or in a later revision the B2 schedule), consists of 75 questions about psychoneurotic tendencies. And the second schedule, the C1 schedule (or in a later revision the C2 schedule), consists of 53 questions about introversion-extroversion.

In constructing the Colgate Mental Hygiene Test, Laird theorized that "all the traits which are characteristic of mental ill health are but exaggerations of traits of behavior present in all humans." Therefore, Laird continues, "the method . . . is to have those traits which are significant as indicators of mental deviation so described for each individual that one can determine whether or not the person being examined deviates from the normal in these traits."

Development. There were just five steps involved in the construction of the Colgate Mental Hygiene Test. These were the collection of a list of statements, their editing, the giving of the test to an experimental population, the determination of deviant answers, and the preparation of percentile norms.

Laird took most of his items from Woodworth's Personal Data Sheet and worded them so that they could be answered by means of a check mark on a graphic scale. The questions were printed on the left-hand side of the test booklet, and the graphic scales were printed on the right. An example is given below:

HAVE YOU BEEN ....
BOTHERED BY   Not to   Only when bawled   Many times
BLUSHING?   know it   out or such   each day

Directions. The schedules were given to more than 2,000 students with these instructions:

In the large type to the left (look at the blank) questions are asked. You will answer these by making a check mark like this / along the dotted line at the place which indicates the right answer for you. One end of this dotted line might be thought of as low, the other high, with each dot representing a step from one extreme to the other.

To help you locate yourself some descriptive phrases are printed below the dotted line. It may be that none of these phrases describe you, in which case the check may be placed between two of the phrases. Check at any dot, using the phrases to help you locate the proper dot easily.

We want to know about your personality for the last few months; say the last six or so. After you read each question in the larger type and then the descriptive phrases, think how you have been in the past half year—not how you would like to have been or how you think the ideal person should have been, but *how you actually were.*

You may use the margins and blank spaces to write in any explanation you want to, but always make a check mark some place along each line of dots.

After you are through you may study it over again and make any changes you think necessary. Do not erase, however; just cross out your first check marks and make new ones.

Remember: you may check any place along the dotted line.

Think how *you* have been *the past half year.*

Scoring. Laird prepared distributions of the answers (check marks) for each question and determined on the graphic scales the points which indicated the top and bottom quarters of the distributions. Then he prepared scoring stencils indicating for each question the portion of each graphic scale included in the deviant quarters of the distributions. A subject's score consisted of the number of answers placed in these deviant quarters. When all schedules had been scored, Laird prepared four sets of percentile norms: two for Schedule B1 and two for Schedule C1. One of the two sets of norms for each schedule was for men, and the other was for women.

Reliability. Laird secured reliability data in three ways: by comparing the results for duplicate sets of questions, by correlating the scores on comparable halves of the schedules, and by the test-retest method. All three methods gave evidence of only moderate degrees of reliability.

The comparisons of duplicate sets of questions consisted in the observation that the distributions on these duplicate questions tended to the same form. Hoitsma, who reported these results for Laird, argues that, since the distributions on most of these questions were non-normal, their similarity can be taken as evidence of substantial reliability. Whether the reader accepts this argument or not (and the author doesn't), it applies to only five of the questions in the two schedules and has little relevance to the reliability of the total scores.

The second determination of reliability was through the correlation of the scores on comparable halves of the schedules. In Schedule B1 these comparable halves were composed, on one hand, of all the questions in the first halves of its several sections and, on the other hand, of all the questions in the second halves of these same sections. In Schedule C1 the two halves were composed of the odd- and even-numbered questions. The correlation between the scores on the comparable halves of the B1 schedule was .79, and that for the C1 schedule was .45. Hoitsma, who reported these coefficients, did not enter them in the Spearman-Brown Prophecy Formula. Had he done so, he would have obtained coefficients of .88 and .62.

As the third bit of evidence on reliability, Hoitsma reports a test-retest correlation of .85 for the B1 schedule and one of .67 for the C1 schedule. These values must be considered low, since the interval involved was only two weeks.

Distinguishing Features. We find in the Colgate Mental Hygiene Test two features not found in any of the other tests we shall discuss. These features are the use of the distribution of answers to each question as a basis for determining which answers are to have deviant significance, and the use of a graphic scale for the recording of the answers. It is undoubtedly the use of the graphic scale feature that led to the low reliabilities. For other investigators, using practically the same set of items, have been able to achieve much higher reliabilities. This fact undoubtedly led to the abandonment of the graphic scale answering continuum and, with its abandonment, to that of the possibility of further use of item distributions as a basis for determining which of the answers were to possess deviant significance.

THE ALLPORTS' ASCENDANCE-SUBMISSION REACTION STUDY

Our third example of a unidimensional approach to the measurement of personality is that exemplified in Gordon W. Allport and Floyd H. Allport's Ascendance-Submission Reaction Study (1928). This is a test which was designed, says Gordon W. Allport, to yield

. . . a score which indicates the incidence in the personality of the two traits ascendance or submission. The method of the test is to present verbally certain situations of life, and to require the subject to select from a few standardized choices that type of behavior which most nearly characterizes his own usual adjustment to each of the situations.

The Allports postulated the existence of two traits, ascendance and submission, and theorized that as one of these traits would be prominent in an individual, the other trait would be subordinate. They proceeded, on this theory, to choose a variety of situations in which they thought a person would tend to be dominant or submissive. An entire trait continuum would be represented, they said, not in any one situation, but by the average behavior of a person in a great number of these situations. An individual might be dominant in one situation and not in another. But a more dominant person would tend to be dominant in a greater number of situations than would a less dominant person, and so forth. A score on the test would be an algebraic summation of the number of situations in which the person was, or felt he would be, dominant. If the situations in the test could be made representative of all situations in which an individual can find himself, it could be assumed that a score represents some general tendency or habit on the part of the subject.

The test is available in one form for men and in another form for women. A typical situation is as follows:

    a. At a reception or tea do you seek to meet the important person present?
       Frequently   _____
       Occasionally _____
       Never   _____
    b. Do you feel reluctant to meet him?
       Yes, usually _____
       Sometimes   _____
       No   _____

This illustration represents 1 situation, 2 items, and 6 choices. Counting in this way, the men's form has 33 situations, 41 items, and 123 choices. The women's form has 35 situations, 49 items, and 140 choices. The directions which a subject is asked to follow in taking the test are as follows:

Most of these situations will represent to you your own actual experiences. Reply to the questions spontaneously and truthfully by checking the answer which most nearly represents your usual reaction. If the situation has not been experienced endeavor to feel yourself into it and respond on the basis of what you believe your reaction would be. If a situation seems totally unreal or impossible to respond to you may omit it.

Development. The steps in the development of the Ascendance-Submission Reaction Study may be listed as follows:

  1. A list of situations was collected.
  2. The test was given to a group of experimental subjects.
  3. These subjects and their close associates completed a seven-step rating scale.
  4. Mean ratings for each of the alternate answers to each question were determined.
  5. Scouring weights were assigned.
  6. Norms were prepared.

All situations were selected by the Allports on an a priori basis. The test was given to 400 men at Dartmouth and to 200 women at Goucher, Wellesley, and Radcliffe. Freshmen were excluded, but all other classes were represented. At the same time that students were asked to take the test, they were also asked to rate themselves and to have four of their close associates rate them on a seven-point rating scale. The directions for making these ratings were as follows:

Kindly rate the student who gives you this paper in regard to the trait of his personality which is described below. Place a check against the phrase which seems to you to represent best his customary level of behavior.

  _____ Strongly marked tendency to take the active role, to dominate, lead, organize, in dealing with his fellows.

____ Marked tendency to take the active role.

____ Slightly above average in tendency to take the active role.

____ AVERAGE: neither distinctly active nor passive.

____ Slightly under average in tendency to take active role.

____ Tendency to be passive in contact with his fellows, to be led rather than to be the leader.

____ Strongly marked tendency to be passive in contacts.

Subjects were divided according to the answers given on each question. Then for each of these groups the average of the five ratings was ascertained. For example, one situation had these alternative answers: "habitually," "occasionally," "never." The average ratings for the subjects giving these answers were 3.35, 3.50, and 3.57. Those who answered "habitually" were rated more dominant than those who answered "occasionally." And these subjects, in their turn, were rated more dominant than those who answered "never."

The average rating assigned to all subjects was 3.48. This average rating was subtracted from each of the foregoing means and yielded the differences .13, −.02, and −.09. These differences were rounded to one decimal, the decimals were discarded, and the results became the scoring weights. In this instance these weights are 1, 0, and −1 for the answers "habitually," "occasionally," and "never." A total score is obtained by an algebraic summation of the values associated with the responses which a subject gives. The maximum possible range of scores extends from −79 to 81 for men and from −91 to 112 for women. The actual range in the original subject population was −55 to 64 for men and −50 to 59 for women.

Reliability. The Allports do not give extensive data on reliability but report that on a six-week retest, comparing an earlier and a later revision, they found an intercorrelation of .78. This value is subject to qualification, however, for only 37 per cent of the situations in the two revisions were identical. For men, a more conventional split-half reliability of .74 is reported. This was obtained from a stepped-up correlation of .58 between the scores based on the situations listed on pages 1, 3, and 5 and the scores based on the situations listed on pages 2, 4, and 6.

Validity. The validity data which the Allports offer consist of correlations between the scores on the test and the ratings used in determining the scoring weights. The ascendance-submission scores correlate .63 with self-ratings; .50 with the total of all ratings (self-and associates' ratings combined); and .46 with associates' ratings. At first glance these coefficients might appear to be quite satisfactory. But since the ratings involved were the same as those used in establishing the scoring system, these coefficients can in no sense be considered remarkable. When the Allports used the records of 42 men and 51 women not included in the item-standardization process, the correlations between scores and total ratings were found to be .29 and .30. These correlations are low, but they still indicate a significant relation between the scores and the ratings.

THE THURSTONES' PERSONALITY SCHEDULE

We have now explained the methods by which three of the historically important unidimensional tests of personality were constructed. And we have found three different methods by which the significance of the items can be determined. These are by judgment, by incidence, and by correlation with an external criterion.

Woodworth, as we have seen, placed chief reliance upon judgment —his own and that of the textbook authors and authorities from whom he collected his questions. Woodworth supplemented this judgment, however, by giving consideration to the incidence of the responses in both normal and psychoneurotic populations.

Laird supplemented Woodworth's judgment with his own but placed his chief reliance for determining item significance upon the incidence of the responses in a normal college population. We recall, for example, that the only responses contributing to the total score on the Colgate Mental Hygiene Test are those in the deviant quarters of the answer distributions.

In the Allports' study we come, for the first time, to a consideration of the use of an external criterion for determining item significance. Perhaps we should say semiexternal criterion rather than external criterion because a part of this criterion was a self-rating. The chief point, however, is that something besides the judgment of the investigator or the incidence of the item responses was used in determining item significance. Another first in the Allports' study is the use of something other than a series of unit weights in scoring. We shall find that this differential weighting of test items has since played an important part in the history of personality-test development, even though the most recent evidence and belief are to the effect that differential systems of weighting do not do all that is claimed for them.

We are now ready to begin our discussion of three more unidimensional approaches to the measurement of personality. And in these we shall find two additional methods of determining item significance. One of these methods will consist of the criterion of internal consistency which we encountered in our discussion of Likert's a posteriori method of attitude-scale construction. And the other method will consist of a criterion of external consistency, somewhat more objectively applied than in the case of the Ascendance-Submission Reaction Study.

Our fourth example of a unidimensional approach to the measurement of personality is that contained in Thurstones' Personality Schedule. This schedule was developed in 1928 by Louis L. Thurstone and Thelma Gwinn Thurstone. It consists of 223 questions to each of which a subject must answer "Yes," "No," or " ?." The schedule was designed, say the Thurstones, to yield a "fairly reliable" index of the neurotic tendencies of university freshmen.

Development. The steps in the development of the Personality Schedule may be listed as follows:

1. A list of statements was collected.
2. These statements were edited.
3. An a priori scoring key was developed.
4. The Schedule was given to a group of subjects.
5. An item analysis was performed.
6. Norms were prepared.

The Thurstones collected a list of over 600 statements. These came from their reviews of the Woodworth Personal Data Sheet, of House's monograph "A Mental Hygiene Inventory," of the Colgate Mental Hygiene Test, of Freyd's monograph "Introverts and Extroverts," and of the Allports' Ascendance-Submission Reaction Study. The 600 questions were typed individually on cards, were classified in various groups, were rearranged, were edited, and were finally reduced to a select 223 items. These items became the Personality Schedule. On an a priori basis the Thurstones decided which answers were to be considered symptomatic of neurotic tendency, and a scoring weight of 1 was assigned to each such answer.

Directions. As an initial tryout the Personality Schedule was given to 694 University of Chicago freshmen. Their instructions were as follows:

In order that your advisers may help you in the best possible way it is desirable that they know something of your personality as well as of your intellectual ability and scholarship. The questions in this blank are intended to indicate various emotional and personality traits. Your answers may reveal a well-adjusted emotional life or they may show that you have some form of nervousness or worry which you may not yourself understand completely. If your answers show emotional maladjustment you will have the opportunity to get advice about this aspect of your development. If your answers reveal a well-adjusted personality, that fact will be known to your advisers.

This is not an examination. It is not a test in any sense because there are no right and wrong answers to any of the questions in this blank. Your admission to the University and your scholastic standing will not be affected in any way by your answers to these questions.

Your answers to particular questions will be confidential. They will be known only to two or three persons who will study these blanks and who will summarize your answers in a brief statement for your Dean. It has been found that some of the brightest students have emotional and personality difficulties which can be overcome with suitable counsel if the difficulties are known. It will therefore be to your own advantage to answer the questions as truthfully as possible.

In front of each question you will find: Yes No ?

Draw a ring around one of these three answers for each question. Try to answer by "yes" or "no" if it is possible. If you are entirely unable to say even a tentative "yes" or "no" to the question, then draw a ring around the question mark.

Norms. Scores were obtained by counting the number of questions to which "neurotic" answers were given. The total possible range of scores extended from 0 (if no "neurotic" answers were circled) to 223 (if all "neurotic" answers were circled). The actual range extended from 5 to 134.

Item Analysis. The Thurstones now wished to check upon the "adequacy" of their a priori assignment of scoring weights. Therefore they selected the 50 most neurotic-scoring subjects and the 50 least neurotic-scoring subjects and counted the number of "neurotic" answers which each of these groups gave in answer to each of the 223 questions. They wanted to find out if the 50 most neurotic-scoring subjects gave "neurotic" answers more frequently than the 50 least neurotic-scoring subjects. The Thurstones found this to be true for all but one of the items. In view of these results they concluded that their a priori assignment of scoring weights had been satisfactory.

TABLE 56. *The Most Differentiating Items in the Personality Schedule**

1. Do you get stage fright?
2. Do you have difficulty in starting a conversation with a stranger?
3. Do you worry too long over humiliating experiences?
4. Do you often feel lonesome, even when you are with other people?
5. Do you consider yourself a rather nervous person?
6. Are your feelings easily hurt?
7. Do you keep in the background on social occasions?
8. Do ideas often run through your head so that you cannot sleep?
9. Are you frequently burdened by a sense of remorse?
10. Do you worry over possible misfortunes?
11. Do your feelings alternate between happiness and sadness without apparent reason?
12. Are you troubled with shyness?
13. Do you day dream frequently?
14. Have you ever had spells of dizziness?
15. Do you get discouraged easily?
16. Do your interests change quickly?
17. Are you easily moved to tears?
18. Does it bother you to have people watch you at work even when you do it well?
19. Can you stand criticism without feeling hurt?
20. Do you have difficulty in making friends?
21. Are you troubled with the idea that people are watching you on the street?
22. Does your mind often wander so badly that you lose track of what you are doing?
23. Have you ever been depressed because of low marks in school?
24. Are you touchy on various subjects?
25. Are you often in a state of excitement?
26. Do you frequently feel grouchy?
27. Do you feel self-conscious when you recite in class?
28. Do you often feel just miserable?
29. Does some particularly useless thought keep coming into your mind to bother you?
30. Do you hesitate to volunteer in a class recitation?
31. Are you frequently in low spirits?
32. Do you often experience periods of loneliness?
33. Do you often feel self-conscious in the presence of superiors?
34. Do you lack self-confidence?
35. Do you find it difficult to speak in public?
36. Do you often feel self-conscious because of your personal appearance?
37. If you see an accident are you quick to take an active part in giving help?
38. Do you feel you must do a thing over several times before you leave it?
39. Are you troubled with feelings of inferiority?
40. Do you often find that you cannot make up your mind until the time for action has passed?
41. Do you have ups and downs in mood without apparent cause?
42. Are you in general self-confident about your abilities?

---

* From Thurstone, L. L., and Thurstone, T. G. A neurotic inventory. *J. soc. Psychol.*, 1930, **1**, 3–30.

The 42 items showing the greatest degree of discrimination are given in Table 56. The content of these most differentiating items suggests, to the Thurstones, "that the fundamental characteristic of the neurotic personality is an imagination that fails to express itself effectively on external social reality."

Reliability. When the Personality Schedule was printed, it was prepared so that two columns of questions appeared on each one of its four pages. In scoring, it was found convenient to enter a subtotal at the foot of each column of questions. The Thurstones utilized these subtotals in determining the reliability of total scores. They correlated the scores obtained from the questions printed in the left-hand columns of the schedule with those obtained from the questions printed in the right-hand columns. When they obtained this coefficient, they entered it in the Spearman-Brown Prophecy Formula and found a total score reliability of .95.

Validity. A score on the Personality Schedule shows the number of "neurotic" answers checked by a subject. But these "neurotic" answers are "neurotic" only because the Thurstones said they were. The author would be one of the last to decry the value of the Thurstones' judgment, but we must recognize the fact that no other standard was used.

Landis and Katz have presented some data which show that the validity of the Personality Schedule varies with the score involved. They find that the answers of psychotic and psychoneurotic subjects with "neurotic" scores agree fairly well with case-history data. But as the scores of psychotic and psychoneurotic subjects recede from the "neurotic" end of the continuum and become more "normal,"

TABLE 57. *Percentage of Answers Agreeing with Case-history Findings*[*]

Percentile	Number	Percentage
90–100	25	91
80– 89	10	79
50– 79	27	73
20– 49	21	70
10– 19	6	60
0– 9	10	60
Total..........	224	

[*] From Landis, C., and Katz, S. E. The validity of certain questions which purport to measure neurotic tendencies. *J. appl. Psychol.*, 1934, **18**, 343–356.

the less becomes their correspondence to case-history data. These findings are summarized in Table 57. These findings agree, by the way, with the Thurstones' own statement indicating greater validity for the "neurotic" than for the "nonneurotic" scores.

BERNREUTER'S SELF-SUFFICIENCY TEST

Our fifth example of a unidimensional approach to the measurement of personality is that contained in Bernreuter's test of Self-sufficiency. This is a test which Bernreuter prepared prior to the development of his widely used Personality Inventory and which, as we said before, we shall discuss in the next chapter.

The Self-sufficiency Test was published in 1933 under the title "Personal Preference Blank." It consists of 60 questions to which a subject is asked to answer "Yes," "No," or "?." These questions are supposed to elicit answers which will be indicative of the extent to which a subject is dependent upon or is not dependent upon other persons. A subject who is *not* dependent upon other individuals is called a self-sufficient person; hence the name of the test.

Development. The steps through which Bernreuter proceeded in the development of the Self-sufficiency Test may be listed as follows:

1. A list of statements was collected.
2. These statements were edited.
3. An a priori scoring key for the "yes" and "no" answers was developed.
4. The test was given to a group of subjects.
5. An item analysis was performed.
6. The test was revised.
7. Scoring weights for " ? " answers were determined.
8. The revised test was given to new groups of subjects.
9. Percentile norms were prepared.

Bernreuter's first step was to collect a list of 132 items. These items were worded in the form of questions so that a subject could answer "Yes," "No," or " ?."

Bernreuter's second step was to develop, with the aid of his colleagues at Washington University (St. Louis), an a priori scoring key for the "yes" and "no" answers. In this key one point was assigned for each answer thought to be indicative of self-sufficiency. At this stage no scoring weights were assigned for " ?" answers.

The next step consisted of giving the 132 items to 127 Washington University elementary-psychology students. Here are their instructions:

The questions on this sheet are intended to indicate your likes and dislikes. It is not an intelligence test, nor are there any right or wrong answers.

In front of each question you will find: Yes   No   ?

If your answer is "Yes" draw a circle around the "Yes." If your answer is "No" draw a circle around the "No." If you are entirely unable to answer either "Yes" or "No" to the question then draw a circle around the question mark.

Item Analysis. Scores were obtained by counting the number of answers which, according to the a priori key, were considered indicative of self-sufficiency. The scores obtained ranged from 16 to 117. The papers were now arranged in order according to these scores, and the 24 highest scoring students and the 24 lowest scoring students were selected as criterion groups for further study. To select these groups Bernreuter noted the scores falling at plus and minus one standard deviation unit from the mean of the distribution and then used the scores nearest these two points that would give him an equal number of cases in the two criterion groups.

To get an index of the discriminatory power of each item Bernreuter counted the number of "Yes," "No," and " ?" answers given by each criterion group and subtracted the number of low-scoring subjects giving a designated answer from the number of high-scoring subjects giving this same answer. For example, if 12 low-scoring subjects and 20 high-scoring subjects answered "Yes," the 12 was subtracted from the 20 to yield a difference of 8 (*i.e.*, $20 - 12 = 8$). This difference was taken as a measure of discriminative value. The range of all differences extended from 0 to 19. When all differences had been computed, Bernreuter selected the 60 most discriminating items to constitute the final form of the Self-sufficiency Test.

At this point Bernreuter determined the significance of the " ?" answers. He did this by comparing the number of high-scoring subjects and the number of low-scoring subjects giving a " ?" as an answer to each of the questions. When Bernreuter found that more of the high-scoring subjects gave a " ?" as an answer, he assigned the " ?" a scoring weight of 1. He also assigned it such a weight if the number of high-scoring and low-scoring subjects were the same *and* if the "high scoring group shows less consistency within itself in responding to that particular item. . . . " On 12 items the " ?" was found to be indicative of self-sufficiency.

Norms. The revised (60-item) edition of the test was then given to 388 men and 456 women. Subjects were secured from Washington University, Stanford University, Chico (California) State College, San Francisco State College, and Menlo (Menlo Park, California) Junior College, and upon the basis of the responses of these subjects percentile norms were prepared.

Reliability and Validity. Bernreuter determined the reliability of the Self-sufficiency Test both by the split-half and by the test-retest techniques. Both techniques led to a coefficient of .84.

The validity of the self-sufficiency scores was established, says Bernreuter, by correlating them with a series of ratings. Three ratings were secured. Two of these were from close associates, and the third was a self-rating. These were on need for sympathy, appreciation, and encouragement; desire to be alone; frequency of asking advice; and ability to handle responsibilities. The correlations between these ratings and self-sufficiency scores were .36, .69, .52, and .18. Self-sufficiency scores correlated .60 with total self-ratings and .54 with ratings supplied by associates. These coefficients were based upon the records for 58 women.

Table 58 shows how 21 high-scoring students and 21 low-scoring

TABLE 58. *Significance of the Differences between the Mean Ratings Assigned to High- and Low-scoring Students on the Self-sufficiency Test**

Trait	Self-rating	Associates' rating	Combined rating
R1 Need for sympathy, appreciation and encouragement	0.83	1.60	1.95
R2 Desire to be alone	8.67	4.55	6.61
R3 Frequency of asking advice	4.69	3.04	4.37
R4 Ability to handle responsibilities	1.28	4.37	1.99

* From Bernreuter, R. G. The measurement of self-sufficiency. *J. abnorm. soc. Psychol.*, 1933, **28**, 291–300.

students (out of a total of 128 students) differ on their own and on their associates' ratings. The figures in the body of the table are critical ratios of the differences between mean ratings assigned to the high-scoring and low-scoring subjects.

These critical ratios show that self-sufficiency scores are more nearly a reflection of "desire to be alone" and of "frequency of asking advice" than they are of "need for sympathy, appreciation, and encouragement" and of "ability to handle responsibilities." Bernreuter does not seem perturbed that the self-sufficiency scores do not correlate so well with these latter traits, but he must have felt that they were integral parts of the trait "self-sufficiency," or there would have been no reason to seek ratings on them in the first place.

The results presented in Table 58 led Bernreuter to compute the correlation between self-sufficiency scores and a sum of the ratings on "desire to be alone" and "frequency of asking advice." The correlation with self-ratings was found to be .62, with associates' ratings, .44, and with combined ratings, .58. The number of subjects was not large, but these correlations can be considered substantial. But even so, it is difficult to see why we should accept as relevant ratings on only two of the traits and discard as irrelevant those which did not result in such high correlations.

THE TERMAN-MILES MASCULINITY-FEMININITY TEST

Our sixth and last example of a unidimensional approach to the measurement of personality is contained in the Terman-Miles Attitude Interest Analysis Test, more popularly known as the M-F test. In it we shall find the use of an external criterion for the determination of item significance in contrast with the use of an internal criterion, such as that used by Bernreuter and the Thurstones.

We shall also find in the M-F test another important contrast with the approaches we have been discussing. In these approaches some trait has been visualized or defined, and a test has been built with the purpose of measuring whatever trait had been visualized or defined. If criterion groups were needed, they were selected upon the basis of the test being constructed.

In the Terman-Miles M-F test we follow a radically different procedure. We define our criterion groups ahead of time and permit our test items to have no part in their selection. We set as our objective the building of a test to distinguish our previously defined and selected criterion groups. The test scores acquire meaning with reference to the nature of these criterion groups. This is in marked contrast with a test based on a criterion of internal consistency, in which case the criterion groups are defined and selected in terms of test scores.

We shall find that the Terman-Miles technique of defining and selecting criterion groups before constructing the test yields results far superior to any secured by internal consistency techniques. We found that this same fact applied in our discussion of interest tests. Dr. Strong used, as we will recall, carefully defined criterion groups and achieved remarkably successful results. Dr. Kuder constructed his Preference Records by techniques which did not make use of criterion groups, and, to date, his test must be considered to possess considerably less validity than we can ascribe to the scores on the Strong Vocational Interest Test. It is admittedly difficult, in the area we are now discussing, to obtain easily identified criterion groups. However, Terman and Miles did this in their development of the M-F test, and to their work we now turn.

Purpose and Content of Test. According to Terman and Miles: The purpose of the investigations which led to the development of the M-F test, [was] the accomplishment in the field of masculinity-femininity of something similar to Binet's early achievement in the field of intelligence—a quantification of procedures and concepts. . . . A measure is needed which can be applied to the individual and scored so as to locate the subject, with a fair degree of approximation, in terms of deviation from the means of either sex. Range and overlap of the sexes must be more accurately determined than is possible by observational and clinical methods. . . . The purpose of the M-F test is to enable the clinician or other investigator to obtain a more exact and meaningful, as well as a more objective, rating of those aspects of personality in which the sexes tend to differ. More specifically, the purpose is to make possible a quantitative estimation of the amount and direction of a subject's deviation from the mean of his or her sex, and to permit quantitative comparisons of groups differing in age, intelligence, education, interests, occupation, and cultural milieu. [And, finally,] it is evident that no clear delineation of sexual temperament is possible on the basis of uncontrolled observation. The M-F test is an attempt to remedy this situation. Its scientific intent is to free the concepts of masculinity-femininity from the irrelevancies and confusions which have become attached to them as a result of superficial consideration of everyday behavior.

The M-F test is available in two equivalent forms. It consists of a variety of stimulus objects to each of which a subject must respond by checking or underlining one or two, three, or four alternate answers. The contents of the test may be classified as in Table 59.

Development of Test. The idea of constructing a masculinity-femininity test first occurred to Dr. Terman when, in 1922, he was working over some sex-difference data for his group of gifted children. Terman had classified a group of games and childhood amusements in accord with their relative preference by boys and girls and was attempting to work out a masculinity index upon the basis of an individual's preference for activities preferred by boys in contrast with those preferred by girls. In preparing separate sex distributions of the masculinity indices, one of Terman's assistants noticed what seemed to be an error. One of the boys received a more feminine score than any of the girls. A recheck was made but no error was found. This called into question the correctness of the sex classification. This was checked and no error was discovered. This led to a careful investigation and to the preparation of a complete case history of the boy in question, with verification of his feminine interests, propensities, attitudes, and behavior.

TABLE 59. *Item Content of the Terman-Miles M-F Test**

Exercise	Number of items	
	Form A	Form B
1. Word association........................	60	60
2. Ink-blot association......................	18	18
3. Information.............................	70	70
4. Emotional and ethical responses...........	105	105
5. Interests..............................	119	118
6. Personalities and opinions................	42	41
7. Introvertive responses....................	42	42
Total.................................	456	454

* From Terman, L. M., and Miles, C. C. *Sex and Personality*. New York: McGraw-Hill Book Company, Inc., 1936.

Terman and Miles give, with more than usual completeness, a step-by-step account of the development of each part of the M-F test. We shall describe these steps in an attempt to give the reader some idea of the tremendous amount of spadework necessary to develop an adequate psychological test.

Word Association. The first step in the preparation of the word-association test was that of scanning a short English dictionary for words which appeared to be capable of eliciting different responses from men and women. These words were rated by three judges as to their probable value in being able to elicit sex differences. As a result of these ratings, 280 words were discarded. The remaining 220 words were divided into two sets of 110 words each. These words were printed, individually, on cards and were given to 200 high-school and college men and to 200 high-school and college women, with instructions to respond to each of the stimulus words with the first word thought of. A scoring system was worked out, and the stimulus words were given to additional subjects. The results were unsatisfactory, however, so a new approach was tried.

This new approach involved printing the stimulus words in a booklet with four possible response words following each stimulus word. The subject was instructed to underline one of the response words, the one which best went with the stimulus word.

For the most part, response words were those which, in the preliminary studies, showed some evidence of yielding sex differences. However, 51 additional and previously untried stimulus words were added, and of these, 28 were found to be usable. In each set of four response words two were preferred by men and two by women.

The test now consisted of 171 stimulus words and was given, in this form, to 600 subjects. A study of the responses yielded 120 items for the final form. The words retained were those that showed sex differences in the same direction for at least three out of four possible responses in all groups tested (100 boys and 100 girls in the seventh grade, 100 boys and 100 girls in junior high school, and 100 men and 100 women in college).

The transition from the first uncontrolled response situation to the second and controlled response situation was dictated by the following reasons. The first method was found disadvantageous in that most of the responses had such low frequencies that large numbers of subjects would be needed to establish sex differences. Many of the responses, for this reason, could not be scored. Scoring, even when possible, was found to be laborious and time-consuming. And some subjects lost their place on the answer sheets and misplaced all subsequent answers. The second and controlled method was found to be better adapted to group testing and to require less time for its administration and scoring.

Ink-blot Association. To initiate work on this section of the test, Terman and Mary A. Bell made 40 ink blots according to Dearborn's directions and used, besides these, 20 blots furnished by Whipple. None of these blots proved satisfactory, so a new series of 100 blots was prepared. These were made with printer's ink with sweeping strokes of a paintbrush. These 100 blots were given to 100 male and

100 female high-school and college students with a request that they write down whatever each blot made them think of. Seventy blots were found to be acceptable (that is, they seemed capable of eliciting sex differences) and were photographed and reproduced on the pages of a 3- by 5-inch booklet, one blot per leaf. These booklets were given to 230 male subjects and to 230 female subjects (seventh grade, high-school freshmen, college, and adult groups) with these instructions:

On each leaf of this booklet is a kind of ink blot or drawing. They are not pictures of anything in particular, but might suggest almost anything to you, just as shapes in the clouds sometimes do. Below each drawing write the *first* thing it makes you think of. (Subjects were given 10 seconds for each drawing.)

The responses were studied in detail and were retained for further trial only if they were given by at least four subjects in at least three of the four groups studied and if they showed a sex difference in the same direction for at least three of these four groups.

The number of items was reduced to 50, and the response words which met the above criteria were printed after each stimulus blot. In this final form the test was given to 600 subjects (300 male and 300 female) and reduced as a result of this new exposure to a total of 36 items. These were equally divided between Form A and Form B.

Information. Two hundred items of information were prepared. These covered history, physical science, biological science, literature, general information, household arts, religion, and mythology. These items were prepared in multiple-choice form and were given to 800 subjects. The successes and failures were separately tabulated for each of four subject groups (seventh graders, high-school students, college students, and adults). The items retained for further trial had to show a significant difference in the same direction for at least three of the four populations. Ninety-one items were retained and given a further tryout on new populations. At this same time 491 additional items were also tried and of this group 95 proved worth retaining. Therefore these 95 items plus the previous 91 gave 186 items for further trial.

On these items a new method of scoring was tried. On all previous trials the scoring procedure was to count the number of masculine items correctly answered and to subtract from this the number of feminine items correctly answered. It was found during the course of investigation, however, that some of the wrong responses and omissions were just as productive of sex difference as were some of the right answers. Therefore steps were taken to include omissions and wrong answers in the scoring formula. The final test consists of 140 items equally divided between the two forms.

Emotional and Ethical Attitudes. Terman and his associates prepared a total of 218 items for this part of the M-F test. They covered the "emotions" of anger, fear, disgust, pity, and a variety of ethical attitudes. The subject was instructed to read each of the stimulus words (*e.g.*, gumchewing) and to indicate to what extent the situation "tended to provoke in him the emotion in question." The subject could answer VM (Very much), M (Much), L (Little), or N (Not at all). The test items were given to over 800 subjects, and items were retained if they showed a significant sex difference on at least two of the four possible responses. Terman and his associates decided to retain 195 items and to divide them between the two forms of the test.

Interests. For this part of the test 456 items were assembled, most of them coming from the Strong Vocational Interest Test. The test was given to 245 subjects, and items were retained if they showed a sex difference on two of the three responses L, I, and D, if they were "probably" significant, and if they were in the same direction for all subject groups tested, *i.e.*, seventh graders, high-school students, college students, and adults. Of these, 170 items were retained and, along with 60 new items on historical characters and 40 items on preferences for contrasting activities, were given to new subject groups. For the final forms 187 items were kept.

Opinions. Ninety-six items were prepared and given to 100 boys and 100 girls in the seventh grade and high school and to 50 men and 50 women in college. Twenty-eight items yielded significant differences in each of the three subject populations and were divided into two groups of 14 items each for the alternate forms.

Introvertive Responses. Cady's revision of the Woodworth Personal Data Sheet was given to 100 children in Terman's gifted group and to 100 controls. The responses of the sexes were compared and the item was retained if it yielded a critical ratio of 2.0 or more for either the "Yes" or "No" response. A series of 47 items from the Laird C-2 and Heidbreder introversion-extroversion schedules was tried out on seventh graders and high-school students. For the final scales 84 items were selected. These had to be significant on both the "Yes" and "No" responses.

Reliability and Validity. In most of the sections of the M-F test weighted and unit-scoring procedures were tried. It was found that the weighted scores added very little in the way of reliability or subtracted very little in the amount of sex overlap, so they were discarded in favor of unit scores throughout.

Reliability. Terman and Miles are meticulous in giving data concerning the reliabilities of many of the preliminary and trial test forms. It will be sufficient for our purposes here, however, if we take note only of the reliabilities of the final forms of each part of the test. They are given in Table 60.

TABLE 60. *Spearman-Brown Reliability Coefficients for the M-F Test**

Exercise	Single sex	Both sexes
1. Word association	.40	.62
2. Ink-blot association	.25	.34
3. Information	.50	.68
4. Emotional and ethical attitudes	.89	.90
5. Interests	.60	.80
6. Opinions	.54	.64
7. Introvertive responses	.24	.32
Either form (A vs. B)	.72	.90
Either form (Spearman-Brown)	.78	.92
Both forms (A and B)	.88	.96

* From Terman, L. M., and Miles, C. C. *Sex and Personality.* New York: McGraw-Hill Book Company, Inc., 1936.

Most of the part reliabilities are low. The only parts that have reasonably satisfactory reliabilities are the emotional and ethical attitudes and the test of interests. The remaining reliabilities can be called into question but particularly those for the ink-blot and introvertive sections.

The reliability of the entire test, of either form or of both forms combined, is satisfactory. Therefore we may, with some degree of assurance, rely upon the total score, even though we must view with considerable suspicion the value of some of the part scores. For this reason Terman and Miles repeatedly warn against profile-type analyses and suggest that until such time as the reliabilities of the parts can be increased, investigators confide only in the total score.

Interrelation of Parts. The correlations among the scores on the different parts of the M-F test are given in Table 61. As the M-F

TABLE 61. *Intercorrelations among the Parts of the M-F Test**

Exercise	Ink-blot association	Infor- mation	Emo- tional and ethical atti- tudes	Inter- ests	Opin- ions	Intro- vertive re- sponses
Word association..............	.05	.14	− .15	.07	− .02	− .04
Ink-blot association...........		.06	.22	.06	− .07	.06
Information...................			.23	.09	.47	.17
Emotional and ethical attitudes...				.15	.09	.36
Interests.....................					.02	.20
Opinions.....................						.05

* From Terman, L. M., and Miles, C. C. *Sex and Personality.* New York: McGraw-Hill Book Company, Inc., 1936.

test is supposed to mirror the differences between men and women in our present Occidental culture, it would lose seriously in value if it did not reflect a large number and variety of these differences. Therefore it is particularly important that a wide variety of psychological functions be tapped by the test. The extent to which the M-F test does tap different functions can, to some degree, be judged by the intercorrelations among part scores. If we should find that the various parts of the test are all highly intercorrelated, we might have some reason to suspect that an insufficient variety of functions were tested. On the other hand, if we find low intercorrelations, we can infer that the test taps at least as many separate functions as there are parts to the test. The correlations among the parts are low, so we can conclude that different areas of personality are tapped. We must temper this conclusion, however, with our knowledge of the low part reliabilities and with our awareness that these low reliabilities undoubtedly contribute to the low interpart correlations.

Validity. The validity of the M-F test is easy to ascertain. First, we restate its purpose: to differentiate between the sexes. All we have to do is see if boys and men get different scores from girls and women. This is almost universally the case. The range of scores for men runs from approximately 200 to −100, while that for women runs from approximately 100 to −200. The average score for men is 52, and that for women is −70. The amount of overlap in the distribution of scores for the two sexes is given in Table 62.

TABLE 62. *Overlap in the Sex Distributions on the M-F Test**

Exercise	*Percentage Overlap*
1. Word association	18.56
2. Ink-blot association	30.61
3. Information	16.97
4. Emotional and ethical attitudes	28.31
5. Interests	8.84
6. Opinions	30.89
7. Introvertive responses	30.07
Total	8.02

* From Terman, L. M., and Miles, C. C. *Sex and Personality*. New York: McGraw-Hill Book Company, Inc., 1936.

According to these data we can conclude that the M-F test as a whole validly distinguishes between the two sexes. We can see that Exercise 5 (interests) is almost as valid as the entire test and that Exercise 2 (ink-blot association), Exercise 6 (opinions), and Exercise 7 (introvertive responses) are the least valid parts of the test.

However, an alternative explanation would be to the effect that men and women do actually differ more in their interests and less in their responses to ink blots and introvertive items. There is really no wholly objective way of deciding between the alternative conclusions: that some parts of the test are more valid than others or that in the functions which to a great extent overlap men and women are really less dissimilar than in some of the other sections of the test.

With our discussion of the Terman-Miles M-F test we bring to a close our chapter on unidimensional approaches to the measurement of personality. There are many other tests that we could, with profit, discuss, but we have selected and discussed those that illustrate a method, point a moral, or, as we said once before, have led to some later development. We shall now find it profitable to turn our attention to these later developments.

7

PERSONALITY: MULTIDIMENSIONAL

APPROACHES

Each of the tests we discussed in Chap. 6 was designed to yield one score. In this chapter we propose to discuss tests designed to yield several scores. These tests are examples of what we call multidimensional approaches to the measurement of personality. A multidimensional approach may consist in the simultaneous use of several tests of the unidimensional type, or it may consist in the use of the same set of items scored in different ways. And there are, of course, gradations between these extremes.

THE PERSONALITY INVENTORY

We shall begin our discussion of multidimensional approaches by describing the Bernreuter Personality Inventory. This test consists of 125 questions to which a subject is asked to answer "Yes," "No," or " ?." It was developed by Robert G. Bernreuter and was first published in 1932. It was designed to do the work of four of the tests we discussed in the preceding chapter and, consequently, yields a series of scores serving the same purposes as the scores on these original tests. These scores are supposed to measure neurotic tendency, self-sufficiency, introversion-extroversion, and dominance-submission. Individuals scoring high and low on each of these variables can, according to Bernreuter, be characterized as follows:

High B1 N. The individuals that score high on this scale show a tendency toward a neurotic condition. Such an individual often feels miserable, is sensitive to blame, and is troubled by useless thoughts, by shyness, and by feelings of inferiority. He feels shut off from other people, he frequently daydreams, and worries both over things that have happened and over things that may happen.

Low B1 N. The individual who scores low on the B1 N scale is an emotionally stable person. He is rarely troubled by moods, by worries, or by the criticism of others. He is self-confident, and is a doer rather than a daydreamer.

High B2 S. The individual who scores high on the B2 S scale is a self-sufficient person. He is able to be contented when by himself. He prefers to work alone and depends upon his own judgment in reaching decisions and in formulating plans.

Low B2 S. The individual who scores low on the B2 S scale is dependent upon others for his enjoyments. He likes to be with other people a great deal and prefers company both while working and during leisure hours. He prefers to talk problems over with others and to receive advice before reaching decisions.

High B3 I. The individual who scores high on the B3 I scale is introverted in the sense that he is introspective and is given to autistic thinking. He shows the symptoms of a neurotic condition which are typical of those individuals who score high on the B1 N scale.

Low B3 I. The individual who scores low on the B3 I scale is extroverted in the sense that he rarely substitutes day dreaming for action. He is emotionally stable and possesses the characteristics of those individuals who score low on the B1 N scale.

High B4 D. The individual who scores high on the B4 D scale is dominant in face-to-face situations with his equals. He is self-confident and aggressive, and readily assumes a position in the foreground at social functions. He converses readily with strangers or with prominent people and suffers no feelings of inferiority when doing so.

Low B4 D. The individual who scores low on the B4 D scale is submissive in face-to-face situations with his equals. He lacks self-confidence, keeps in the background at social functions, and rarely takes the initiative in directing people or activities. He experiences feelings of inferiority and is reluctant to meet important personages.

Development of Test. Personality tests prior to the advent of the Bernreuter Personality Inventory were constructed upon the basis of the proposition that a given behavioral element reflected, or could be explained by, one trait. Not all psychologists accepted this hypothesis, but those concerned with the construction of personality tests used no other alternative. It remained for Bernreuter to take the all-important step and to proceed to test the assumption that the "behavior of an individual in a single situation may be symptomatic of several traits. . . . " If this proposition could be established, Bernreuter reasoned, an item could be assigned one diagnostic weight for one trait and a different diagnostic weight for another trait. This would make possible the "construction of tests . . . which could be used in the simultaneous analysis of several traits. . . . "

To test this hypothesis Bernreuter assembled the items which had been used in four of the tests we described in Chap. 6 and proceeded to demonstrate that a common core of these items could measure each of the original variables just about as accurately as the original tests. The tests Bernreuter selected as a basis for his operations were Laird's Introversion-Extroversion Schedule, the Allports' Ascendance-Submission Reaction Study, the Thurstones' Personality Schedule, and his own test of Self-sufficiency.

Subjects. Bernreuter initiated his work by giving a trial form of his inventory and the four tests from which its items were taken to several groups of students. These students were located at Menlo (Menlo Park, California) Junior College, Chico (Chico, California) State Teachers College, San Francisco State Teachers College, and Stanford University. Approximately 400 students were tested. The exact number for each test is given in Table 63.

TABLE 63. *Number of Subjects Used by Bernreuter in Developing the Personality Inventory**

Test	Men	Women
Laird's Introversion-Extroversion............	182	202
Allports' Ascendance-Submission.............	200	174
Thurstones' Personality Schedule...........	208	205
Bernreuter's Self-sufficiency................	203	244

* From Bernreuter, R. G. The theory and construction of the personality inventory. *J. soc. Psychol.*, 1933, **4**, 387–405.

Bernreuter prepared a distribution of scores for each of these tests, and upon the basis of these distributions he selected a number of criterion groups to represent extreme deviants on each of the tests. He selected 50 cases to represent "introverts" and 50 cases to represent "extroverts." He selected 50 cases to represent "dominant" individuals and 50 cases to represent "submissive" individuals, and so on. There were included in each criterion group 25 men and 25 women. For each trait these were the 25 highest and 25 lowest scoring men and the 25 highest and 25 lowest scoring women.

Item Analysis. Bernreuter then proceeded to find out how well the items in his inventory could differentiate between the two contrasting criterion groups on each of the four variables. To do this he computed the number and percentage of each criterion group that answered "Yes," "No," and " ?" to each question.

Bernreuter's next step should have consisted of the computation of the difference between the percentages of each contrasting pair of criterion groups and of the assignment of diagnostic weights upon the basis of these differences. Bernreuter did not have to make these computations, however. He utilized one of Dr. Strong's item-weighting charts which makes these intermediate computations unnecessary. Dr. Strong's chart gives item weights directly from the percentages characterizing the criterion groups to be contrasted with each other. So when Bernreuter wished to determine the significance of a "Yes" answer, he entered in the chart the percentages of the two criterion groups answering "Yes." When he wished to determine the significance of a "No" answer, he entered in the chart the percentages of the two criterion groups answering "No." And when he wished to determine the significance of a " ? " answer, he entered in the chart the percentages of the two criterion groups answering with a " ?."

The weights resulting from this procedure ranged from 0 to ± 30. Now, wondered Bernreuter, what standard of elimination should be used? Obviously, responses with diagnostic values of 0 should be ignored. But should responses with diagnostic values of ± 1, ± 2, or ± 3 be ignored? To answer this question, Bernreuter tried several successive eliminations (additions, we should say) of items in attempting to develop a scale for self-sufficiency. First, he used all responses with a diagnostic value of ± 7 or more. He weighted these responses equally (*i.e.*, ± 1) and computed the reliability of total scores. It turned out to be .73. Second, he added all responses having a diagnostic value of ± 6, and recomputed the reliability. Then he added all responses having a diagnostic value of ± 5, and recomputed the reliability, and then added all responses having a diagnostic value of ± 4 and, again, recomputed the reliability. Each time it increased over the previous value and was then .87. Next, Bernreuter added all items having a diagnostic value of ± 3, but found that this did not further increase reliability. Therefore, concluded Bernreuter, responses with diagnostic values of 0, ± 1, ± 2, and ± 3 should not be used.

The elimination of responses with diagnostic values of ± 3, or less, still left a range of values extending from ± 4 to ± 30. This series of values proved too cumbersome to retain in the actual scoring process, so at this point Bernreuter substituted a reduced but proportional series of weights ranging from 0 to ± 7. When these new weights were used in the Self-sufficiency Scale, a reliability of .92 was obtained. The development of the remaining scales followed the pattern established by the Self-sufficiency Scale. Responses with diagnostic values of 0, ±1, ±2, and ±3 were eliminated, and new weights ranging from ±1 to ±7 were assigned to the responses retained.

Reliability. Bernreuter then gave his inventory to new groups of subjects and obtained the split-half reliability coefficients reported in Table 64.

TABLE 64. *Reliability Data for the Personality Inventory**

Scale	Average	Men			Women		
		High school	College	Adult	High school	College	Adult
B1 N	.87	.88	.90	.89	.85	.84	.86
B2 S	.83	.78	.84	.83	.85	.84	.84
B3 I	.85	.87	.88	.91	.82	.83	.80
B4 D	.88	.87	.88	.88	.87	.89	.91

* From Bernreuter, R. G. The theory and construction of the personality inventory. *J. soc. Psychol.*, 1933, **4**, 387–405.

Validity. Bernreuter's thesis in constructing the Personality Inventory was that one set of items could be weighted differentially to do the work previously done by four separate tests. The data in Table 65 show the extent to which Bernreuter was able to verify this hypothesis. These figures show that the scales on the Personality

TABLE 65. *Correlations between the Scores on the Personality Inventory and Those of the Tests It Was Designed to Replace**

Bernreuter scale	Fall quarter students			Winter quarter students		
	Number	r	r_c	Number	r	r_c
B1 N	70	.94	1.00	32	.91	.99
B2 S	70	.89	1.00	46	.86	1.00
B3 I	70	.76	.99	44	.69	.92
B4 D (Men)	55	.81	1.00	29	.67	.84
B4 D (women)	..	...	....	55	.82	.99

* From Bernreuter, R. G. The theory and construction of the personality inventory. *J. soc. Psychol.*, 1933, **4**, 387–405.

Inventory are highly correlated with the scores on the tests they were designed to replace. We must agree with Bernreuter that one set of items can be weighted differentially and can serve several purposes at one time.

But, granting this point, we can still ask, "Are the scales on the Personality Inventory valid for measuring neurotic tendency, self-sufficiency, introversion-extroversion, and dominance-submission?" Bernreuter offers no direct evidence in answer to this question. All that Bernreuter can claim is that if the original tests measure these traits in a valid way, then the Personality Inventory does so also. But if the original tests do not measure these traits in a valid way, then neither does the Personality Inventory.

In Chap. 6 we discussed the validation of these original tests and found that, at best, it must be considered meager. Laird's Introversion-Extroversion Schedule and the Thurstones' Personality Inventory went through no validation process whatsoever. The Allports' Ascendance-Submission Reaction Study and Bernreuter's Self-sufficiency Scale were validated against various sets of ratings, but the validity coefficients obtained left much to be desired.

Criticisms. Three popular criticisms of the Bernreuter Personality Inventory are that the responses it elicits are due to chance, that they are slanted in a direction to win social approval, and that they are actually dishonest. Bernreuter agrees that these possibilities exist, but he feels that they do not vitiate completely, as his critics would have it, the value of the inventory scores.

Chance. Bernreuter cites the standard errors of estimate in Table 66 as evidence that chance alone cannot account for the

TABLE 66. *Standard Errors of Estimate for the Scores on the Personality Inventory**

Bernreuter scale	Men			Women		
	High school	College	Adult	High school	College	Adult
B1 N	17.7	18.2	16.9	20.8	21.5	20.4
B2 S	16.0	14.8	14.5	14.5	14.8	15.0
B3 I	11.4	12.2	10.0	13.8	12.8	14.0
B4 D	13.7	15.5	14.2	14.9	14.0	13.6

* From Bernreuter, R. G. The validity of the personality inventory. *Person. J.*, 1933, **11**, 383–386.

variation in scores. He arrives at this conclusion by noting that these standard errors of estimate, computed according to the formula $\sigma_{est} = \sigma_{dis} \sqrt{1 - r^2}$, are considerably smaller than the standard deviations of the original raw-score distributions. If chance were the only factor accounting for the variation in test scores, the standard errors of estimate would be equal to the original distribution standard deviations.

The formula for the standard error of estimate shows that if the reliability of a test is 1.00, the standard error of a single score will be 0; that is, if a test is perfectly reliable, there will be no error. On the other hand, if a test possesses no reliability, the standard error of a single score will be equal to the standard deviation of the distribution, and the test will not reliably distinguish one individual from another. In other words, a person may secure one score today and a completely unrelated score tomorrow. When the reliability of a test is .866, our standard error of estimate formula shows that the standard error of a single score is one-half the standard deviation of the distribution. Therefore a reliability of .866 enables us to reduce by 50 per cent our error in locating the score of a single individual.

The standard errors of estimate in Table 66 average only four-tenths of the original raw-score standard deviations. Therefore our error in locating the score for a single individual is 60 per cent less than if chance were the only factor causing score variation. Therefore, says Bernreuter, chance does not account for the scores on the Personality Inventory.

We can agree that this is true. But the elimination of chance as an important explanatory factor does not mean that the non-chance factors operating are those we choose to have operating. Could the scores be due, we wonder, to a slanting of responses in a direction to win social approval or could they be downright dishonest?

Social Approval. Bernreuter, to check upon the extent to which responses might be slanted to win social approval, asked a group of students to take the Personality Inventory under two different conditions. The first of these conditions was the standard one, and the second consisted of asking students to respond to the test items in such a way as to win the greatest possible degree of social approval. Bernreuter found the scores under these two conditions practically uncorrelated. The correlation between the two series of "neurotic" scores was −.07, that between the two series of "self-sufficiency" scores was .19, and that between the two sets of "dominance" scores was −.03. Under the second set of conditions students indicated that social approval would go to emotionally stable, self-sufficient, and dominant individuals. But the first answers of many of the students who replied thus indicated emotional instability, lack of self-sufficiency, and submissiveness. This result, argues Bernreuter, shows that emotionally unstable individuals, individuals lacking in self-sufficiency, and submissive individuals will, in many cases, give responses that are not controlled by the desire to win social approval.

Dishonesty. And now the last question. Is it possible that a subject will respond to the items in the Personality Inventory by indicating the kind of person he would like to be rather than the kind he actually is? Bernreuter, to check upon this possibility, asked each one of several students who had taken the test under standard conditions to take it a second time and to indicate by his second responses the kind of a person he would most like to be. The scores secured under these two sets of conditions were compared with each other. Bernreuter found a correlation of .22 between the two series of "neurotic" scores, a correlation of .39 between the two series of "self-sufficiency" scores, and a correlation of .14 between the two series of "dominance" scores. These correlations are sufficiently low, argues Bernreuter, to show that most subjects do not, under standard conditions, indicate what they want to be like rather than what they actually are like.

We can grant, with Bernreuter, that chance does not account for all test-score variation and that many subjects will give honest responses. But Bernreuter has not demonstrated that dishonest answers can be dismissed as of infrequent occurrence. It would be desirable, therefore, if some method could be devised to indicate how honest or how dishonest any given set of responses is likely to be. Floyd L. Ruch has attacked this problem and reports on what he calls an honesty scale for the Personality Inventory. This scale, applied to the responses secured under standard conditions, is supposed to indicate the degree of honesty or dishonesty involved.

Ruch developed his honesty scale by comparing the responses of 245 subjects acting under "honest" and under "dishonest" conditions. "Honest" conditions were the normal ones. "Dishonest" conditions were induced with these instructions:

Imagine that you are applying for a position as salesman. Your showing in this test will decide whether or not you get the job. You know the characteristics of a good salesman. See if you can answer these questions as a good salesman would, whether you really feel that way or not.

Ruch scored both the "honest" blanks and the "dishonest" blanks on the introversion scale and found, as he expected, that the results were quite different. On the first set of blanks, *i.e.*, on those completed "honestly," the median score corresponded to the 50th percentile for male college students. But on the second set of blanks, *i.e.*, on those completed "dishonestly," the median score corresponded to the 98th percentile (for extroversion) for male college students. Ruch tabulated the number of "Yes," "No," and " ?" answers for each question under the "honest" and "dishonest" conditions, computed the differences, and assigned scoring weights in accord with these differences.

Then he had a second group of 100 students take the Personality Inventory, first under "honest" and then under "dishonest" conditions. Then he scored both sets of papers for introversion and for honesty. He divided the students, upon the basis of their introversion scores, into those more introverted than the average college male and into those less introverted than the average college male. The honesty scores for these two groups of subjects are given in Table 67.

Under "honest" conditions honesty scores range from 15 to 60 and have a median value of 39. But under "dishonest" conditions they range from 5 to 35 and have a median value of 14. Introverts changed their responses and their honesty scores to a remarkable extent. There is a clean-cut separation between their honesty scores in the "honest" and in the "dishonest" situations. If we can assume, with Ruch, that all introverts were originally honest, scores from 35 and up can be taken as indicative of honesty, and scores from 34 and down can be taken as indicative of dishonesty. However, we must note that if we adopt 35 as a critical score separating honest from dishonest answers, more than 50 per cent of the extroverts must be considered to have answered dishonestly even under "honest" conditions. If this is not an artifact of the experiment, the data

TABLE 67. *Honesty Scores of Introverts and Extroverts under "Honest" and "Dishonest" Conditions**

Honesty score	Introverts		Extroverts	
	"Honest"	"Dishonest"	"Honest"	"Dishonest"
60	1			
55	1			
50	5	..	1	
45	10	..	4	
40	16	..	11	
35	6	..	11	
30	..	2	10	
25	..	..	12	2
20	..	3	11	4
15	..	17	1	19
10	..	14	..	31
5	..	3	..	5
Total.........	39	39	61	61

* From McNemar, Q., and Merrill, M. A. (Eds.) *Studies in Personality.* New York: McGraw-Hill Book Company, Inc., 1942.

lead to the conclusion that extroverts, as measured by the Personality Inventory, are less honest than introverts. And this should have important implications for the measurement of personality.

Intercorrelations. The scales on the Bernreuter Personality Inventory exhibit substantial intercorrelations. Those published by Bernreuter are given in Table 68. The correlation between the

TABLE 68. *Intercorrelations among the Bernreuter Scales**

Scale	B1 N	B2 S	B3 I
B2 S	−.49		
B3 I	.96	−.38	
B4 D	−.83	.58	−.72

* From Bernreuter, R. G. The theory and construction of the personality inventory. *J. soc. Psychol.*, 1933, **4,** 387–405.

neuroticism and introversion-extroversion scale is particularly high and suggests that only one or the other, but certainly not both, of these scales need be scored. The other intercorrelations are lower, but there are none that approach zero. This state of affairs led Flanagan to wonder whether it would be possible, by means of a factor-analysis approach, to reduce the number of scales on which the Bernreuter test needs to be scored. Therefore he analyzed the intercorrelations in Table 68 in accord with Hotelling's method of principal components. And he found that two independent factors would "account for all but about four percent of the non-chance variance."

One of these factors, says Flanagan, "may be interpreted as distinguishing between the self-confident, well-adjusted, socially-aggressive, 'thick-skinned' individual and the self-conscious, shy, emotionally unstable individual." Eight of the items which indicate the character of this factor, which Flanagan calls self-confidence, are given in Table 69.

TABLE 69. *Items Related to Self-confidence**

Do you blush very often?
Do you feel self-conscious in the presence of superiors in the academic or business world?
Are you troubled with shyness?
Are your feelings easily hurt?
Do you often find that you cannot make up your mind until the time for action is passed?
Are you troubled with feelings of inferiority?
Do you have difficulty in starting a conversation with a stranger?
Are you troubled with the idea that people on the street are watching you?

* From Flanagan, J. C. *Factor Analysis in the Study of Personality*. Stanford University, Calif.: Stanford University Press, 1935.

The second factor is "best described," says Flanagan, "as differentiating between the social and the non-social or independent." Eight items which indicate the nature of this factor, which Flanagan calls sociability, are given in Table 70.

TABLE 70. *Items Related to Sociability**

Do athletics interest you more than intellectual affairs?
Do you think you could become so absorbed in creative work that you would not notice a lack of intimate friends?
Do you prefer traveling with someone who will make all the necessary arrangements to the adventure of traveling alone?
Have books been more entertaining to you than companions?
Do you usually enjoy spending an evening alone?
Do you get as many ideas at the time of reading a book as you do from a discussion of it afterwards?
Do you prefer making hurried decisions alone?
Do you like to be with people a great deal?

* From Flanagan, J. C. *Factor Analysis in the Study of Personality*. Stanford University, Calif.: Stanford University Press, 1935.

When Flanagan had isolated these factors and had reworked his data to give each of his subjects scores on these new factors, he picked those with scores above one standard deviation and those with scores below one standard deviation as new criterion groups. Then he compared these groups with each other (two on each factor), and, using an item-analysis chart which he devised, he assigned scoring weights to the various responses. When the tests were rescored with these new item weights, Flanagan found values which correlated .98 and .84 with the original factor scores. Using the scores computed from the item weights, Flanagan repeated his entire item-analysis procedure and this time secured scores which correlated .98 and .91 with his original factor scores. Also, the correlation between these two series of scores was now nearly zero, whereas in the first trial it was .18. When Flanagan tried his keys out on new groups of cases, he found reliabilities of .86 and .78 and an interscale correlation of .04.

Now, wondered Flanagan, how well could the scores on Bernreuter's original scales be predicted from these new scales? Very well, indeed, as the correlations in Table 71 amply demonstrate. We can

TABLE 71. *Multiple Correlations between Flanagan's New Scales and the Original Bernreuter Scales**

Neurotic tendency................ .97
Self-sufficiency.................... .87
Introversion-extroversion.......... .95
Dominance....................... .87

* From Flanagan, J. C. *Factor Analysis in the Study of Personality*. Stanford University, Calif.: Stanford University Press, 1935.

agree with Flanagan "that scores on the two new variables . . . contain such a large amount of the available information that it . . . is not . . . worthwhile to score the blanks for more than these two factors." But the economy involved in scoring the Bernreuter test for two independent factors rather than for four substantially correlated variables does nothing to augment or to change the degree of validity which these scores may or may not possess.

THE PERSONAL AUDIT

Our second example of a multidimensional approach to the measurement of personality is contained in the Personal Audit, a test devised by Clifford R. Adams and William L. Lepley. It is available in two forms, LL and SS. Form LL consists of nine parts of 50 items each, and Form SS consists of the first six parts of Form LL. The parts of the test are relatively independent of each other and were designed to assist in "the measurement of those traits of personality essential to the vocation for which an individual is preparing."

According to Adams, these traits are seriousness-impulsiveness, firmness-indecision, tranquillity-irritability, frankness-evasion, stability-instability, tolerance-intolerance, steadiness-emotionality, persistence-fluctuation, and contentment-worry. The scores on these traits are to be interpreted, says Adams, as follows:

1. *Seriousness-Impulsiveness.* High scores indicate a serious disposition characterized by quietness, ambition, and studiousness. Low scores indicate pronounced sociability (or the need for it), aggressiveness, and dominance.

2. *Firmness-Indecision.* High scores indicate positiveness and conscientiousness. The individual tends to be cooperative, poised and confident. Low scores indicate a tendency to accept momentarily and impulsively suggestions of others. Frequently this leads to an inability to make or maintain a decision.

3. *Tranquillity-Irritability.* High scores indicate evenness of temperament and lack of irritability. There is little tendency to fly off the handle or become impatient. Low scores indicate readiness and unevenness of response, often accompanied by annoyance and fault-finding toward subordinates.

4. *Frankness-Evasion.* High scores indicate dependability, frankness, and truthfulness. Low scores indicate unwillingness to face reality and inability to take responsibilities.

5. *Stability-Instability.* High scores indicate pronounced confidence in self and willingness to carry responsibilities. Low scores indicate a lack of self-confidence accompanied by feelings of inferiority.

6. *Tolerance-Intolerance.* High scores indicate broadminded, easygoing attitudes. Standards and ideals tend to be flexible, practical and realistic. Low scores indicate strong attitudes, usually unfavorable, toward others. Intolerance and prejudice, often disguised as high standards and ideals may be present.

7. *Steadiness-Emotionality.* High scores indicate normal ways of thinking. Feelings are not intense. Low scores indicate that the individual is atypical. Usually sensitive, feelings are volatile and deep-seated.

8. *Persistence-Fluctuation.* High scores indicate stable attitudes and interests with little likelihood of pronounced changes occurring after age 25. Low scores indicate that interests and attitudes are in a state of flux.

9. *Contentment-Worry.* High scores indicate few unsolved problems and absence of worry about them if they do exist. The person is usually stable, cooperative, and well adjusted to his work and social life. Low scores indicate worry, uneasiness, and indecision brought about by unsolved problems. Lacking confidence, the individual is usually uncertain and beset by conflicts often revolving around adjustments to the opposite sex.

Five parts of the Personal Audit require a response of "much," "some," "little," or "no." These parts are I, III, V, VI, and IX. Part I requires a subject to indicate whether he has much, some, little, or no *liking* for various activities. Part III requires a subject to indicate whether he has much, some, little, or no *dislike* for annoyances. Part V requires a subject to indicate whether he has much, some, little, or no *fear* in reaction to various possible events. Part VI requires the subject to indicate whether he has much, some, little, or no *dislike* for activities not already given in Part I. And Part IX requires a subject to indicate whether he has done much, some, little, or no *thinking* on various topics.

Part II requires a subject to show whether he agrees, agrees with reservations, or disagrees with different statements. Part IV requires a subject to indicate whether he believes certain statements to be true, doubtful, or false. Part VII is a word-association test which requires the subject to indicate which one of four response words best goes with the stimulus word. Finally, Part VIII requires the subject to indicate if his feelings about a variety of subjects are the same, partly different, or different from what they were three or four years ago.

Development of Test. There have been to date five editions of the Personal Audit. Adams alone developed the original test and the first and second revisions. Lepley helped on the third and fourth revisions, thus bringing the test into its fifth and current edition.

We can tell very little about the development of the first and second editions. The only comment Adams offers is that they were "experimental and exploratory." This being the extent of our information concerning the first two forms, we begin our discussion with the third edition. This edition consisted of ten parts, each containing 25 to 50 items. Adams does not describe the sources of these items, but we can guess that they came from the usual sources such as surveys of appropriate textbook and journal material, from other personality tests, from his own ideas, and, of course, from the first two versions of the test. Adams assigned a priori weights of 1, 2, 3, etc., for scoring. Using these weights, he found split-half reliabilities ranging from .72 to .99 and intercorrelations among the scales ranging from .01 to .46. These figures show that Adams achieved what he was seeking: scales with fairly high reliabilities and with fairly low intercorrelations. Unfortunately, Adams has not described for us the exact procedures by which he assigned items to the various scales. We are left in doubt, therefore, as to whether he was just fortunate in achieving these results or whether he went through some of the same processes used by Kuder in the development of his Preference Records (see Chap. 3).

In contemplation of the fourth revision of the Personal Audit, Adams and Lepley gave the third form to 356 college students. Using a priori scoring keys as before, they scored these tests and determined which students fell into the upper and lower quarters of each trait distribution. Next, they determined the mean rating assigned to each item by the appropriate contrasting criterion groups, computed the differences between these mean ratings, and determined the significances of these differences by computing a series of t ratios. Then, says Adams, items with t values less than 3 were eliminated. These processes resulted in the elimination of one entire part of the test and, of course, reduced the number of items available for the nine parts of the test which survived. To remedy this, Adams and Lepley collected new items and finally achieved a total of 60 items for each of the nine parts of the fourth revision of the Personal Audit.

The fourth revision of the Personal Audit was administered to 400 college students. Again, Adams and Lepley selected the students falling into the upper and lower fourths of each trait distribution and, again, went through a complete item analysis. This time, however, each item was related to the total scores on each scale which correlated .30 or more with the scale of which it formed a constituent part. This made it possible for Adams and Lepley to eliminate items with the lowest t values within a scale *and* items with the highest t values in relation to other scales. Adams and Lepley eliminated 90 items, 10 from each scale, leaving 50 items in each of the nine parts of the test. These items constitute the fifth and currently available revision of the Personal Audit.

A final step consisted of giving the fifth revision to 231 high-school boys and to 230 high-school girls. The 50 highest scoring boys and 50 lowest scoring boys, and the 50 highest scoring girls and 50 lowest scoring girls were isolated as criterion groups, and a third item analysis was performed. This time only three items were found to have a t value less than 3, so no further revision was, or has been, attempted.

Validity. Adams discusses six sets of "validation" data. We cannot agree that all the data which Adams discusses are relevant to the validity problem, but we shall find it worth while to review Adams's arguments. The six types of data relate to the internal consistency of the trait scores, the intercorrelations among the scales, consensus of opinion, ratings, correlations with other tests, and clinical evaluations.

Internal Consistency. We see the criterion of internal consistency applied with a vengeance in the development of the Personal Audit test. This was, in fact, the only criterion used, and it was used repeatedly. As we have already indicated, all except three items have *t* values of 3 or more, indicating significant correlations with total scores. We can agree with Adams that his data show that each scale is internally consistent, but this certainly does not show that they are valid.

Intercorrelations. The intercorrelations among the scales in the Personal Audit are shown in Table 72. These correlations are based upon the records of 442 college students not included in any of the standardization groups. The correlations range from −.07 to .56 and have an average algebraic value of .12. Adams offers these data

TABLE 72. *Intercorrelations among the Scales on the Personal Audit**

Scale	Seriousness-impulsiveness	Firmness-indecision	Tranquillity-irritability	Frankness-evasion	Stability-instability	Tolerance-intolerance	Steadiness-emotionality	Persistency-fluctuation	Contentment-worry
Seriousness-impulsiveness..........	.90	−.05	.08	−.04	.00	.04	−.03	−.07	.27
Firmness-indecision...............		.91	.09	.37	.15	.24	−.03	−.02	.14
Tranquillity-irritability...........			.91	.14	.45	.56	.03	.05	.24
Frankness-evasion.................				.90	.18	.17	.08	.03	.13
Stability-instability...............					.96	.33	.04	.03	.30
Tolerance-intolerance.............						.95	−.07	.04	.30
Steadiness-emotionality...........							.91	.18	.05
Persistency-fluctuation............								.93	.08
Contentment-worry...............									.92

* From Adams, C. R. *Manual of Directions for Using and Interpreting the Personal Audit.* Chicago: Science Research Associates, 1945.

as "evidence for validation by negation. . . . " He says that "since the nine parts do *not* overlap one another to any appreciable extent . . . nine relatively independent factors are measured." We can grant the last part of this statement to the effect that the scales are relatively independent, but we cannot agree that this fact has any relevance to the validity problem. To assert that a scale is valid means that it must do a specific measuring job with some minimum degree of accuracy. Proving that scales are independent of each other in no way shows that they provide accurate measures of personality traits which are said to be involved.

The diagonal entries in Table 72 represent reliability coefficients. These were computed by the split-half technique with the aid of the Spearman-Brown Prophecy Formula.

Consensus of Opinion. Adams asked 30 psychologists, caliber not specified, to tell him what each part of the Personal Audit appeared to measure. He says that their combined judgment coincides with the descriptions he himself has prepared. All that this indicates, we fear, is a common-sense agreement upon names for the several traits. But just because we can agree on the name for a trait is no proof that we can accurately measure it. Consensus on trait names are completely irrelevant to the fundamental validity problem.

Ratings. Adams discusses five sets of rating data, but, unfortunately, he is vague on many of the details which we need in order to make an adequate evaluation of the procedures which he used. He cites, for example, a study by Mrs. C. R. Adams. She "asked nine teachers and four upper class students to identify the boys and girls in the four high school grades ($N = 461$: 231 boys, 230 girls) who represented extremes on 12 different personality traits. Although the differences found were small they tended," says C. R. Adams, "to support the descriptions of Audit traits as tentatively given. . . . " The number of students rated on each of the 12 traits varies from 17 to 23, but little other information of value can be gathered from the Adams's account.

The second set of rating data mentioned by Adams was secured by Reppert and Borow. About the only information which Adams gives is that "correlations between Audit scores and 'personality' ratings of 120 chemical operator trainees were . . . small. . . . " Again, we are left in the dark as to the nature of the ratings and so cannot properly make any evaluation of them.

The third set of data refers to two groups of "clerical employees in three government agencies." In these groups, 50 employees were selected as being "most unsatisfactory" in their jobs, and 50 as "most satisfactory" or "excellent." Adams states that on Frankness-Evasion the satisfactory employees received a percentile average of 54 and that the unsatisfactory employees received a percentile average of 39. Furthermore, Adams reports that the percentile scores for satisfactory employees ranged from 11 to 99 but that those for the unsatisfactory employees ranged from 3 to 60.

We can accept with Adams the fact that the scores on Frankness-Evasion seem to differentiate the satisfactory employee from the unsatisfactory employee. But this hardly has any bearing upon the question as to how valid the scores in Part IV may be for the measurement of that which it is asserted to measure, namely, frankness-evasion.

Adams's fourth set of rating data is presented by Gilliard. He "compared Audit scores of 100 R.O.T.C. students judged by their officers to be leaders with 100 R.O.T.C. students judged *not* to be leaders. . . . The leaders tended to be more stable, more steady and less emotional, and more persistent and less cycloidal."

And, finally, Adams says that he has found "happy husbands . . . high on Tranquillity, Frankness and Tolerance," and "happy wives . . . high on Frankness, Stability and Contentment." Data for unhappy husbands and unhappy wives Adams fails to give, however.

In no one of these five sets of rating data can we find much evidence strictly relevant to the problem of determining the validity of the scores on the Personal Audit. Where, for example, do we find any data showing that the traits measured by the Personal Audit are "essential to the vocation for which an individual is preparing"? And, after all, Adams did state this as being the major purpose of the test.

Correlations with Other Tests. Adams presents some data showing how the scores on the Personal Audit correlate with the scores on the Guilford-Martin Inventories, the Strong Vocational Interest Test, the Bernreuter Personality Inventory, the Allports' Ascendance-Submission Reaction Study, and Terman's Scale of Marital Happiness. All the correlations are low and, again, are irrelevant to the basic validity problem of the Personal Audit scores. We might, of course, make an exception in the case of the Strong Vocational

Interest Test, for Strong has validated his scales against occupational groups of known composition. But Strong certainly has never claimed (nor has anyone else) that the Vocational Interest Test can serve as a basis for the validation of a personality test of the type represented in the Personal Audit.

Clinical Evaluations. Adams offers as his last validating procedure a comparison between 100 maladjusted individuals and 100 adjusted individuals. Adams selected the 100 maladjusted individuals "from his clinical practice" and the controls from (presumably) routine college records. He says that comparisons between these two groups justify (among others) the following conclusions:

1. That seriously maladjusted students are characterized by extreme deviations from the means
2. That fearful, anxious and depressed subjects make low scores on Firmness, Frankness and Stability
3. That stubborn, aggressive and generally obnoxious individuals make low scores on Seriousness, Tranquillity, and Frankness; high scores on Stability, Persistence and Contentment
4. That cases characterized by lying, hallucinations and delusions make low scores on Frankness, Steadiness and Firmness and Stability; high scores on Seriousness and Persistence

These few facts hardly give us any ground for being enthusiastic about the validity of the scores on the Personal Audit. We must consider the results as a striking condemnation of the utility of the criterion of internal consistency as the sole standard of personality-test construction.

THE MINNESOTA PERSONALITY SCALE

Our third example of a multidimensional approach to the measurement of personality is that contained in the Minnesota Personality Scale. This scale, constructed by John G. Darley and Walter J. McNamara, was designed by them to do in a more efficient manner the work done by a number of previously published tests. These tests were the Minnesota Scale for the Survey of Opinions (Rundquist and Sletto), the Bell Adjustment Inventory, and the Minnesota Inventories of Social Attitudes (Williamson and Darley). These tests, collectively, yield 13 scores. It was Darley and McNamara's purpose to reduce the number of these scores without sacrifice of useful information.

The Minnesota Personality Scale consists of 218 items and is divided into five parts. Parts I and V contain impersonal statements which require a subject to check one of these five responses: "strongly agree," "agree," "undecided," "disagree," or "strongly disagree." Sample items from Part I read, "Life is just a series of disappointments," and "A high school education makes a man a better citizen." Sample items from Part V read, "Most great fortunes are made honestly," and "Cooperative housing plans should be encouraged." Parts II, III, and IV contain personal questions which require a subject to check one of these responses: "almost always," "frequently," "occasionally," "rarely," or "almost never." Sample items from Part II read, "Are you eager to make new friends?" and "Do you dislike social affairs?" Sample items from Part III read, "Do you become nervous at home?" and "Was your father your ideal of manhood?" Sample items from Part IV read, "Are your feelings easily hurt?" and "Are your eyes sensitive to light?" We see that the items in Parts I and V are phrased as statements and that items in Parts II, III, and IV are phrased as questions.

The Minnesota Personality Scale yields five scores, one based on each part. Each item contributes to one score only and not to several, as in the case of the Bernreuter Personality Inventory. The traits measured by the Minnesota Personality Scale as defined by Darley and McNamara are as follows:

Part I. *Morale.* High scores are indicative of belief in society's institutions and future possibilities. Low scores usually indicate cynicism or lack of hope in the future.

Part II. *Social Adjustment.* High scores tend to be characteristic of the gregarious, socially mature individual in relations with other people. Low scores are characteristic of the socially inept or undersocialized individual.

Part III. *Family Relations.* High scores usually signify friendly and healthy parent-child relations. Low scores suggest conflicts or maladjustments in parent-child relations.

Part IV. *Emotionality.* High scores are representative of emotionally stable and self-possessed individuals. Low scores may result from anxiety states or over-reactive tendencies.

Part V. *Economic Conservatism.* High scores indicate conservative economic attitudes. Low scores reveal a tendency toward liberal or radical points of view on current economic and industrial problems.

The first step in the development of the Minnesota Personality Scale was that of giving to several hundred subjects the tests it was designed to replace. These tests, the Minnesota Scale for the Survey of Opinions, the Bell Adjustment Inventory, and the Minnesota Inventories of Social Attitudes were given in 1935 and again in 1936. They were given to 326 men and to 217 women at the University of Minnesota. From these records Darley and McNamara selected for intensive analysis 100 test and 100 retest records for men and 100 test and 100 retest records for women.

The second step in the development of the Minnesota Personality Scale was that of analyzing the test-retest correlations on each of the 13 test variables. These variables, together with their test-retest correlations (over a nine-month interval) are given in Table 73.

TABLE 73. *Test-Retest Correlations on 13 Personality Variables**

Scale	Men	Women
Morale	.65	.63
Inferiority	.61	.53
Attitude toward family	.64	.76
Attitude toward the legal system	.55	.57
Economic conservatism	.79	.59
Education	.46	.63
General adjustment	.61	.64
Home adjustment	.71	.82
Health adjustment	.72	.81
Social adjustment	.84	.78
Emotional adjustment	.68	.70
Social preferences	.73	.62
Social behavior	.64	.69

* From Darley, J. G. Changes in measured attitudes and adjustments. *J. soc. Psychol.*, 1938, **9**, 189–199.

Darley and McNamara decided that these coefficients "revealed a reasonable degree of stability" and that because of this "reasonable degree of stability," it would be desirable for them to proceed further with their plans.

The third step in the development of the Minnesota Personality Scale was that of computing the intercorrelations among the 13 test variables. These correlations were computed separately for the test and retest scores and separately, also, for men and women. The results are presented in Tables 74 and 75. Table 74 shows the intercorrelations for men, and Table 75 shows the intercorrelations for women. In both tables the figures above the diagonal are based upon the original test scores, and those below the diagonal are based upon the retest data.

The fourth step in the development of the Minnesota Personality Scale was that of performing centroid factor analyses upon the four intercorrelational matrices presented in Tables 74 and 75.

TABLE 74. *Intercorrelations among 13 Personality Variables (Men)*†*

Scale	1. Morale	2. Inferiority	3. Attitude toward family	4. Attitude toward legal system	5. Economic conservatism	6. Education	7. General adjustment	8. Home adjustment	9. Health adjustment	10. Social adjustment	11. Emotional adjustment	12. Social preferences	13. Social behavior
1		.50	.30	.48	.19	.43	.74	.26	.08	.29	.34	.20	.30
2	.63		.17	.24	.12	.23	.45	.17	−.06	.52	.28	.22	.48
3	.42	.32		.37	−.16	.32	.40	.40	.22	.14	.09	.29	.18
4	.54	.30	.38		.21	.40	.58	.15	.06	.13	.28	.06	.14
5	.14	.18	−.03	.29		.08	.39	.06	.02	.17	.22	.20	.14
6	.47	.23	.24	.44	.05		.52	.10	−.06	−.15	.01	−.06	−.04
7	.76	.57	.38	.55	.40	.54		.25	.11	.28	.30	.15	.29
8	.35	.35	.60	.24	.12	−.02	.25		.32	.31	.48	.32	.18
9	−.01	.14	.04	.08	−.09	−.15	−.09	.28		.16	.38	.20	.13
10	.34	.60	.07	.05	.04	.11	.34	.26	.12		.46	.43	.69
11	.31	.55	.22	.26	.08	−.04	.19	.58	.41	.54		.20	.32
12	.31	.38	.25	.12	.11	.13	.22	.18	.03	.49	.23		.49
13	.34	.61	.18	.14	.06	.16	.29	.22	.16	.77	.43	.66	

* Correlations above the diagonal are based on original test data and those below the diagonal are based on retest data.

† From Darley, J. G., and McNamara, W. J. Factor analysis in the establishment of new personality tests. *J. educ. Psychol.*, 1940, **31**, 321–334.

Now, continue Darley and McNamara, the "problem was to regroup the thirteen scales in such a way that all would be accounted for within five factors, that no one scale would appear in more than one factor, and that the groupings would be the same for both test and retest, and men and women." The realignment which appeared to meet these conditions Darley and McNamara give as follows:

    I. Morale, attitude toward law, education, general adjustment
   II. Inferiority, social adjustment, social preferences, social behavior
 III. Family adjustment, home adjustment

IV. Health adjustment, emotional adjustment
V. Economic conservatism

Darley and McNamara conclude "that the thirteen separate scores in the battery can be accounted for by five psychologically meaningful factors, and that these factors [are] sufficiently stable from test to retest to represent significant aspects of personality."

TABLE 75. *Intercorrelations among 13 Personality Variables (Women)**†

Scale	1. Morale	2. Inferiority	3. Attitude toward family	4. Attitude toward legal system	5. Economic conservatism	6. Education	7. General adjustment	8. Home adjustment	9. Health adjustment	10. Social adjustment	11. Emotional adjustment	12. Social preferences	13. Social behavior
1		.58	.54	.69	.38	.56	.86	.36	.04	.25	.32	.20	.17
2	.64		.40	.41	.28	.36	.50	.32	.15	.47	.42	.29	.50
3	.47	.45		.50	.19	.32	.60	.58	.11	.23	.21	.02	.15
4	.62	.33	.37		.49	.51	.67	.27	.10	.09	.18	.16	.02
5	.12	.02	.23	-.27		.18	.38	.14	.07	.08	.04	.19	.18
6	.56	.19	.19	.42	-.07		.58	-.02	-.08	.07	.11	.04	.01
7	.80	.52	.54	.62	.36	.54		.33	.05	.19	.28	.13	.15
8	.26	.33	.71	.16	.04	.06	.33		.38	.23	.50	.11	.20
9	.10	.14	.14	-.02	-.26	-.02	-.03	.39		.05	.38	.06	.06
10	.14	.50	.20	-.03	-.01	-.14	.08	.26	.17		.42	.42	.67
11	.33	.50	.43	.14	-.10	.14	.33	.65	.53	.43		.15	.34
12	.30	.29	.20	.24	.18	.05	.14	.00	.06	.28	.05		.58
13	.34	.62	.25	.15	.11	.04	.32	.23	.14	.72	.40	.40	

* Correlations above the diagonal are based on original test data and those below the diagonal are based on retest data.

† From Darley, J. G., and McNamara, W. J. Factor analysis in the establishment of new personality tests. *J. educ. Psychol.*, 1940, **31**, 321–334.

The fifth step in the development of the Minnesota Personality Scale was that of converting the raw scores on each of the 13 original variables into standard scores. This done, these scores were appropriately weighted and summed to give scores on the five factor variables. These scores were then intercorrelated with the results shown in Table 76. Theoretically, all these intercorrelations should be zero. They are not zero, but they are low enough to suggest that five different aspects of personality are under consideration.

The sixth step in the development of the Minnesota Personality Scale was that of reducing the number of items needed to produce the five factor scores. Darley and McNamara selected separately for each factor and separately for men and women the 25 highest scoring subjects and the 25 lowest scoring subjects to serve as criterion groups. Then they determined how many subjects in each of these groups gave each of the alternate answers to the various items. Having done this, they applied the Rundquist-Sletto internal consistency technique and found 302 items (out of 368) which yielded critical ratios of 2.0 or more and, of these, 223 which yielded critical ratios of 3.0 or more. Darley and McNamara reviewed these items carefully, eliminated unnecessary duplications, made editorial changes in some of them, and, finally, added 21 new items. This gave them a total of 290 items for further tryout.

TABLE 76. *Intercorrelations among the Factor Scores Underlying the Minnesota Personality Scale**

Factors intercorrelated	100 men		100 women	
	Test	Retest	Test	Retest
Morale vs. social adjustment.....................	.29	.39	.30	.32
Morale vs. family relations.....................	.39	.37	.45	.39
Morale vs. emotionality.........................	.19	.10	.18	.18
Morale vs. economic conservatism................	.27	.28	.39	.20
Social adjustment vs. family relations...........	.32	.28	.29	.32
Social adjustment vs. emotionality...............	.33	.41	.31	.34
Social adjustment vs. economic conservatism......	.23	.11	.22	.09
Family relations vs. emotionality................	.40	.38	.41	.50
Family relations vs. economic conservatism.......	−.05	.04	.16	.18
Emotionality vs. economic conservatism..........	.13	−.01	.05	−.14

* From Darley, J. G., and McNamara, W. J. *Manual of Directions. Minnesota Personality Scale.* New York: The Psychological Corporation, 1941.

The seventh step in the development of the Minnesota Personality Scale was that of assembling the 290 items we have just mentioned into a new test form. This new test form was given to 100 men and 100 women at Rochester (Minnesota) Junior College, Carleton College, and the University of Minnesota. Following this, the 290 items surviving the first item analysis were subjected to a second analysis. Darley and McNamara do not say so explicitly, but we can assume that their procedure in this second analysis was the same as in their first. This would mean that the 25 highest scoring men and 25 highest scoring women and that the 25 lowest scoring men and 25 lowest scoring women served as the criterion groups. When the results from this second item analysis became available, Darley and McNamara proceeded to eliminate from any further consideration those items falling into either one of the following two categories:

1. Items with critical ratios below 3.00 in all analyses
2. Items with critical ratios above 3.00 in the second analysis but with critical ratios below 3.00 in the original analyses (both test and retest)

The ninth step in the development of the Minnesota Personality Scale was that of rescoring 200 test papers on the 218 items which met all criteria for retention in the scale. And, coupled with this, it included the giving of the final form of the test to 577 men and 557 women upon their entrance to the College of Science, Literature, and the Arts of the University of Minnesota. When all these papers were scored, the intercorrelations presented in Table 77 were obtained.

FIG. 77. *Intercorrelations among the Scores on the Second Edition of the Minnesota Personality Scale**

Factors intercorrelated	100 men	100 women	577 men	557 women
Morale vs. social adjustment	.43	.53	.41	.36
Morale vs. family relations	.44	.50	.26	.34
Morale vs. emotionality	.41	.53	.38	.38
Morale vs. economic conservatism	.14	.28	.21	.18
Social adjustment vs. family relations	.37	.22	.25	.26
Social adjustment vs. emotionality	.56	.47	.53	.48
Social adjustment vs. economic conservatism	.05	.12	.17	.13
Family relations vs. emotionality	.55	.42	.52	.54
Family relations vs. economic conservatism	.15	.18	.24	.16
Emotionality vs. economic conservatism	.08	.10	.21	.15

* From Darley, J. G., and McNamara, W. J. *Manual of Directions. Minnesota Personality Scale.* New York: The Psychological Corporation, 1941.

We see that these correlations are very similar to those in Table 76.

The tenth step in the development of the Minnesota Personality Scale was that of determining score reliabilities. The stepped-up Spearman-Brown coefficients computed by Darley and McNamara are given in Table 78. We see that they range from a low of .84 to a high of .97 and that they average .93. Since each coefficient is based upon a relatively small number of items, we can consider these reliabilities as eminently satisfactory.

TABLE 78. *Reliability Data for the Minnesota Personality Scale**

Scale	Number of items		Corrected coefficients	
	Men	Women	Men	Women
Part I. Morale............................	40	44	.84	.91
Part II. Social adjustment...................	61	53	.97	.95
Part III. Family relations....................	30	36	.95	.95
Part IV. Emotionality.......................	35	44	.94	.93
Part V. Economic conservatism...............	33	32	.92	.92

* From Darley, J. G., and McNamara, W. J. *Manual of Directions. Minnesota Personality Scale.* New York: The Psychological Corporation, 1941.

The eleventh and last step in the development of the Minnesota Personality Scale was that of preparing norms for the interpretation of scores. Darley and McNamara prepared separate norms for men ($N = 1083$) and women ($N = 888$) and for hand-scored and machine-scored editions of the test. These norms are given in their *Manual of Directions.*

Darley and McNamara conclude their discussion of the steps in the development of the Minnesota Personality Scale by saying their

. . . procedures . . . have resulted in: a smaller number of tests for the counselor to interpret in diagnosing five important aspects of personality; a smaller and more homogeneous number of items in each of these tests than in the groupings of tests from which the items were derived; and a higher set of reliability coefficients than was characteristic of the original scales.

THE GUILFORD INVENTORIES

Our fourth multidimensional approach to the measurement of personality is found in the Guilford inventories. These inventories are three in number, contain 511 questions to be answered "Yes," "No," or " ?," and provide scores on 13 "temperament-traits."

The first inventory, "An Inventory of Factors STDCR," contains 175 questions and provides, says Guilford, for the measurement of social introversion-extroversion, thinking introversion-extroversion, depression, cycloid disposition, and rhathymia. The second inventory, "The Guilford-Martin Personnel Inventory I," contains 150 questions and provides for the measurement of objectivity, cooperativeness, and agreeableness. And the third inventory, "An

Inventory of Factors GAMIN," contains 186 questions and provides for the measurement of general activity, ascendance-submission, masculinity-femininity, inferiority feelings, and nervousness. Guilford's definitions of these 13 traits are as follows:

Social Introversion-Extroversion. A high score indicates sociability, a tendency to seek social contacts and to enjoy the company of others. A low score indicates shyness, a tendency to withdraw from social situations and to be seclusive. A high score is more desirable for mental health than is a low score. A very low score indicates a need for guidance toward increased social participation.

Thinking Introversion-Extroversion. A high score indicates a lack of introspectiveness and an extrovertive orientation of the thinking processes. A low score indicates an inclination to meditative thinking, philosophizing, analyzing one's self and others, and an introspective disposition. The middle range of scores is more desirable for mental health than either extreme. Each extreme, however, may have its value for certain types of occupation.

Depression. A high score indicates freedom from depression, a cheerful, optimistic disposition. A low score indicates a chronically depressed mood including feelings of unworthiness and guilt. The higher the score the better is likely to be the emotional adjustment of the individual.

Cycloid Disposition. A high score indicates stable emotional reactions and moods, and freedom from cycloid tendencies. A low score means the presence of cycloid tendencies as shown in strong emotional reactions, fluctuations in mood, and a disposition toward flightiness and instability. The higher the score the better will be the emotional adjustment of the individual, except that scores too high may indicate a colorless, inert individual.

Rhathymia. A high score indicates a happy-go-lucky or carefree disposition, liveliness and impulsiveness. A low score indicates an inhibited disposition and an overcontrol of the impulses. Both extremes of scores may represent psychological maladjustments and a score in the middle range is desirable for mental health.

Objectivity. A high score on this trait indicates a tendency to view one's self and surroundings objectively and dispassionately. A low score indicates a tendency to take everything personally and subjectively and to be hypersensitive. The higher the score the better for mental health.

Cooperativeness. A high score indicates a willingness to accept things and people as they are and a generally tolerant attitude. A low score indicates an overcriticalness of people and things and an intolerant attitude. The higher the score the better for mental health unless the score on General Activity or clinical signs indicate a torpid and sluggish condition to be the basis of the lack of criticalness. Overcriticalness is often a compensation for hidden feelings of inadequacy. Pathological cases may exhibit a paranoid projection of their conflicts and impulses.

Agreeableness. A high score indicates an agreeable lack of quarrelsomeness and a lack of domineering qualities. A low score indicates a belligerent, domineering attitude and an overreadiness to fight over trifles. Very low scores indicate an extreme craving for superiority as an end in itself developed as a compensation for some chronic frustration and in pathological cases may lead to paranoid delusions of grandeur. It is possible that a sadistic component may occur in some of the pathological cases.

General Activity. A high score indicates a tendency to engage in vigorous overt action. A low score indicates a tendency to inertness and a disinclination for motor activity. An extremely high score may represent a manic tendency while an extremely low score may be an indication of a hypothyroid condition or other causes of inactivity. Thus, for good mental health a score in the middle range is usually most desirable.

Ascendance-Submission. A high score indicates social leadership and a low score social passiveness. The score of a person on this trait must be interpreted in the light of his other characteristics of temperament, and no general rule can be set forth as to what scores are most desirable for mental health.

Masculinity-Femininity. A high score on this trait indicates masculinity of emotional and temperamental make-up and a low score indicates femininity. The scores of the majority of males are above 5 and the majority of females have scores below 5. Males whose scores are very low are sometimes found either to lack their full quota of male hormones or to have an oversupply of female hormones.

Inferiority Feelings. A high score indicates self-confidence and a lack of inferiority feelings. A low score indicates a lack of confidence, underevaluation of one's self, and feelings of inadequacy and inferiority. The higher the score the better for mental health, with the exception of extremely high cases in which clinical investigation may reveal a superiority compensation for hidden inferiority feelings. Many psychoneurotics have very low scores.

Nervousness. A high score indicates a tendency to be calm, unruffled, and relaxed; a low score indicates jumpiness, jitteriness, and a tendency to be easily distracted, irritated, and annoyed. The higher the score the better for mental health unless there are clinical indications that an overly sluggish and torpid condition is the basis for an extremely high score. Extremely low scores in some cases may involve a lack of calcium in the blood. In many cases, a mental conflict may be the basis for the emotional tension expressed in jitteriness and irritability.

Development of the Inventories. We shall see in the development of the Guilford inventories an extensive use of the technique of factor analysis. We have already encountered this technique in our discussion of the Bernreuter Personality Inventory and the Minnesota Personality Scale. But in these two instances the factor analyses were based upon intercorrelations among test scores, while in the present instance they will be based upon intercorrelations among items.

The Nebraska Personality Inventory. Work was begun on what eventually became the Guilford inventories sometime prior to 1936. Professor J. P. Guilford and his wife, Ruth B. Guilford, scanned a number of sources pertinent to the measurement of introversion-extroversion. They reviewed Jung's writings, Freyd's monograph "Introversion-Extroversion," and the Laird, Marston, Neyman-Kohlstedt, and Gilliland and Morgan introversion-extroversion inventories. In these sources they found 75 "unrepeated" items. From these unrepeated items they selected 35 as representing the "essence" of introversion-extroversion. These are given in Table 79. These 35 items were those which showed the least duplication of content from one item to another and were those upon which the consulted authorities showed most agreement. All items selected were mentioned by three or more of these authors.

The Guilfords attempted to word the items so that an answer of "yes" would indicate introversion as often as it would indicate extroversion and so that both the "yes" and "no" answers would appear equally desirable. Furthermore, they included the phrases "Do you like . . . " and "Are you inclined to . . . " on the theory that subjects would be more honest in indicating their likes and dislikes, inclinations and disinclinations, than they would be in reporting actual behavior.

The Guilfords gave this list of questions to 930 subjects (430 men and 500 women) and one month later asked 277 of these subjects (163 men and 114 women) to take the test again. The directions accompanying the list were as follows:

Below you will find 36 questions which are to be answered either "Yes" or "No." Read each question in turn. Think what your behavior has usually been and underline either "Yes" or "No" whichever answer describes your behavior better. If you cannot decide, then guess. *Be sure to answer every question.* There is no implication of right or wrong in any of these items.

The Guilfords' next step was to compute a series of contingency coefficients showing how each item was related to each of the other items in the list. This meant the computation of 630 coefficients These coefficients were found to range, with two exceptions, between −.50 and .50. The Guilfords subjected these coefficients to a Spearman-type factor analysis to determine whether one general factor could account for all the correlations. They found a large general factor but a number of specific factors also. They concluded that the 36 items could not be said to lie along just one linear dimension. Actually they extracted 18 factors from their interitem correlational matrix.

Later the Guilfords replaced their contingency coefficients by

TABLE 79. *Items Which the Guilfords Selected to Represent the "Essence" of Introversion-Extroversion**

1. Do you express yourself better in speech than in writing?
2. Are you inclined to limit your acquaintances to a select few?
3. Do you generally prefer to take the lead in group activities?
4. Do you prefer to read about a thing rather than experience it?
5. Do you like work which requires considerable attention to details?
6. Are you generally very particular about your personal property, i.e., do you take very good care of your things?
7. Are you inclined to be considerate of other people's feelings?
8. Are you inclined to act on the spur of the moment without thinking things over?
9. Have you ever kept a personal diary of your own accord?
10. Do you work much better when you are praised?
11. Do you like to change from one type of work to another frequently?
12. Are you inclined to study the motives of others?
13. Do you daydream frequently?
14. Do you prefer to work with others rather than alone?
15. Are you inclined to worry over possible misfortunes?
16. Are you frequently somewhat absent-minded?
17. Do you like to persuade others to your point of view?
18. Are you inclined to keep in the background on social occasions?
19. Are you more interested in athletics than intellectual things?
20. Do you usually dislike to change opinions you have already formed?
21. Do you like to speak in public?
22. Do you prefer to work things out for yourself rather than accept suggestions from others?
23. Do you have frequent ups and downs in mood, either with or without apparent cause?
24. Are you inclined to be slow and deliberate in movement?
25. Are your feelings rather easily hurt?
26. Do you enjoy getting acquainted with most people?
27. Are you inclined to keep quiet when out in company?
28. Do you adapt yourself easily to new conditions, i.e., to new environments, situations, places, etc?
29. Do you like to confide in others?
30. Do you express such emotions as delight, sorrow, anger, etc., readily?
31. Are you inclined to think about yourself much of the time?
32. Do you like to have people watch you when you are working?
33. Do you frequently rewrite social letters before mailing them?
34. Do you like to sell things?
35. Do you get rattled easily in exciting situations?
36. Are you a male?

* From Guilford, J. P., and Guilford, R. B. An analysis of the factors in a typical test of introversion-extroversion. *J. abn. soc. Psychol.*, 1934, **28**, 377–399.

computing tetrachoric intercorrelations. These were found to average slightly higher than the contingency coefficients and ranged in value from −.60 to .69. These were subjected to a Thurstone centroid factor analysis, and five psychologically meaningful factors were extracted.

The first of these factors appeared to be social introversion-extroversion. "At one end of the scale the individual seeks to withdraw, to remove himself from social contacts and social responsibilities; at the other end of the scale he seeks social contacts and depends upon them for his satisfactions."

The second factor appeared to be an emotionality factor. "Running throughout the list of characteristics is a thread of emotional immaturity or emotional dependency. The individual having those traits would seem to lack self-sufficiency."

The third factor appeared to represent a masculine ideal, that is, maleness, agressiveness, dominance, and so forth.

The fourth factor appeared, say the Guilfords, to be a "happy-go-lucky" factor. One end of the scale represented the slow, methodical, deliberate person, and the other end of the scale represented the careless person, the person careless about dress, personal property, and the feelings of others. It is best described, say the Guilfords, by the Greek word *rhathymia*.

And finally, the fifth factor indicated a liking for thinking and for tackling problems requiring thought as opposed to a liking for prompt overt action. It can be called, say the Guilfords, a thinking introversion-extroversion factor.

Following this factor analysis, the next step essayed by the Guilfords was that of building more adequate scales for the measurement of the factors social introversion-extroversion, emotionality, and masculine ideal. They added 87 new items to their original list of 36, bringing it up to a total of 123. The Guilfords gave this augmented list of items to 815 new subjects (382 men and 433 women). This time, answers of "Yes," "No," and "?" were permitted. The plan was, say the Guilfords, "to separate these subjects into highest and lowest quartiles for factors, S, E, and M separately, and from the three pairs of criterion groups to validate every test item and to derive a scoring weight for it in one or more of the factors."

All items in the 36-item test were assigned scoring weights in "rough agreement with their factor loadings." Using these weights, factor scores were secured, and for each factor the highest scoring 25 per cent and the lowest scoring 25 per cent of the subjects were selected as criterion groups. The number of subjects in each criterion group answering "Yes," "No," and "?" was determined. Then weights were assigned in accord with Strong's item-weighting procedure. To make this clear, consider the data for the question "Do you express yourself more easily in speech than in writing?" The number in each criterion group answering "Yes," "No," and " ? " and the calculations leading to the assignment of scoring weights are set forth in Table 80.

TABLE 80. *Determination of Scoring Weights**

Group	Yes	?	No
High criterion group..........	61	6	133
Low criterion group...........	142	8	50
Difference...................	−81	−2	83
Weight...................	−2	0	2
Add constant...............	4	4	4
Final weight...............	2	4	6

* From Guilford, J. P., and Guilford, R. B. Personality factors S, E, and M, and their measurement. *J. Psychol.*, 1936, **2**, 109–127.

The Guilfords found 101 items with significant scoring weights for one or more of the factors. These items were assembled into a new form and became the Nebraska Personality Inventory. The reliabilities of these scores for one group of 100 cases and for one group of 665 cases are given in Table 81. Via the Spearman-Brown formula

TABLE 81. *Reliability Data for the Nebraska Personality Inventory**

Scale	$(N = 100)$	$(N = 665)$
Social introversion-extroversion...........	.93	.85
Emotionality.........................	.89	.86
Masculine ideal......................	.65	.75

* From Guilford, J. P., and Guilford, R. B. Personality factors S, E, and M, and their measurement. *J. Psychol.*, 1936, **2**, 109–127.

these values were stepped-up from the correlations between the items in the first half and the items in the second half of each scale.

By design, factor scores should not be correlated with each other, but in practice they frequently are. Those obtained from the short 36-item form are presented in Column 2 of Table 82, and those obtained from the long form are presented in Column 3.

TABLE 82. *Intercorrelations among the Scoring Weights and among the Scores of the Nebraska Personality Inventory**

Scale	Weights	Short form	Long form
Social introversion-extroversion vs. emotionality...........	−.02	.18	.46
Social introversion-extroversion vs. masculine ideal........	.02	.09	.40
Emotionality vs. masculine ideal........................	−.21	−.24	−.01

* From Guilford, J. P., and Guilford, R. B. Personality factors S, E, and M, and the measurement. *J. Psychol.*, 1936, **2**, 109–127.

An Inventory of Factors STDCR. The results presented in Table 82, particularly those for the long form, were not exactly what the Guilfords had intended. Therefore, they set about getting new weights and new criterion group separations. They did this by using "pure" items, *i.e.*, those with large and significant loadings on one factor and with zero loadings on all others. Double weight was given to any item with a factor loading of .50 or more. These items are given in Table 83.

TABLE 83. *Items Highly Saturated with Factors S, E, and M**

Social introversion-extroversion
Do you express yourself better in speech than in writing?
Do you prefer to read about a thing rather than experience it?
Are you inclined to keep in the background on social occasions?
Are you inclined to be slow and deliberate in movement?
Do you enjoy getting acquainted with most people?
Are you inclined to keep quiet when out in company?

Emotionality
Do you daydream frequently?
Are you inclined to worry over possible misfortunes?
Do you have frequent ups and downs in mood, either with or without cause?
Are your feelings rather easily hurt?
Are you inclined to think about yourself much of the time?

Masculine ideal
Have you ever kept a personal diary of your own accord?
Are you frequently somewhat absent-minded?
Do you adapt yourself easily to new conditions, i.e., to new environments, situations, places, etc?
Do you like to sell things?
Are you a male?

* From Guilford, J. P., and Guilford, R. B. Personality factors S, E, and M, and their measurement. *J. Psychol.*, 1936, **2**, 109–127.

At this point the Guilfords set up a new questionnaire to cover more adequately the "happy-go-lucky" and thinking dimensions. They added to this list their questions on social introversion-extroversion and gave the combined list of 89 questions to 1,000 subjects (610 men and 390 women). Then they selected 30 of these items, the

TABLE 84. *Items Giving Rise to Factors S, T, D, C, and R**

1. Are you ordinarily a carefree individual?
2. Do you usually have difficulty in starting a conversation with strangers?
3. Do you prefer to read about a thing rather than to experience it?
4. Do you hesitate to lend your personal property even to close friends?
5. Are you inclined to be considerate of other people's feelings?
6. Are you relatively unconcerned about what others think of your actions?
7. Are you inclined to analyze the motives of others?
8. Do you consider yourself a practical individual rather than one who theorizes?
9. Do you usually keep in close touch with things going on around you?
10. Are you inclined to worry over possible misfortunes?
11. Do you often have the "blues"?
12. Are you inclined to keep in the background on social occasions?
13. Are you more interested in athletics than in intellectual things?
14. Would you rate yourself as an impulsive individual?
15. Do you enjoy getting acquainted with most people?
16. Do you frequently find yourself in a meditative state?
17. Are you inclined to be over-conscientious?
18. Do you often crave excitement?
19. Are you inclined to ponder over your past?
20. Are you inclined to stop and think things over before acting?
21. Are you less attentive than most individuals to things going on around you?
22. Do you like to discuss the more serious questions of life with your friends?
23. Do you like to try your wits in solving puzzles?
24. Would you rate yourself as a happy-go-lucky individual?
25. Do you enjoy thinking out complicated problems?
26. Are you inclined to be introspective, that is, to analyze yourself?
27. Are you usually concerned about the future?
28. Do you usually become so absorbed in watching an athletic contest that you completely forget yourself?
29. Can you relax yourself easily when sitting or lying down?
30. Are you more alert to your immediate surroundings than the average person?

* From Guilford, J. P., and Guilford, R. B. Personality factors D, R, T, and A. *J. abn. soc. Psychol.*, 1939, **34**, 21–36.

30 items given in Table 84, computed their tetrachoric intercorrelations, subjected these intercorrelations to a Thurstone centroid factor analysis, and extracted nine factors.

The social introversion-extroversion factor was rediscovered, the rhathymia factor was verified, the thinking dimension was split into two subfactors, and two new factors, depression and alertness, were defined.

We have now described the sources from which Guilford chose many of his items for "An Inventory of Factors STDCR." Guilford has not explicitly described the development of the final form of this inventory, but we can surmise that it was done much after the fashion involved in setting up his initial scales for Factors S, E, and M. Guilford states that "the 175 items of the inventory were retained after successive tests of internal consistency of the responses of 400 university students. . . . "

An Inventory of Factors GAMIN. The Guilfords then constructed a questionnaire designed to test G. L. Freeman's hypothesis of an activity drive. They prepared, with Freeman's help, a list of 100 questions and gave this list to 600 University of Nebraska and Northwestern University students. They selected 24 items for intensive study, computed their tetrachoric intercorrelations, subjected the resulting matrix to a Thurstone centroid factor analysis, and extracted seven factors. Two of these factors were fairly clear-cut, and indicated dimensions of nervousness and general drive.

Guilford and Howard G. Martin then selected a list of over 300 items covering the following factors:

G. General pressure for overt activity
A. Ascendancy in social situations as opposed to submissiveness; leadership qualities
M. Masculinity of attitudes and interests as opposed to femininity
I. Lack of inferior feelings; self-confidence
N. Lack of nervous tenseness and irritability

The items for factors G and N were suggested by the analysis just discussed, the items for factor I were suggested by a study conducted by Mosier, and the items for factors M and A were suggested by some of the material in the Guilfords' earlier analyses.

This new list of items was given to 500 students (250 men and 250 women) attending colleges and universities in Southern California. Preliminary scoring keys, based upon previous factor analyses, were applied to 400 papers, the 100 highest scoring cases and the 100 lowest scoring cases were selected as criterion groups (on each factor), and item analyses were conducted.

"Scoring weights were found for each response to every item by using Guilford's abac method. This procedure yielded final scoring keys consisting of 41 items for trait G, 50 items for trait A, 52 items for trait M, 69 items for trait I, and 69 items for trait N. Only 9 items were scored for more than one trait."

The Guilford-Martin Personnel Inventory. This inventory "was designed with two primary purposes in mind. It was first of all designed as a means of assisting supervisors of workers in business and industry to single out and diagnose those individuals who are personally maladjusted. . . . As a second motive, the test was designed to extend the list of temperamental traits already assessed by Guilford's Inventory of Factors STDCR."

Guilford and Martin's intent in the construction of their Personnel Inventory was to cover the "paranoid disposition." They selected 200 items which they felt might be diagnostic of "subjectivity (taking things personally; ideas of reference; touchiness); belligerence (domineering attitude; craving for superiority); suspiciousness; and faultfinding or hypercriticalness." Guilford and Martin gave their list of questions to 500 industrial and business employees (250 men and 250 women), scored 400 of the papers on the basis of a priori scoring keys, applied their test of internal consistency (using top and bottom fourths as criterion groups), and selected 150 items to comprise the final form of the inventory. As finally developed, however, it gives only three rather than four scores. These are "objectivity (as opposed to personal reference or a tendency to take things personally); agreeableness (as opposed to belligerence or a dominating disposition and an overreadiness to fight over trifles); and cooperativeness (as opposed to fault finding or overcriticalness of people and things)."

Objectivity is measured by the responses to questions such as, "Do people near you sometimes whisper or look knowingly at one another when they think you are not noticing them?" "Are there some things about yourself concerning which you are rather touchy?" and "Are you continually comparing yourself with other people?" Agreeableness is measured by the responses to questions such as, "Have you frequently wished for enough money or power to impress people who regard you as an inferior?" "Have you very much resented having friends or members of your family give you orders?" and "Do you believe that most people require someone to tell them what to do?" Finally, cooperativeness is measured by the responses to questions such as, "Do you believe that most people shirk their duties whenever they can without appearing to do so?" "Do you believe that only people with money can be sure of getting a square deal in courts of law?" and "Do you feel that many young people get ahead today because they have 'pull'?"

Scoring weights were determined for these and for the remaining items in the inventory in accord with Guilford's procedure for determining phi coefficients (see pages 245 to 248 of his text *Fundamental Statistics in Psychology and Education*). The weights which result from this procedure are directly proportional to the phi coefficients and inversely proportional to the standard deviations of the distributions of item responses.

Reliability. The reliabilities of the scores on the Guilford inventories range from .80 to .94. They are summarized in Table 85. Those

TABLE 85. *Reliability Data for the Guilford and Guilford-Martin Inventories**

Social introversion-extroversion	.90	Masculinity-femininity	.85
Thinking introversion-extroversion	.84	Inferiority feelings	.91
Depression	.94	Nervousness	.89
Cycloid disposition	.88	Objectivity	.83
Rhathymia	.90	Agreeableness	.80
General activity	.89	Cooperativeness	.91
Ascendance-submission	.88		

* From Guilford, J. P. *Manual of Directions*. (Rev. Ed.) *An Inventory of Factors STDCR; Manual of Directions and Norms. The Guilford-Martin Inventory of Factors GAMIN;* and *Manual of Directions and Norms. The Guilford-Martin Personnel Inventory.* Beverly Hills, Calif.: Sheridan Supply Company.

for factors STDCR were determined from the correlations between alternate sixths of the items divided into two equal pools. Those for factors GAMIN, O, Ag, and Co were determined from the correlations between random halves of the items. All reliabilities reported in Table 85 were determined on 100 cases not included in the standardization groups.

Intercorrelations. Final score intercorrelations are presented in Tables 86, 87, and 88. Those among factors STDCR are given in Table 86, those among factors GAMIN are given in Table 87, and those among factors O, Ag, and Co are given in Table 88. These intercorrelations are, in several instances, rather far removed from the ideal intercorrelation of .00. But they are sufficiently moderate to suggest that sensibly different variables are measured by the different scales.

Validity. We come now to the question of validity and find three sets of data to report. The first consists of a comparison between the scores on factors STDCR and a series of self-ratings and a composite rating by five associates. The scales on which these ratings were made are given in Fig. 6. Table 89 shows the reliabilities of these ratings and their correlations with the factor scores. Correlations

TABLE 86. *Intercorrelations among Factors S, T, D, C, and R**

Factor	T	D	C	R
S	.15	.49	.33	.54
T		.15	.14	.21
D			.85	.36
C				.02

* From Guilford, J. P. *Manual of Directions.* (Rev. Ed.) *An Inventory of Factors STDCR.* Beverly Hills, Calif.: Sheridan Supply Company.

TABLE 87. *Intercorrelations among Factors G, A, M, I, and N**

Factor	A	M	I	N
G	.51	.16	.39	.27
A		.34	.54	.16
M			.43	.34
I				.70

* From Guilford, J. P. *Manual of Directions and Norms. The Guilford-Martin Inventory of Factors GAMIN.* Beverly Hills, Calif.: Sheridan Supply Company.

TABLE 88. *Intercorrelations among Factors O, Ag, and Co**

Factor	Ag	Co
O	.64	.55
Ag	. . .	.63

* From Guilford, J. P. *Manual of Directions and Norms. The Guilford-Martin Personnel Inventory.* Beverly Hills, Calif.: Sheridan Supply Company.

between the ratings and scores on factor S vary from .43 to .70; those between the ratings and scores on factor D vary from .39 to .60; and those between the ratings and scores on factor R vary from .39 to .65. The correlations for factors T and C are not so satisfactory. For factor T they are .08 and .46, and for factor C they are .20 and .34.

The second set of validity data relate to the Personnel Inventory.

This was given by Guilford and Martin to 51 aircraft employees. Upon the basis of the distributions of scores obtained (on objectivity, agreeableness, and cooperativeness), Guilford and Martin predicted that anyone "below the median on two or more traits" would be found unsatisfactory, *i.e.*, would be found to be a troublemaker, etc.

S—Shuns society of others; is shy   1 2 3 4 5 6 7 8 9   Seeks society of others; is a "good mixer."

T—Frequently indulges in meditative thinking   1 2 3 4 5 6 7 8 9   Shuns meditative or reflective thinking

D—Emotions and moods predominantly unpleasant; worried; depressed   1 2 3 4 5 6 7 8 9   Emotions and moods predominantly pleasant; cheerful; optimistic

C—Has frequent or radical changes in mood   1 2 3 4 5 6 7 8 9   Very uniform in mood

R—Happy-go-lucky; carefree   1 2 3 4 5 6 7 8 9   Serious minded; conscientious

Fig. 6. Rating scales used in validating factors STDCR. (*From Guilford, J. P. Personality factors D, R, T and A. J. abnorm. soc. Psychol.*, 1939, **4**, 21–36.)

TABLE 89. *Reliability and Validity Data for the Rating Scales in Fig. 6**

Year	Number	S	T	D	C	R	Rating by
				Validity			
1938	50	.68	.46	.51	.34	.65	Self
1939	51	.60	...	.45	...	.39	Self
1938	50	.70	.08	.60	.20	.48	Others
1939	51	.43	...	.39	...	.46	Others
				Reliability			
1938	50	.55	.33	.51	.58	.68	Self and others
1939	51	.63	...	.54	...	.63	Self and others
....	22	.69	.01	.73	.38	.54	Others

* From Guilford, J. P., and Guilford, R. B. Personality factors D, R, T and A. *J. abnorm. soc. Psychol.*, 1939, **34**, 21–36.

Twenty-two of the workers in the group of 51 actually were considered troublemakers by management, and the remaining 29 were considered satisfactory. Without knowing management's classification, Guilford and Martin correctly classified 73 per cent of the unsatisfactory workers and 66 per cent of the satisfactory workers. This result argues for some basic validity, Guilford and Martin believe, for the scores on their Personnel Inventory.

The third set of validity data relate to factor M. To validate the scores on this factor, Guilford and Martin compared the scores of men and women not included in their standardization or item analysis groups. They found that 92 per cent of 50 men secured scores "above the median of the distribution . . . of the two sexes combined, and that 92 per cent of 50 women secured scores "below the median of this distribution." A phi coefficient was computed and found to be .84. This value Guilford and Martin consider "highly satisfactory."

Norms. All norms for the Guilford inventories are given in terms of what Guilford calls a C scale, a normalized distribution with 11 intervals. Guilford assumes a normal distribution underlying each of his factor distributions and a predetermined percentage of cases in each score interval. These norms will be found in his *Manuals of Directions*.

THE ALLPORT-VERNON STUDY OF VALUES

Our fifth example of a multidimensional approach to the measurement of personality is contained in the Allport-Vernon Study of Values. This test was designed in 1931 by P. E. Vernon and Gordon W. Allport (and revised in 1951 by Allport, Vernon, and Gardner Lindzey) to measure six pervasive or broad evaluative attitudes first defined by the philosopher Edouard Spranger. Vernon and Allport feel that

. . . the isolation and measurement of single habits, traits or capacities within personality give an incomplete and frequently misleading picture. It is evident [they say] that in some fashion . . . the significance of these single factors is dependent upon the total personality in which they are set. [Therefore] an investigator must find within a personality broad functions that are common to all other personalities.

These functions are to be found, argue Vernon and Allport, in Spranger's list of evaluative attitudes. The Spranger attitudes, as redefined by Allport and Vernon, are as follows:

Theoretic. The dominant interest of the theoretical man is the discovery of truth. In the pursuit of this goal he characteristically takes a "cognitive attitude, one that looks for identities and differences; one that divests itself of judgments regarding the beauty or utility of objects, and seeks only to observe and to reason. Since the interests of the theoretical man are empirical, critical, and rational, he is necessarily an intellectualist, frequently a scientist or philosopher. His chief aim in life is to order and to systematize his knowledge.

Economic. The economic man is characteristically interested in what is useful. Based originally upon the satisfaction of bodily needs (self-preservation), the interest in utilities develops to embrace the practical affairs of the business world, the production, marketing and consumption of goods, the elaboration of credit, and the accumulation of tangible wealth. This type is thoroughly practical and conforms well to the prevailing conception of the average American businessman.

Aesthetic. The aesthetic man sees his highest value in form and harmony. Each single experience is judged from the standpoint of grace, symmetry or fitness. He regards life as a manifold of events; each single impression is enjoyed for its own sake. He need not be a creative artist; nor need he be effete; he is aesthetic if he but finds his chief interest in the artistic episodes of life.

Social. The highest value for this type is love of people, whether of one or many, whether conjugal, filial, friendly, or philanthropic. The social man prizes other persons as ends, and is therefore himself kind, sympathetic, and unselfish. He is likely to find the theoretical, economic, and aesthetic attitudes cold and inhuman. In contrast to the political type, the social man regards love as itself the only suitable form of power, or else repudiates the entire conception of power as endangering the integrity of personality. In its purest form the social interest is selfless and tends to approach very closely to the religious attitude.

Political. The political man is interested primarily in power. His activities are not necessarily within the narrow field of politics; but whatever his vocation he betrays himself as a Macht mensch. Leaders in any field generally have a high power value. Since competition and struggle play a large part in all life, many philosophers have seen power as the most universal and most fundamental of motives.

Religious. The highest value for the religious man may be called unity. He is mystical, and seeks to comprehend the cosmos as a whole, to relate himself to its embracing totality. Spranger defines the religious man as one "whose mental structure is permanently directed to the creation of the highest and absolutely satisfying value experience."

Edouard Spranger, a philosopher of the *Verstehende* school, postulated in his book *Types of Men* that men are guided primarily by one or the other of these six predominant all-pervasive attitudes. Thus one man will behave or act, says Spranger, primarily from a theoretical point of view, another primarily from a religious point of view, another primarily from an aesthetic point of view, and so on. It is not hard for us to find examples illustrative of Spranger's theory. We can cite the poet or musician who looks at things from an aesthetic point of view, the politician who looks at things from a political point of view, the minister who looks at things from a religious point of view, and so on. Spranger so carefully defined his types that we can see them almost on every hand. Spranger rested his case at the arm-chair level, however, and did not attempt any empirical verification of his theory. This latter task was undertaken by P. E. Vernon and Gordon W. Allport in their development of the Study of Values.

Allport and Vernon constructed the Study of Values to show the relative predominance of Spranger's six evaluative attitudes. The scoring is such that we can discover only whether a man is governed *more* or *less* by a theoretical attitude than by, let us say, a religious attitude, and so forth. This is in contrast with most scales of personality measurement in which the score on a scale is obtained independently of, and without reference to, the other ways in which the test may be scored.

The Study of Values consists of two parts. There are 30 items in Part I and 15 items in Part II. The first item in Part I is worded this way:

The main object of scientific research should be the discovery of pure truth rather than its practical applications.

The subject must answer "Yes" or "No," thus indicating whether he agrees or disagrees with the statement. In this instance if he answers "Yes," the inference is that he is guided more by a theoretical attitude, but if he answers "No," the inference is that he is guided more by an economic attitude. The remaining questions in Part I offer similar comparisons. Each evaluative attitude is represented in 10 of these comparisons. The first item in Part II reads as follows:

Do you think that a good government should aim chiefly at:
a) more aid for the poor, sick and old
b) the development of manufacturing and trade
c) introducing more ethical principles into its policies and diplomacy
d) establishing a position of prestige and respect among nations

The subject is instructed to rank these alternatives in order. He must put a 1 in front of the alternative he prefers over all others, a 2 in front of the alternative which is his second choice, a 3 in front of his third choice, and a 4 in front of his last choice. This particular item represents (*a*) social, (*b*) economic, (*c*) religious, and (*d*) political attitudes. Thus throughout Part II four attitudes are represented in each item, and each attitude is represented ten times.

Development of Test. Allport and Vernon prepared the items for the Study of Values "upon the basis of their fidelity in representing Spranger's six types." The only evidence of this fidelity, however, is Allport and Vernon's claim that such is the case.

In any test requiring the choice between two or more alternative answers, care must be taken to see that choices are made upon the basis of the crucial issue. If they are made upon the basis of factors irrelevant to the main issue, this will defeat the purpose of the test. In the present instance Allport and Vernon wanted the popularity of the alternatives to be equated so that a subject would not choose an alternative because of its greater popularity. Allport and Vernon tried a number of alternatives for each item until they satisfied themselves that the alternatives left in the final form of the test differed little or not at all in terms of their relative popularity.

Vernon and Allport's next step consisted of making an internal consistency analysis, using the top and bottom fourths on each variable as their criterion groups. They made this analysis on three different groups of subjects. There were more than 160 subjects in each group, so that there were at least 40 subjects included in each one of the criterion groups. Vernon and Allport then tabulated the "average marks which these extreme groups gave to each of the proposed answers, that referred to the value in question." Then they computed the difference between the average scores, and divided this difference by its probable error. All items retained had differences greater than three times their own probable errors, and the average difference for the items retained was six times its probable error. In the 1951 revision, Vernon, Allport, and Lindzey report similar item analyses on 780 subjects and state that each item in the test correlates significantly with the total scale of which it is a part.

In Part I a subject can secure 1, 2, or 3 points for each answer. Since each evaluative attitude is represented ten times, this means that the score for each scale can range from 10 to 30. In Part II a subject can give ranks of 1, 2, 3, or 4. These are summed, and since each evaluative attitude is represented ten times, the scores on each scale can range from 10 to 40. In this instance, since these scores are ranks, they are subtracted from 40 so that a high numerical value will represent the predominance of an attitude. In two of the scales, the scores are subtracted from 36 and 42 (not from 40). The first of these is for the social scale, and the second is for the religious scale.

These subtractions correct these scores for the greater popularity of the items indicating social attitudes and the lesser popularity of the items indicating religious attitudes in comparison with the items in the other four scales. The final scores can range from 0 to 60, with 30 being the average or neutral score on each scale. The predominance of an evaluative attitude is indicated by a score of 40 or more, and its lack of predominance by a score of 20 or less.

Reliability. Allport and Vernon, Whitely, and Allport, Vernon, and Lindzey report the split-half and repeat reliabilities given in Table 90. On the old form, the social scale had the lowest reliability

TABLE 90. *Reliability Data for the Allport-Vernon Study of Values* *

Scale	Revised edition	Original edition		Whitely
	Allport, Vernon, and Lindzey	Vernon and Allport		
	Split-half	Split-half	Repeat	Repeat
Theoretic..........	.73	.62	.66	.68
Economic..........	.87	.72	.71	.79
Aesthetic..........	.80	.84	.84	.86
Social..............	.82	.49	.39	.50
Political...........	.77	.53	.55	.76
Religious..........	.90	.84	.80	.87

* From Vernon, P. E., and Allport, G. W. A test for personal values. *J. abnorm. soc. Psychol.*, 1931, **26**, 231–248; Whitely, P. L. A study of the Allport-Vernon test for personal values. *J. abnorm. soc. Psychol.*, 1933, **28**, 6–13; and Allport, G. W., Vernon, P. E., and Lindzey, G. *Study of Values*. (Rev. Ed.) *Manual of Directions*. Boston: Houghton Mifflin Company, 1951.

and the aesthetic scale the highest. On the new form, the aesthetic scale has the lowest reliability and the religious scale the highest. In general, the new form possesses a considerably greater degree of reliability than did the original form.

Validity. In determining the validity of the Vernon-Allport Study of Values, we have two questions to answer: How well does the test represent Spranger's theoretical types? And how well do the scores on the test identify individuals who are governed by different evaluative attitudes?

We have no way to provide an adequate answer to the first question. We have Allport and Vernon's statement that they tried to select items representing Spranger's types, but no objective evidence on this point is available. However, we can note that the correlations between the scales on the original and revised editions of the test vary between .31 and .75. These values would seem to raise some question as to how validly the scales on either edition represent the original Spranger types.

Evidence on the second question is more plentiful. Vernon and Allport, Stone, Cantril and Allport, and Allport, Vernon, and Lindzey have secured evidence of differences in mean scores of men and women and of students engaged in different studies. Table 91

TABLE 91. *Mean Study of Values Scores for Men and Women* *

Scale	Revised edition		Original edition	
	Men N = 851	Women N = 965	Men N = 1,163	Women N = 1,592
Theoretic..........	43.3	36.4	30.8	27.7
Economic..........	42.1	38.8	32.0	27.0
Aesthetic..........	37.2	42.2	27.0	33.0
Social.............	37.7	41.2	29.7	31.6
Political..........	42.7	38.1	32.1	27.9
Religious..........	37.0	43.2	28.0	33.3

* From Cantril, H., and Allport, G. W. Recent applications of the Study of Values. *J. abnorm. soc. Psychol.*, 1933, **28**, 259–273; and from Allport, G. W., Vernon, P. E., and Lindzey, G. *Study of Values.* (Rev. Ed.) *Manual of Directions.* Boston: Houghton Mifflin Company, 1951.

TABLE 92. *Mean Study of Values Scores for Students with Different College Majors* *

Subject	Number	Theoretic	Economic	Aesthetic	Social	Political	Religious
Banking	21	29	38	31	29	34	19
Business............	110	28	37	28	30	33	24
Commercial.........	125	32	34	22	29	32	31
Education..........	21	29	26	35	30	32	29
Engineering.........	64	32	35	26	29	31	26
Law...............	33	26	31	30	31	37	26
Literature..........	24	24	27	40	29	30	30
Medical............	45	36	27	31	30	28	28
Missionary..........	80	27	23	26	35	22	49
Psychology.........	10	44	23	37	31	22	22
Salesmen...........	110	28	39	24	27	36	26
Science.............	18	35	26	31	31	28	28
Theological.........	13	26	22	23	34	26	49

* From Cantril, H., and Allport, G. W. Recent applications of the Study of Values. *J. abnorm. soc. Psychol.*, 1933, **28**, 259–273.

shows mean scores for men and women, and Table 92 shows mean scores for students majoring in different subjects. Vernon and Allport conclude:

The Study of Values test . . . affords a method of scaling the relative predominance of the theoretical, economic, aesthetic, social, political and religious values in personality. The results indicate that Spranger is on the whole justified in regarding these values as constituting generalized motives in men, and that the test succeeds in determining with some precision the prominence of each value in any single individual.

Biographical Application. Personality tests are designed to be used by living individuals. The questions are usually too detailed and too specific for use in connection with historic personages. One attempt at such an application has been made, however, with the Study of Values. We give this study in some detail, for to date it represents, apart from the work of Cox in estimating the intelligence quotients of 300 eminent men from biographical data, a unique application of a personality test. This application consists of an attempt to fill out the Study of Values for Jonathan Swift, author of *Gulliver's Travels* (to Lilliput, Brobdingnag, Laputa, and the country of the Houyhnhnms, etc.).

From various biographies, as well as from the works of Swift himself, data were secured which enabled the author to fill out for Swift the Study of Values. It was hoped that by the use of the standard set of questions furnished by the Study of Values an impartial and fairly accurate evaluation of Swift's basic motives could be achieved. The quantitative results are given in Fig. 7.

According to this figure, Swift was governed first of all by religious motives, secondarily (and perhaps equally) by political, social, and economic motives, then by aesthetic motives, and last of all by theoretical motives. The numerical scores are 42.0, 33.0, 31.5, 30.0, 25.5, and 18.0 for the religious, political, social, economic, aesthetic, and theoretic scales, respectively. Scores on the political, social, economic, and aesthetic scales do not differ significantly from the average, but scores on the religious and theoretic scales differ markedly. Ferguson reports

A detailed analysis of the item "responses" shows that Swift would have preferred reading about Protestant reconciliation rather than about improvement in market conditions; he would have preferred reading about threats to constitutional governments rather than about physicists' discoveries concerning the nature of atoms; and he would have preferred reading accounts of the lives and works of such men as Aristotle, Plato and Socrates rather than those of Alexander, Julius Caesar and Charlemagne.

If a series of popular lectures had been offered Swift would have preferred one on the progress and needs of social service work to one on contemporary painters;

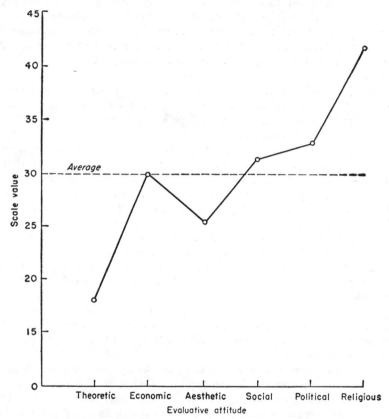

Fig. 7. Profile of the evaluative attitudes of Jonathan Swift. (From Ferguson, L. W. The evaluative attitudes of Jonathan Swift. *Psychol. Rec.*, 1939, **3**, 26–44.)

and under like circumstances would have preferred one on the comparative development of the great religious faiths to one on the comparative methods of government.

Swift would have preferred to write on the defects of the educational system rather than on the role of church-going in religion; and he would have preferred writing on the distribution of one's income between the necessities of life, luxuries and savings rather than on the personality of a close friend.

It was not justifiable, according to Swift, for great artists to be negligent of the feelings of others; and unselfishness and sympathy he considered more desirable character traits than high ideals and reverence. Because of the aggressive and self-assertive nature of man he thought the abolition of war an illusory ideal. He did not think that one who analyzes his emotions was any less sincere than one who did not; and he did not believe that contemporary charitable policies should be curtailed.

Swift thought the world would be a much better place if people took to heart the teaching "Lay not up for yourselves treasures upon earth . . . but lay up for yourselves treasures in heaven," etc; he thought the aim of churches should be to convey spiritual worship and a sense of communion with the highest rather than to attempt to bring out altruistic and charitable tendencies; taking the Bible as a whole, he did not consider it as beautiful mythology but rather as spiritual revelation.

If Swift had been a university professor he would rather have taught poetry than physics or chemistry; he would have preferred teaching economics to law. If nothing of the kind had existed in the college he would have preferred founding a debating society rather than a classical orchestra.

The main objects of scientific research were not, according to Swift, the discovery of pure truth rather than its practical applications; he did not believe that the universe had evolved to its present state in accord with mechanistic principles, thus doing away with the necessity of assuming a God; he did not believe our modern developments a sign of a greater degree of civilization than those attained by any previous race.

Swift thought a good government, first of all, should aim at introducing ethical principles into its policies and diplomacy, and last of all at establishing a position of prestige and respect among nations. Between each of these extremes lay the aims of providing more aid for the poor, sick, and old; and the developing of manufacturing and trade.

If Swift could have influenced the educational policies of schools he would have undertaken, first of all, to develop cooperativeness of spirit and service; secondarily, to promote the study and performance of drama; and last of all to provide additional laboratory facilities.

Swift's excess income first was used to endow **his** church and to establish hospitals; secondarily it would have been applied to industrial development; and last of all, would he have given it to a university for scientific research. He would have preferred establishing a mental hygiene clinic to aiming at a seat in the Cabinet, and the latter to entering into banking and finance, and this to making a collection of sculptures or paintings.

Swift preferred for personal friends those who possessed qualities of leadership; secondly those of refinement and emotional sensitivity; thirdly, those seriously interested in thinking out their attitude toward life as a whole; and lastly, those who were efficient, industrious, and of a practical turn of mind. At evening discussions with these friends he preferred talking about literature rather than about socialism and social amelioration; about this rather than about the meaning of life; and about the latter rather than about philosophy and psychology.

Swift preferred being a clergyman to being a politician; this in turn to being a sales manager; and this to being a mathematician. He thought one should guide his conduct in accord with his religious faith rather than in accord with his business organization and associates; in accord with the latter rather than in accord with the ideals of beauty; and in accord with these rather than in accord with the precepts of society as a whole.

We must remember that this qualitative description of Swift is based solely upon the alternatives suggested by the Study of Values. Answers said to be characteristic of Swift are characteristic of him only in reference to the rejected alternative or alternatives. Alternatives not suggested by the Study of Values might easily have been possible.

Relation to the Strong Vocational Interest Test. We have seen by the data in Table 92 that students of literature get high aesthetic scores that law students get high political scores, that commerce students get high economic scores, and that engineering and science students get high theoretical scores. Stone has supplemented these results by reporting practically identical findings. His only addition is that medical students get high theoretical scores. These results suggest a degree of parallelism between the areas of personality probed by the Study of Values and by the Strong Vocational Interest Test. This parallelism has not gone unnoticed and has been examined by Sarbin and Berdie, by Duffy and Crissy, and by Ferguson, Humphreys, and Frances W. Strong.

Ferguson, Humphreys, and Strong gave both tests, that is, the Strong Vocational Interest Test and the Study of Values, to 93 male Stanford University students. They scored the Strong Vocational Interest Test on eight scales: teacher, office worker, life insurance salesman, certified public accountant, physician, lawyer, Y.M.C.A. secretary, and chemist, and then correlated these scales with each other as well as with all six scales on the Study of Values. These intercorrelations are presented in Table 93.

Next Ferguson, Humphreys, and Strong subjected the intercorrelations in Table 93 to a centroid factor analysis and interpreted the factors they extracted as follows:

Factor I. Strong scales for lawyer (.77), physician (.51), and office worker (−.78); and Allport-Vernon scales for aesthetic (.38), theoretic (.35), and economic (−.67).

Factor II. Strong scales for teacher (.76), Y.M.C.A. secretary (.79), certified public accountant (.53), office worker (.56), and physician (−.40).

Factor III. Strong scales for chemist (.95), physician (.65), teacher (.38), lawyer (−.40), and life insurance salesman (−.93), and Allport-Vernon scales for theoretic (.59) and political (−.58).

TABLE 93. *Intercorrelations among the Scores of the Study of Values and Selected Scales from the Strong Vocational Interest Test**

	Scale	Allport-Vernon						Strong						
		Theoretic	Economic	Aesthetic	Social	Political	Religious	Teacher	Life insurance salesman	Certified public accountant	Office worker	Physician	Lawyer	Y.M.C.A. secretary
Allport-Vernon	Economic	−.34												
	Aesthetic	.13	−.26											
	Social	−.05	−.29	−.28										
	Political	−.57	.16	−.17	−.26									
	Religious	−.28	−.46	−.44	.22	−.20								
Strong	Teacher	.24	−.31	.07	.15	−.41	.24							
	Life insurance salesman	−.60	.18	−.27	.08	.35	.24	−.23						
	Certified public accountant	−.05	.04	.07	.13	−.14	.07	.32	.26					
	Office worker	−.39	.51	−.30	−.08	.19	−.04	.16	.20	.32				
	Physician	.59	−.49	.18	.09	−.32	.02	.08	−.60	−.30	−.66			
	Lawyer	.01	−.43	.12	.10	−.03	.29	.03	.36	.28	−.53	.18		
	Y.M.C.A. secretary	−.27	.01	−.14	.16	−.03	.21	.65	.36	.36	.57	−.57	−.09	
	Chemist	.64	−.20	.14	−.04	−.36	−.17	.18	−.90	−.27	−.28	.73	−.35	−.44

* From Ferguson, L. W., Humphreys, L. G., and Strong, F. W. A factorial analysis of interests and values. *J. educ. Psychol.*, 1941, **32**, 197–204.

Factor IV. Allport-Vernon scales for religious (.89), social (.47), and aesthetic (−.47).

Factor V. Allport-Vernon scales for political (.72) and economic (−.60).

Ferguson, Humphreys, and Strong state that we cannot argue "from the above results that the Allport-Vernon Study of Values contains factors which the Vocational Interest Test does not, for all of the scales from the latter test were not included in the analysis. Since Factor II, on the other hand, is described entirely in terms of Strong scales, it can be asserted that the Vocational Interest Test measures at least one factor that the Study of Values does not." Finally, these investigators conclude that "tests for any one of the . . . five factors which they isolated should be more significant in the analysis of behavior than any one of the Strong or Allport-Vernon scales by itself." Unfortunately these authors have not followed up this suggestion.

Duffy and W. J. E. Crissy gave the Allport-Vernon Study of Values and the Strong Vocational Interest Test to 108 women freshmen at Sarah Lawrence College. They scored the Vocational Interest Test on the scales for nurse, lawyer, librarian, secretary-stenographer, physician, artist, author, housewife, office worker, and social worker, and correlated the scores on these scales with those on the Study of Values. Their results are presented in Table 94. They subjected these correlations to a centroid factor analysis and, after rotations had been made, secured the following factor interpretations.

TABLE 94. *Intercorrelations between the Scores on the Study of Values and Certain of the Scores on the Strong Vocational Interest Blank for Women**

Scale	Theoretic	Economic	Political	Aesthetic	Social	Religious
Nurse	−.02	−.06	.11	−.24	.28	.00
Lawyer	.22	.25	.24	−.36	.00	−.25
Librarian	.12	−.12	−.09	.36	−.32	.05
Secretary	−.32	.21	.32	−.19	.22	−.12
Physician	.44	−.06	−.12	−.16	−.08	−.05
Artist	.08	−.31	−.22	.45	−.35	.22
Author	−.01	−.26	−.15	.37	−.25	.20
Housewife	−.32	.11	.14	−.17	.34	−.02
Office worker	−.26	.37	.34	−.32	.19	−.17
Social worker	.15	−.11	−.09	−.07	.22	−.08

* From Duffy, E., and Crissy, W. J. E. Evaluative attitudes as related to vocational interests and academic achievement. *J. abnorm. soc. Psychol.*, 1940, **35**, 226–245.

On Factor I scales for political (.65), economic (.64), and lawyer interest (.36) are opposed to scales for religious (−.51), aesthetic (−.40), and author interest (−.33). Duffy and Crissy call this a Philistine factor because of the association of economic, political, and lawyer interest values.

Duffy and Crissy's second factor is described by scales for social (.60), housewife (.38), and secretary (.30) which are opposed to the theoretic scale (−.38). This factor Duffy and Crissy call an "interest in people."

Finally, Factor III contrasts the theoretic scale (.55) with the religious scale (−.48). Duffy and Crissy call this a "theoretic" factor.

Scores from both the Study of Values and the Vocational Interest Test are represented on two of the factors, but the third factor is defined entirely in terms of scales from the Study of Values. But just as in Ferguson, Humphreys, and Strong's study, we cannot conclude that the Study of Values measures anything which the Vocational Interest Test does not measure. This is because Duffy and Crissy, like Ferguson, Humphreys, and Strong, did not score all of the scales on the Vocational Interest Test.

Sarbin and Berdie gave the Study of Values and the Vocational Interest Test to 59 male students at the University of Minnesota and treated their data somewhat differently than did Ferguson, Humphreys, and Strong, and Duffy and Crissy. Sarbin and Berdie scored the Vocational Interest Test on 26 occupations and then arranged these according to Strong's classification (Table 14, Chap. 2). Then they classified the students as having or not having the interests in each *group* of occupations rather than in each *specific* occupation. Following this classification Sarbin and Berdie computed mean Study of Values scores for each of their several contrasting pairs of students, computed *t* ratios to indicate the significance of the differences between the contrasting pairs of means, and secured the results discussed below.

Their data indicate that theoretical attitudes are related positively to the interests of scientific and professional occupations and negatively to the interests of salesmen. They indicate that economic attitudes are related positively to the interests of businessmen and negatively to the interests of scientific, professional, and "language" occupations. They show aesthetic attitudes are related positively to the interests of professional men, positively to the interests of "language" occupations, and negatively to the interests of business-men. The social attitude appears related positively to the interests of salesmen and to "language" occupations but related negatively to the interests of businessmen. Political attitudes are related posi-tively to the interests of businessmen and are related negatively to the interests of scientific and professional men, farmers, etc. Finally the religious attitude is related positively to "interest in people" and is related negatively to the interests of certified public accountants.

Table 95 brings together the data for three occupations common to both the men's and women's Vocational Interest blanks. Duffy and

TABLE 95. *Correlations between the Allport-Vernon Study of Values Scales and the Lawyer, Physician, and Office Worker Vocational Interest Scores**

Scale	Lawyer			Physician			Office worker		
	Fergu-son, Hum-phreys, and Strong	Duffy and Crissy	Sarbin and Berdie	Fergu-son, Hum-phreys, and Strong	Duffy and Crissy	Sarbin and Berdie	Fergu-son, Hum-phreys, and Strong	Duffy and Crissy	Sarbin and Berdie
Theoretic...	.01	.22	−1.4	.59	.44	4.1	−.39	−.26	−1.5
Economic..	−.43	.25	−2.0	−.49	−.06	−2.3	.51	.37	1.5
Aesthetic...	.12	−.36	1.8	.18	−.16	2.4	−.30	−.32	−1.9
Social......	.10	.00	1.7	.09	−.08	0.2	−.08	.19	−1.6
Political....	−.03	.24	1.0	−.32	−.12	−3.5	.19	.34	2.0
Religious...	.29	−.25	−0.8	.02	−.05	−1.1	−.04	−.17	1.6

* Adapted from: Duffy, E., and Crissy, W. J. E. Evaluative attitudes as related to voca-tional interests and values. *J. abnorm. soc. Psychol.*, 1940, **35**, 226–245; Ferguson, L. W., Humphreys, L. G., and Strong, F. W., Jr. A factorial analysis of interests and values. *J. educ. Psychol.*, 1941, **32**, 197–204; and from Sarbin, T. R., and Berdie, R. F. Relation of measured interests to the Allport-Vernon Study of Values. *J. appl. Psychol.*, 1940, **24**, 287–296.

Crissy's data, and Ferguson, Humphreys, and Strong's data are given in terms of correlations, while Sarbin and Berdie's data are given in terms of *t* ratios. In the latter case we must realize, too, that the *t* ratios refer, not to the specific occupation alone, but to the group of occupations in which each is included.

All three sets of data show that the theoretical attitude is related positively to physician interest and related negatively to office worker interest. They also agree in showing that the economic atti-tude is related positively to office worker interest and negatively to physician interest. All three studies agree in showing the aesthetic attitude to be related negatively to office worker interest. Finally, they agree in showing the political attitude to be related positively to office worker interest and related negatively to physician interest.

For men the economic attitude appears to be related negatively to lawyer interest, the aesthetic attitude appears to be related positively to lawyer interest and to physician interest, and the religious attitude appears to be related negatively to lawyer interest. Either these same trends do not hold for women, or Duffy and Crissy's data are in disagreement with those of Ferguson, Humphreys, and Strong and with those of Sarbin and Berdie.

We can conclude by saying that the agreements we have been discussing are interesting and suggest a basic parallelism between the areas of personality probed by the Strong Vocational Interest Test and by the Study of Values. But the disagreements indicate that further research is in order before we can make completely definitive the relations we have been examining.

8

ADJUSTMENT: DIAGNOSTIC APPROACHES

One of our most important daily tasks is that of making adjustments. We must adjust ourselves to the other members of our family, to our neighbors, to our friends, to our school chums, to our business associates, and so forth. And, of course, we expect the other members of our family, our neighbors, our friends, our school chums, and our business associates to make adjustments in our behalf, also. We already know from the doctrine of individual differences that a few people will be very adept at making these adjustments, a few will seem incapable of making any degree of adjustment whatsoever, and the rest of us will fall somewhere between these two extremes.

The task which confronts us in this and in the next chapter is that of describing some of the methods devised to measure the degree of adjustment which an individual can make. We shall find it convenient to discuss these methods under two general categories: diagnostic approaches and prognostic approaches. Under the latter heading we shall discuss the devices measuring adjustment in relation to a specific object and for which a definite prediction of adjustment in a specified situation is desired. For example, under this heading we shall discuss adjustment in marriage, vocational adjustment, and adjustment in military service. We could discuss other specific situations also, but these three will suffice to illustrate the types of methodology which are generally involved.

Under the heading of diagnostic approaches, the subject of our present chapter, we shall discuss adjustment in general. We shall be concerned with the internal (if we can call it that) emotional adjustment of the individual. Is he inwardly happy? Is he at harmony with himself, or is there some basic conflict that keeps him in an inner turmoil? We shall be concerned with the diagnosis of the presence or absence of such adjustment, for we can see, without elaboration, that such general adjustment is basic to a person's adjusting himself in specific situations. We shall discuss two of the most widely used general adjustment inventories. These are the Bell Adjustment Inventory and the Minnesota Multiphasic Personality Inventory.

THE BELL ADJUSTMENT INVENTORY

According to Bell, the first list of adjustment questions appearing in psychological literature is that prepared in 1905 by Heymans and Wiersma. It was prepared for, and used by, 400 Dutch physicians in determining the maladjustments of 2,415 of their patients. Some of the questions in this list, as given by Bell, are presented in Table 96.

TABLE 96. *Some of the Questions Used by Heymans and Wiersma to Determine Maladjustment**

Is the particular person active and busy (gesticulating, jumping lightly from the chair, walking back and forth in the room), or sitting quiet?

Is the particular person discouraged easily in disagreeable tasks or is he persevering in the completion of his intentions?

Is the particular person impulsive (grasps a situation on the impulse of the moment), does he think it over and not act without deliberation of pro and con, or is he a man of principles acting only in accordance with rules of conduct already established?

Is the particular person excitable (that is, is he moody over little things and easily hurt) or is he of a happy mood (that is, moves easily among his fellows, is at ease among others); or is he absolutely incapable of being aroused to anger (cannot be hurt, does not let himself be aroused)?

Is the particular person happy and joyful (that is, enjoys life), is he of heavy mood and depressed, does he fluctuate from one to the other, or is he always quiet and the same?

Is the particular person inclined to sink himself in abstract speculations?

Is the particular person a lover of intellectual games, puzzles, et cetera?

Is the particular person inclined to talk about things, persons, or about himself?

Is the particular person domineering, or inclined to let everyone have his freedom, or is he easy to guide and control?

* From Bell, H. M. *The Theory and Practice of Personal Counseling.* Stanford University, Calif.: Stanford University Press, 1939.

The next list of questions in the adjustment area was prepared, says Bell, by Hoch and Amsden. Their list differed from that prepared by Heymans and Wiersma in being longer and in placing greater emphasis upon sexual adjustment. A few of the questions in their list are given in Table 97.

The third list of note is that prepared by F. L. Wells in 1914. This list Wells based directly upon those prepared by Heymans and

Wiersma, and by Hoch and Amsden, and he also drew to some extent from some personal trait lists prepared by Cattell and by Davenport.

The next step in this field was that undertaken by Woodworth when he prepared his Personal Data Sheet. We have already discussed this (in Chap. 6) and have given the list of questions which Woodworth prepared. We have also indicated that there have been many revisions of Woodworth's list and that his list can be considered the grandfather of practically all personality and adjustment schedules now in existence. We shall find that the Bell Adjustment Inventory is no exception to this and that it is a direct descendant of the Woodworth list through just one intermediary, the Thurstones' Personality Schedule.

TABLE 97. *Some of the Questions Used by Hoch and Amsden to Determine Maladjustment**

In childhood was he active in play and work?
Does he make friends easily?
As a child did he play freely with other children?
Does he daydream frequently?
Does he think the world treats him ill?
Does he readily adapt himself to a new environment?
Does he get despondent without apparent reason?
Is he up and down in his moods?
Is he irritable, quick-tempered?
Does he have a marked preference or antagonism for any member of his family?
Is he natural and at ease with the opposite sex?
Does he read much?

* From Bell, H. M. *The Theory and Practice of Personal Counseling.* Stanford University, Calif.: Stanford University Press, 1939.

Development of Test. In 1930 Bell gave the Thurstones' Personality Schedule to entering freshmen students at Chico (California) State College. He interviewed these students during the course of the school year and found that the test did not tap, as well as he thought it ought to tap, all areas of student maladjustment. Therefore he began a revision of the Thurstones' schedule, and this ultimately led to Bell's own Adjustment Inventory.

The first step which Bell took was to classify the items in the Thurstones' schedule into various groups. These groups were:

Home life	Attitude toward others
Health	Social reaction
Use of time	Attitude toward life
Emotional control	Attitude toward sex
Self-feeling	Pathological tendencies

Bell next constructed "a differential scoring stencil" and used this stencil in scoring the Thurstones' schedule for the entering freshman class of 1931. Bell reports that this materially increased the usefulness of the schedule.

Bell's third step was to devise 188 new questions and to add these to the 223 already in the Thurstones' schedule. Bell, with the assistance of Dr. C. Gilbert Wrenn, prepared an a priori scoring key and used this key to derive an adjustment score based upon all 411 questions. This key was validated, says Bell, "through subsequent use and analysis of the test." But Bell gives no other details.

As the fourth step in the development of the Adjustment Inventory, Bell performed an item analysis. This analysis was performed separately for each of the 10 adjustment areas previously defined. Bell selected for his criterion groups the upper and lower 15 per cent of the score distributions. Items were not retained if they failed to differentiate between these two criterion groups.

Bell next applied what he called a criterion of applicability. He wanted items that would apply to a large number of students and so eliminated any item which did not apply to 25 per cent or more of the "maladjusted" group.

Bell's sixth step was to eliminate items which were misunderstood or which aroused resentment. These items were detected via his interviews with students over a period of three years.

The criteria we have just described caused Bell to discard 271 of his (or the Thurstones') questions, leaving 140 for the final form of the Adjustment Inventory. His criteria also caused him to eliminate or to combine some of the original adjustment categories. Finally there remained only four categories in the scale. These are home adjustment, health adjustment, social adjustment, and emotional adjustment. The items are equally divided among these areas.

Scoring. Bell experimented with both weighted and unweighted scoring procedures. The unweighted system makes use of the a priori scoring key developed by Bell and Wrenn, whereas the weighted system makes use of a key developed by Strong's item-weighting technique. But Strong's technique cannot be applied, of course, until some other system segregates the cases into criterion groups. Bell found that total scores derived from the weighted and unweighted scoring systems correlate .95 to .97 for the four scales. Therefore he recommends the use of the unweighted system in scoring.

Reliability. The reliabilities of the scores on the Adjustment Inventory range between .80 and .93. These were determined by the split-half technique and are given in Table 98.

TABLE 98. *Reliability Data for Bell's Adjustment Inventory**

Home adjustment.............. .89
Health adjustment.............. .80
Social adjustment.............. .89
Emotional adjustment.......... .85
Total adjustment.............. .93

* From Bell, H. M. *The Theory and Practice of Personal Counseling.* Stanford University, Calif.: Stanford University Press, 1939.

Validity. Bell states that we may consider the matter of student adjustment from two points of view: from the standpoint of the individual himself or from the standpoint of a disinterested party. The point in making this distinction is that a person may feel himself perfectly well adjusted, but a disinterested party might think otherwise. Or a disinterested party might consider a subject well adjusted when the individual himself thinks he is maladjusted. Bell's interest was in the viewpoint of the individual himself—in the individual's evaluation of his own behavior. The Adjustment Inventory is supposed to "get at" this aspect of adjustment. We must keep this point clearly in mind as we review the data Bell offers as relevant for determining the validity of his Adjustment Inventory.

The first bit of evidence Bell offers is that the items in the Adjustment Inventory show a significant differentiation between the students falling in the upper and lower 15 per cent segments of the score distributions. We cannot accept this as evidence for validity. In the first place, the criterion groups were themselves selected upon the basis of the items whose validity is at stake, and in the second place, the results are pertinent only to item reliability, not to item validity.

Bell's second type of validation data lies in his interview material. He states that item responses were found to be consistent with remarks made during these interviews. This may well be true, but it would seem that all that this proves is that a person will put down on paper the same things he is willing to divulge in an interview. This does not answer the basic question as to whether these responses are really indicative of adjustment, or of maladjustment, as the case may be.

Bell's third type of validating data consists of the correlations of the scores on his inventory with other measures of adjustment. He submits correlations with the scores on the Thurstones' Personality Schedule, the Allports' Ascendance-Submission Reaction Study, and Bernreuter's Personality Inventory. These correlations are presented in Table 99.

TABLE 99. *Correlations between Certain Bell Adjustment Scores and Scores on Other Inventories**

Scales intercorrelated	N	r
Social adjustment vs. Allports' Ascendance-Submission score (men)	46	.58
Social adjustment vs. Allports' Ascendance-Submission score (women)	50	.67
Emotional adjustment vs. Thurstones' Personality Schedule	96	.83
Total adjustment vs. Thurstones' Personality Schedule	96	.89
Social adjustment vs. Bernreuter's B4-D scale	39	.79

* From Bell, H. M. *The Theory and Practice of Personal Counseling.* Stanford University, Calif.: Stanford University Press, 1939.

These correlations are highly questionable as indices of validity. They involve the assumption that the Allports', the Thurstones', and Bernreuter's inventories are, themselves, valid indicators of maladjustment. And of this assumption, as we pointed out in Chap. 6, there is no positive proof. Next, many of the questions in Bell's inventory were taken from the Thurstones' schedule. And both Bernreuter and the Thurstones took many of their items from the Allports' Ascendance-Submission Reaction Study. Thus Bell, in reporting the correlations in Table 99, is not reporting correlations with *independent* measures of adjustment. This makes these correlations spuriously high. They cannot be taken as indicating validity in the adjustment scores. If the Bell Adjustment Inventory is a valid test, we must look elsewhere for supporting data.

The last type of validity data which Bell presents is to the effect that the scores on his inventory differentiate between counselor-selected groups of well-adjusted and poorly adjusted students. Bell asked a number of student counselors to select groups of adjusted and maladjusted students so that he could determine if they secured differentiating scores on the Adjustment Inventory. The groups used in connection with each scale were located in schools in the following cities: Chico, California (home and health adjustment); Hasbrouck Heights, New Jersey (home and health adjustment); Redwood City,

California (health adjustment); Sacramento, California (social adjustment); and Pasadena, California (emotional adjustment). Clearly, the students used in connection with the social adjustment and emotional adjustment scales are different from each other, and both are different from those used in connection with the home adjustment and health adjustment scales. Bell is not entirely clear, however, as to whether there is or is not any overlap in the student groups used in connection with the home adjustment and health adjustment scales. The adjustment scores for these various groups of adjusted and maladjusted students are given in Table 100.

TABLE 100. *Bell Adjustment Scores for Counselor-selected Adjusted and Maladjusted Students**

Scale	Number	Adjusted	Maladjusted	Difference	Standard deviation of the difference
Home adjustment......	51	4.65	10.27	5.62	.80
Health adjustment.....	42	5.40	11.53	6.13	.93
Social adjustment......	24	8.40	16.80	8.40	1.52
Emotional adjustment..	36	8.28	16.28	7.50	1.42

* From Bell, H. M. *The Theory and Practice of Personal Counseling.* Stanford University, Calif.: Stanford University Press, 1939.

These data are interesting and indicate, without doubt, that Bell's Adjustment Inventory can differentiate between counselor-selected groups of well-adjusted and counselor-selected groups of poorly adjusted students. These would seem to be evidence for validity until we recall Bell's assertion that his test was designed to measure adjustment or maladjustment from a student's point of view and not necessarily from a counselor's point of view. Therefore we must reject the data in Table 100 as irrelevant to the hypothesis to be tested. We have now exhausted the evidence which Bell himself has presented, and we must conclude that the validity of the Adjustment Inventory has in no way been substantially demonstrated.

THE MINNESOTA MULTIPHASIC PERSONALITY INVENTORY

We have discovered throughout this volume that one of the most popular methods of test construction is that which relies upon some method of internal consistency. The second most popular method is that which utilizes the scores of other tests as a criterion. One of the least used methods of personality-test construction is that of using criterion groups which have been selected independently of the test to be validated. So far in this volume we have run into this technique only twice—in our discussion of the Strong Vocational Interest Test and in our discussion of the Terman-Miles Masculinity-Femininity Test. We are now to see it used again, however, in the development of the Minnesota Multiphasic Personality Inventory. The authors of this inventory, Hathaway and McKinley, have developed several adjustment questionnaires based directly upon the responses of preselected and carefully defined groups of adjusted and maladjusted individuals.

Development of the Inventory. In the development of their inventory Hathaway and McKinley's first step, as it is of all investigators, was that of collecting a list of suitable items. In their search for items their goals were to secure a varied subject-matter coverage, simpler wording than that in preexisting inventories, and a larger reservoir of items from which different scales could later be constructed. Altogether Hathaway and McKinley collected 1,000 items. Then they edited these items to eliminate duplications and finally ended up with a total of 504 usable items. These items had been suggested by Hathaway and McKinley's own clinical experience, by their reviews of psychiatric examination forms and textbooks on psychiatry, by their reviews of the directions used in case studies, and by their reviews of preexisting personality and adjustment scales. All items were phrased as declarative statements in the first person singular and covered the subjects listed in Table 101.

These items Hathaway and McKinley printed in two forms. In one form they are printed in a booklet with instructions for giving the answers on an IBM answer sheet. In the other form, and this is the original form, the items are printed individually in large type on 3- by 5-inch cards. These cards are divided about equally into two sections, and each group of cards is distinctively marked with a colored stripe along the top edge. The two groups of cards are housed in appropriate file boxes with three guide cards marked: "True," "False," "Cannot Say." After a subject has been tested and after his responses have been recorded, the cards are shuffled so that they will be presented to the next subject in a random order.

Hathaway and McKinley set up this system to eliminate the effect

TABLE 101. *Classification of Items in the Minnesota Multiphasic Personality Inventory* *

Topic	Number of items	Topic	Number of items
1. General health................	9	15. Religious attitudes...........	20
2. General neurologic...........	19	16. Political attitudes (law and	
3. Cranial nerves................	11	order)......................	46
4. Motility and coordination.....	6	17. Social attitudes..............	72
5. Sensibility...................	5	18. Affect, depressive............	32
6. Vasomotor, trophic speech, se-		19. Affect, manic.................	24
cretory......................	10	20. Obsessive, compulsion........	15
7. Cardiorespiratory.............	5	21. Delusions, hallucinations, illu-	
8. Gastro intestinal.............	11	sions, ideas of reference.......	31
9. Genito-urinary...............	6	22. Phobias.....................	29
10. Habits......................	20	23. Sadistic.....................	7
11. Family and marital...........	29	24. Morale......................	33
12. Occupational................	18	25. Is individual trying to place	
13. Educational.................	12	himself in improbably accept-	
14. Sexual attitudes.............	19	able or unacceptable light.....	15

* From Hathaway, S. R., and McKinley, J. C. A multiphasic personality schedule: I. Construction of the schedule. *J. Psychol.*, 1940, **10**, 249–254.

of item position and to facilitate the addition or deletion of items to or from any scale. The directions for taking the test are as follows:

Take the cards out from the front, one at a time and decide whether each is true or not.

If it is *mostly* true about you, put it *behind* the card that says TRUE.

If it is *not mostly* true about you, put it *behind* the card that says FALSE.

If a statement does not apply to you, or is something that you don't know about, put it *behind* the card that says CANNOT SAY.

There are no right or wrong answers.

Remember to give *your* opinion of *yourself*.

There are two boxes in this set.

In order that we may use your results, both boxes must be completed.

To date, Hathaway and McKinley have developed eight scales designed "to assay those traits that are commonly characteristic of disabling psychological abnormality," a scale for masculinity-femininity, and four special validating scales. Of primary importance at this point are the eight diagnostic scales. These are for the measurement of hypochondriasis, symptomatic depression, psychasthenia, hysteria, hypomania, psychopathic deviate, paranoia, and schizophrenia. Each of these scales has been based upon a comparison of item responses between a clinically diagnosed group and a control group of normals. We shall discuss these criterion groups in greater detail later, but here we can point out that they represent as carefully selected criterion groups as have been available for the purposes of personality-test construction. All abnormal criterion groups consist of hospital patients and fall clearly into the classification or clinical syndrome involved. Diagnoses have been made directly by a clinician from a mimeographed symptomatic tabulation sheet or have been made following a review of the records supplied by a neuropsychiatric hospital staff.

Normal controls have been drawn from a variety of sources, but the great majority have been visitors at the hospital and high-school graduates tested at the University of Minnesota testing bureau. They have also included nonpsychiatric patients in the general ward of the hospital.

Hypochondriasis. The first scale which Hathaway and McKinley developed was for hypochondriasis, that is, "abnormal, psychoneurotic concern over bodily health." The criterion groups were 50 clinically selected hypochondriac patients (abnormal group) and two groups of normal controls. These latter groups consisted of 109 adult married males and 153 adult married females (first normal control group) and 265 University of Minnesota freshmen, the great majority of whom were adolescent and single (second normal control group).

Hathaway and McKinley tabulated the responses given by these subjects and determined the percentages of the normal and abnormal groups giving each possible answer to each one of the 504 items. Then they determined the differences between the percentages for the normal and abnormal groups, computed the standard errors of these differences, and determined a critical ratio for each item. Then Hathaway and McKinley eliminated all items which failed to yield a difference twice as large as its own standard error. They also eliminated items for other reasons, one of these other reasons being that the item occurred with greater frequency in the college normal group than in the hypochondriac group. In other instances, the difference seemed to be more closely related to a difference in marital status or in attitude toward children than to the clinically diagnosed disorder of the abnormal criterion group. As might be surmised, Hathaway and McKinley had to revise their scale a number of times before they felt it to be maximally effective. In these revisions they tried various methods of weighting the items, some methods being based upon clinical judgments of importance and other methods being based upon the reliability of the differences between the criterion groups. None of the weighting systems of scoring were found to be better than a simple unit-weighting system, so the latter was adopted. As a result of these procedures, 55 items were selected to comprise the scale for hypochondriasis.

The next step undertaken by Hathaway and McKinley was that of scoring all hospitalized psychiatric cases on the Hypochondriasis scale. Hypochondriacs received, as they should, significant scores. And normals received, as they should, nonsignificant scores. But a large group of psychiatric patients, not hypochondriacs, received high scores. To correct this Hathaway and McKinley selected from the nonhypochondriacs the 50 cases who on the Hypochondriasis scale received the highest scores. They compared the responses of this group with those of the 50 clinically diagnosed hypochondriacs and prepared a new scale differentiating these two groups from each other. In selecting items for this scale, those that were already included in the Hypochondriasis scale were omitted, but from the remainder Hathaway and McKinley retained all items yielding significant differences. Forty-eight items met the criterion of significance and were included in the Hypochondriasis Correction scale.

To determine the final hypochondriacal score, it is necessary to use both the Hypochondriasis and Hypochondriasis Correction scales and to subtract the score on the latter from the score on the former. This score is designated the $H - C_h$ score. What this correction accomplishes is illustrated in Table 102.

The normal control group and the hypochondriac criterion groups are clearly segregated as they should be, and this differentiation holds up on new cases, as shown in the cross-validating groups. Note, however, that the nonhypochondriac groups who secure high scores on the Hypochondriasis scale receive much lower scores on the $H - C_h$ scale. Yet the differentiation on this scale between the two original criterion groups and the two new cross-validating groups is just as satisfactory as on the Hypochondriasis scale alone. It is clearly worth while, argue Hathaway and McKinley (and in view of these data we have no reason to doubt them), to make this correction and to use the $H - C_h$ score as the measure of hypochondriasis.

The logic involved in correcting the original scale by means of a second scale is simple. Psychiatric cases differ from normals, but also differentially diagnosed groups of psychiatric cases differ among themselves. The Hypochondriasis scale differentiates hypochondriacs from normals, but the $H - C_h$ scale is needed to differentiate hypochondriacs from nonhypochondriacal psychiatric patients.

TABLE 102. *Validity Data for Hathaway and McKinley's Hypochondriasis Scales**

Group	Normal	Hypo-chondriac	Critical ratio	$H - C_h$	Critical ratio†
Normal married males.................	123	10.9			
Hypochondriacs (critical cases)..........	50	29.1	15.4	14.3	14.9
C_h group............................	50	26.2	13.0	0.3	4.5
Cross validating groups:					
Hypochondriacs.....................	25	29.1	13.0	14.0	13.1
Symptomatic hypochondriacs.........	28	20.9	5.0	3.6	5.1
High hypochondriasis score without symptomatic hypochondriasis.......	17	22.3	10.4	1.2	3.6

* From McKinley, J. C., and Hathaway, S. R. A multiphasic personality schedule: II. A differential study of hypochondriasis. *J. Psychol.*, 1940, **10**, 255–268.

† Each group compared with normal controls.

Symptomatic Depression. The second scale which McKinley and Hathaway developed was one designed to measure symptomatic depression. Symptomatic depression is, according to Hathaway and McKinley, "a clinically recognizable general frame of mind characterized by a poor morale, lack of hope in the future, and dissatisfaction with the patient's own status generally."

In the development of the Depression scale, Hathaway and McKinley utilized the responses of the following criterion groups:

1. 139 normal married males, age 26 to 43
2. 200 normal married females, age 26 to 43
3. 256 college students
4. 50 carefully selected depressed patients (in the depressed phase of manic-depressive psychosis)

The item responses of the depressed cases were compared with those of the normal controls, and, as in the development of the Hypochondriasis scale, items with a difference twice their standard error were retained. Items showing sex differences were eliminated, however, and this left 70 items. This scale of 70 items was found to make significant differentiation between normal and depressed cases, but some patients not depressed received high depression scores. Therefore two additional criterion groups were selected for study. One of these groups consisted of 50 nondepressed patients with high depression scores, and the other group consisted of 40 depressed normals. Item responses for these groups were tabulated. Then, to be included in the final Depression scale, an item had to show a progressive increase in frequency from normal through depressed normal to depressed psychotics, and the percentage for the non-depressed patients was required to approach that for normals. Sixty items met these criteria and they now constitute the Depression scale. Data on its validity are set forth in Table 103. There is clearly

TABLE 103. *Validity Data for Hathaway and McKinley's Depression Scale**

Group	Number	Mean	Critical ratio†
Criterion	50	36.68	26.9
Test depressed	35	32.49	11.0
Non-depressed	50	28.86	11.8
Symptomatically depressed	223	28.20	19.0
Random psychiatric cases	413	24.44	15.8
Physically ill	229	21.70	8.9
Normals	690	18.14	

* From Hathaway, S. R., and McKinley, J. C. A multiphasic personality schedule: III. The measurement of symptomatic depression. *J. Psychol.*, 1942, **14**, 73–84.

† Each group compared with normal controls.

no question that it differentiates between normal and depressed individuals.

Psychasthenia. This term signifies "individuals whose thinking is characterized by excessive doubt, by compulsions, obsessions, and unreasonable fears; . . . by great doubts as to the meaning of his reactions in what seems to be a hostile environment"; and by "a weakened will that cannot resist the behavior regardless of its maladaptive character."

The criterion groups which Hathaway and McKinley used in the development of this scale were as follows:

1. 139 normal married males, age 26 to 43, and 200 normal married females, age 26 to 43

2. 20 psychasthenia patients

Hathaway and McKinley constructed a preliminary scale by selecting all items that yielded differences with critical ratios of 2.0 or more between the criterion groups. Then they computed tetrachoric correlations between the responses for each item and total

TABLE 104. *Validity Data for Hathaway and McKinley's Psychasthenia Scale**

Group	Number	Mean	Standard deviation	Critical ratio	Percentage equal to or greater than mean of normals
Normals....................	690	11.70	7.7		
Criterion cases.............	20	27.05	9.4	7.2	95
Symptomatic psychiatric.....	50	21.02	9.1	7.1	90
Other psychiatric...........	576	16.15	10.1	8.6	63
Physically ill...............	266	12.12	7.9	0.7	48
College students............	270	7.99	6.0	7.9	28

* From McKinley, J. C., and Hathaway, S. R. A multiphasic personality schedule: IV. Psychasthenia. *J. appl. Psychol.*, 1942, **26**, 614–624.

TABLE 105. *Intercorrelational Data for the Minnesota Multiphasic Personality Inventory**

Group	100 normals			100 psychopathics		
	Hysteria	Hypo-mania	Psycho-pathic deviate	Hysteria	Hypo-mania	Psycho-pathic deviate
Psychopathic deviate............	.37	.49	...	.18	.43	
Hysteria......................	...	.05	.37	.....	−.13	.18
Depression....................	.55	−.02	.29	.68	−.21	.14
Hypochondriasis...............	.52	.28	.42	.71	−.08	.37
Psychasthenia.................	.13	.39	.48	.33	.14	.23
Paranoia.....................	.44	.30	.38	.40	.31	.40
Hypomania...................	.05	.....	.49	−.13	.....	.43
Schizophrenia.................	.28	.56	.60	.23	.36	.31

* From McKinley, J. C., and Hathaway, S. R. The MMPI: V. Hysteria, hypomania, and psychopathic deviate. *J. appl. Psychol.*, 1944, **28**, 153–174.

scores for 100 normals and for 100 "randomly selected psychiatric patients." Then they selected for their final scale all items that yielded a significant correlation in one or the other or in both of these groups. Forty-eight items met their test, and these items now constitute the Psychasthenia scale.

Data relevant to the validity of the Psychasthenia scale are presented in Table 104. The number of psychiatrically diagnosed psychasthenia patients is small, and no cross-validating group was available.

Hysteria, Hypomania, and Psychopathic Deviate. Scales for hysteria, hypomania, and psychopathic deviate were developed in much the same fashion as those already described, so we need not discuss their detailed development. Their intercorrelations with the other scales on the Minnesota Multiphasic Personality Inventory are set forth in Table 105.

SPECIAL VALIDATING SCALES

We have commented before upon the problem of getting honest, objective, and straightforward responses to the items in a personality test. The Minnesota Multiphasic Personality Inventory is, of course, not immune from this problem. Hathaway and McKinley have been well aware of this fact and have attempted to mitigate the seriousness of the problem by developing four special validating scales. These are the Question score (?), the Lie score (L), the Validity score (F), and the Correction score (K). The development of these scales has been rather different from that of the diagnostic scales we have already discussed, so we shall have to give them separate treatment.

The Question Score. This consists of nothing more than the total number of items classified in the "cannot say" category. The average subject will place 30 or fewer items in this category. When the number of items so classified exceeds 30, Hathaway and McKinley feel that the scores on the various diagnostic scales are automatically lowered. And if the number of items classified as "cannot say" is 130 or more, Hathaway and McKinley feel that all of the diagnostic scores must be considered invalid. Hathaway and McKinley's only validation for the Question score consists in their own clinical judgment that subjects with high Question scores do not appear to have responded to the test items in a properly objective manner.

The Lie Score. This score "affords," say Hathaway and McKinley, "a measure of the degree to which the subject may be attempting to falsify his score by always choosing the response that places him in the most acceptable light socially." High Lie scores, according to Hathaway and McKinley, indicate that the scores on the diagnostic scales are too low.

The Lie scale consists of 15 items on which a completely honest person is apt to get a very low score. They are representative of socially desirable situations which are rarely apt to be true. Therefore, when a subject secures a fairly high score on the 15 items in the Lie scale his entire record becomes suspect. Like the Question scale, the only validation for the Lie scale lies in Hathaway and McKinley's clinical judgment.

The Validity Score. This scale is composed of 64 items which are answered infrequently by normal subjects. Therefore a high score is considered as evidence for faking, for careless marking, or as evidence that the subject could not understand the meaning of the items. A low score is considered as evidence that the scores on the diagnostically significant scales are valid. Here again Hathaway and McKinley fail to give us supporting evidence.

The Correction Score. This scale consists of 30 items. Twenty-two of these items Hathaway and McKinley found useful in differentiating clinically diagnosed abnormals with normal profiles from normal control groups. The remaining 8 items were included because they were found to differentiate depressed or schizoid subjects from normal controls. The first of these two groups of items taps, Hathaway and McKinley argue, the test-taking attitude of trying to look better than one actually is, and the second set of 8 items taps the test-taking attitude of trying to look worse than one actually is. The net score, as a result of the operation of these two sets of items, indicates a correction to increase the validity of each of the diagnostic scales. This correction varies for the different scales, being the full amount of the score in two instances, one-half in one instance, four-tenths in another, and two-tenths in another. These corrections are added to the scores on the diagnostic scales and thus augment these latter scores. Thus the tendency of a subject to refrain from indicating undesirable traits is thought to be counterbalanced to some extent by the use of the Correction scale.

That the Correction scale does, in fact, increase the validity of the diagnostic scales was proved by Hathaway and McKinley in the following manner. They selected cases with one or more diagnostic scores of 65 or over but not more than 80. In this group they included the records for 337 clinically diagnosed abnormal cases and

174 normal controls, all with borderline profiles. Then they divided the entire group of 511 cases into two groups. This division was based upon the median correction score, so that 50 per cent of the cases were placed in each of the two groups. This division of cases made it possible for Hathaway and McKinley to identify correctly more than half of both the normal and abnormal groups. The exact percentages of cases correctly identified are as follows:

72 per cent of the normal men
59 per cent of the normal women
61 per cent of the abnormal men
66 per cent of the abnormal women

Some of these percentages may not seem high, but they are all better than chance and appear to increase by a significant margin the accuracy of the diagnoses based upon the scores of the Minnesota Multiphasic Personality Inventory.

9

ADJUSTMENT: PROGNOSTIC APPROACHES

Our discussion in the last chapter centered around diagnostic approaches to the measurement of adjustment. By diagnostic approaches we mean approaches concerned with immediate adjustment and adjustment related to the general mental health of an individual. We want to turn our attention in this chapter to prognostic approaches to the measurement of adjustment. Prognostic approaches are designed to predict adjustment at some future date and, usually, in a defined and specific situation. Thus, we shall discuss adjustment in marriage, adjustment in an individual's occupational calling, and adjustment in military service. We shall be concerned with the prediction of the degree of adjustment in these specific situations before the person has actually entered them. We shall have to concern ourselves also with the measurement of adjustment after the fact, for we need some criterion for the validation of our predictions. Our first two examples of prognostic approaches will be the Burgess and Cottrell, and the Terman, marital-happiness prediction scales. Our third will be the Aptitude Index for predicting success in life insurance selling. And our fourth example will be Shipley and Graham's Personal Inventory for predicting adjustment in military (naval) service.

BURGESS AND COTTRELL

Burgess and Cottrell were interested in determining the extent to which adjustment in marriage could be predicted from a subject's responses to a variety of background and personal-history items. They constructed an adjustment questionnaire to measure adjustment in marriage and a background and personal history questionnaire from which these predictions were to be made, and then they

244

established empirically the extent to which each of the personal-history and background items, and all of these items together, could give forehand knowledge of the score on their marital adjustment scale. In Burgess and Cottrell's own words, they "first sought to define the problem of marriage adjustment; second, to find what factors present at the time of marriage are associated with marital success or failure; and third, to determine whether or not it is possible to devise a method of predicting before marriage its outcome in marital happiness or unhappiness."

Burgess and Cottrell began their study by collecting a large number of personal-history, personality, background, and marital adjustment items. They divided these items into two sets, one including the items of a more personal nature and the other including the items of a less personal nature. It is this latter set that chiefly concerns us, for it was prepared in questionnaire form, and we are to discuss the data secured in response to it.

Subjects. Burgess and Cottrell prepared a preliminary form of this questionnaire and tried it out on 100 subjects before it was made ready for final use. The questionnaire completed, Burgess and Cottrell's next task was to secure subjects. They located these through students, interested individuals, social agencies, the general mail, and apartment-house mailboxes. They distributed over 7,000 copies of their questionnaire and received 1,300 replies. From these replies they selected 526 for intensive study. Of these 526 questionnaires, 153 were completed by the husband, 317 by the wife, 30 were completed together, 15 were completed by the wife or husband with an interviewer's assistance, and 11 were completed in an unknown way. The questionnaires selected for study had to represent:

1. Couples resident in Illinois
2. Couples married more than one year but not more than six years
3. Divorced couples married not more than six years

Of the questionnaires selected for study 80 per cent represented subjects from north European cultural groups, more than half of the questionnaires represented Protestant subjects, and more than half represented college subjects. The great majority represented subjects reared in cities, and 80 per cent represented subjects resident in or near Chicago. Husbands came primarily from the white-collar and professional groups. About one-third of the couples had one child, and the average length of time married (for all couples) was three years. Husbands averaged 26 years in age and wives, 23.

Marital Happiness Scale. The criteria which Burgess and Cottrell set forth as indicative of marital adjustment are agreement between husband and wife on family finances, recreation, religious matters, demonstrations of affection, friends, intimate relations, table manners, matters of conventionality, philosophy of life, and ways of dealing with in-laws; the possession of a substantial number of common interests and activities; frequent overt demonstrations of affection; few complaints; infrequent or no feelings of loneliness, miserliness, irritability, or lack of self-confidence; and an over-all feeling of happiness. Altogether 28 items were involved.

Happiness Ratings. Burgess and Cottrell considered the most basic of these criteria to be the over-all feeling of happiness. Their questionnaire required each respondent to rate the happiness of the marriage (not that of each spouse individually) on a five-step rating scale. The distribution of ratings which they secured is given in Table 106.

TABLE 106. *Distribution of Subjective Happiness Ratings**

Very happy	42.6%
Happy	20.5
Average	14.4
Unhappy	13.5
Very unhappy	8.0
No reply	1.0
Total	100.0%

* From Burgess, E. W., and Cottrell, L. S., Jr. *Predicting Success or Failure in Marriage.* New York: Prentice-Hall Inc., 1939.

How adequate can these ratings be considered? Are they objective? Are they reliable? Are they valid? To answer these questions Burgess and Cottrell compared the distribution in Table 106 with a distribution showing the happiness of parents, compared the rating given by one member of a couple with that assigned by an outsider, compared the rating given by one member of a couple and that assigned by each of two judges who assigned ratings upon the basis of case histories, compared the ratings given by a member of a couple upon two different occasions, and compared the ratings given independently by husband and wife.

The comparison of the distribution of the spouses' happiness ratings with that of parental happiness ratings was apparently intended to "get at" the objectivity of the first distribution of ratings. Burgess and Cottrell found that these two series of ratings did not differ appreciably from each other and took this as evidence supporting the claim of objectivity in the spouses' ratings. We cannot be enthusiastic about this "proof," however, since there is little reason to suppose that halo or error, if present, will not affect both sets of ratings.

The remaining comparisons mentioned in the first of the two foregoing paragraphs are relevant to reliability. Burgess and Cottrell report than 251 husbands and 251 wives provided independent ratings of the happiness of their marriage and that these independent ratings were highly correlated (coefficient of contingency = .80). We cannot accept this evidence uncritically. All that Burgess and Cottrell can mean by independent ratings is that both husband and wife furnished a rating. But the replies were received by mail, and, in most cases, there was no contact with the respondent. Therefore there was no way for Burgess and Cottrell, or for us, to determine the extent of collaboration which may have taken place in making these ratings.

In 272 cases an outsider rated the happiness of the marriage. These ratings correlated .91 on a tetrachoric basis, or .68 on a coefficient of contingency basis, with those furnished by a member of the couples themselves. For 38 couples two judges assigned ratings upon the basis of case histories. Their first ratings (averaged) correlated .86 (tetrachoric) with their second ratings, and .96 (tetrachoric) with those assigned by a member of the couples themselves.

Objections can be raised against the use of happiness ratings as a criterion for marital success or failure. Those specifically listed by Burgess and Cottrell are that marital happiness cannot be defined in an objective manner, that the meaning of marital happiness varies from one person to another, that an individual's own conception of marital happiness varies from day to day, that a marriage may be happy for one spouse and unhappy for the other, that people may not be honest in giving their ratings, and that there is no completely adequate method of checking the reliability and validity of the ratings. In spite of these recognized objections, Burgess and Cottrell argue that the happiness ratings as they secured them can be made to serve a useful purpose.

Table 107. *The Relation of Adjustment Item Responses to Over-all Ratings of Marital Happiness**

Item	Contingency coefficient	Tetrachoric coefficient	Maximum weight
State approximate extent of agreement or disagreement on following items:			
Handling family finances.............................	.50	.69	10
Matters of recreation.............................	.48	.65	10
Religious matters.................................	.28	.38	5
Demonstrations of affection........................	.45	.65	10
Friends...	.47	.60	10
Intimate relations...............................	.50	.61	10
Caring for the baby...............................	.41	.40	
Table manners....................................	.22	.33	5
Matters of conventionality.........................	.43	.51	10
Philosophy of life................................	.48	.62	10
Ways of dealing with in-laws.......................	.46	.66	10
When disagreements arise, they usually result in: husband giving in . . . ; wife giving in . . . ; agreement by mutal give and take . . .	.45	.70	10
Do husband and wife engage in outside interests together: all of them . . . ; some of them . . . ; very few of them . . . ; none of them . . .	.48	.76	10
In leisure time husband prefers: to be on the go . . . ; to stay at home . . . ; wife prefers to be on the go . . . ; to stay at home . . .	.44	.70	10
Do you kiss your husband (wife): every day . . . ; occasionally . . . ; almost never . . .	.45	.69	10
Do you confide in your husband (wife): almost never . . . ; rarely . . . ; in most things . . . ; in everything . . .	.47	.53	10
Do you ever wish you had not married? Frequently . . . ; occasionally . . . ; rarely . . . ; never . . .	.63	.86	15
If you had your life to live over, do you think you would: marry the same person . . . ; marry a different person . . . ; not marry at all . . .	.58	.87	15
What things annoy and dissatisfy you most about your marriage?.................................	.41	.55	10
What things does your husband (wife) do that you don't like?..	.35	.53	7
Do you often feel lonesome, even when you are with other people? Yes . . . No . . . ? . . .	. . .	−.31	1
Are you usually even-tempered and happy in your outlook on life?.......................................	. . .	.30	1
Do you often feel just miserable?.....................	. . .	−.31	1
Does some particular useless thought keep coming into your mind to bother you?........................	. . .	−.30	1
Are you usually in good spirits?......................	. . .	.35	1
Do you often experience periods of loneliness?..........	. . .	−.47	1
Are you in general self-confident about your abilities? . . .	. . .	.27	1

* From Burgess, E. W., and Cottrell, L. S., Jr. *Predicting Success or Failure in Marriage.* New York: Prentice-Hall Inc., 1939.

Adjustment Ratings. But as the ratings stand in Table 106, they cannot be said to yield a very refined series of discriminations. Furthermore, a change of a rating from one step to another would constitute a major variation. To secure a scale capable of making finer discriminations and one on which any given fluctuation would not constitute such a violent change in meaning, Burgess and Cottrell proceeded to compute the correlation between each of the adjustment items and the over-all happiness ratings. These correlations, together with the adjustment items, are given in Table 107.

Item Weights. Next Burgess and Cottrell assigned scoring weights. These are also given in Table 107. The maximum weight for each item was made proportional to its correlation with the happiness ratings, and the other answers were assigned points in accord with the way in which happy and very unhappy ratings were distributed among these answers. A concrete example of this weighting process is given in Table 108.

TABLE 108. *The Assignment of Scoring Weights**

Percentage	Weight	Rating
71.3	15	Never
18.2	4	Rarely
8.0	2	Occasionally
2.5	0	Frequently

* From Burgess, E. W., and Cottrell, L. S., Jr. *Predicting Success or Failure in Marriage.* New York: Prentice-Hall, Inc., 1939.

The weight of 15 was assigned upon the basis of the correlation between the responses to this item and the self-ratings on marital happiness. A value of 4 was assigned to the response "rarely" because the percentage for this response was roughly one-fourth that for the response "never." A value of 2 was assigned to the response "occasionally" because the percentage for this response was roughly one-half that for the response "rarely." According to this scheme it appears logical that the response "frequently" should be assigned a weight of 0.

Third, using the scoring values we have just described, Burgess and Cottrell scored all the questionnaires and used the total scores as their measure of marital adjustment. The distribution of these adjustment scores is given in Table 109.

TABLE 109. *Distribution of Marriage Adjustment Scores for 526 Marriages**

Adjustment scores	Number	Percentage	Cumulative percentage
190–199	19	3.6	100.0
180–189	51	9.7	96.5
170–179	82	15.6	86.8
160–169	74	14.1	71.2
150–159	50	9.5	57.1
140–149	32	6.1	47.6
130–139	41	7.8	41.5
120–129	33	6.3	33.7
110–119	25	4.7	27.4
100–109	20	3.8	22.7
90– 99	23	4.4	18.9
80– 89	19	3.6	14.5
70– 79	16	3.0	10.9
60– 69	21	4.0	7.9
50– 59	12	2.3	3.9
40– 49	5	1.0	1.6
30– 39	2	0.4	0.6
20– 29	1	0.2	0.2
Total.........	526	100.0	

* From Burgess, E. W., and Cottrell, L. S., Jr. *Predicting Success or Failure in Marriage.* New York: Prentice-Hall, Inc., 1939.

A number of correlations pertinent to the evaluation of these adjustment scores are given in Table 110. The first two of these correlations may, perhaps, be considered as measures of reliability, and the third may be considered a measure of validity.

TABLE 110. *Adjustment Score Correlates**

Variables	Number	*r*
Correlation between scores for husband and wife....................	66	.88
Correlation between adjustment scores and happiness ratings.........	68	.95
Correlation between adjustment scores and divorce or separation.....	526	−.89

* From Burgess, E. W., and Cottrell, L. S., Jr. *Predicting Success or Failure in Marriage.* New York: Prentice-Hall, Inc., 1939.

Happiness Prediction Scale. The next step which engaged Burgess and Cottrell's attention was that of determining what premarital data could be utilized as significant predictors of marital adjustment. The search for these predictors led Burgess and Cottrell through questions covering the cultural background of both husband and wife, through questions on their psychogenetic characteristics, through questions on their social characteristics, through questions on economic factors, and through questions on response attitudes and patterns.

For each possible predictor Burgess and Cottrell prepared a scatter diagram to show its relation to the marital adjustment scores. An example is given in Table 111. This table shows the relationship

TABLE 111. *The Relation between Marital Adjustment and Duration of Premarital Acquaintance**

Period of acquaintance	Marital adjustment			Mean adjustment score
	Poor, per cent	Fair, per cent	Good, per cent	
Under six months................	47.0	30.6	22.4	120
Six—twenty-three months.........	37.7	24.6	37.7	132
Two—four years..................	27.8	28.4	43.8	141
Five years and more..............	14.7	32.0	53.3	153
Total........................	28.5	28.3	43.2	

* From Burgess, E. W., and Cottrell, L. S., Jr. *Predicting Success or Failure in Marriage.* New York: Prentice-Hall, Inc., 1939.

between marital adjustment and duration of acquaintance prior to marriage. The adjustment scores are trichotomized into good, fair, and poor scores, and the duration of acquaintance is broken down into four categories. We can read across any row in the table or down any column to find a demonstration of the relationship which the table is intended to portray. For example, we see in the first column that as length of premarital acquaintance increases, the percentage of poorly adjusted couples steadily decreases from 47 to 14.7 per cent. In the third column we see the converse: that the percentage of couples with "good" adjustment steadily increases from 22.4 to 53.3 per cent as length of premarital acquaintance increases. Reading across the table in the top row, we find that the percentages decrease as we go from couples with "poor" adjustment to couples with "good" adjustment. And, in the last row of the table, we find the converse: that the percentages increase as we go from couples with "poor" adjustment to couples with "good" adjustment.

Besides these scatter plots Burgess and Cottrell also computed mean marital adjustment scores for subjects giving each of the possible responses to the various predictor items. Those for the various categories of duration of premarital acquaintance are given in column 4 of Table 111. They steadily increase from a minimum value of 120 to a maximum value of 153 as length of premarital acquaintance increases.

Processing their data in the manner we have just described, Burgess and Cottrell found 35 items with significant predictive value. Of these items, 21 were for husbands and 17 were for wives. Three of the items were useful for both husbands and wives.

Scoring Weights. Burgess and Cottrell's next problem was to assign scoring weights. For each predictor they assigned a maximum value to the response given by the highest proportion of couples with "good" adjustment scores and a value of 0 to the response given by the smallest proportion of couples with "good" adjustment scores. The magnitude of the maximum value was made to approximate the difference between the highest and lowest proportions of couples with "good" adjustment scores, and intermediate values were assigned, say Burgess and Cottrell, "by inspection." In short, this process was very much like the one illustrated in Table 108.

When these weights had been determined, Burgess and Cottrell applied them to their predictor items and derived marital-happiness prediction scores for all of their subjects. These scores were found to have a reliability of .88, measured either by the intercorrelation between the scores for husband and wife or by a test-retest correlation.

Significant Items. Several items which Burgess and Cottrell found to be predictive of marital happiness for men, together with the scoring weights for the alternative responses to them, are given in Table 112. The items for women are so similar in character that their reproduction would constitute a needless duplication.

Validity. Burgess and Cottrell determined the validity of their marital-happiness prediction scores in two ways: by correlating them with the adjustment scores and by comparing the scores secured by divorced, separated, and nondivorced couples.

Correlations with adjustment scores were found to be .51 and .48. The first of these coefficients is based upon cases included in the standardization group, so it cannot be taken seriously. The second coefficient can be accepted, however. It is based upon 155 cases not included in the original group.

Table 113 shows a comparison between the scores of divorced, separated, and nondivorced couples. It is clear that there are sub-

TABLE 112. *Several of the Items in Burgess and Cottrell's Marital Adjustment Prediction Scale for Men**

	Scoring Weight
1. Place in family:	
Only child	0
Oldest child	15
Middle child	20
Youngest child	15
No reply	0
2. Most attached to which sibling:	
Only child	0
No special attachment but has sibling	20
Older brother	20
Older sister	10
Younger brother	15
Younger sister	15
No reply	10
3. Area of residence at time of marriage:	
Chicago rooming house area	0
Chicago area of first settlement	15
Chicago area of second settlement	20
Chicago hotel area	0
Chicago apartment and apartment hotel area	10
Chicago private homes of better class	20
Chicago suburbs	30
Other city	10
Small town not a Chicago suburb	20
Rural	15
No reply	5
4. Education at marriage:	
Grades only	5
High school	0
Professional school but not college	0
College	15
Graduate or professional work beyond college	20
No reply	0

* From Burgess, E. W., and Cottrell, L. S., Jr. *Predicting Success or Failure in Marriage.* New York: Prentice-Hall, Inc., 1939.

stantial differences between the groups and that these differences are in the expected directions.

It is evident that Burgess and Cottrell derived their marital-happiness prediction scores without reference to item intercorrelations. Burgess and Cottrell were well aware that these intercorrelations are important and that it would have been desirable to take them into account. But to do this would have required much more time and effort than Burgess and Cottrell felt they could devote to the problem. Therefore they attempted a compromise by classifying their predictor items into five categories: psychogenetic, cultural

TABLE 113. *Percentage Distribution of Prediction Scores for Those Who Are Divorced, Are Separated, Have Contemplated Divorce or Separation, and Have Not Contemplated Divorce or Separation**

Prediction score	Number	Divorced	Separated	Have contemplated divorce or separation	Have not contemplated divorce or separation
700–779	11	0.0	0.0	9.1	90.9
620–699	68	2.9	0.0	5.9	91.2
540–619	139	2.9	4.3	6.5	86.3
460–539	173	13.9	15.0	13.9	57.2
380–459	100	25.0	17.0	16.0	42.0
300–379	41	34.2	21.9	21.9	21.9
220–299	8	50.0	37.5	12.5	0.0
Total..........	540	73	61	64	342

* From Burgess, E. W., and Cottrell, L. S., Jr. *Predicting Success or Failure in Marriage.* New York: Prentice-Hall, Inc., 1939.

impress, social type, economic role, and response patterns, and by computing the intercorrelations among these five categories of items rather than those among all individual items. The intercorrelations among these five groups of items are given in Table 114. Burgess and Cottrell used these intercorrelations and the correlation of each group of items with the marital adjustment scores to determine a multiple correlation. This multiple correlation turned out to be .56

TABLE 114. *Intercorrelations of Scores among Five Prediction Areas**

Prediction areas	Psycho-genetic	Cultural impress	Social type	Economic role
Cultural impress............	.30			
Social type................	.45	.47		
Economic role..............	.29	.32	.53	
Response patterns..........	.30	.32	.42	.34

* From Burgess, E. W., and Cottrell, L. S., Jr. *Predicting Success or Failure in Marriage.* New York: Prentice-Hall, Inc., 1939.

and represents only a slight increase over the value of .51 previously reported.

Contingency Factors. Burgess and Cottrell point out that there are a number of factors not included either in their adjustment scale or in their prediction scale that influence the happiness of a marriage. These factors are called contingency factors and take place or occur after marriage. Such items are number of years married, size of community, distance of residence from Chicago, characteristics of neighborhood, type of residence (number of rooms, and whether home is owned, is being rented, or is being purchased), amount of rent, changes in residence, relatives (living with them or not, and visits to or from), children (number of, and desire for), average length of employment in each position held since marriage, extent of unemployment, and financial status.

Burgess and Cottrell found that all items except "residence after marriage with relatives, number of rooms in residence and monthly rent per room" were significant in relation to marital adjustment. Therefore it is important for us to realize that individuals having the same marital-happiness prediction scores may end up with different marital adjustment scores, and this by itself can be taken in no way as evidence for lack of validity in the prediction scores. One person may run into one set of contingency factors and a second person may run into a second set, and these two sets of contingency factors operate to produce a difference in what had originally been predicted to be equal degrees of marital adjustment. Burgess and Cottrell content themselves with discussing this problem but do not make any attempt to include the effects of contingency factors in their predictions of adjustment from their marital happiness scale.

TERMAN

Our second example of a prognostic approach to the measurement of adjustment also lies in the field of marital happiness. It consists of the scale developed by Terman and his collaborators at Stanford University. We shall find that Terman's study differs in several important respects from Burgess and Cottrell's study, and it will be important for us to evaluate these differences from the standpoint of personality measurement. Before we can make these evaluations, however, we must review the steps involved in Terman's study.

Terman, like Burgess and Cottrell, was interested in the measurement and prediction of marital happiness. "We have selected as the theme of our study," says Terman, "that aspect of the successful marriage which may be designated as marital happiness, and we wish to ascertain, if possible, what psychological factors are demonstrably associated with this state."

This purpose necessitates, as it did in Burgess and Cottrell's study, a measure of marital happiness. This measure of happiness must be used as the standard to which all premarital predictor items must be related. Terman borrowed most of his items from the marital adjustment scale constructed by Burgess and Cottrell. Thus Terman's criteria of marital happiness are "subjective ratings of the happiness of the marriage, and factual information on husband-wife agreement or disagreement about various matters, on methods used in resolving disagreements, on specific things in the marriage that are unsatisfactory, on regret over the choice of a mate, and on consideration that may have been given to separation or divorce." The way Terman requested these ratings (from his respondents) differed in only minor ways from those used by Burgess and Cottrell.

Terman, in the opening chapter of his book *Psychological Factors in Marital Happiness*, lists several points of methodological technique which require consideration. These are that the researcher be fully cognizant of the pitfalls of sampling, of the fact that he must design his questionnaire to elicit the kind of information that a respondent will be willing to give, of the importance of getting complete answers from each subject, of the necessity of securing data in a way that makes them amenable to statistical treatment, and last, but certainly not least, of the caution and care needed in the interpretation of his findings.

Terman's questionnaire was divided into seven parts. Part I consisted of 71 items taken from the Bernreuter Personality Inventory. Part II consisted of 128 items taken from the Strong Vocational Interest Test. Part III consisted of 34 opinion items. Part IV consisted of the items used as the criterion index of marital happiness. Part V consisted of 12 items of childhood background. Part VI consisted of 50 items relevant to sex adjustment. And Part VII consisted of 25 miscellaneous items.

Subjects. Terman secured his data through personal contact. The general procedure was for Terman, or for one of his associates, to give a talk at a parent-teacher or other civic gathering, to explain the purpose of the study, and to ask for volunteers to stay after the talk to complete the questionnaires.

Terman assured his subjects of complete anonymity and guaranteed this anonymity. First, he explained to the subjects that the schedules could be completed by drawing circles around preprinted answers or by inserting check marks in appropriate places—the point being that no telltale handwriting would be required. Second, the schedules were not to be signed. Third, all schedules were to be mingled with hundreds of others so that the identity of each schedule would be lost in the general calculations. Subjects were asked to come to the front of the lecture-room (husband and wife were to come forward together) and to take any envelope they chose out of a large basket marked A. This envelope contained two smaller unsealed envelopes with one schedule for the husband and one for the wife. The husband took his envelope and schedule to one side of the room, and the wife took her envelope and schedule to the other side of the room. When the husband completed his schedule, he inserted it in the appropriate envelope and sealed it. The wife did the same thing with hers. Then both husband and wife came to the front of the room, put their two sealed envelopes together in a larger envelope, sealed this larger envelope, and dropped it into a basket marked B. This procedure assured anonymity, prevented collaboration, and made it possible to keep the schedules of a husband-wife pair together. Terman justifiably claims that no other investigator has availed himself of a technique so airtight with respect to the prevention of collaboration and to the assurance of anonymity to the respondents.

Terman secured completed schedules from 792 couples. These couples came from the middle and upper-middle class of urban and semiurban Californians. Over 50 per cent of the husbands were employed in business or in the professions. The average school grade completed was 14, and 48 per cent of the husbands and 38 per cent of the wives had graduated from college. The mean age of the husbands was 39 and that of the wives was 36. The average length of time married was slightly more than eleven years but one-third of the couples still had no children.

Marital Happiness Scale. The items which Terman used as a basis for constructing a criterion index of marital happiness are presented in Table 115. We also give in this table the scoring weights

TABLE 115. *Distributions of Answers to Questions in Terman's Marital Happiness Scale**

Item	Husbands	Wives	Weight
Do you and your wife (husband) engage in outside interests together?			
All of them	13.7	19.8	7
Most of them	54.6	55.9	5
Some of them	26.7	18.7	3
Very few of them	4.9	4.4	1
None of them	0.1	1.2	0
Approximate extent of agreement or disagreement on:			
Handling family finances			
Always agree	29.2	34.6	8†
Almost always agree	46.8	44.2	6
Occasionally disagree	19.6	14.0	4
Frequently disagree	3.5	5.3	2
Almost always disagree	0.5	1.1	1
Always disagree	0.4	0.8	0
Matters of recreation			
Always agree	19.2	24.1	
Almost always agree	57.8	53.1	
Occasionally disagree	18.1	18.6	
Frequently disagree	4.2	2.9	
Almost always disagree	0.6	1.0	
Always disagree	0.1	0.3	
Religious matters			
Always agree	46.6	49.6	
Almost always agree	38.1	34.6	
Occasionally disagree	10.9	11.1	
Frequently disagree	2.7	2.8	
Almost always disagree	0.8	0.8	
Always disagree	0.9	1.1	
Demonstrations of affection			
Always agree	31.4	40.0	
Almost always agree	44.1	38.7	
Occasionally disagree	17.1	14.8	
Frequently agree	5.1	4.7	
Almost always disagree	1.8	1.3	
Always disagree	0.5	0.5	
Friends			
Always agree	21.4	29.4	
Almost always agree	50.8	44.6	
Occasionally disagree	22.8	21.8	
Frequently disagree	4.2	3.4	
Almost always disagree	0.4	0.4	
Always disagree	0.4	0.4	

TABLE 115. *Distributions of Answers to Questions in Terman's Marital Happiness Scale.* * (Continued)*

Item	Husbands	Wives	Weight
Caring for the children			
Always agree	25.7	31.2	
Almost always agree	46.9	41.6	
Occasionally disagree	21.8	21.4	
Frequently disagree	4.4	4.4	
Almost always disagree	0.9	1.0	
Always disagree	0.3	0.3	
Table manners			
Always agree	36.4	41.6	
Almost always agree	42.5	36.1	
Occasionally disagree	17.4	17.5	
Frequently disagree	3.0	3.9	
Almost always disagree	0.4	0.6	
Always disagree	0.3	0.3	
Matters of conventionality			
Always agree	23.9	29.8	
Almost always agree	47.9	42.8	
Occasionally disagree	23.3	21.3	
Frequently disagree	4.2	5.1	
Almost always disagree	0.6	0.4	
Always disagree	0.1	0.6	
Philosophy of life			
Always agree	25.3	32.0	
Almost always agree	48.7	43.3	
Occasionally disagree	20.8	17.3	
Frequently disagree	4.1	5.1	
Almost always disagree	0.8	1.8	
Always disagree	0.8	0.9	
When disagreements arise, they usually result in:			
You giving in	14.9	16.0	0
Your wife (husband) giving in	3.8	4.7	2
Mutual give and take	81.3	79.3	5
Do you ever regret your marriage?			
Frequently	3.4	3.5	0
Occasionally	12.4	12.8	4
Rarely	28.9	25.3	7
Never	55.3	58.4	10
If you had your life to live over do you think you would:			
Marry the same person	82.7	86.1	10
Marry a different person	10.1	10.4	0
Not marry at all	7.2	3.5	0
Have you ever seriously contemplated separation?			
Yes	16.3	21.0	0‡
No	83.7	79.0	8§

TABLE 115. *Distributions of Answers to Questions in Terman's Marital Happiness Scale.* (Continued)*

Item	Husbands	Wives	Weight
Have you ever seriously contemplated divorce?			
Yes	8.8	11.5	
No	91.2	88.5	
Everything considered, how happy has your marriage been?			
Extraordinarily happy	29.5	34.6	15
Decidedly more happy than average	36.8	35.9	12
Somewhat more happy than average	16.3	14.7	9
About average	12.9	9.2	6
Somewhat less happy than average	2.9	3.0	3
Decidedly less happy than average	1.6	1.8	0
Extremely unhappy	0.1	0.8	0
If your marriage is now unhappy, how long has that been true?			
Unanswered	92.1	90.6	11
One year or more specified	7.9	9.4	0
Complaint score (computed by counting 1 for each annoyance circled 1 and 2 for each annoyance circled 2. Annoyances circled 0 not counted)‖			
0	38.2	43.1	13
1– 2	22.4	20.3	11
3– 9	20.5	22.1	9
10–19	13.0	8.7	6
20–29	3.9	3.2	3
30 or over	2.0	2.6	0

* From Terman, L. M. *Psychological Factors in Marital Happiness.* New York: McGraw-Hill Book Company, Inc., 1938.

† These weights were assigned in accord with the average amount of agreement on this and the following nine items.

‡ A weight of 0 was assigned for an answer of "Yes" to this *or* the following question.

§ A weight of 8 was assigned for an answer of "No" to *both* this and the following question.

‖ The instructions preceding the list of complaints called for circling of "0" if the thing mentioned was present in the marriage but had not interfered with happiness, "1" if the thing had made the marriage less happy than it should be, and "2" for things that had done most to make the marriage unhappy.

and the distribution of answers among the alternate item-response categories. The items show variable intercorrelations with each other, ranging from a low of .22 to a high of .84. Their average intercorrelation is .57. These intercorrelations make it evident that some factor underlies all items, and this common factor Terman assumes is, of course, the variable *marital happiness.*

Item Weights. To weight the items for scoring, two criteria were considered: "the average magnitude of the correlation of the item with each of the other eight items, and the size of the husband-wife correlation for the item in question." Terman says that "items which showed the highest intercorrelation received greatest weight on the supposition that they were most heavily saturated with the general happiness factor and hence more valid indicators of the trait to be measured. Account was taken of the husband-wife correlation on the ground that this was a rough indication of reliability."

Scoring values were assigned to the various response categories in such a way that the standard deviations of the distribution of answers would be proportional to the weight desired. When the blanks for the 792 couples were scored with the weights given in Table 115, the distributions presented in Table 116 were obtained.

TABLE 116. *Distribution of Happiness Scores**

Happiness score	Husbands	Wives
85–87	72	101
80–84	138	172
75–79	161	143
70–74	116	96
65–69	68	66
60–64	50	40
55–59	39	32
50–54	41	33
45–49	23	15
40–44	14	17
35–39	16	17
30–34	13	13
25–29	10	10
20–24	10	5
15–19	10	12
10–14	7	7
5– 9	3	10
0– 4	1	3

* From Terman, L. M. *Psychological Factors in Marital Happiness*. New York: McGraw-Hill Book Company, Inc., 1938.

These distributions are decidedly nonnormal in appearance. There is a great preponderance or piling-up of the scores at the upper (happy) ends of the distribution.

Nonnormality. Terman discusses three possible causes of this nonnormality. First, he posits inequality of the scale units at different parts of the scale. To explain the skewness, this would require the assumption that the "units of happiness" at the upper end of the scale are much broader than those at the lower end of the scale. This would make for a bunching of the top ratings and for a spreading of the poorer ratings. This inequality of scale unit cannot, of course, be proved, but it is assumed upon the basis of a fact in psychophysics: that the units of a psychological measuring scale are proportional to the number of cases falling within it. When a trait is distributed in a normal manner, we require fewer cases at each extreme than we do in the middle part of the range in order to indicate a unit of equal length. Therefore when we see a bunching up, as we do in the marital happiness distributions, we assume that the intervals in part of the distribution are not sufficiently narrow in scope to allow for an adequate differentiation among the individuals in question.

The second factor Terman mentions is that of selection. Normal distributions are to be expected only for sample populations drawn at random with respect to the variable being investigated. In the present case this has not been done. Terman's subjects, for the most part, were secured via the medium of lecture and group meetings. Since both husband and wife were to participate, it was necessary that both be in attendance at the meeting. The only couples who attend such meetings are those sufficiently well adjusted to each other to attend group functions together. Thus the proportion of seriously unhappy marriages represented in Terman's sample is undoubtedly far short of that in the general population.

The third factor Terman mentions is generosity. This tendency is present in almost every rating scheme that has been devised. And this is particularly true when one has the task of rating himself. There is certainly no reason to suppose that this factor has not contributed its share in the skewness of the marital happiness distributions.

Item Correlations. The extent to which each item in the happiness scale makes a contribution to it can be seen by reference to the correlations presented in Table 117. This table shows the extent to which each item correlates with total happiness scores. To keep these correlations from containing a spurious element, the part of the total score due to the item in question was subtracted from it, so that the correlation between an item and the total score indicates

TABLE 117. *Correlations between Marital Happiness Scores and Responses to Individual Items**

Item	Husband	Wife	Combined
Degree of outside interests in common:			
Husband's answer	.45	...	.43
Wife's answer	...	.56	.51
Degree of agreement on:			
Family finances			
Husband's answer	.41	...	.40
Wife's answer	...	.47	.44
Recreation			
Husband's answer	.46	...	.43
Wife's answer	...	.52	.49
Religion			
Husband's answer	.30	...	.30
Wife's answer	...	.40	.39
Demonstrations of affection			
Husband's answer	.58	...	.53
Wife's answer	...	.60	.60
Friends			
Husband's answer	.45	...	.43
Wife's answer	...	.50	.49
Care of children			
Husband's answer	.45	...	.41
Wife's answer	...	.53	.50
Table manners			
Husband's answer	.38	...	.36
Wife's answer	...	.42	.38
Matters of convention			
Husband's answer	.40	...	.38
Wife's answer	...	.44	.39
Philosophy of life			
Husband's answer	.45	...	.42
Wife's answer	...	.57	.52
Dealing with in-laws			
Husband's answer	.40	...	.36
Wife's answer	...	.40	.38
Average degree of agreement on above 10 items			
Husband's answer	.54	...	.53
Wife's answer	...	.63	.60
Degree of reciprocity in settling disputes			
Husband's answer	.49		
Wife's answer	...	.53	
Combined answer	...	...	.49
Lack of regret over marriage			
Husband's answer	.76	...	.80
Wife's answer	...	.79	.84

TABLE 117. *Correlations between Marital Happiness Scores and Responses to Individual Items.* (Continued)*

Item	Husband	Wife	Combined
Satisfaction with choice of mate			
Husband's answer...............................	.82		
Wife's answer......................................	...	.82	
Combined answer.................................	...	...	.85
No contemplation of separation or divorce			
Husband's answer...............................	.76		
Wife's answer......................................	...	.82	
Combined answer.................................	...	...	.74
Degree of happiness of marriage (self-rating)			
Husband's answer...............................	.76	...	.73
Wife's answer......................................	...	.78	.75
No admission of unhappiness			
Husband's answer...............................	.80		
Wife's answer......................................	...	.83	
Combined answer.................................	...	...	.85
Total of husband's complaints......................	.66	...	.62
Total of wife's complaints.........................	...	.72	.69
Sum total of husband's and wife's complaints..........	.67	.68	.81

* From Terman, L. M. *Psychological Factors in Marital Happiness.* New York: McGraw-Hill Book Company, Inc., 1938.

its correlation with that part of the total score not due to the item in question.

Terman found that the correlation between the marital happiness ratings and the marital happiness scores was .76 for husbands and .78 for wives. These are both lower than the value of .95 reported by Burgess and Cottrell. This discrepancy can be attributed to two facts: a tetrachoric coefficient, the type used by Burgess and Cottrell, usually provides a higher estimate than a Pearson correlation, and in the Burgess and Cottrell study the basic criterion consisted of nothing more than the happiness ratings. In Terman's study the items were included or excluded upon the basis of their intercorrelation with *all* other items in the scale, not alone upon the basis of their correlation with the marital happiness ratings.

Terman gives three reasons for not wishing to accept self-happiness ratings as a sole or chief criterion. These are the known unreliability of such ratings, the complex character of the variable being rated, and the extreme skewness in the distribution. Terman felt, as did Burgess and Cottrell, that a greater number of discriminations, that more normal distributions, and that greater score reliability would be secured by using data concerning areas of agreement and disagreement, satisfaction and dissatisfaction, and so forth, in addition to the happiness ratings.

Terman derived and used throughout his study separate happiness scores for husbands and wives. This contrasts with the technique of Burgess and Cottrell, who concerned themselves with the happiness of the marriage and not with that of each individual partner. Terman found a correlation of .59 between the happiness scores of husbands and wives. Thus, either the scale cannot be considered a very reliable index of the happiness of a marriage (*à la* Burgess and Cottrell) or else the happiness of the two spouses can vary in considerable degree.

The next step after the construction of the marital happiness index was the determination of its personality, background, and sexual correlates. The ways in which the values of these correlates were determined differ from one area to another, so we shall have to discuss them separately.

Personality Correlates. Terman investigated 233 personality variables. Of these variables, 71 were taken from the Bernreuter Personality Inventory, 128 were taken from the Strong Vocational Interest Test, and the remaining 34 items were designed to gain knowledge of opinions about the ideal marriage. As we already know, the Bernreuter items can be answered by "Yes," "No," or " ?," and the Strong items by L, I, or D. The opinion items, which are new to us, allowed for five alternative responses.

The first step in the analysis of the personality correlates of marital happiness consisted in the picking of two matched criterion groups of happy and unhappy couples. The first group selected were the 150 couples with the lowest combined happiness scores. Then 300 happy couples were matched with these 150 unhappy couples. These 300 couples had, of course, high happiness scores, but they were selected to have the same average age, the same average number of years married, the same average number of years of schooling, and the same average occupational status as the 150 unhappy couples. The husbands in each group averaged 39 years in age and the wives 36. Both groups had been married, on the average (median), for eleven years and had had a little over fourteen years of schooling. This matching made it certain that differences in the personality correlates to be investigated could not be attributed to differences in age, length of time married, education, or occupation.

Terman studied his personality variables in two ways. He compared the happy and unhappy groups with respect to the proportion of each group giving answers in different item-response categories, and he compared the tetrachoric correlations expressing husband-wife agreement in the happy group with those in the unhappy group. The data in Table 118 illustrate how these techniques of

TABLE 118. *Analysis of Personality Items**

Item	Happy	Unhappy	Critical ratio	Weight
Do you prefer a play to a dance?				
Husbands:				
Yes.........................	74.3	63.3	2.4	1
No..........................	19.0	26.0	−1.6	
Wives:				
Yes.........................	72.0	58.0	2.9	1
No..........................	21.7	30.0	−1.9	
Husband-wife correlation...........	.58	.08	.....	2

* From Terman, L. M. *Psychological Factors in Marital Happiness.* New York: McGraw-Hill Book Company, Inc., 1938.

comparison were applied. We find, in this table, that the proportion of couples preferring a play to a dance is greater for happy couples than it is for unhappy couples, and that husband-wife agreement is greater for happy couples than it is for unhappy couples.

Terman retained for his marital happiness prediction scale all items yielding one or more critical ratios of 1.5 or more. This critical ratio could refer to the difference in proportions of the couples giving a designated item response or to the difference between the husband-wife agreement correlations. Terman assigned two series of scoring weights. One was based upon the critical ratios for the difference between proportions and the other was based upon the husband-wife agreement correlations. In each series these weights were three in number (0, 1, and 2), so the total possible range of weights varied from 0 to 4.

Terman generally assigned a weight of 0 when the critical ratio was below 1.5, a weight of 1 when it was between 1.5 and 2.9, and a weight of 2 when the critical ratio was 3.0 or higher. The assignment of these weights was not carried out in a strictly mechanical manner, however, as Terman tempered many of them with his own common-sense judgment.

Terman retained 132 of the 233 personality items for his prediction scale. There were 54 Bernreuter items, 54 Strong interest items, and 24 opinion items. From these items Terman prepared the following characterizations of the temperaments of happy and unhappy husbands and of happy and unhappy wives.

Happily Married Men. Happily married men show evidence of an even and stable emotional tone. Their most characteristic reaction to others is that of cooperation. This is reflected in their attitudes toward business superiors, with whom they work well; in their attitude toward women, which reflects equalitarian ideals; and in their benevolent attitudes toward inferiors and underprivileged. In a gathering of people they tend to be unself-conscious and somewhat extroverted. As compared with unhappy husbands, they show superior initiative, a greater tendency to take responsibility, and greater willingness to give close attention to detail in their daily work. They like methodological procedures and methodical people. In money matters they are saving and cautious. Conservative attitudes are strongly characteristic of them. They usually have a favorable attitude toward religion and strongly uphold the sex mores and other social conventions.

Unhappily Married Men. Unhappy husbands, on the other hand, are inclined to be moody and somewhat neurotic. They are prone to feelings of social inferiority, dislike being conspicuous in public, and are highly reactive to social opinion. This sense of social insecurity is often compensated by domineering attitudes in relationships where they feel superior. They take pleasure in commanding roles over business dependents and women, but they withdraw from a situation which would require them to play an inferior role or to compete with superiors. They often compensate this withdrawal by daydreams and power fantasies. More often than happy husbands they are sporadic and irregular in their habits of work, dislike detail and the methodical attitude, dislike saving money, and like to wager. They more often express irreligious attitudes and are more inclined to radicalism in sex morals and politics.

Happily Married Women. Happily married women, as a group, are characterized by kindly attitudes toward others and by the expectation of kindly attitudes in return. They do not easily take offense and are not unduly concerned about the impressions they make upon others. They do not look upon social relationships as rivalry situations. They are cooperative, do not object to subordinate roles, and are not annoyed by advice from others. Missionary and ministering attitudes are frequently evidenced in their responses. They enjoy activities that bring educational or pleasurable opportunities to others and like to do things for the dependent or underprivileged. They are methodical and painstaking in their work, attentive in detail, and careful in regard to money. In religion, morals, and politics they tend to be conservative and conventional. Their expressed attitudes imply a quiet self-assurance and a decidedly optimistic outlook upon life.

Unhappily Married Women. Unhappily married women, on the other hand, are characterized by emotional tenseness and by ups and downs of moods. They give evidence of deep-seated inferiority feelings to which they react by aggressive attitudes rather than by timidity. They are inclined to be irritable and dictatorial. Compensatory mechanisms resulting in restive striving are common. These are seen in the tendency of the unhappy wives to be active "joiners," aggressive in business, and overanxious in social life. They strive for wide circles of acquaintances but are more concerned with being important than with being liked. They are ego-centric and little interested in benevolent and welfare activities, except in so far as these offer opportunities for personal recognition. They also like activities that are fraught with opportunities for romance. They are more inclined to be conciliatory in their attitudes toward men than toward women and show little of the sex antagonism that unhappily married men exhibit. They are impatient and fitful workers, dislike cautious or methodical people, and dislike types of work that require methodical and painstaking effort. In politics, religion, and social ethics they are more often radical than happily married women.

Background Correlates. The background items which Terman investigated as possible predictors of marital happiness are given in Table 119.

TABLE 119. *Background Items Investigated by Terman*

1. Husband's occupation
2. Income
3. Presence or absence of children
4. Present age
5. Length of marriage
6. Age at marriage
7. Age differences
8. Number of years of schooling
9. Differences in years of schooling
10. Relative mental ability
11. Acquaintance before marriage
12. Length of engagement
13. Marital happiness of parents
14. Sibling relationships
15. Conflict with and attachment to parents
16. Physical appearance of parents
17. Childhood happiness
18. Home discipline and punishment
19. Religious training
20. Sex education
21. Childhood curiosity about sex
22. Premarital attitudes toward sex
23. Sexual shock
24. Age of first menstruation
25. Adolescent petting
26. Association with opposite sex during adolescence
27. Desire to be of opposite sex

For most of these items the relation to marital happiness was determined by the critical ratio technique, but, in addition, for many of the items Terman computed a tetrachoric or Pearsonian coefficient of correlation. Most of the items have predictive value, if they have predictive value at all, at a very low level. And therefore most of the items listed above need not be discussed. We shall pick out some of the more important items, however, and use them to illustrate the types of analyses which were involved.

Length of Marriage. Table 120 shows the mean happiness scores of husbands and wives according to number of years married. It starts at values of 73 for husbands and 74 for wives and drops to values of 65 for husbands and 67 for wives for six to eight years and then gradually increases for twenty-five years or more. These trends appear to be reasonable and to be in accord with our common-sense judgment that the honeymoon years should be happier than those several years later but that after this initial decline there should be greater understanding and happiness which should mature through the years. There is, then, a relationship between happiness and

TABLE 120. *Mean Happiness Scores According to Length of Marriage**

Years	Number	Husband	Wife
0– 2............	110	73.0	74.2
3– 5............	103	68.5	69.2
6– 8............	142	65.1	66.9
9–11............	92	68.4	69.0
12–14............	116	67.7	68.5
15–17............	73	65.9	65.5
18–20............	64	67.6	67.4
21–23............	32	71.3	69.9
24–26............	26	68.9	70.5
27 or over.........	34	69.4	70.3

* From Terman, L. M. *Psychological Factors in Marital Happiness.* New York: McGraw-Hill Book Company, Inc., 1938.

length of marriage which the correlation coefficients of −.03 and .05 do not reveal. This is because the relationship is *curvilinear*, and for such relationships Pearsonian coefficients of correlation are not appropriate. To note what we mean by a curvilinear relationship, let us first understand that a linear relationship demands a steady and consistent change in one direction on one variable for corresponding changes on the other. In the present case a linear relationship would mean a consistent and steady increase or decrease in happiness scores for each additional year of marriage. Instead of this we find an initial decline followed by a more gradual increase in mean scores for each additional year of marriage. In other words the relationship is consistent, but the direction changes. This is what we mean by a nonlinear or a curvilinear relationship.

Schooling. Terman finds that amount of schooling is related to marital happiness scores as follows:

Husband's schooling with his own happiness.......... .06
Husband's schooling with wife's happiness............ .17
Wife's schooling with her own happiness.............. .07
Wife's schooling with husband's happiness............ .05

When these correlations are divided by their respective standard errors, it is found that the correlation for husband's schooling with wife's happiness is the only significant one. This suggested to Terman the comparison presented in Table 121.

TABLE 121. *Mean Happiness Scores According to Relative Amount of Schooling*

Schooling of husband	Husband	Wife [*]
Five or more years greater...........	68.3	72.0
Five or more years less..............	67.8	62.8
Critical ratio of difference...........	0.2	3.0

* From Terman, L. M. *Psychological Factors in Marital Happiness.* New York: McGraw-Hill Book Company, Inc., 1938.

Thus the schooling of a husband is, again, found to be unrelated to his own happiness but significantly related to that of his wife. Wives whose husbands have had five or more years less schooling than they themselves have had tend to be significantly less happy than wives whose husbands have had five or more years more schooling than they have had.

Our point in mentioning this item is to show that even though a difference is significant it must still be interpreted. And in this instance Terman interprets this difference as not due to the effect of schooling difference per se. He considers that the schooling difference reflects a difference in relative mental ability between spouses and that it is this latter factor which is the better explanation of the results. Let us consider the data relevant to this hypothesis.

Relative Mental Ability. Each spouse was asked to indicate whether the other spouse was equal to the rater in mental ability or possessed more or less mental ability than the rater. Obviously these ratings were subject to the usual types of error, but certain consistencies, nevertheless, emerge. The optimum state of marital happiness, that is, both partners being equally happy, occurs when they are equal to each other in mental ability. When there is a difference in mental ability, the partner of superior ability tends to be less happy than the partner of lesser mental ability.

Marital Happiness of Parents. The marital happiness of parents correlates .25 and .21 with the happiness of the present marriage. These correlations are clearly significant, although moderate, and are consistent with the mean scores presented in Table 122. We

TABLE 122. *Mean Happiness Scores According to Rated Happiness of Parents' Marriage**

Rated happiness of parent	Number	Husband	Number	Wife
Extraordinarily happy	83	76.1	90	73.2
Decidedly more happy than average	163	73.3	129	71.8
Somewhat more happy than average	91	66.8	78	71.8
About average	182	65.4	165	69.9
Somewhat less happy than average	53	63.6	66	63.9
Decidedly less happy than average	39	58.3	55	62.9
Extremely unhappy	40	65.6	67	61.0

* From Terman, L. M. *Psychological Factors in Marital Happiness.* New York: McGraw-Hill Book Company, Inc., 1938.

present these data to show the remarkable consistency in trend to which a fairly moderate degree of correlation can give rise.

Oedipus Complex. We should like to show now a type of analysis taking into account the interrelationships of two factors with each other and their individual and joint relationships to marital happiness. This is the type of data subject to treatment by partial or multiple correlation or by the analysis of variance. But we have in mind here a simpler type of analysis and one which can be used by a person not versed in some of the more advanced statistical techniques. The data we shall discuss are the rated attractiveness of the opposite sex parent, the rated resemblance between the opposite sex parent and the spouse, and the marital happiness of the rater. The data we shall discuss are presented in Table 123.

The arrangement of the table shows that the first thing necessary is the preparation of a scatter plot designed to show the relation between the rated attractiveness of the opposite sex parent and the rated resemblance between the opposite sex parent and spouse. Then, having prepared such a table and knowing the number of cases in each cell, and their identity, we must compute the mean happiness scores for the cases represented. This done, we are in a

TABLE 123. *Mean Happiness Scores According to Rated Attractiveness of Opposite Sex Parent and Rated Resemblance between Spouse and Opposite Sex Parent**

	Resemblance between wife and mother			
	Very close	Some	None	Opposite types
Husband's rating of mother:				
Exceptionally attractive..........	68	63	71	69
Above average...................	63	70	70	66
Just average....................	68	68	70	68
Below average..................	8	..	65	60
	Resemblance between husband and father			
Wife's rating of father:				
Exceptionally attractive........	78	72	75	61
Above average................	74	72	69	66
Just average..................	54	74	69	69
Below average................	..	39	67	72

* From Terman, L. M. *Psychological Factors in Marital Happiness.* New York: McGraw-Hill Book Company, Inc., 1938.

position to discover and to study the relationship between rated attractiveness of opposite sex parent and marital happiness, with influence of rated resemblance of opposite sex parent to spouse held constant; rated resemblance of opposite sex parent to spouse and marital happiness, with influence of rated attractiveness of opposite sex parent held constant; and joint relation of rated attractiveness of opposite sex parent and rated resemblance of opposite sex parent to spouse and marital happiness.

First, we can study the mean happiness scores in each column and see how they vary with differing degrees of attractiveness of the opposite sex parent. In the first column (that for very close resemblance between opposite sex parent and spouse) we see that mean happiness scores decline as attractiveness declines. This same trend holds for the second column and also for the third. We discover in the column for opposite types, however, that the trend is reversed. Next, we can follow the mean happiness scores across by rows and find that for the first three rows the greater the resemblance between opposite sex parent and spouse, the greater the marital happiness. But for the last row (when the opposite sex parent is rated below average in attractiveness) the trend is reversed. To consider the joint relation between rated attractiveness of opposite sex parent and rated resemblance of opposite sex parent to spouse, let us start with the highest mean we can find. This is 78 in the upper left-hand cell. In other words, the happiest wives are those whose fathers were exceptionally attractive and whose husbands resemble these fathers very closely. As we go down the column from the first cell or as we go across the row, we find that the happiness scores decrease. In other words, from the optimum condition a lessening in either the attractiveness of the father or in the resemblance between husband and father, a lessening also in the happiness of the wives concerned. This finding is consistent with that which we reach by starting with the mean value of 72 in the lower right-hand cell. This represents the mean happiness of wives whose fathers are below average in attractiveness but whose husbands are opposite in type. As we proceed up the column, we find a lowering of happiness score, or as we proceed left along the bottom row, we find a lowering of the happiness scores. In other words, if the father is below average in rated attractiveness, it is well for the wife to take to herself a husband of opposite type. We might summarize this discussion by saying that we have been attempting to prove in a hard and laborious and devious statistical way that which any young maiden could have told us: that physical attractiveness is important in the choice of a husband, and in general, the more attractive *he* is, the happier *she* will be.

Sex Adjustment. We can now turn to a study of some of the sex-adjustment items and examine their relationship to marital happiness. First we shall list the topics which Terman investigated. They are given in Table 124. We shall not need to discuss Terman's findings for each one of these topics, but we shall, as we did in the case

TABLE 124. *Sex-adjustment Items Investigated by Terman*

1. Frequency of intercourse
2. Preferred frequency of intercourse
3. Relative passionateness
4. Refusal of intercourse
5. Orgasm adequacy
6. Duration of intercourse
7. Desire for extramarital intercourse
8. Homosexual attraction
9. Wife's response to first intercourse
10. Contraceptive practices
11. Wife's rhythm of sexual desire
12. Sexual complaints

of the background items, select a few to show the methods of analyses which Terman employed.

Frequency of Sexual Intercourse. We shall first discuss Terman's findings on the significance of the frequency of sexual intercourse in relation to marital happiness. We do this to show how the influence of a third variable, in this case, age, must be eliminated before the true relation between frequency of intercourse and marital happiness can be adequately ascertained.

Let us start naïvely, however, and examine the over-all data. Table 125 shows mean happiness scores for husbands and wives

TABLE 125. *Mean Happiness Scores in Relation to Monthly Intercourse Frequency**

Monthly frequency	Number	Men	Women
Over 10.............	80	69.8	73.4
7–10..............	159	70.2	70.3
3– 6..............	374	68.5	69.1
1– 2..............	153	65.7	67.4
0..............	18	60.0	51.5

* From Terman, L. M. *Psychological Factors in Marital Happiness.* New York: McGraw-Hill Book Company, Inc., 1938.

reporting different intercourse frequencies. There certainly appears to be a relation to marital happiness, rather more striking for wives than for husbands, but the Pearsonian coefficients are only .09 and .12 for husbands and wives respectively.

But now we ask whether we can accept these data without considering age, for it does not seem unreasonable for us to expect a decline in intercourse frequency with advancing age. We should like to know how this decline might affect our conclusion with regard to the relation of intercourse frequency to marital happiness.

We give in Table 126 the median intercourse frequency as it varies with the age of Terman's subjects. There is no doubt about a striking relationship. Intercourse frequency definitely declines with advancing age. The Pearsonian coefficients expressing this relationship are −.30 for husbands and −.33 for wives.

TABLE 126. *Monthly Intercourse Frequency in Relation to Age**

Men			Women		
Age	Number	Median	Age	Number	Median
60–	15	1.4	55–	20	1.2
50–59	80	2.9	45–49	88	2.8
40–49	219	4.1	35–44	281	4.1
30–39	340	5.0	25–34	333	5.5
20–29	127	6.3	24	60	7.2

* From Terman, L. M. *Psychological Factors in Marital Happiness.* New York: McGraw-Hill Book Company, Inc., 1938.

Now that we have verified the hypothesis that age affects intercourse frequency, how is age to be eliminated as an unwanted factor in the data we presented in Table 125? Terman eliminated it by preparing a second table in which age was held constant. Before he did this, however, he divided his total subject population into the following four age groups: below 30; 30 to 39; 40 to 49; and 50 and over. Then he computed the correlation between intercourse frequency and marital happiness for each of these groups. These correlations were .03, .18, .08, and .03. Thus there is a change in the importance of intercourse frequency with different age groups. The most marked relation occurs in the age range 30 to 39, so we present Terman's additional data for this group in Table 127.

Here we see the same trend we saw in Table 125, but it is brought out much more clearly. Thus the elimination of age clarifies the interpretation of the original set of data.

Preferred Intercourse Frequency. Table 128 shows mean happiness scores in relation to preferred frequency of intercourse. There is, here, no question of a marked relationship. This result is straightforward and requires no additional comment.

Terman points out that more important, probably, than intercourse frequency per se or preferred intercourse frequency per se is the relationship between them. That is, in spite of the relationships we have demonstrated, it would be possible for a person to be unhappy if his preferred and actual intercourse frequency were not in

TABLE 127. *Monthly Intercourse Frequency in Relation to Marital Happiness for Ages 30 to 39**

Frequency	Number	Husbands	Wives
Over 10..........	32	69.2	74.0
7–10.............	81	70.9	72.2
3– 6.............	153	66.0	68.6
1– 2.............	56	61.4	65.7
0.............	3	44.8	42.5

* From Terman, L. M. *Psychological Factors in Marital Happiness*. New York: McGraw-Hill Book Company, Inc., 1938.

near agreement with each other. To get at this relationship, Terman computed a hunger-satiety index by dividing reported frequency of intercourse by preferred frequency of intercourse. When this ratio is 1.00, actual frequency and preferred frequency are in agreement. When it is more than 1.00, actual frequency exceeds preferred frequency and a state of satiety is approached. When the ratio is

TABLE 128. *Mean Happiness Scores in Relation to Preferred Monthly Frequency of Intercourse**

Frequency	Number	Husbands	Number	Wives
Over 10..........	119	64.1	73	76.5
7–10.............	217	68.0	151	69.4
3– 6.............	295	69.7	288	68.8
1– 2.............	86	71.6	134	67.1
0.............	9	57.3	22	57.8

* From Terman, L. M. *Psychological Factors in Marital Happiness*. New York: McGraw-Hill Book Company, Inc., 1938.

less than 1.00, preferred frequency exceeds actual frequency and a state of sex hunger is approached. A summary of the ratios for all of Terman's subjects is given in Table 129, and Table 130 shows the relation of these ratios to marital happiness. This last table looks like an old friend, so our interpretation of the data it contains should not be difficult. We see that happiness scores increase as we proceed either from marked hunger or from marked satiety toward a position of optimum ratios. This is true for husbands and wives separately as well as jointly considered.

TABLE 129. *Percentage of Subjects with Different Sex Hunger-Satiety Ratios**

Hunger-satiety ratio	Husbands	Wives
A. Under .59 (marked hunger)...........	24.3	13.6
B. .59–.90 (moderate)....................	19.4	8.8
C. .91–1.10 (optimum)...................	52.9	54.1
D. 1.11–1.70 (moderate).................	1.1	8.1
E. 1.71 up (marked satiety)..............	2.3	15.4

* From Terman, L. M. *Psychological Factors in Marital Happiness.* New York: McGraw-Hill Book Company, Inc., 1938.

TABLE 130. *Mean Happiness Scores in Relation to Sex Hunger-Satiety**

Hunger-satiety ratio	Marked hunger	Moderate	Optimum	Moderate	Marked satiety	Total
Marked hunger.............	56	64	65	71	57	61
Moderate..................	57	72	74	64	64	68
Optimum..................	64	71	75	73	69	73
Moderate and marked satiety	54	65	75	78	63	66
Total...................	58	69	73	70	64	69

* From Terman, L. M. *Psychological Factors in Marital Happiness.* New York: McGraw-Hill Book Company, Inc., 1938.

Relative Passionateness. One of the questions which Terman asked his subjects was worded as follows:

Do you think your wife (husband) is *more* or *less* passionate than you are? (check) Much more____, somewhat more____, same____, somewhat less____, much less____.

The "replies to this item were treated," Terman says, "by averaging the ratings of husband and wife and coding the result so as to yield nine degrees of difference in the composite ratings." Table 131 shows the results and the relationship of relative passionateness to marital happiness. As we should have been led to expect from the preceding section, optimum happiness results when the husband and wife are equally passionate. When a discrepancy in passion occurs, the less passionate partner appears to be the less happy member of the couple.

The data in columns 4 and 5 of Table 131 offer a type of validation of the passionateness ratings. We see a definite equality in preferred monthly intercourse frequency when husbands and wives consider themselves equally passionate, and we see discrepancies in the expected directions as we depart from this optimum state of equality.

TABLE 131. *Mean Happiness Scores in Relation to Relative Passionateness**

Relative passion	Number	Mean happiness		Number of copulations preferred per month	
		Husband	Wife	Husband	Wife
1. Husband more..............	112	60	61	9.0	4.6
2. Husband more..............	106	68	67	8.5	5.8
3. Husband more..............	130	73	75	8.1	6.4
4. Husband more..............	110	73	73	8.2	8.0
5. Equality..................	121	74	75	8.6	8.7
6. Husband less..............	67	68	70	8.3	9.1
7, 8, 9. Husband less..............	51	64	65	6.2	7.6

* From Terman, L. M. *Psychological Factors in Marital Happiness*. New York: McGraw-Hill Book Company, Inc., 1938.

TABLE 132. *Sex-adjustment Items Related to Marital Happiness**

1. Sex hunger and satiety (ratio of reported to preferred frequency of intercourse)
2. Duration of intercourse (wife only)
3. Rated relative passionateness of spouses
4. Wife's orgasm adequacy
5. Husband's asserted ability to prolong intercourse
6. Release and satisfaction from intercourse
7. Forwardness of wife
8. Overmodesty or prudishness of wife
9. Wife's demand for foreplay
10. Desire for extramarital intercourse
11. Refusal of intercourse
12. Attitude on being refused intercourse
13. Number of sexual complaints
14. Wife's fear of pregnancy
15. Wife's pain at first intercourse
16. Wife's enjoyment of first intercourse
17. Time before wife experienced first orgasm
18. Premarital intercourse

* From Terman, L. M. *Psychological Factors in Marital Happiness*. New York: McGraw-Hill Book Company, Inc., 1938.

It will not be necessary for us to continue further this item-by-item review of Terman's sex-adjustment items. We have illustrated all the different techniques involved and can list the sex-adjustment items showing a significant relation to marital happiness. They are given in Table 132.

Relative Predictions. One of Terman's main purposes was to determine the relative importance of personality, background, and sex-adjustment factors in predicting or influencing marital happiness. We have reviewed his studies separately in each of these areas, but now we wish to bring the various results together. This can best be done by means of the data presented in Table 133. This table shows the correlations between the various factors we have discussed and marital happiness.

TABLE 133. *Correlations between the Scores on the Various Prediction Scales and Marital Happiness**

Item	Husbands	Wives
1. Bernreuter items	.38	.42
2. Strong items	.36	.35
3. Opinion items	.22	.22
4. Personality total	.47	.46
5. Background items	.35	.29
6. Personality and background	.54	.47
7. Sex adjustment items	.49	.49
8. Personality, background and sex	.49	.57

* From Terman, L. M. *Psychological Factors in Marital Happiness*. New York: McGraw-Hill Book Company, Inc., 1938.

Unfortunately, these correlations have an element of spuriousness in them because they are based upon the same group of cases that was used in deriving the various scoring weights. Nevertheless, we are probably safe in concluding that there is a significant relationship between the total of all factors and marital happiness.

The sex-adjustment items, according to the data in Table 133, show the highest correlation with marital happiness, the personality factors run a close second, and the background items are third. Background and personality factors are just about equal to the sex-adjustment factors in relation to marital happiness. This is important, for the only information available prior to the marriage, and the information upon the basis of which our predictions have to be made, is that concerning the personality and background items.

Table 134. *Relation of Mean Adjustment Prediction Scores (Burgess and Cottrell) to Number of Cases*

Score	Total N	Number of cases												
		1–25	26–50	51–75	76–100	101–125	126–150	151–175	176–200	201–225	226–250	251–275	276–300	301–325
160	1			1										
158	3			1	1			1						
156	3		1	1		1								
154	6		3	1		1		1						
152	5		1	1	1	1		1						
150	10			3	2	2	3	2						
148	19	1	3	6	3	2	6	2						
146	26	1	4	3	5	3	7	5	3	1	1	3		4
144	35	1	1	3	3	3	3	6	1	1	2	2		4
142	38		2	7	5	6	3	6	2	1	1	1	1	5
140	33	1	2	4	2	1	3	2	1	2				1
138	31		3	4	5	7	6	2	2	3		1	1	2
136	34	1	4	4	1	5	2	2	2	3	4			
134	20	1	5	3		1	3			1				
132	11		3	3	3	3	2							1
130	10	1	1	1		3	1	1						
128	11		2	3	1	4	2							
126	4	2		2	1	1								
124	10	1	2	4		1								
122	2		1											
120	7		4	3										
118														
116	4	1	1	1		1								
114	1		1											
112	1	1												
110														
Below 110	3	1	1	1										
Total	328	13	46	60	33	47	41	31	11	12	8	7	2	17
Mean	139.31	129.42	135.50	138.87	140.44	138.84	141.55	142.69	141.77	139.50	139.50	142.50	138.50	140.85
SD	8.90	12.71	12.23	10.23	7.02	8.24	5.74	5.64	3.74	3.42	3.16	2.14	2.00	3.23

TABLE 135. *Relation of Mean Happiness Prediction Scores (Terman) to Number of Cases*

Score	Total N	Number of cases												
		1–25	26–50	51–75	76–100	101–125	126–150	151–175	176–200	201–225	226–250	251–275	276–300	301–325
76	5	3	1	1	1					3	1			3
74	21	5	3	1	....			1		4	1	....	....	8
72	47	11	3	2	3	3	1	5	....	5	5	1	2	16
70	98	7	11	17	6	6	1	9	....	10	8	5	5	38
68	166	8	15	9	18	2	5	16	5	3	6	6	5	9
66	104	6	6	11	15	12	12	7	9	2	1	6	1	1
64	59	6	10	13	5	13	9	3	12			....	....	
62	33	4	10	7	4	9	5	....	4					
60	15	2	....	4	2	4	2	1	2					
58	22	5	7	5	2	5	1							
56	11	5	5	1		2	1							
54	5	4	1											
52	6	....	3	1		2								
50	2	1	1											
48	2	1	....	1										
46	2	1	1											
44	2	1	....	1										
42	1	1	....											
40														
38	1		1											
36														
34														
32	1	1												
Total..........	603	72	77	74	56	58	38	42	32	27	22	18	13	75
Mean..........	66.86	64.67	64.32	65.61	67.11	66.22	66.29	68.74	67.19	69.61	68.68	68.61	69.73	69.30
SD..........	5.29	8.87	6.73	5.47	3.38	4.70	6.35	2.63	2.16	2.74	2.25	1.82	1.67	2.01

SAMPLING INTERDEPENDENCE

In the two studies we have just reviewed, it was necessary for Burgess and Cottrell, and for Terman, to sort their subjects according to their answers to one question at a time and to determine separately for each of these sortings what significance it had in relation to marital happiness. This creates a situation in which the successive samples (obtained from the successive sortings) cannot be considered independent of each other with regard to the variables under study. A corrective course of action is obvious, but this course of action is usually so prohibitively expensive that it cannot be followed. Let us realize, therefore, the limitations with which the course of action actually followed leaves us.

We bring out one of the most important of these limitations in Tables 134 and 135. Both of these tables show distributions of marital happiness or marital adjustment scores in relation to the number of cases upon which they are based. Table 134 presents the results for Burgess and Cottrell's study and Table 135 presents the results for Terman's. Two facts stand out clearly from these tables. Mean marital adjustment scores or marital happiness scores are related to the number of cases upon which they are based, and the standard deviations of the distributions of marital adjustment or marital happiness scores are also related to the number of cases upon which the means are based. The greater the number of cases giving any one alternate item response, the less chance there is of finding that the variable under study has a significant relation to marital adjustment or to marital happiness. Most of the items found to be significant must be those based upon a fairly moderate number of cases. This is an artificial limitation caused by our finite sample. This limitation is a serious one and calls into question the value of any study which does not include a means of processing data in such a way as to make allowance for it.

THE APTITUDE INDEX

Our third example of a prognostic approach to the measurement of adjustment is contained in the Aptitude Index. This is a test designed to predict success in life insurance selling. If a person is well adjusted in this business, he will become successful in it. But if he finds himself maladjusted, he will be unsuccessful and will soon leave it. We could say this about many other occupations, but since it is relatively so easy to get into the life insurance business—and so easy to leave it—it has become a glaring example whenever we think of poor occupational adjustment.

The Aptitude Index was designed to cut down on this degree of maladjustment. It was designed to be used by life insurance companies to weed out ahead of time a large proportion of those applicants who cannot adjust themselves satisfactorily to the life insurance business. It can also be used by applicants themselves as an aid to them in reaching their own decisions as to whether the selling end of life insurance is a suitable line of endeavor for them.

The Aptitude Index is a unique test. It is the product of the Life Insurance Agency Management Association (formerly the Life Insurance Sales Bureau) and is published by this agency for the use of its member companies. Since the Life Insurance Agency Management Association has more than 200 members, this means that the Aptitude Index is available for use by a large segment of the life insurance business.

There are two parts to the Aptitude Index. Part I consists of 10 items similar to those on many a business application blank. It calls for an applicant's age, number of dependents, occupation, number of organizations in which membership is held, net worth, and so forth. Part II consists of 81 personality items of the Bernreuter type and 15 questions similar to those in Part II of the Allport-Vernon Study of Values.

Development of Test. Those responsible for the development of the Aptitude Index (chiefly Albert K. Kurtz and Arthur W. Kornhauser) have not published fully on the methodology used in its development. However, we can report on the general ideas which were involved. Kurtz reports that the study leading to Part I was

. . . based upon the records of 10,111 men without previous life insurance selling experience, who were contracted as full-time agents during 1933, 1934, and 1935. These men were contracted by eleven different companies operating throughout the United States.

Data were gathered and analyzed on 24 personal history items and a scoring system was devised so as to give good prediction in terms of the following measures:

1. Whether or not the agent remained under contract for 12 months
2. Whether or not the agent remained under contract for 24 months

3. Paid-for production during the first 12 months—for agents who remained in the business that long

4. Paid-for production during the first 24 months—for agents who remained in the business that long

After determining the relative importance of each of the 24 items, 10 were selected as giving the best predictions of first and second year production, and also giving good predictions of whether or not an agent would remain in the business.

The scoring weights assigned to the various items, and their alternate answers, vary from 0 to 13. Those assigned for net worth, which will suffice for an example, are given in Table 136.

TABLE 136. *Scoring Weights for Net Worth**

$15,000 or more.......... 10
$10,000–$14,999.......... 8
6,000– 9,999.......... 6
1,000– 5,999.......... 4
0– 999.......... 2

* Adapted from Kurtz, A. K. *How Well Does the Aptitude Index Work?* Hartford, Conn.: Life Insurance Sales Research Bureau, 1941.

The total score for an applicant is obtained by adding the weights for his answers to each of the 10 items. When this total is obtained, it is compared with the norms for an appropriate age group and is converted into a letter rating. This letter rating, which can be A, B, C, D, or E, indicates a given probability that the applicant will be able to achieve success as a life insurance salesman. In one study of 408 agents not included in the original standardization group, it was found that applicants who rated A produced 300 per cent more business in their first year than did applicants who rated E. In a second study of 211 agents, it was found that applicants who rated A produced 400 per cent more business than applicants who rated E.

Part II of the Aptitude Index was designed to measure some of the personality characteristics which . . . experimentation has demonstrated to be important in determining the success or failure of the new life insurance agent. In the development of this part of the Aptitude Index, a very large number of questions designed to measure a number of different traits believed to be important were tried out. The specific questions . . . retained are those which have actually proved their value in differentiating between groups of successful and unsuccessful agents. The traits that these questions are measuring are therefore those which experience has shown to be of definite importance in determining whether or not a new man is likely to succeed in the life insurance business.

In the course of this experimentation approximately 500 questions and 8 different tests designed to measure 38 personality characteristics were tried. These were all tried, however, on men already in the life insurance business. Therefore the questions which seemed of value were printed in a booklet called the "Personnel Blank" and were given to 1,433 applicants in 24 companies. When study on this group was complete, a final summary was prepared for the group of 211 agents we have already mentioned. The results are shown in Table 137.

TABLE 137. *Predictive Value of Aptitude Index**

Score	Percentage of average	
	Part I	Parts I and II
A	195	206
B	120	137
C	63	78
D	76	39
E	47	41
Average..........	100	100

* From Kurtz, A. K. *How Well Does the Aptitude Index Work?* Hartford, Conn.: Life Insurance Sales Research Bureau, 1941.

Predictive Value. Column 1 of Table 137 shows the results when Part I of the Aptitude Index is used alone, and column 2 shows the results when Parts I and II are used together. Agents who score A produce 195 per cent more business (column 1) or 206 per cent more business (column 2) than the average agent whose production was equated to 100 per cent. Agents who score E produce only 47 per cent as much business (column 1) or 41 per cent as much business (column 2) as does the average agent. Clearly, the personality characteristics measured by Part II of the Aptitude Index are of value in predicting adjustment in the life insurance business. Kurtz, in reporting some of these results, says:

There are a large number of factors other than the ability of the man in question which have an important bearing on the degree of success attained by a new man after entering the life insurance business. Nevertheless, for any given set of circumstances, the probability of success is much higher for men with high ratings on the Aptitude Index than for those with low ratings.

In our discussion we have not attempted to cover the many follow-up studies which have repeatedly demonstrated the value of the

Aptitude Index in predicting adjustment in the life insurance business. But we must comment that these repeated validity studies demonstrate another way in which the Aptitude Index is a unique test. Few other tests in existence have received the thorough and persistent study that has been devoted to the Aptitude Index to give it its present degree of predictive or prognostic value.

THE PERSONAL INVENTORY

Our fourth example of a prognostic approach to the measurement of adjustment is that contained in the Personal Inventory developed by Shipley and Graham during World War II. Shipley and Graham developed this inventory in response to a request from the Office of the Commander in Chief, U.S. Fleet, and the Bureau of Naval Personnel, who asked them "to develop a test for emotional stability."

As their first step in the development of the Personal Inventory, Shipley and Graham made "a detailed analysis of 100 psychiatric case histories drawn from the records of the Chelsea Naval Hospital." From these records they selected 300 items which seemed capable of differentiating psychiatric patients from normal men. They prepared all items in pairs, such as

I have felt bad more from head colds. I have felt bad more from dizziness.

so that a recruit in answering the questionnaire would always have to choose one or the other of two alternatives. Shipley and Graham prepared two forms of this inventory, one having 145 items (60 of which were scored) and one having 20 items (all of which were scored).

Bray, who reports the development of the Personal Inventory, states that "after the test had been standardized and the scoring system stabilized, it was administered to various groups of men; the results were filed and compared later with the psychiatrist's verdict on each man . . . care was exercised to insure that the psychiatrist was in ignorance of the test score at the time of the psychiatric examination." Thus the nature of the validation was to be a comparison between test scores and psychiatric judgment as to whether recruits were normal or sufficiently abnormal to be discharged from the Navy. Two sets of results are presented in Table 138. The figures in the first two columns of the table are the "best" results which

Bray reports and the figures in columns 3 and 4 are the "poorest." The figures given are cumulative percentages, so as one proceeds from the bottom to the top of the table, he will find the figures increase in magnitude. In each row he will find the percentages of normal and discharged groups receiving the designated or less favorable scores on the inventory. Both sets of data indicate that the Personal Inventory is useful in predicting psychiatric classification.

TABLE 138. *Predictive Value of the Personal Inventory**

Score	Cumulative percentages			
	Best results		Poorest results	
	Normal	Discharged	Normal	Discharged
7– 8	68	96	76	89
10–11	47	91	50	80
12–13	29	85	29	67
14–15	21	82	17	58
16–17	10	76	6	49

* Adapted from Bray, C. W. *Psychology and Military Efficiency.* Princeton, N.J.: Princeton University Press, 1948.

Bray reports that "the Personal Inventory was more successful as a psychiatric screen than any other test with which it was compared. . . . " Its reliability (split-half) varied in different samples from .66 to .91, and it was found to be useful in saving the time of a psychiatrist by showing him the men most in need of a psychiatric examination.

IO

RATINGS: NONANALYTICAL APPROACHES

We are now to consider one of the most frequently used, and at the same time most frequently abused, methods of personality measurement: the rating technique. This technique is used whenever all other methods seem inadequate, whenever no other method is available, as a supplement to other techniques, and as an integral part of many other techniques of personality measurement. The method is frequently abused, however, because its apparent simplicity leads many untrained individuals to construct and to make use of rating scales without any concern whatsoever as to the objectivity, reliability, or validity of the results that may be secured. It is also abused because of the fact that it is used even when better methods of assessment are known to be available.

We shall try in this and in the next chapter to describe some of the better standardized rating techniques, to point out some of the dangers of inadequate techniques, and to show in what ways the various varieties of the technique should and should not be applied. We can begin our discussion by pointing out that there should be in the use of any rating technique we have in mind, as in the use of any other technique of measurement, the accomplishment of two objectives. We want to be able to classify individuals upon some meaningful trait or variable, and we want to know the reasons for the placement of an individual in one category rather than in another. In accord with these two objectives, we shall classify all rating methods in two broad categories: analytical if they provide both classifications and supporting reasons; nonanalytical if they provide classifications without supporting reasons. With this distinction in mind we proceed with a discussion of several varieties of nonanalytical rating techniques.

MULTIPLE-CHOICE RATING FORMS

A great many of the employee rating forms used by business and industrial organizations require ratings on personality traits and are secured on what we can call multiple-choice merit-rating forms. The term *multiple-choice* is more commonly applied to tests than to merit-rating forms, but its use in this connection is appropriate. Most of the merit-rating forms used by business and industrial organizations suggest several traits upon which an employee is to be rated and provide for several alternative ratings with respect to each of these traits. These alternatives are generally lettered or numbered, but frequently they may consist of a series of unlettered or unnumbered descriptive phrases set off in separate blocks. The following paragraphs contain a number of examples of rating forms in current or recent use by various business and industrial organizations.

Allison Division of General Motors. Provision is made for rating employees on volume of work, quality of work, knowledge of job, attitude toward supervision, cooperation with fellow workers, and 10 other traits. On each of these traits the supervisor is asked to indicate whether the employee is (O) outstanding, (AA) above average, (A) average, (BA) below average, or (US) unsatisfactory.

Chase Brass & Copper Company. Provision is made for rating employees on quality of work, quantity of work, reliability, attitude, and flexibility. On each of these traits the supervisor is asked to indicate whether the employee is (O) outstanding, (G) good, (F) fair, (MS) minimum satisfactory, (BS) below standard, or (U) unsatisfactory.

Graybar Electric Company. Provision is made for rating employees on quality of work, volume of work, knowledge of assigned job, interest in assigned job, dependability, initiative and ingenuity, personal appearance, personality, cooperation, health and vitality, and six other traits. On each of these traits the supervisor is asked to indicate whether the employee is (1) poor, (2) fair, (3) average, (4) good, or (5) best.

John Hancock Mutual Life Insurance Company. Provision is made for rating employees on appearance, character, influence on others, mental flexibility, concentration, imagination, ability to coordinate, and inspirational and executive influence. On each of these traits the supervisor is asked to indicate whether the employee is outstanding, above standard, satisfactory, below standard, or unsatisfactory; or, alternatively, whether the employee is one who far exceeds requirements, exceeds requirements, meets requirements, partially meets requirements, or does not meet requirements.

J. L. Hudson Company. Provision is made for rating employees on management and direction, leadership, coordination, and dependability. On each of these traits the supervisor is asked to indicate whether the employee is superior, good, fair, or poor.

London Life Insurance Company. Provision is made for rating employees on personality, disposition and cooperation, dependability, initiative, and judgment. On each of these traits the supervisor is asked to indicate whether the employee is outstanding, above average, average, or below average.

McKesson & Robbins Company. Provision is made for rating employees on accuracy, output, adaptability, dependability, and cooperation. On each of these traits the supervisor is asked to indicate whether the employee is outstanding, superior, better than satisfactory, satisfactory, or unsatisfactory.

National City Bank & Trust Company. Provision is made for rating employees on cooperation, thoroughness, resourcefulness, grooming, manner of speech, tactfulness, self-confidence, judgment, and initiative. On each of these traits the supervisor is asked to indicate whether each employee is superior, above average, average, below average, or unsatisfactory.

Pure Oil Company. Provision is made for rating employees on quantity of work, quality of work, knowledge of work, use of working time, cooperation, and initiative. On each of these traits the supervisor is asked to indicate whether the employee is to be rated in a first, second, third, fourth, or fifth class.

Union Central Life Insurance Company. Provision is made for rating employees on quantity of work, quality of work, knowledge of work, carrying out instructions, judgment, and working with others. On each of these traits the supervisor is asked to indicate whether the employee is above average, average, or below average.

The foregoing list is rather long, but by it the author hopes to demonstrate the great preponderance of personality traits, the "multiple-choice" nature of the scales, and the great variation from one company to another. Unfortunately there is very little published information (the author will hazard a guess there is none) concerning the objectivity, reliability, and validity of any of the foregoing techniques. We cannot say, therefore, how well or how poorly these and many other rating scales used in business and industry serve their intended purposes.

NUMERICAL RATING SCALES

In the preceding section we made several references to numerical-type rating scales. The rating method used by the Graybar Electric Company requires a supervisor, in rating an employee, to circle or underline a 1, 2, 3, 4, or 5. The method used by the Pure Oil Company is similar but instead of the numbers 1, 2, 3, 4, 5, the adjectives first, second, third, fourth, and fifth, are used. It is to be noted that most of the other rating methods described, even those making use of descriptive adjectives, could also have been set up on a numerical basis.

Crooks. It is not uncommon for us to find a numerical type scale combined with a descriptive-adjective scale. Obviously the two extremes of any scale must be defined, and it is a small step from this to providing a descriptive term for each of the positions on a numerical rating scale. We find, however, that most numerical scales with descriptive adjectives for all alternatives are frequently limited to five steps. It is difficult to think of a sufficient number of descriptive adjectives for all steps on a 7, 9, or 11 step scale. This can be done, however, and is illustrated in a rating form developed by William R. Crooks in cooperation with the Clerical Salary Study Committee of the Life Office Management Association. This scale is reproduced in Fig. 8. Its purpose is to provide a means of permitting a supervisor to rate an employee on the same variables as those underlying the Life Office Management Association's Point Plan of Job Evaluation.

Ferguson. A second illustration in which a numerical scale is combined with a descriptive adjective scale is given in Fig. 9. This form was developed by the author and has been used, among others, by the Clerical Salary Study Committee of the Life Office Management Association. It was used by this committee to secure ratings on 30 traits for more than 3,000 clerical employees.

The instructions for the use of the scale we have just mentioned

EMPLOYEE RATING RECORD

NAME _____   DATE _____

DEPARTMENT _____   DIVISION _____

Instructions: For each of the factors listed below place a check mark (✓) above the phrase which most accurately describes the employee being rated.

FACTOR	SCALE POINTS							RATING
	1	2	3	4	5	6	7	
TEACHABILITY: Ability to grasp new ideas and methods	Needs repeated instructions	Requires detailed instructions	Slightly below average	Average	Slightly above average	Readily grasps new ideas and methods	Ability to grasp new ideas outstanding	____
SUPERVISORY RESPONSIBILITY: Capability in organizing and directing the work of others	Lacks leadership qualities	Supervisory ability is inadequate	Slightly below average	Average	Slightly above average	Well developed supervisory ability	Exceptional supervisory ability	____
INITIATIVE: Resourcefulness, ingenuity and aggressiveness of the individual on the job	Is not very resourceful	Requires considerable urging	Slightly below average	Average	Slightly above average	Very resourceful	Exceptionally resourceful	____
PUBLIC RELATIONS: Capability in maintaining the good-will of people outside the Home Office	Lacks ability to maintain good-will	Very little ability	Slightly below average	Average	Slightly above average	Very capable in handling people	Exceptionally capable	____
ANALYTICAL ABILITY: Ability to grasp essentials, reach sound conclusions and plan necessary action	Lacks ability to grasp essentials	Very little ability	Slightly below average	Average	Slightly above average	Very quick in grasping essentials	Exceptional ability in analysis	____
PERSONAL REQUIREMENTS: Individual's effectiveness in working with others in harmony	Constant friction with others	Difficult to work with	Slightly below average	Average	Slightly above average	Good team worker	Exceptionally cooperative	____
MONETARY RESPONSIBILITY: Interest and ability in guarding against monetary wastes or losses	Lacks ability to control cost or risk	Infrequently considers cost or risk	Slightly below average	Average	Slightly above average	Very capable in reducing cost or risk	Exceptional monetary ability	____
APPLICATION: Ability to apply self to work	Wastes time	Poor concentration	Slightly below average	Average	Slightly above average	Very good concentration	Exceptionally conscientious	____
VOLUME OF WORK: Amount of work completed in a given period of time	Unsatisfactory output	Very slow worker	Slightly below average	Average	Slightly above average	Rapid worker	Outstanding amount of work	____
NEATNESS AND ACCURACY: Neatness and accuracy of the work as habitually done by the individual	Work almost valueless	Frequent errors	Slightly below average	Average	Slightly above average	Very few errors	Exceptionally accurate and neat	____
DEPENDABILITY: Thoroughness and reliability of the individual in the performance of the job	Very erratic	Often erratic	Slightly below average	Average	Slightly above average	Very trustworthy	Exceptionally reliable	____

AVERAGE RATING: (Average of the ratings in the right-hand column) . . . . ____

Note: The following factor is intended as an over-all rating or recommendation and therefore should not be considered as part of the average rating.

PROMOTABILITY: Capacity of the individual for growth or advancement	1	2	3	4	5	6	7	
	Unsatisfactory for present job	Decreasing in efficiency	Has about reached limit of ability	Advance in rank questionable	Should advance slowly	Promising- should advance steadily	Should advance rapidly Very capable	____

Rated by: _____

Use the reverse side of the blank for any remarks that you may have regarding the employee.

Title: _____

Date: _____

FIG. 8. Rating scale developed by William R. Crooks for the Life Office Management Association. (From *Life Office Job Evaluation Plans.* New York: Life Office Management Association, 1941.)

If the Agent's performance is DISTINCTLY SUPERIOR..................circle the.....9   (4%)*

If the Agent's performance is CONSIDERABLY ABOVE AVERAGE.......circle the.....8   (7%)

If the Agent's performance is MODERATELY ABOVE AVERAGE.........circle the.....7   (12%)

If the Agent's performance is SLIGHTLY ABOVE AVERAGE.............circle the.....6   (17%)

If the Agent's performance is AVERAGE................................circle the.....5   (20%)

If the Agent's performance is SLIGHTLY BELOW AVERAGE.............circle the.....4   (17%)

If the Agent's performance is MODERATELY BELOW AVERAGE........circle the.....3   (12%)

If the Agent's performance is CONSIDERABLY BELOW AVERAGE.......circle the.....2   (7%)

If the Agent's performance is DISTINCTLY INFERIOR..................circle the.....1   (4%)

```
................................................  1  2  3  4  5  6  7  8  9
................................................  1  2  3  4  5  6  7  8  9
................................................  1  2  3  4  5  6  7  8  9
................................................  1  2  3  4  5  6  7  8  9
................................................  1  2  3  4  5  6  7  8  9
................................................  1  2  3  4  5  6  7  8  9
................................................  1  2  3  4  5  6  7  8  9
................................................  1  2  3  4  5  6  7  8  9
................................................  1  2  3  4  5  6  7  8  9
................................................  1  2  3  4  5  6  7  8  9
................................................  1  2  3  4  5  6  7  8  9
................................................  1  2  3  4  5  6  7  8  9
................................................  1  2  3  4  5  6  7  8  9
................................................  1  2  3  4  5  6  7  8  9
................................................  1  2  3  4  5  6  7  8  9
```

*Percent of Agents who should receive each rating.

Fig. 9. A descriptive adjective numerical rating scale. (From *Agents' Experimental Performance Ratings*. New York: Metropolitan Life Insurance Company, 1950.)

are given in Table 139. In one of the studies in which this scale was used, more than 50 cooperating life insurance companies were asked to rate typical cross sections of their home-office-employee groups. In spite of this admonition the rating distributions showed a marked degree of skewness. Therefore the cooperating companies did not select random or representative cross sections of their employees, or the supervisors were not so objective as might have been desired, or the employees rated represent a truly superior portion of the general

TABLE 139. *Instructions for Using the Rating Scale in Fig. 9**

(*a*) Draw a circle around the figure 9 after the name of each Agent whose present job performance is distinctly superior and is better than that of at least 96 per cent of all Agents with whose job performance you are acquainted.

(*b*) Draw a circle around the figure 8 after the name of each Agent whose present job performance is considerably above average and is better than that of at least 89 per cent, but not better than that of 95 per cent, of all Agents with whose job performance you are acquainted.

(*c*) Draw a circle around the figure 7 after the name of each Agent whose present job performance is moderately above average and is better than that of at least 77 per cent, but not better than that of 88 per cent, of all Agents with whose job performance you are acquainted.

(*d*) Draw a circle around the figure 6 after the name of each Agent whose present job performance is slightly above average and is better than that of 60 per cent, but not better than that of 76 per cent, of all Agents with whose job performance you are acquainted.

(*e*) Draw a circle around the figure 5 after the name of each Agent whose present job performance is average and is better than that of at least 40 per cent, but not better than that of 59 per cent, of all Agents with whose job performance you are acquainted.

(*f*) Draw a circle around the figure 4 after the name of each Agent whose present job performance is slightly below average and is better than that of at least 23 per cent, but not better than that of 39 per cent, of all Agents with whose job performance you are acquainted.

(*g*) Draw a circle around the figure 3 after the name of each Agent whose present job performance is moderately below average and is better than that of at least 11 per cent, but not better than that of 22 per cent, of all Agents with whose job performance you are acquainted.

(*h*) Draw a circle around the figure 2 after the name of each Agent whose present job performance is considerably below average and is better than that of at least 4 per cent, but not better than that of 10 per cent, of all Agents with whose job performance you are acquainted.

(*i*) Draw a circle around the figure 1 after the name of each Agent whose present job performance is distinctly inferior and is no better than that of at least 3 per cent of all Agents with whose job performance you are acquainted.

For the small group of Agents whose performance you will rate, it is difficult to determine the proper proportions, if any, of the various ratings to be assigned. If, however, you were to rate the performance of 100 (or, better, 1,000) Agents, you would find that the ratings would distribute themselves approximately as follows:

Rating	Description of rating	Per cent of agents who should receive each rating
9	Distinctly superior performance.....................	4
8	Considerably above average performance............	7
7	Moderately above average performance.............	12
6	Slightly above average performance................	17
5	Average performance.............................	20
4	Slightly below average performance................	17
3	Moderately below average performance.............	12
2	Considerably below average performance...........	7
1	Distinctly inferior performance...................	4

* From *Agents' Experimental Performance Ratings*. New York: Metropolitan Life Insurance Company, 1950.

population. Probably all three of these factors contributed to the results, but the first two must carry the greatest responsibility.

It cannot be proved, of course, that skewed distributions are erroneous. But neither can it be proved that they are correct. Psychologists are usually wary of accepting such skewed distributions, however, as representing the true state of affairs with respect to the distributions of the variables in the population being studied. We can think of too many reasons: the tendency for a supervisor to be lenient, the tendency for a supervisor to give the employee the benefit of the doubt, the tendency for a supervisor to rate an employee high on all traits because of his superiority in only one trait, or the fear on the part of a supervisor that low ratings will indicate that he is a poor supervisor. These, and many other reasons that could be cited, make us wary of accepting as fact a skewed distribution of ratings.

But since these are the kinds of distributions we will usually get on numerical rating scales, what can we do about them? Three courses of action are open: we can discard them; we can modify them; or we can ask supervisors to do the job over. Which course of action we choose will depend upon the particular object we have in mind. If our object is to get supervisors to understand the errors made so that we can get a more correct set of ratings from them, we shall choose the third alternative. If we feel that another technique will prove suitable, we shall choose the first alternative. But if we have secured the ratings for a one-time use, it is possible that we may choose the second alternative. And by this alternative we mean some process, such as regrouping the intervals, which would give more nearly normal distributions. In our example this was the course adopted. (See Table 149, Chap. 11.) The scale was changed from a nine-step scale to a five-step scale. Step 9 was reassigned a value of 5, step 8 was reassigned a value of 4, steps 7 and 6 were grouped together and assigned a value of 3, step 5 was reassigned a value of 2, and steps 4, 3, 2, and 1 were grouped together and reassigned a value of 1. The regrouping does no violence to the original order of the ratings, it looks more reasonable from a common-sense point of view, and it lends itself a little more easily to treatment by normal curve statistics.

The ratings just discussed were solicited and received by mail. The instructions were written, and accompanied the request for the ratings. Let us turn, therefore, to a second situation in which this rating form was used in a series of conference sessions during which raters were given careful oral instruction. The distributions resulting in this situation are decidedly improved over those secured in the unsupervised situation. Therefore, it appears that close supervision over the rater while he is making his ratings is a major factor in securing adequate distributions on a numerical-type rating scale.

OSS. A third example of a combination numerical and descriptive-adjective rating scale is that developed by the Assessment Staff of the Office of Strategic Services and used by them in the studies we shall describe in Chap. 14. This scale is given in Table 140. Like the

TABLE 140. *Rating Scale Developed by the OSS Assessment Staff**

5	Very superior	7%
4	Superior	18
3	High average	25
2	Low average	25
1	Inferior	18
0	Very inferior	7

* From *Assessment of Men*. New York: Rinehart & Company, Inc., 1948.

scales we have just discussed, the OSS scale consists of a series of numbers, a series of descriptive adjectives, and a series of percentages indicating the proportion of ratings expected in each step of the scale. "One of the advantages of this scale is that it can easily be converted into a two-point, three-point, or four-point scale, or, by using pluses and minuses in marking, into an eighteen-point scale . . . ." The OSS Assessment Staff developed this scale to provide a summary of a large number of judgments, to transmute clinical observations into a form amenable to statistical treatment, and to provide a brief mode of communicating observational results to other individuals.

RANKING METHODS

The numerical methods of rating which we have just discussed have as one of their chief objects the spacing of subjects along a series of equidistant steps or intervals. Many of them do not achieve this hoped-for result, but this does not alter the fact that the steps on a numerical rating scale are supposed to be placed at known distances from each other.

There are few measurements in psychology, and there are none in the field of personality, that possess a very high degree of accuracy. Therefore, some psychologists assert that it is foolish for us to use numerical scales and other similar scales because we are fooled into thinking we have done some real measuring when in reality we have not. They contend that all we can do in psychology, and particularly in the field of personality, is to rank-order our subjects. Somebody is more this or less that, but we do not know how much more or how much less. This being the case, it is argued that we might just as well use ranking scales to start with, and it is our purpose in this section to present three studies in which ranking scales have played important roles.

Landis. The first of these studies was conducted by Professor Carney Landis and is reported in his book *Sex in Development.* Landis and his collaborators were interested in evaluating "the importance of . . . psychosexuality in psychopathology." Their procedure was to study "the growth and development of emotional and sexual patterns of personality in two groups of women, one normal, the other psychotic or neurotic." Landis and his coworkers were interested "in determining whether the psychosexual components of the adult personality" can be considered as "the end product of earlier incidents, events and relationships." "The essential object of their study . . . " says Landis, "revolved around the following questions: What is the normal (average) pattern of psychosexual development? How do deviations in this pattern affect the adult personality? What are the characteristics of psychosexual development of different types of adult personalities?"

Landis defines the term *psychosexual development* as "the growth and changes in the biological, psychological, and sociological aspects of sex in the course of the life history of the individual." We understand, then, that Landis was interested in discovering the early and developmental antecedents of the adult or mature stage of psychosexuality. He was interested, also, in finding what departures from the normal developmental sequence could occur and in what way these departures from the normal or typical developmental sequence affect the character of adult psychosexuality.

Interview Data. Landis secured his data via a controlled-interview technique, supplemented with questionnaire forms and physical examinations. The data came from 153 normal women and 142 abnormal women. The material of chief interest for us is that secured in the controlled interview. In this interview a total of more than 50 questions was put to each subject. These questions concerned "the facts and phantasies related to psychosexual development. The subjects were asked to describe both the incidents of their early lives and the emotional value of such incidents."

Each subject was asked these questions in a natural interview, and the interviewer took down near verbatim notes of all answers. Each question was pursued until the subject began responding with material irrelevant to the question involved. When all interviews had been completed, it was necessary for Landis and his coworkers to quantify the material in some meaningful and useful way. And this is our reason for being interested in Landis's study.

Quantification was accomplished, says Landis, by a careful reading of all case histories "in order to determine just what personality variables" could be evaluated. Then "the general divisions or steps of the scales were set up arbitrarily. The frame of reference for these arbitrarily set limits was the entire group of 295 individuals studied. . . . The number of steps in each scale of evaluation depended upon the amount of discrimination appropriate to the material at hand." Further, "the steps or divisions on the evaluation scales did not constitute a continuum nor was there any particular attempt to establish equal intervals between the steps."

We see here an important dichotomy with certain other scale-construction techniques. For example, in the equal-appearing-interval method of attitude-scale construction we assume a continuum on which attitudes may be graded. And we assume that it is possible for an individual to have an attitude at any position on the scale from one extreme to the other. The scale-construction work proceeds without reference to the empirical distribution of attitude in a group. In contrast, the method used by Landis in the development of his various psychosexual scales makes no assumption about the general type of distribution to be expected. The empirical facts are first secured, these are examined, and scales are constructed in accord with whatever discriminations exist for the group being studied.

The first method has the advantage, if it is otherwise acceptable, that the steps involved transcend any particular group that may be tested. It may have the disadvantage, of course, of not being sufficiently tied down to empirical data to be realistic. The second method has the advantage of being based directly upon empirical data but may have the disadvantage of being so restricted by the particular data at hand that the scales cannot be applied to other groups.

Scale Development. Landis says that "after a particular personality concept or variable had been selected for analysis, the case histories of all individuals were reread and each step of the evaluation scale was defined in terms of the actual responses of the subjects." Then these scales were used by three judges independently of each other. To eliminate or to minimize the effects of halo, a judge would read only that part of the case history which was pertinent and would not review the entire case.

Final evaluations or ratings were not assigned to a subject unless two of the raters were in complete agreement and the third rater disagreed not more than one step. If this criterion could not be met for any given rating, the matter was settled in a group conference. According to Landis, only 5 per cent of several hundred ratings had to be settled in group conference.

The criteria by which the adequacy of each psychosexual scale was judged may be listed as follows:

1. The steps in each scale had to be sufficiently clear and exact to produce consistency (as above defined) among the judges.

2. The steps in each scale had to provide "for differentiations" among the subjects rated.

3. The steps in each scale had to differentiate between individuals "exhibiting ogically different reaction patterns."

Altogether, 14 scales were developed. There were two scales with three steps each, four scales with four steps each, and eight scales with five steps each. An example of one of the scales is given in Table 141.

Reliability. We can gain some idea of the reliability of these scales by reference to the data presented in Table 142. The entries in this table show the percentage of cases upon which, for each scale, all three judges were in complete agreement. According to these data, the scales for prepuberty sex aggressions (affective response), masturbation (occurrence), and menstruation (affective response)

TABLE 141. *Landis's Psychosexual Scales**

1. Early sex information
Judges' rating of factual adequacy
    1. No instruction or information. Subject denies all knowledge of sex differences as a child.
    2. Fantastic explanations by adults; inadequate information from playmates; childish gossip; dirty stories; inadequate factual information (parents, schools).
    3. Adequate factual information from parents, books, school hygiene lectures, etc.

Subjects' rating of adequacy
    1. Early information adequate, subject satisfied as to manner in which acquired whether from parents or otherwise.
    2. Early information from parents fairly adequate, but wish parents' attitude had been more frank. Felt she should have been given more information.
    3. Parents gave no information, did not discuss, or gave inadequate information. No apparent resentment toward parents for lack of frankness. Accepted as natural attitude, no information from other sources. Would give her own daughter more information.
    4. Parents gave no information, or inadequate information. Resentment toward parents' attitude. Felt information should have come from parents rather than from other sources.
    5. Lack of information, misinformation, or extreme unpleasantness of sources of information. Early information so disgusting she has never been able to view as pleasant. Too much information when she did not want it. Disliked being told about sex.

* From Landis, C. *Sex in Development*. New York: Paul B. Hoeber, Inc., 1940.

TABLE 142. *Percentage of Cases on Which All Three Judges Were in Complete Agreement on Original Rating**

Prepuberty sex aggressions (affective response)	79
Early sex information (subjective rating)	17
Menstruation (affective response)	62
Problem of family ties (importance)	51
Homoerotism (occurrence)	37
Homoerotism (affective response)	45
Masturbation (occurrence)	64
Masturbation (affective response)	56
Heterosexual experience (affective response)	51
Narcissism (importance)	45
Masculine protest (importance)	54
General compatability in marriage	52
Sex adjustment in marriage	37
General adjustment in marriage	45

* From Landis, C. *Sex in Development*. New York: Paul B. Hoeber, Inc., 1940.

are the most reliable; and scales for early sex information (subjective rating), homoerotism (occurrence), and sex adjustment in marriage are the least reliable.

Psychosexual Development. After a complete application of the scales to all case histories, Landis states:

. . . the course of personality development of most of our group showed certain common characteristics which made it possible to classify each subject in terms of expected levels of development. We found that certain experiences, attitudes and practices were common and usual at certain ages in most of these women. We considered these findings as the basis of approximate age norms for the psychosexual development of the individual. A brief characterization of each of these levels is as follows:

15 to 17 years. The average girl of 15 to 17 years has gone out with boys fairly frequently but has not had complete sex experience. Her relationship with boys has been carried to the extent of mild petting. She is still somewhat tied to her family emotionally, and economically has not reached an independent adult status. Her sex information is fairly complete, but she feels quite constrained in discussing such matters with her family. She still takes a good deal of pleasure in associating with girls of her own age but is definitely interested in boys, more as dates than in any more serious fashion. She has fairly strong emotional attachments to members of her family, and to her friends of either sex, but is not exclusively attached to any one of them as an individual.

An immature girl at this age evinces no interest in boys and restricts her interests and activities to members of the family or to girl friends. She has a definitely unfavorable attitude toward sex which may show itself in a complete lack of interest or in disgust toward sexual matters. Her attachments to members of the family may be so strong that she has no interests or activities outside the home.

18 to 21 years. The average girl between these ages may be expected to show the following characteristics. She has many friends and activities outside the family circle which keep her away from home a large part of the time. She is not yet wholly independent of her family financially, however. She has had a fairly complete knowledge of sex since she was 16 years old. She had gone out with six or more boys on different occasions, and feels that she is attracted to one of them, but has not been thinking specifically in terms of marriage. Her attitude toward sex is one of healthy interest. She is not preoccupied with boys although more and more of her time is spent in planning or day-dreaming about particular individuals.

The immature girl of this age has little interest in boys and has had few dates. Her physical contact with them has never gone beyond kissing, and such intimacies as have occurred have not been particularly enjoyable. She probably has a negative attitude toward all sexual matters. Her sex information was not complete until she was 18 years old, but she does not remember any strong curiosity about sex. She probably masturbates occasionally and shows evidence of being primarily interested in herself.

An extremely immature person of this age has never had any dates or any love affairs, her sex information is still incomplete, and she masturbates frequently or excessively. She is still very closely emotionally attached to her family, and extremely narcissistic. Her attitude toward sex is one of disgust or apathy.

22 to 25 years. The mature woman has completely resolved her family ties and is free from any pronounced signs of narcissism. Her heterosexual intimacies have included some sex play or petting. She is free from any unfavorable sex attitudes.

The immature women 22 years old or more had her first date after the age of 19 years and since that time has gone out with less than six men. Her physical intimacy with men rarely has gone beyond a kiss. Her sex information was not complete until after she was 18 years old. She may masturbate occasionally, show evidence of narcissism and of a poorly resolved family situation.

An extremely immature women of this age is one who has had no dates or attachments to men, and has not yet acquired complete sex information. She masturbates frequently or excessively, shows extreme narcissism, and close attachment to her parents.

It now becomes possible to compare the psychosexual level of any given subject with these various stages and to determine whether this person has reached a state of psychosexual level appropriate for her age, or whether she is advanced or retarded with respect to it. We can also compare different adult groups with each other: abnormal vs. normal, single vs. married, happily married vs. unhappily married, and so forth. It is also possible for us to determine the differential antecedents for abnormality in contrast with normality, for remaining single in contrast with getting married, and for being unhappy in contrast with being happy.

Mead. A second study in which ranking scales have played a major part is that conducted by Margaret Mead on *Cooperation and Competition among Primitive Peoples*. Mead's purpose was to see if some insight could be gained relative to the factors which, on the one hand, appear to lead to cooperative behavior and which, on the other hand, appear to lead to competitive behavior. Her source material consisted of the studies of 13 primitive groups of people: the Arapesh of New Guinea, the Eskimo of Greenland, the Ojibway of Canada, the Bachiga of East Africa, the Ifugao of the Philippine Islands, the Kwakiutl of Vancouver Island, the Manus of the Admiralty Islands, the Iroquois, the Samoans, the Zuñi of New Mexico, the Bathonga of South Africa, the Dakota, and the Maori of New Zealand. Mead, with her associates Mirsky, Landes, Edel, Goldman, Quain, and Mishkin, prepared accounts of the behavior of each of the afore-mentioned groups and then undertook to analyze each culture from the standpoint of those factors relevant to cooperative and competitive behavior.

Mead prepared a series of questions and asked each of her associates, as well as herself, to attempt to find an answer to each of these questions for the various groups studied. To give the reader an account of the nature of these questions, we can do no better than to quote Mead herself. We give a portion of her list of questions below and remind the reader that these and similar questions in five other areas (social organization, political structure, social structure, view of life, and educational process) had to be kept in mind as Mead and each of her associates prepared their accounts of the 13 primitive societies. With reference to the study of economics, Mead asked each of her associates to

Watch closely the correspondence between the group habits and the actual economic conditions, that is, the amount of genuine environmentally determined social cooperation which is necessary. Do they use boats needing several people to build them, to man them? Try to estimate the extent to which environment dictates cooperation, and at what ages, in what activities, etc., so that later you can form a judgment on whether this factor is important in dictating habits in other spheres. For instance, are the customary occupations of women solitary or social as compared with the men? Distinguish carefully between individual activities performed in groups—as when a group of women meet to weave mats together, and activities which require each member of the group actually to contribute to one end, as in a drive of game or fish. (In mat weaving, for instance, the women may meet to make mats for the dowry of the chief's daughter; they are engaged in social cooperation, but there is nothing in the actual work they are doing which dictates cooperation, and in fact each one may compete with the other to make the best mat, or work the fastest.) When an activity does require group effort, as a fishing drive, is the contribution of individual effort assessed individually so that the actively existing cooperation is given no social expression? (E.g., when four men fish in the canoe which belongs to each man, and the owner of the canoe receives two-fifths of the catch, each other man a fifth; or when the fish is devoted without comment to some communal purpose.) How many differential skills are involved in the economic life? Is a high quality of skill demanded in any particular activity? Is it socially recognized? Is there a different organization of behavior in the activities demanding skill and those which do not?

Is the food supply plentiful, seasonal, unreliable? Does the acquisition of food depend upon skill, luck, foresight, aggressiveness in securing a share of a fixed supply? Is the absence of cooperative effort, or the absence of a partner in cooperative effort, such as a wife or parents, economically penalized in the society? Are other materials besides food—such as wood, clay, metal—limited in supply, difficult to secure, etc?

Is the community self-contained? Is there division of labor? Is there dependence on trade? How is the trading situation organized: cooperation between members of the community as over against members of other communities, or cooperation between trade partners, across community lines? Is this extended to groups? Among manufactured articles how much differentiation is there between the items of a given type, in value, beauty, etc? When considerations are used to evoke trade, free barter, compulsive barter (where one subject will be traded only for another of a particular type): magical compulsion, maintenance of alliances, etc?

What are the property arrangements? Here note particularly whether individuals own a share of ground, but not a definite piece of ground, etc. Does one inherit property, or the right to share in a cooperative agricultural group, etc? What are the rules in regard to newly created property as over against old property? What are the proportions between old property which is inherited and new property which an individual can create by skill, industry, social manipulation, etc? Is property perishable?

What is the position of the skilled worker? Is he set apart, given different rewards from others? Do skilled workers compete or cooperate among themselves?

What is the nature of the economic activity? Does it require long-time planning, unremitting daily activity? Does a sick man fall inevitably behind? Are misfortunes individual—like the loss of a valuable fishing trap—or communal in incidence —as a crop failure? Can you estimate the time spent in different kinds of activities, cooperative and competitive?

Conclusions. When all accounts had been prepared, Mead attempted a classification of the societies upon three variables: co-

Fig. 10. The individual, cooperative, and competitive behavior classification of 13 primitive societies. (From Mead, M. (Ed.) *Cooperation and Competitition among Primitive Peoples.* New York: McGraw-Hill Book Company, Inc., 1937.)

operative, competitive, and individualistic. We can show her results, as Mead did herself, in the form of a diagram (see Fig. 10).

The Kwakiutl are listed as most competitive, the Ojibway and Eskimo as most individualistic, and the Zuñi and Bathonga as most cooperative. From each of these extreme positions the other societies shade off in mild gradation, as in most other types of classifications of human behavior.

Having classified the 13 primitive societies upon the relative predominance of individualistic, cooperative, or competitive behavior, Mead studied each group with respect to character formation and ego development. In other words, she wished to use the variables individualistic, cooperative, and competitive as her predictors, and character formation and ego development as her predictands. Let us see what conclusions she reached.

1. "Strong ego development can occur in individualistic, competitive or cooperative societies." In other words, the characterization of a society as individualistic, as competitive, or as cooperative is of no value in predicting the type of ego development. Its correlates must be looked for elsewhere.

2. "Whether a group has a minimum or a plentiful subsistence level is not directly relevant to the question of how cooperative or competitive in emphasis a culture will be." Here Mead was interested in subsistence level as a predictor and in the variables cooperative, competitive, and individualistic as predictands. No useful relationships were discovered.

3. "The social conception of success and the structural framework into which individual success is fitted are more determinative than the state of technology or the plentifulness of food." In other words, social conceptions of success and structural framework as just defined can be used as useful predictors and will indicate to some degree whether the culture can be classed primarily as individualistic, cooperative, or competitive in nature.

4. "There is a correspondence between: a major emphasis upon competition, a social structure which depends upon the initiative of the individual, a valuation of property for individual ends, a single scale of success, and a strong development of the ego."

5. "There is a correspondence between: a major emphasis upon cooperation, a social structure which does not depend upon individual initiative or the exercise of power over persons, a faith in an unordered universe, weak emphasis upon rising in status, and a high degree of security for the individual."

To classify these 13 primitive societies, Mead considered the following questions:

What are the principal ends to which an individual devotes his time? What are the principal ends to which group activities are directed? What are the proportions of time and energy devoted by individuals and by groups to ends which are shared, competitive, and individual? [Mead states that] the application of these criteria is admittedly rough since it involves a judgment of more or less upon data themselves incomparable. . . . Nevertheless the range of difference in the thirteen cultures in these aspects of life was so great, and the extremes of the gamut so clear, that all those engaged in the study were unanimous in their agreement.

Objectivity. In anthropological studies data on objectivity are extremely hard to obtain and, as in the study just discussed, are seldom given. Because such data are hard or even impossible to get does not, however, mean that we should, as many do, ignore the subject altogether. Let us review Mead's study with a view to determining the points on which we should concern ourselves with the factor of objectivity.

The first point is in connection with the informants, the natives of the primitive groups giving the anthropologist his information. If the anthropologist had interviewed a different set of informants, would he have secured the same information? The only way an anthropologist can be sure of this is to interview several informants independently of each other and see if the data he gets from these various sources is the same. If it is, he can have some assurance that his informants have been objective.

The second place at which we need to show concern is in the observations which the anthropologist himself makes. Would another anthropologist have seen the same things and have interpreted them in the same way? The only way to be sure is to have another anthropologist make a parallel study, and this, of course, is expensive and is seldom possible. It must be understood, however, that unless such studies can be made, the anthropologist's observations and interpretations cannot be said to be beyond doubt as to their objectivity. This is a serious matter, for there is abundant evidence to indicate that different observers, equally well-trained from a technical standpoint, will persist in seeing different things and in interpreting the same things seen in different ways.

The third point where we need to concern ourselves with objectivity in Mead's study is with the reinterpretation of a study by an anthropologist not involved in securing the original data. The reasons for our concern here are much the same as those mentioned in the preceding paragraph.

And last we might be concerned with Mead's own over-all interpretation of the results. Would another equally competent anthropologist have interpreted the data in the same manner that Mead did? Perhaps so, but there is presented no proof that this would have been the result.

Our purpose in raising the foregoing questions on objectivity is not to lessen our faith in, and regard for, Dr. Mead as anthropologist.

Our purpose, however, has been to point out the places in which anthropological studies can be lacking in objectivity and so make us all aware and ever on the alert to see that due care has been taken, whenever possible, to provide proof for the objectivity of the data which are presented.

Reliability. Mead presents no data on reliability. This would refer, of course, to the extent to which upon a subsequent occasion, or by another observer, the 13 primitive societies would be ranked in the same way. This would be impossible for Mead herself to carry out, for she could not, undoubtedly, forget completely her first classification. And since she could not do this, she is not in a position to render a completely independent classification. The only way to get at the reliability of the classifications would be to have another observer make a separate classification. And this too would probably be impossible, for any anthropologist capable of making such an independent classification would, in the course of his early training, have familiarized himself with Dr. Mead's studies. Therefore all we can do is point to the problem but have no solution to offer as to a way in which appropriate reliability data could be obtained.

Validity. Here we are concerned with the accuracy of the results. Do our classifications correspond with actual fact as determined in some completely independent manner? Here, again, we are stymied in the solution of the problem, but here, again, we cannot ignore its existence.

THE PAIRED-COMPARISONS METHOD

The rating methods we have been discussing require us to make a series of judgments on a number of isolated stimuli. If we have the problem of rating employees on proficiency, adolescent girls on psychosexual development, and primitive societies on cooperative and competitive behavior, we consider our stimuli one at a time and assign a number, a rank order, or a letter grade, and then go on to the next. The judgments we are called on to make are frequently not easy, but the procedure is simple and straightforward.

We can point to several disadvantages, however. If we have a large number of stimuli to rate, we may not be able to keep in mind exactly the same set of standards throughout all our ratings. One case may call to mind certain items of information or behavior which we forget to reconsider in rating a second case. And the standards we use one time may be higher or lower than those we apply a second time. Also any of the methods we have discussed suggest that we keep in mind some "absolute" standard which we proceed to apply case by case.

A method designed to overcome some of these difficulties is the paired-comparisons method of rating. This method, as its name implies, requires that stimuli be rated in pairs and not one by one. It is thought that this pairing of stimuli makes it possible for a rater to give a more accurate judgment than any technique requiring him to judge stimuli, one by one, in terms of some previously established standard.

The paired-comparisons method of rating requires the rater to compare each stimulus to be rated with each of the other stimuli to be rated and to render a judgment as to which stimulus in each pair is the larger, the better, the preferred, and so on. For example, if five people are to be rated on courtesy, it is necessary that the rater compare each individual with every other individual and for each of these pairs render a judgment as to which individual in the pair is the more courteous. This requires the rater to make 10 judgments. If 10 people were to be rated, the rater would have to make 45 judgments. The number of judgments required for any given number of stimuli can be determined by the formula $N(N - 1)/2$, in which N is the number of stimuli to be rated.

Variations. There are several methods by which paired-comparisons ratings can be secured. One method is to list all pairs and to ask the rater to underline or circle the preferred member of each pair. A second method is to present the pairs on 3- by 5-inch cards; and still another method is to use a diagram such as that presented in Fig. 11. The first of these methods possesses the advantage that the pairs can be randomized, and this gives the experimenter some control over the order in which the rater will consider the various pairs of stimuli. The second method has the advantage of being useful in a shop or industrial situation when the investigator wishes to present for consideration one stimulus pair at a time and to have the rater indicate his choice before moving on to the next pair. The experimenter can shuffle his cards to have them in a new random order for the next rater. The last method has the advantage of being easy to prepare, and for this reason it is suitable for use in a conference situation, *e.g.*, when 20 or 30 raters are instructed simultaneously and when each rater has a different set of stimuli to rate.

Treatment of Results. We can begin our explanation of the details of the paired-comparisons method with this last variation. The

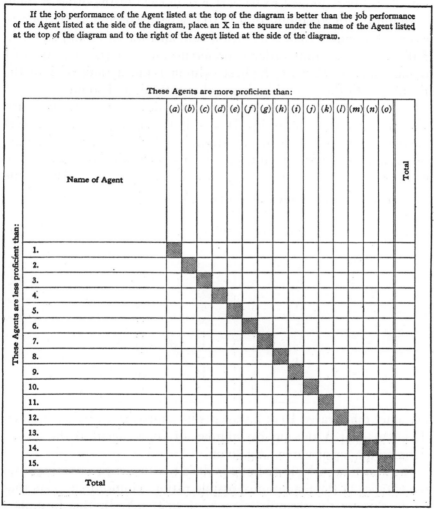

Fig. 11. A chart to facilitate paired comparisons ratings. (From *Agents' Experimental Performance Ratings*. New York: Metropolitan Life Insurance Company, 1950.)

rater is instructed to place an X in the square under the better man and to the right of the poorer man. When he has completed his consideration of all individual pairs, he is asked to count the number of X's in each column and the number of X's in each row. This gives him a check on accuracy. For the number of checks in the column plus the number of checks in the corresponding row should be equal to one less than the number of stimuli available for comparison.

The column sums indicate the number of times that each stimulus is preferred or is judged to be better than each of the other stimuli. A stimulus with a column total of 10 is a better or a more frequently preferred stimulus than one with a column total of 8, and so forth. If all we want is a rank order of preference, we can assign a rank of 1 to the stimulus with the highest column total, a rank of 2 to the stimulus with the second highest column total, and so on.

But the paired-comparisons method was designed to give us much more than a mere rank order. It was designed to give us the actual scalar separations between our stimuli. To illustrate how we may arrive at these scalar separations, let us start with the data given in Table 143. This table shows how a manager of a district life

TABLE 143. *The Statistical Treatment of Paired-comparisons Ratings*

Agent	Votes	Percentage	Standard score
A	9	95	82
B	8	85	70
C	7	75	63
D	6	65	58
E	5	55	52
F	4	45	48
G	3	35	42
H	2	25	37
I	1	15	30
J	0	5	18

insurance office rated 10 of his agents in comparison with each other. He gave agent A the highest number of votes, agent B the second highest number of votes, and so on.

The first thing which we have to do is to convert these ratings into percentages of the maximum possible rating. Guilford suggests that we do this by the formula $\% = (c + n/2)/nN$. In this formula c represents the total number of votes given to a stimulus, N represents the number of judges, and n represents the number of stimuli. When only one judge's ratings are required, our formula reduces to $\% = (c + \frac{1}{2})/n$. In our example we shall assume we have only one judge for each set of stimuli. This will simplify our discussion.

Agent A, with nine votes, has a percentage rating of 95, agent B, with eight votes, secures a percentage rating of 85, and so on. Next, we must convert these percentages into standard scores. This we do by means of a table prepared by Hull. Long ago, Professor Hull showed how rank orders or percentage ratings could be translated into a series of standard scores ranging from 0 to 100. We shall not reproduce Hull's table here, but we shall merely give the results of its application to our data. These results are presented in column 3 of Table 143.

The conversions that Hull's table effects give a series of standard scores with a predetermined mean of 5.0 (or 50) and a predetermined standard deviation of 2.0 (or 20). In terms of this scale, we can now visualize actual scale separations, and this we could not do from the original votes in Table 143. If we compare the final standard scores with the original votes, we shall see that we have merely stretched out both ends of the scale in relation to its more central portion and that the farther out the scale we proceed, the more stretching we have done. This stretching is considered legitimate in view of our common assumption that the steps at the extremes of a distribution are usually broader than those in the more central parts of the scale. Our original votes do not show this, so we go through the procedures we have described to secure this result.

Basic Assumptions. To understand the nature of the assumptions required to provide a rationale for the foregoing calculations, we shall have to take a brief excursion into psychophysics. Suppose that we have a series of stimuli: S1, S2, S3, S4, and S5, and wish to present them to a group of subjects and evoke their responses. For the sake of our illustration, we shall suppose that the proper responses to our stimuli are R1, R2, R3, R4, and R5, respectively. In other words when we present stimulus S1, we expect response R1. When we present stimulus S2, we expect response R2, and so on. We know, however, that because of the variability of human nature, chance, and other factors, we do not always get the response we expect. So once in a while in response to stimulus S3, we shall get response R2 or R4 instead of R3. But if we can exert sufficient control over the conditions under which the stimuli are presented and over the situation in which the responses are to occur, we can postulate that in response to stimulus S3 we shall most frequently get response R3. Responses R2 and R4 will occur but less frequently than R3. And responses R1 and R5 will also occur but much less frequently than R2 and R4. In fact we can expect a normal distribution on the response continuum for each stimulus on the stimulus continuum. Thurstone calls the response which occurs most frequently for any given stimulus the *modal discriminal process,* and the standard deviation of all responses about this modal response he calls the *discriminal dispersion.*

It is to be understood that there is a modal discriminal process and a discriminal dispersion for every stimulus on our stimulus continuum. A plot of these results for two stimuli is given in Fig. 12.

FIG. 12. The modal discriminal processes and discriminal dispersions for two stimuli.

We know from our elementary statistics that any difference can be evaluated in terms of its standard error. And by the standard error of a difference we mean a measure of the dispersion of all possible differences about the difference we have in hand. If our standard error is small, our obtained difference will be considered a more significant (that is, a larger) difference than if our standard error is large. This suggests that we can use the standard error of a difference as a measure of the extent to which two stimuli on our stimulus distribution depart from each other. The formula which we have under consideration is as follows:

$$S_b - S_a = X_{ba}\sqrt{\sigma_1{}^2 + \sigma_2{}^2 - 2r\sigma_1\sigma_2}.$$

To get the standard error of a difference we must know the standard error of the mean of each of the two distributions and the correlation between the individual pairs of the two distributions. It is frequently not possible for us to get this information when all we have is a series of paired comparisons, but Thurstone has demonstrated that certain assumptions can be made to enable us to get around this difficulty.

The first assumption is that there is no correlation between the responses made to different stimuli. This eliminates the factor $2r\sigma_1\sigma_2$. The second assumption is that the discriminal dispersions for different stimuli are equal to each other. This enables us to reduce our formula to $S_b - S_a = X_{ba}\sqrt{2\sigma_b{}^2}$. In this formula, $S_b - S_a$

represents the difference in scale values between two stimuli, X_{ba} equals "the deviate corresponding to the proportion of judgments R_b greater than R_a," and σ_b represents one discriminal dispersion. Now if we let σ_b become our unit of measurement, our formula becomes $S_b - S_a = X_{ba}\sqrt{2}$. This formula requires only that we multiply each of our proportions X_{ba} by 1.414.

A Combination Method. The author has used a rating form that utilizes both numerical ratings and paired-comparisons ratings. This rating form consists of three work sheets. The first is an acquaintance-rating form, the second is a numerical rating form, and the third is a paired-comparisons rating form. We have already discussed the last two types of rating, so the acquaintance-rating form is the only thing that is new to us. On this form the rater indicates whether he is extremely well acquainted, moderately well acquainted, only slightly acquainted, or not at all acquainted with each ratee.

There are six steps involved in the use of the combination rating form. These are the securing of acquaintance ratings, the securing of numerical ratings, the securing of paired-comparisons ratings, the correction of the numerical ratings by their comparison with the paired-comparisons ratings, the converting of the paired-comparisons ratings into standard scores, and the averaging of the standard paired-comparisons scores and the numerical ratings.

The application of steps 1, 2, and 3 are obvious, since we have already explained them. Step 4, however, requires additional comment. When a rater has completed both steps 2 and 3, he is asked to compare the two sets of ratings. He is instructed to do this in the following way:

1. By means of the column total entered at the bottom of the paired comparisons diagram identify the person to whom the greatest number of votes (X's) has been given. Then find the numerical rating assigned to this person.

2. By means of the column totals entered at the bottom of the paired comparisons diagram locate the person to whom the second largest number of votes (X's) has been given. And then find the numerical rating assigned to this person. This rating will be found to be (*a*) higher than, (*b*) the same as, or (*c*) lower than that assigned to the person identified in step 1. If contingency (*a*) occurs the numerical rating is too high. It should be adjusted by reducing it to a value which is the same as, or lower than, that assigned to the person identified in step 1.

3. By means of the column total entered at the bottom of the paired comparisons diagram locate the person to whom the third largest number of votes (X's) has been given. And then find the numerical rating assigned to this person. This rating

will be found to be (*a*) higher than, (*b*) the same as, or (*c*) lower than the numerical rating assigned to the person identified in step 2. If contingency (*a*) occurs the numerical rating is too high. It should be adjusted by reducing it to a value which is the same as, or lower than, that assigned to the person identified in step 2.

4. Continue this process, person by person, until complete consistency between the paired comparisons ratings and the numerical ratings is achieved.

When the paired-comparisons ratings have been checked for internal consistency and have been used to adjust the numerical ratings, composite ratings are computed. To do this the paired-comparisons ratings are converted into standard scores, and these standard scores are averaged with the numerical ratings.

Were the use of the method of rating just described to stop at this point, there might be little to be said in favor of this technique in contrast with others which might be used. It is significant, therefore, that the technique makes possible the combination of ratings when these are assigned by mutually exclusive groups of raters. Before going into this matter, however, it will be necessary to show the treatment accorded the ratings assigned when one rater is required to rate more than 15 persons (the maximum number for which provision is made on the rating form). The treatment to be discussed refers only to the paired-comparisons ratings. Whenever it is necessary for one rater to rate more than 15 persons, two forms should be used, and five of the ratees should be repeated on both forms. Usually the last five names on one form, those in spaces 11 to 15, can be copied in the first five spaces, 1 to 5, on the second form. Additional names, up to a maximum of 10, can be added to the second form. Thus two forms provide for the ratings of 25 individuals.

The first step in combining the ratings from the two forms is that of computing the average paired-comparisons ratings assigned to the five persons common to the two forms. If we find their average on one form to be 42 and on the other to be 51, we can add nine points to everyone's rating in the first form to bring the 42 up to the 51. Or we can subtract nine points from everyone's ratings in the second form to bring the 51 down to 42. The final score assigned to each person is the average of the adjusted score and the score in the form in which no adjustment was made.

The comparison of the paired-comparisons ratings and the numerical ratings possesses several advantages. It leads to the discovery and correction of gross errors in the numerical ratings. It forces a greater number of discriminations in the numerical ratings. And it allows the mean of the distribution of the numerical ratings (when corrected) to be used as an anchoring point to equate different groups of ratees with each other.

This method requires an adequate preliminary training period and supervision and help during the completion of the forms. These factors are sometimes considered to be disadvantages, but any procedure that is expected to yield valid, objective, and reliable results is worth the effort, training, and supervision required.

II

RATINGS: ANALYTICAL APPROACHES

The rating methods we discussed in Chap. 10 were nonanalytical in nature. They enable us to make classifications, but they do not provide supporting reasons for these classifications. Nevertheless, they serve a useful purpose because there are many situations in which we can be satisfied with classifications without supporting reasons. Many times, however, we need these supporting reasons. So we turn in this chapter to methods of rating that can give us supporting reasons in addition to classifications. We shall be dealing with what we call analytical methods of rating.

Our first example will consist of the forced-choice technique—the Army's current system of appraisal. Our second example will consist of a series of forms designed to assess a number of personality traits in clerical employees. Our third example will consist of a form developed for use in appraising the work performance of traveling field training division representatives of the Metropolitan Life Insurance Company. In each of these examples we shall see a method that provides a set of reasons to support the resultant classifications. These reasons are found in a series of statements about various aspects of a person's behavior.

THE FORCED-CHOICE TECHNIQUE

One of the major difficulties or disadvantages of the rating techniques that we discussed in Chap. 10 is that they can be manipulated by the rater to give any result that he wishes to produce. It would be most advantageous, therefore, if we could find a method that could not easily be manipulated by the rater. Unfortunately there are no such techniques, but one which has been alleged to suffer somewhat less from rater manipulability than others is the forced-choice rating technique. It will be useful for us to examine this method to see in what way the attempt is made to reduce the extent to which the results can be manipulated by the rater. We shall describe the scale which was developed and used by the United States Army.

The essential and important part of this rating scale consists of 24 sets of adjectives, phrases, or statements such as:

A. Commands respect by his actions
B. Coolheaded
C. Indifferent
D. Overbearing

The rater must choose from each such set the adjective, statement, or phrase that best describes the person being rated and also indicate the adjective, statement, or phrase that least describes the person being rated. Thus of the four alternatives presented, the rater is forced to choose two of them, one as descriptive and the other as nondescriptive. Now there would be no point in forcing a rater to choose among the alternatives offered unless we knew ahead of time something about the fundamental nature of the choices offered. Therefore let us examine the nature of these choices and see in what way it is thought they disguise to some extent the ratings which will indicate the highest or lowest degree of proficiency.

We would certainly guess, in reviewing our example, that the first two items, "commands respect by his actions" and "coolheaded," would be considered favorable to the individual being rated and that the last two items, "indifferent" and "overbearing," would be considered unfavorable. We would be wrong, however, because only one of the first two items is really favorable and only one of the last two items is really unfavorable. How is this result achieved? We can understand this only by reviewing in detail all steps leading to it. Rundquist and Sisson give these steps as follows:

1. Army officers were asked to write brief essay type descriptions of other officers. They were asked to write essays describing both successful and unsuccessful officers.

2. When these essays had been prepared they were reviewed in detail and upon the basis of the material contained in them a series of descriptive adjectives, phrases, or statements was prepared. Some of these described successful officers and the remainder described unsuccessful officers.

3. This list of descriptive adjectives, phrases and statements was given to a group of army officers who were instructed to select other officers well known to them and

to indicate the extent to which each of the statements characterized each of these officers. Each statement could be said to apply to an officer to an exceedingly high or to the highest possible degree, to an unusual or outstanding degree, to a typical degree, to a limited degree, or to a slight degree or not at all.

4. For each statement, a preference value and a discriminative value were determined. The first of these indices was computed to show the extent to which the alternative answers to each statement were used to describe officers in general regardless of any differences in proficiency among them. The discriminative value was determined to show the extent to which the alternative answers were said to apply to successful officers in contrast to unsuccessful officers. The computation of these indices is illustrated in Table 144.

TABLE 144. *The Computation of Preference and Discriminative Values**

Response	1	2	3	4	5	Sum
Weight	0	1	2	3	4	
Frequency:						
Upper third	1	0	6	6	87	100
Middle third	3	5	13	15	64	100
Lower third	4	11	27	23	35	100
Total frequency	8	16	46	44	186	300
Frequency × weight	0	16	92	132	744	984
Difference in frequency for upper and lower thirds	3	11	21	17	52	104

* From Sisson, E. D. Forced choice—the new Army rating. *Person. Psychol.*, 1948, **1**, 365–381.

The ratees are first divided into three groups: an upper third, a middle third and a lower third. Then for each of these groups the frequency of occurrence for the alternative answers is ascertained. Each of these frequencies is multiplied by an appropriate weight and these products are added and their sum is taken as the preference index. In our example, alternative 1 is used only 8 times; alternative 2 is used 16 times; alternative 3 is used 46 times; alternative 4 is used 44 times; and alternative 5 is used 186 times. It is obvious that alternative 5 is the most popular answer and is applied frequently to all officers regardless of any differences in merit that may obtain. The calculation of the preference index is as follows

$$\frac{984 \times 100}{300} = 328$$

This item has a high preference index and therefore is not a particularly popular item.

The discriminative index is computed by getting the sum of the differences in the frequencies applying to the upper and lower third of the group rated. In our example this value is 104 which is the sum of the differences for each alternative $(3 + 11 + 21 + 17 + 52 = 104)$.

5. Next it is necessary to select pairs of adjectives, phrases or statements (these can be mixed) such that two of equal preference value but different discriminative value are selected. These pairs are then grouped in tetrads (two of the elements have high preference value and two of the elements have low preference value).

6. The items are then tried out on new groups of officers and the preference values and discriminative values redetermined. This step is necessary for assurance that the grouping of items into pairs and tetrads does not do anything to change their values from those originally determined.

Sisson claims that the forced-choice technique calls for objective ratings, minimizes subjective judgments, reduces a rater's ability to produce any desired or predetermined outcome, diminishes the effects of favoritism and personal bias, produces a better distribution of ratings, is less subject to influence by the rank of the officer being rated, and produces more valid ratings.

It may be possible that the forced-choice technique possesses many of these advantages, but the evidence which Sisson presents is not entirely clear and leaves some of these alleged advantages open to doubt. One of the major doubts concerns the alleged better distribution of ratings. By a better distribution of ratings one usually means a more normal distribution, that is, a less skewed distribution of ratings. However, in the figure that Sisson gives, the distribution of ratings is not much less skewed than that secured from the older graphic army rating scale. This being the case, it may still be an open question as to whether the forced-choice technique eliminates entirely or even lessens to any considerable extent the possibility that a rater can manipulate the scale in such a way as to produce any desired or predetermined outcome. In fact Sisson points out that as soon as it became known that the ratings were to be official rather than experimental, a marked shift in the mean (upwards) took place.

As described by Sisson, it is evident that the forced-choice technique differs from the typical rating form not only in the forced-choice element but also in the fact that the items are validated against independently secured criterion groups of successful and unsuccessful officers. To date it has not been demonstrated by the proponents of the forced-choice technique that any merit it may possess is not due to this validation factor rather than to the forced-choice element. We cannot rule out the possibility that the forced-choice element is the important factor giving the technique its value, but its proponents have been careless in assuming and in suggesting that the increased effectiveness of the technique is due entirely to the forced-choice factor.

We may summarize certain of the basic assumptions in the forced-choice system of rating. These assumptions are not necessarily unique to the forced-choice system of rating, however.

1. Any real difference between one officer and another can be described in terms of objective, observable items of behavior.

2. These objective, observable items of behavior differ in the extent to which raters tend to use them in describing the people they rate. That is, some of them are used frequently and others are used infrequently. Some are popular and some are not.

3. These objective, observable items of behavior differ from each other in the extent to which they can discriminate between good and poor officers.

4. Pairs of items can be selected in such a way that both items have the same preference value and therefore eliminate the possibility of choice of one of them as being more acceptable than the other. And at the same time the two items can differ in discriminative or diagnostic value and so offer a real possibility for choice (although hidden) as to the ratee's being a better or a poorer officer in terms of these items.

An important assumption in the forced-choice technique is that the relative diagnostic value of the elements in a pair is unknown and undetectable by the rater. In other words we are going on the assumption that a rater can pick out a more acceptable item and can distinguish it from a less acceptable item but that he cannot pick out a more diagnostic item and distinguish it from a less diagnostic item. This assumption is not entirely well founded, for there is abundant evidence that a person can, when he so desires, get pretty close to any predetermined or desired score on the Terman-Miles Masculinity-Femininity test or on the Strong Vocational Interest Test. To do this the person taking the test must be able to pick out the diagnostically significant items as well as the popular answers or responses. Also in the development of the equal-appearing-interval type of attitude or merit-rating scale, it must be assumed that the rater is capable of picking out the really significant items and of actually estimating fairly well their diagnostic value.

Insofar as clues from preferences are concerned, the forced-choice technique is useful in eliminating them as a basis for choice. Thus if the preference values are related to diagnostic values (in the original group of items), we can eliminate this as a cue. This does not mean, however, that the rater still may not have access to other cues and may nevertheless be able to secure any predetermined or desired result.

Some of the more ardent proponents of the forced-choice technique claim that the method is entirely new and of recent origin. This is patently untrue. In the Strong Vocational Interest Test one of the sections asks a subject to indicate which three activities he most prefers and which three activities he least prefers. This leaves four activities to be marked as neutral. In the Terman-Miles Masculinity-Femininity test certain of the sections present four choices, two of which are known to be preferred by men and the other two by women. The subject is forced to choose only one of the responses, however. In the Allport-Vernon Study of Values a subject is forced to choose between different alternatives known to have different diagnostic values but the same preference values. These examples could be multiplied severalfold.

THE L.O.M.A. MERIT RATING SCALES

Despite their frequently demonstrated lack of reliability, validity, and objectivity, certain varieties of nonanalytical rating scales continue to be found in general use for employee evaluation. The reasons for this probably lie in the ease with which supervisors can complete such forms, in their acceptability and apparent face validity, and in the illusion that they are easy to design. It is this last point, probably, that is responsible for many of the faults of the nonanalytical methods of rating. All too often, a rating scale results from a conference in which several people sitting around a table "dream up" a rating form. The characteristics to be rated, their scaling, and the scoring of the items are far removed from the realities of the situation in which the ratings are to be made.

In 1944 the Clerical Salary Study Committee of the Life Office Management Association took cognizance of this situation and instigated a series of research studies designed to lead to the development of an adequate, reliable, and objective series of merit-rating scales to be used in employee evaluation. These scales have been described in an article called "The L.O.M.A. Merit Rating Plan—Manual of Directions for Use."

In designing the research which led to the L.O.M.A. Merit Rating Scales, consideration was given to the following factors:

1. The traits to be used would be those found on the basis of research to be considered most important by the people who were in the best position to know: first line supervisors.

2. Of the traits found most important, those in which employees were found to differ most from each other would be used. The purpose of an employee evaluation system is to differentiate among the degrees to which workers can be of value to an organization. Thus, even for a characteristic of utmost importance, e.g., honesty, if all employees possess or demonstrate it to the same degree, it is of little use in determining the relative value of each employee to the organization.

3. Ratings, to be of value, must be pertinent to "on-the-job" performance. If characteristics to be evaluated are not tied down to the work situation, there is the ever-present danger that raters will base their judgments, in part at least, on observations made in other than work situations, and on characteristics which have no relationship whatever to the employees' "on-the-job" effectiveness.

4. Characteristics on which workers are to be evaluated must have known and constant meaning. Unless this is true, ratings by different supervisors cannot meaningfully be compared with each other.

5. It is a well-established psychological fact that the distribution of scores on such devices as tests and rating scales is a function not only of differences among employees who are evaluated, but also of irrelevancies introduced by the particular set of items employed, their interrelationships to each other, and so forth. When the nature of the distribution of measured ability is known raw scores should be scaled to that distribution. When such information is not available, an informed guess is an improvement over that which is likely to result from a number of uncontrolled factors.

6. Not all characteristics important in employee evaluation are best measured by supervisors' ratings. General intelligence, spelling and arithmetic ability and the like are better assayed by objective tests. They have no place in a rating scale.

With these six principles as basic guides, the Clerical Salary Study Committee of the Life Office Management Association initiated an extensive research project. It resulted in the development of 16 scales, one for the measurement or evaluation of each of the traits listed in Table 145.

Each of these scales is available in two equivalent forms (A and B), and each of these alternate forms contains descriptions of 26 elements to be rated. Form A of Scale 1 is presented in Table 146.

Trait Importance. On the basis of an extensive review of the literature and an examination of many rating forms, the L.O.M.A. Clerical Salary Study Committee assembled 100 trait names. These

TABLE 145. *The L.O.M.A. Merit Rating Scales*

1. Ability to work with others	9. Efficiency
2. Adaptability	10. Initiative
3. Attitude toward company	11. Interest in work
4. Common sense	12. Loyalty
5. Cooperativeness	13. Punctuality
6. Courtesy	14. Reliability
7. Dependability	15. Tactfulness
8. Disposition	16. Trustworthiness

TABLE 146. *L.O.M.A. Merit Rating Scale No. 1—Form A**

1. Feels that he owes nothing to anybody.
2. Is inclined to "tattle."
3. Provides just the "spark" that is needed for effective teamwork.
4. Promotes harmony.
5. Plans his own activities with every consideration for their effect upon other people.
6. Is unwilling to lend a helping hand.
7. Works well with any group of employees.
8. Has an excellent group spirit.
9. Goes his own way regardless.
10. Pays little attention to any time schedule even though the work of others depends upon his close adherence to such a schedule.
11. Gets mad if things don't go to suit him.
12. Is on his toes to help in any emergency.
13. Tries to lord it over other employees.
14. Helps others over any difficult situation.
15. Annoys other people.
16. Works with others at every opportunity.
17. Is adept in adapting himself to the needs and wishes of fellow employees.
18. Takes much pride in group accomplishment.
19. Refuses to see other fellow's point of view.
20. Belittles the work of others.
21. Accepts group policy even though it may differ from his own.
22. Hinders the work of fellow employees.
23. Is discourteous to those with whom he has to work.
24. Talks against any group with which he is associated.
25. Works only for the welfare of the group.
26. Is careful not to let any failure on his part to complete work interfere with that of others.

* From Ferguson, L. W. (Ed.) *Manual of Directions for Use—L.O.M.A. Merit Rating Scales.* New York: Life Office Management Association, 1950.

were sent to 320 supervisors in 50 companies. Each supervisor was asked to indicate:

1. The 10 most important traits
2. The 20 next in importance
3. The 10 least important
4. The 20 next least important

The middle 40 traits were left unchecked. This "forced-check list" procedure was used to preclude the possibility of the supervisors' assigning a large number of traits to a single category, particularly to the most important category. The frequencies with which the traits were assigned to the various categories were reduced to percentages, and weighted mean ratings, one for each trait, were computed. Weights extending from 5.00 (for traits of greatest importance) to 1.00 (for traits of least importance) were used. These weighted means ranged from 4.63 for "accuracy" to 1.29 for "dominance." The total possible range extended, of course, from 5.00 (for a trait that was universally assigned to the "top ten" category) to 1.00 (for a trait always listed among the bottom ten).

Trait Variability. Many merit-rating scales fail to provide the basis for an adequate degree of variation in assigning ratings, and many raters are nondiscriminating with respect to the relative degrees of proficiency which can be exhibited by a group of employees. These two facts made it desirable, it seemed, to secure evidence concerning the extent of variability "inherently" associated with each trait and concerning the degree to which this "inherent" variability would become evident in supervisors' ratings. To secure appropriate data, the 30 most important traits were incorporated into rating scales of the type illustrated in Fig. 9 (Chap. 10). These 30 scales were divided into three subsets, as illustrated in Table 147.

TABLE 147. *Traits Important for Evaluating Clerical Performance**

Ability to work with others	Adaptability	Attitude toward work
Accuracy	Attitude toward company	Job skill
Ambition	Common sense	Judgment
Conscientiousness	Cooperativeness	Knowledge of work
Disposition	Courtesy	Loyalty
Initiative	Dependability	Productivity
Interest in work	Efficiency	Neatness
Perspective	Punctuality	Thoroughness
Quality of work	Tactfulness	Trustworthiness
Reliability	Volume of work	Willingness to accept responsibility

* From Ferguson, L. W. The L.O.M.A. Merit Rating Scales. *Person. Psychol.*, 1950, **3**, 193-216.

The directions for making the ratings on these scales followed closely those presented in Table 139 (Chap. 10). In accord with these directions the ratings were completed by 112 supervisors using

Set 1, 105 supervisors using Set 2, and 109 supervisors using Set 3. The distributions of ratings secured are presented in Table 148. The

TABLE 148. *Recapitulation of the Distributions of 32,600 Ratings on 30 Traits**

Rating of performance	Number	Per cent	Cumulative percentage
9. Distinctly superior...................	4621	14.17	14.17
8. Considerably above average...........	7108	21.81	35.98
7. Moderately above average............	6607	20.27	56.25
6. Slightly above average...............	4816	14.77	71.02
5. Average............................	6278	19.26	90.28
4. Slightly below average...............	1927	5.91	96.19
3. Moderately below average............	746	2.29	98.48
2. Considerably below average..........	365	1.12	99.60
1. Distinctly inferior...................	132	.40	100.00
Total.............................	32,600	100.00	

* From Ferguson, L. W. The L.O.M.A. Merit Rating Scales. *Person. Psychol.*, 1950, **3**, 193–216.

majority of the ratings fall into the upper third (that is, the more favorable third) of each scale. Approximately 56 per cent of the ratings (total for all traits) were allocated to positions 7, 8, and 9 (moderately above average, considerably above average, and distinctly superior), and 90 per cent were average or better. In contrast only 4 per cent of the ratings were allocated to positions 1, 2, and 3 (moderately below average, considerably below average, or distinctly inferior).

To eliminate a large measure of the skewness evident in Table 148, the ratings were reallocated on a five-step scale. This reallocation involved the reassignment given in Table 149.

TABLE 149. *Reallocation of Ratings Presented in Table 148**

Original category	New category	Per cent
9	5	14.17
8	4	21.81
7, 6	3	35.04
5	2	19.26
4, 3, 2, 1	1	9.72

* From Ferguson, L. W. The L.O.M.A. Merit Rating Scales. *Person. Psychol.*, 1950, **3**, 193–216.

Skewness was not entirely eliminated, but the reallocated ratings approximate much more closely those of a normal distribution than did those on the nine-step scales. Following this reallocation of ratings, standard deviations were computed for each of the 30 traits.

TABLE 150. *Distribution of Means (by Trait) of Equal-appearing-interval Statements**

Trait	No. of raters	Value of mean							Total
		1.0– 2.49	2.5– 3.49	3.5– 4.49	4.5– 5.49	5.5– 6.49	6.5– 7.49	7.5– 9.00	
Ability to work with others......	75	3	22	21	2	29	21	2	100
Adaptability...................	80	2	24	22	2	26	21	3	100
Attitude toward company.......	81	7	16	23	8	24	17	5	100
Common sense................	80	4	20	25	3	25	18	5	100
Cooperativeness...............	83	7	19	17	10	20	20	7	100
Courtesy......................	78	8	14	24	6	20	24	4	100
Dependability.................	79	6	19	18	9	21	23	4	100
Disposition	78	8	18	20	7	21	22	4	100
Efficiency.....................	77	3	24	20	6	21	22	4	100
Initiative.....................	79	5	19	24	4	21	22	5	100
Interest in work...............	76	4	19	24	6	22	20	5	100
Loyalty......................	81	4	24	19	7	21	22	3	100
Punctuality...................	82	5	18	25	6	25	18	3	100
Reliability....................	82	6	15	26	3	28	17	5	100
Tactfulness...................	82	6	18	26	2	22	22	4	100
Trustworthiness...............	79	5	18	25	4	20	27	1	100
Total......................	..	83	307	359	85	366	336	64	1,600

* From Ferguson, L. W. The L.O.M.A. Merit Rating Scales. *Person. Psychol.*, 1950, **3**, 193–216.

Descriptive Statements. The L.O.M.A. Clerical Salary Study Committee decided that the 30 traits which had been found most important and, of these, the 16 which had produced the greatest variability in ratings (that is, which had the largest standard deviations) would provide the basis for the preparation of items for the final scales. Therefore for each of these 16 traits, 100 statements descriptive of behavioral elements to be rated were prepared. For each trait half of the statements were so worded that affirmation of their applicability to an employee would indicate the presence of the trait to an average or greater than average degree. The other 50 statements in each set were so worded that their affirmation would indicate the presence of the trait to an average or less than average degree. Statements were prepared to be as unambiguous as possible and they were written in language that supervisors ordinarily use in evaluating employees.

The next step was to have the statements in each of the 16 sets scaled by the equal-appearing-interval technique. From 75 to 83 supervisors scaled each set of 100 statements. A nine-point scaling system was employed. The technique used here differed from that ordinarily employed in that it restricted the number of statements that could be placed in each of the nine categories. This restriction was imposed so that each supervisor would have to give careful consideration to a statement before deciding that it had high diagnostic value. Frequency distributions were prepared, and the mean and standard deviation of the ratings for each statement were computed. Table 150 presents the distribution of means for the 16 traits, and Table 151 presents the 16 distributions of standard deviations.

TABLE 151. *Distribution of Standard Deviations (by Trait) of Equal-appearing-interval Statements**

Trait	No. of raters	Value of standard deviation								Total
		.25–.54	.55–.69	.70–.84	.85–.99	1.00–1.14	1.15–1.29	1.30–1.44	1.45–1.74	
Ability to work with others	75	..	3	14	27	28	19	9	..	100
Adaptability	80	..	1	13	32	33	17	3	1	100
Attitude toward company	81	..	11	26	31	22	7	2	1	100
Common sense	80	..	2	11	32	40	10	5	..	100
Cooperativeness	83	3	11	22	36	16	8	4	..	100
Courtesy	78	..	12	26	31	18	10	1	2	100
Dependability	79	..	9	24	34	12	17	4	..	100
Disposition	78	3	5	23	33	21	12	1	2	100
Efficiency	77	2	8	10	29	32	15	3	1	100
Initiative	79	..	3	15	27	32	18	4	1	100
Interest in work	76	..	4	15	37	28	14	2	..	100
Loyalty	81	1	4	19	26	32	14	4	..	100
Punctuality	82	1	2	6	25	36	18	7	5	100
Reliability	82	..	2	17	25	34	17	4	1	100
Tactfulness	82	1	..	10	29	35	20	5	..	100
Trustworthiness	79	3	5	13	29	29	15	4	2	100
Total	..	14	82	264	483	448	231	62	16	1,600

* From Ferguson, L. W. The L.O.M.A. Merit Rating Scales. *Person. Psychol.*, 1950, **3**, 193–216.

The selection of statements for the final forms was confined largely to those whose mean values were 6.5 or higher and 3.5 or lower and to those whose standard deviations did not exceed 1.30. Ninety-four and one-half per cent of 416 statements had mean values of 6.5 or over, 93.0 per cent of 416 additional statements had values under 3.5, and 93.3 per cent of all 832 statements had standard deviations less than 1.30.

No independent criterion population was available for item analysis purposes, so the L.O.M.A. Clerical Salary Study Committee established an arbitrary scoring system. First, the mean value of each statement was rounded to the nearest whole number. For the "positive" statements, that is, those with means of 9, 8, or 7, the weights given in Table 152 were established. Conversely, for the items at the opposite extreme, that is, those with means of 1, 2, or 3, the weights given in Table 153 were assigned. In the interest of

TABLE 152. *Scoring Weights for "Positive" Statements**

Response	Mean value		
	7	8	9
Always or completely characteristic..............	7	8	9
Usually or almost characteristic.................	6	7	8
Sometimes or moderately characteristic..........	5	6	7
Seldom or slightly characteristic................	4	5	6
Never or not at all characteristic................	3	4	5

* From Ferguson, L. W. The L.O.M.A. Merit Rating Scales. *Person. Psychol.*, 1950, **3**, 193–216.

TABLE 153. *Scoring Weights for "Negative" Statements**

Response	Mean value		
	1	2	3
Always or completely characteristic..............	1	2	3
Usually or almost characteristic.................	2	3	4
Sometimes or moderately characteristic..........	3	4	5
Seldom or slightly characteristic................	4	5	6
Never or not at all characteristic................	5	6	7

* From Ferguson, L. W. The L.O.M.A. Merit Rating Scales. *Person. Psychol.*, 1950, **3**, 193–216.

making one uniform scoring key for all 16 scales, several slight departures from this system were allowed.

Standardization. To obtain data for standardization purposes, the L.O.M.A. Clerical Salary Study Committee secured experimental ratings for more than 17,000 employees. To reduce bias in the selection of employees for this purpose, the following instructions were sent to the cooperating companies:

Some person other than the supervisor who is to do the rating should select the employees who are to be rated. This will make it impossible for a supervisor to select his favorite (or vice-versa) as a basis for the ratings. To insure the greatest degree of comparability from company to company, will you please include employees representing all levels of performance. In terms of a nine-step scale of overall ability, we should like the entire employee group for your company to consist of approximately

    4% classified as distinctly superior
    7% classified as considerably above average
  12% classified as moderately above average
  17% classified as slightly above average
  20% classified as average
  17% classified as slightly below average
  12% classified as moderately below average
    7% classified as considerably below average
    4% classified as distinctly inferior

If the norms which we intend to prepare are to serve their purpose, it is absolutely essential that we include employees differing widely in, and representing all, level of performance.

Ratings were secured for 500 or more employees for each of the 16 scales. In spite of the instructions issued there was considerable

TABLE 154. *Interpretation of Standard Scores on L.O.M.A. Merit Rating Scales**

Score	%	Rating	Interpretation
85–90	4	A	Distinctly superior
75–84	7	B+	Considerably above average
65–74	12	B−	Moderately above average
55–64	17	C+	Slightly above average
45–54	20	C	Average
35–44	17	C−	Slightly below average
25–34	12	D+	Moderately below average
15–24	7	D−	Considerably below average
1–14	4	E	Distinctly inferior

* From Ferguson, L. W. The L.O.M.A. Merit Rating Scales. *Person. Psychol.*, 1950, **3**, 193–216.

skewness in the raw-score distributions. Therefore these distributions were normalized before final standards were set up. The interpretation applying to the standard scores is given in Table 154.

THE APPRAISAL OF FIELD TRAINING REPRESENTATIVES

One of the pressing problems in any organization is that of making adequate and fair appraisals of the work done by its employees. These appraisals are needed as an aid in determining salaries and wages and in deciding upon promotions, demotions, transfers, and other personnel changes.

The Metropolitan Life Insurance Company uses five analytical rating forms in its field organization. Two of these forms are for agents, two are for assistant managers, and one is for traveling field training division representatives. Our task now is to describe the development of one of these forms and to show how it differs, as do the L.O.M.A. scales we have just described, from the nonanalytical methods we discussed in Chap. 10. We shall concern ourselves with the form developed for appraising the work performance of the Metropolitan's staff of traveling field training division representatives.

Step 1. The first step in the development of this form was that of collecting a large variety of statements pertaining to all major phases of the work performed by field training division representatives. This work relates to the training of managers and assistant managers so that they in turn can better train agents under their supervision. Samples of the statements collected are: "Has little work to take pride in." "Is a real student of the life insurance business." "Uses poor methods of prospecting and selling" and "Helps management determine the real needs for training." This list of statements was secured as a result of previous informal investigation in the field training division, suggestions offered by field training division representatives and others who possessed knowledge of the duties and characteristics of field training division representatives, and prior research and study by the investigator. When the complete list of statements was assembled, it was submitted to field training division representatives for review, and, as a result, some of the statements were reworded to assure more adequate terminology. Upon the completion of this editing process, the statements were segregated into two groups of 100 statements each and were designated experimental appraisal forms A and B.

Step 2. Next, field training supervisors (these are first-line supervisors) were asked to complete these trial appraisal forms for all field training instructors.

Step 3. Field training division supervisors (these are second-line supervisors) were asked to supply criterion data consisting of degree of acquaintance ratings, numerical performance ratings, and paired-comparisons performance ratings. These ratings were made on forms similar to those presented in Figs. 9 and 11 (Chap. 10) and were secured for 64 field training instructors.

Step 4. Two criterion groups of 20 field training instructors were selected. One group consisted of the 20 field training instructors with the highest composite criterion ratings, and the other group consisted of the 20 field training instructors with the lowest composite criterion ratings. These two groups were compared with each other so that the responses characteristic of each group could be identified. To illustrate, consider the statement "Bases suggested training program on agent's individual needs." This statement was said to be always or completely characteristic of 45 per cent of the high-scoring field training instructors and of only 20 per cent of the low-scoring field training instructors. It was said to be usually or almost characteristic of 50 per cent of the high-scoring field training instructors and of 55 per cent of the low-scoring field training instructors. It was said to be sometimes or moderately characteristic of 5 per cent of the high-scoring field training instructors and of 25 per cent of the low-scoring field training instructors. We see that the response "always or completely characteristic" applies to a larger percentage of high-scoring than of low-scoring field training instructors but that the responses "usually or almost characteristic" and "sometimes or moderately characteristic" apply to a larger percentage of low-scoring than of high-scoring field training instructors. The two remaining responses, "seldom or slightly characteristic" and "never or not at all characteristic," are nondifferentiating, since they did not apply to the instructors in either criterion group. When these comparisons were complete, the 78 items showing the greatest degree of differentiating power were selected to comprise the final appraisal form.

Step 5. Field training supervisors were asked to reappraise all field training instructors on the 78 items retained for use in the final form. This reappraisal was requested because a review of the field training supervisors' responses to the statements in the preliminary forms indicated a considerable degree of overrating. A series of meetings was held to caution field training supervisors against overrating, and in these meetings they proceeded with their re-appraisals. When these reappraisals were complete, each field training supervisor was asked to cite instances of behavior on the part of each field training instructor that would support the answers he had given. If a field training supervisor could not do this, he was asked to lower his rating.

Step 6. When the work of all field training instructors had been reappraised, the appraisal forms were scored on the basis of a formula which assigned a weight of 5 to the most favorable response, a weight of 4 to the next most favorable response, and so on, down to a weight of 1 for the least favorable response to each statement. Consequently, on 46 statements the response "always or completely characteristic" carried a weight of 5, and on 30 statements the response "never or not at all characteristic" carried a weight of 5. Since two statements were ambiguous in nature, they were not used.

When a distribution of the scores secured on this basis became available, the diagnostic values of the 78 statements in the form were recomputed. To ensure the highest possible degree of internal consistency, 19 field training instructors who secured scores in the upper 27 per cent of the distribution just described and who also secured scores in the upper 27 per cent of the distribution of criterion scores described in Step 4 were chosen to represent successful field training instructors. And 19 field training instructors who secured scores in the lowest 27 per cent of the distribution which has just been described and who also secured scores in the lowest 27 per cent of the distribution of criterion scores described in Step 4 were selected to represent unsuccessful field training instructors. Then the comparison procedure illustrated in Step 5 was repeated. Field training supervisors reported that the statement "Demonstrates effectively good debit management" is always or completely charac-teristic of 58 per cent of the successful field training instructors but of none of the unsuccessful field training instructors. This gives a difference of 58 per cent in favor of successful field training instructors. Field training supervisors reported that this statement is usually or almost characteristic of 42 per cent of the successful field training instructors and of 63 per cent of the unsuccessful field training instructors. This gives a difference of 21 per cent in favor of unsuccessful field training instructors. The response "sometimes or moderately characteristic" was said to apply to 32 per cent of the successful field training instructors and to none of the unsuccessful field training instructors. And the response "seldom or slightly characteristic" was said to apply to 5 per cent of the successful field training instructors and to none of the unsuccessful field training instructors. The response "never or not at all characteristic" applied to neither group. Final scoring weights were determined upon the basis of these differences. For example, when a given response, say "usually or almost characteristic," was found to yield a difference of 35 per cent in favor of successful field training instructors, it was assigned a scoring weight of 35. If it was found to yield a difference of, say, 42 per cent in favor of unsuccessful field training instructors, it was assigned a scoring weight of −42. When it was found that a strict application of this procedure would yield a logically inconsistent series of scoring weights, certain of the responses were combined before the weights were assigned. In one case, a strictly literal application of the rule for determining weights gave the series in Table 155.

TABLE 155. *An Illogical Series of "Scoring Weights"*

Always or completely characteristic	58
Usually or almost characteristic	−21
Sometimes or moderately characteristic	−32
Seldom or slightly characteristic	− 5
Never or not at all characteristic	0

This series is illogical. Fewer points are subtracted from the accumulating score for the response "seldom or slightly characteristic" than for the response "sometimes or moderately characteristic." And fewer points still (in fact, none at all) are subtracted for the response "never or not at all characteristic." In this instance, therefore, it seemed proper to combine the last three responses and to make no differentiation between them. This means that only three effective discriminations are provided by the statement in question. The scoring weights become 58 for the response "always or completely characteristic," −21 for the response "usually or almost characteristic," and −37 for the responses "sometimes or moderately characteristic," "seldom or slightly characteristic," or "never or not at all characteristic." This gives a logically consistent series of scoring weights.

Step 7. Reliability was determined by correlating the scores on the odd-numbered statements with those on the even-numbered statements and by stepping this correlation up with the Spearman-Brown Prophecy Formula. The figure arrived at in this way is .97. This value compares favorably with that pertaining to the great majority of appraisal forms used by business and industrial organizations.

Step 8. The validity of the scores on the field training instructor's appraisal form was determined by correlating them with the criterion ratings discussed in Step 4. This correlation is .60. This value is spurious, however, because it is based upon the data used in the derivation of the scoring weights. On the other hand, the correlation is low because the criterion scores do not possess perfect reliability.

Uses. This appraisal form has been found useful in several ways. It has served as a criterion for the validation of a test for selecting new field training instructors, and it has served as a basis for the determination of salaries. It has served as a basis for making promotions, and it has served as a basis for deciding upon training assignments. In connection with this last purpose, it has indicated which field training instructors have needed additional training, and it has indicated in what areas of their performance this additional training was needed.

12

PROJECTIVE TECHNIQUES: A PERCEPTUAL

APPROACH

All the personality-measuring techniques we have discussed have been based upon the theory that responses to test items must be controlled. They must be controlled, it is thought, so that we can determine what they mean. Imagine our problem, for example, if we did not provide a limited number of responses to the items in the Strong Vocational Interest Test or in the Bernreuter Personality Inventory. As it is, there still are an enormous variety of responses available. Let us stop and figure a moment. To each item on the Strong Vocational Interest Test a subject can respond with an L, an I, or a D. So if we consider just two items, there are the following nine possible responses:

Item 1	Item 2
L	L
L	I
L	D
I	L
I	I
I	D
D	L
D	I
D	D

When we add a third item, the number of possible responses increases to 27. But there are 400 items in Dr. Strong's test, so the total number of possible responses is 3^{400}, that is, 3 raised to the 400th power. We do not need to figure this out to realize that we have an enormous number on our hands.

Of course, not all tests provide for as many possible responses as the Strong Vocational Interest Test. But they all provide for a goodly number. This being the case, most of our methods of analysis are designed to classify and organize these responses into general categories amenable to statistical treatment.

Some psychologists object to this procedure. They claim that we lose a great deal of valuable information by ignoring the vast number of response variations which could take place if we did not restrict them. Therefore, they have devised a number of techniques called projective techniques in which responses are completely uncontrolled. They have prepared these techniques on the theory that personality can exert its full sway and exhibit itself completely only in such unrestricted and uncontrolled responses. They feel that this projection cannot take place in the responses allowed by the classical test-measuring techniques.

In this chapter, and in Chap. 13, we propose to discuss the two most widely used projective techniques: the Rorschach test and the Thematic Apperception Test. There are other projective techniques, to be sure, but no others which compare with these in the widespread usage which they enjoy.

CONTENT OF TEST

The Rorschach test is an ink-blot test. It was developed by Hermann Rorschach, a Swiss psychiatrist, on the theory that what we see in ink blots, and how we see these things, provides clues to our personality. If you see a beautiful tree because of the color and if I see a skeleton because of the shape (in the same ink blot), we may have different personalities. At least, this is the theory.

There are 10 blots in the Rorschach test. Five have color and five do not. These blots are reproduced on cards measuring 7 by $9\frac{1}{2}$ inches, and these cards are shown one at a time to a subject. We ask the subject to tell us what he sees in each blot, we record his responses, we take notes on his behavior, and later we ask him to explain the features of the blot which formed the bases for the pictures they suggested to him.

There is very little extant about the way in which Rorschach constructed or selected the particular ink blots that comprise the Rorschach test. Klopfer and Kelley surmise, however, that they are the selected residue of thousands of experimental blots. We shall have little to say, therefore, about the construction of the Rorschach test. In fact, we have nothing further to add on this point. We shall try instead to describe what the test is supposed to do, how it is supposed to do these things, and how well it does them.

PURPOSE OF TEST

First, what is the Rorschach test supposed to do? Klopfer and Kelley, the authorities we shall follow in this chapter, say that it gives us

. . . a configurational picture which reveals the interplay between various major intellectual and emotional factors in the personality of the subject. From this picture the following structural aspects of personality are to be deduced:

1. The degree and mode of control with which a subject tries to regulate his experiences and actions

2. The responsiveness of his emotional energies to stimulations from outside and promptings from within

3. His mental approach to given problems and situations

4. His creative or imaginative capacities, and the use he makes of them

5. A general estimate of his intellectual level and the major qualitative features of his thinking

6. A general estimate of the degree of security or anxiety, of balance in general, and specific unbalances

7. The relative degree of maturity in the total personality development

[Klopfer and Kelley continue] This list does not represent a complete account of the personality aspects revealed by the Rorschach method. It simply enumerates the major structural elements in the configurational picture which the Rorschach material reflects.

A SAMPLE PROTOCOL

Complete or not, this list represents a big order. To understand in what ways a Rorschach record can provide this information, we had best start with a complete protocol. Then we can base our discussion on what we observe in this protocol. The protocol we shall give lists the reactions of Carmen, one of the subjects discussed by Merrill in her volume on *Problems of Child Delinquency*. Carmen gave a total of 30 responses, an average of 3 per card. It took her approximately eighteen minutes to give them. They are given in Table 156.

This protocol constitutes a record of Carmen's *performance*, the first phase of the Rorschach method. The protocol as it now stands

TABLE 156. *Carmen's Protocol**

Response	Card	Position	Time, seconds	Performance
1	1	rsu†	5	Cliff or precipice with two people on it
2	1	rsu	20	Cat
3	1	usd	45	Skeleton of a prairie cow
			60	Interval 1
4	2	rsu	4	Insides of a person
5	2	usd	15	Lamp—and a flame
			35	Interval 2
6	3	rsu	5	Skeleton—body and arms. Red blotches are the blood, middle red is the heart
7	3	usd	30	Bogey man
8	3	usd	35	Profiles, man with mustache
9	3	usd	45	Branches, dried, no leaves
			60	Interval 3
10	4	rsu	5	Bear rug, eyes, queer kind of bear
11	4	rsu	10	Pair of boots
12	4	rsu	18	Ears of a dog
			45	Interval 4
13	5	rsu	3	Bat
14	5	rsu	10	Snail. Head here, and horns stick up here.
			27	Interval 5
15	6	rsu	1	Fish
16	6	rsu	9	Special kind of butterfly
17	6	rsu	33	Bedpost
			35	Interval 6
18	7	rsu	3	Two ladies gossiping together. Funny hair-do's. Both pointing toward places.
19	7	usd	20	Couple dancers, old fashioned kind
			29	Interval 7
20	8	usd	11	Sweet peas
21	8	tor	22	Hyenas with that shape
22	8	usd	43	Back bones
23	8	rsu	50	Face of a man, long beard, long hat on, like in funny books
			61	Interval 8
24	9	rsu	4	Sunset. Sun coming up over here; forest, road here, coming right down through here
25	9	usd	30	Big fat lady, two arms and legs; pink
			60	Interval 9
26	10	rsu	2	Bunch of bugs and insects
27	10	usd	20	Big angel floating down from heaven on a parachute
28	10	usd	30	Crab
29	10	usd	33	Two people holding hands over cliff or bucket or object
30	10	usd	56	Two devils climbing up a tree
			60	Interval 10

* From Merrill, M. A. *Problems of Child Delinquency*. Boston: Houghton Mifflin Company, 1947.

† rsu = right side up; usd = upside down; tor = top on right.

undoubtedly has very little meaning, even if you bothered to read it. So let us go over it again and see what we should look for. First, we see that Carmen looked at Card 1 for five seconds and said she saw a cliff or precipice with two people on it. She looked at it for twenty seconds more and said she saw a cat. Then she turned the card upside down, looked at it this way for forty-five seconds, and said she saw the skeleton of a prairie cow. Now she laid Card 1 aside, taking sixty seconds to do this, and picked up Card 2. She looked at Card 2 for four seconds and said she saw the insides of a person. She turned the card upside down, looked at it this way for fifteen seconds, and said she saw a lamp and a flame. Then she laid Card 2 on the table, picked up Card 3, and proceeded as indicated in the protocol. With this record before us, we can do two things: we can determine the content of Carmen's responses, and we can analyze the time relationships involved. Let us begin with the content.

Content. How many things did Carmen see? In Card 1 she saw two people, in Card 3 she saw a bogeyman, in Card 7 she saw two ladies gossiping together and two dancers, in Card 9 she saw a big fat lady, and in Card 10 she saw an angel, two people holding hands, and two devils climbing up a tree. This gives a total of eight responses involving human beings or the human form. Carmen also saw many animal forms. For example, in Card 1 she saw a cat, in Card 5 she saw a bat, in Card 6 she saw a fish and a butterfly, in Card 8 she saw hyenas, and in Card 10 she saw a bunch of bugs and insects and some blue crabs. Thus eight of her responses had an animal content. A complete review of Carmen's responses gives us the tabulation in Table 157.

TABLE 157. *The Content of Carmen's Responses*

Content	No.	Content	No.
Animal	8	Human anatomy	1
Animal detail	3	Animal anatomy	1
Human	7	Objects	3
Human detail	2	Objects created from parts of animals	1
Nature	4	Total	30

Now if you were to take the Rorschach test or if I were to take it, we would probably see many things that Carmen did not see, and some of the things she saw we would not see. Thus the content of our responses might be quite different from the content of Carmen's responses. And in these differences lie, say the Rorschach experts, important clues to the nature of Carmen's, of your, and of my personalities.

One of the major things we want to note about the content of Carmen's responses is the percentage involving animals. We want to know this because if it is large, it indicates, say the Rorschach experts, a stereotyped or a narrow range of interests. It indicates this, they say, because the choice of animal concepts is obvious. Therefore, a person who cannot choose a reasonable proportion of concepts not involving animals is merely reacting to the obvious. Carmen gave a total of 11 animal responses. This is just 37 per cent of the total number of responses which she gave, so we conclude that there is no evidence that Carmen's interests are stereotyped or narrow.

We were able to classify Carmen's responses into nine content categories. These include those most important in any Rorschach analysis, but they by no means exhaust the possibilities. Bell has compiled a list of 34 frequently used content categories, and we give this list, for general information, in Table 158.

TABLE 158. *Content Categories of Rorschach Responses**

Animal	Emblem	Sex
Animal detail	Fire	Statues
Abstract	Fountains	Structures
Alphabet	Geographical	Symbolic
Anatomy	Ice	Volcanic
Art	Mask	Water forms
Architecture	Mountains	Imaginary
Human	Blood	Cave
Human detail	Botanical forms	Color
Clouds, mist, fog	Nature	Numbers
Plants	Objects	Scenery

* From Bell, J. E. *Projective Techniques*. New York: Longmans, Green & Co., Inc., 1948.

Time. The second thing we said we could do with Carmen's protocol was to analyze the time relationships involved. The protocol itself contains the time it took Carmen to make each response and the time elapsing between cards. From these figures we can compute Carmen's total response time, average response time, total reaction time, and average reaction time. This last represents the average time required for the first response to each card. We should also compute, say the Rorschach experts, the average reaction time for the cards with color and compare this with the average reaction time for the cards without color.

Carmen's total response time was 617 seconds, or 10 minutes 17 seconds. This makes her average response time not quite 21 seconds. Her total reaction time was 472 seconds, or 7 minutes 52 seconds. This makes her average response time a trifle over 47 seconds. Finally, Carmen's average response time for the cards without color was 45 seconds while that for the cards with color was 49 seconds. These data would lead the Rorschach expert to conclude that Carmen has quick reaction and response time (less than one-half minute per response) and no color shock (that is, no practical difference in average response time for the colored and noncolored blots).

Response and reaction times averaging over one and one-half minutes are considered by Rorschach experts to be symptomatic of severe pathology or of extreme inhibitions. And large differences in the average response and reaction times for the colored and un- colored blots are supposed to be symptomatic of severe emotional disturbance. We see that Carmen, in her response and reaction time, gives no evidence of such psychological malfunction.

THE INQUIRY

We must now mention the inquiry, the second, and a very impor- tant, phase of the Rorschach method. In the performance proper the task of the examiner is to record whatever the subject says. But in the inquiry, which follows the performance, the task of the examiner is to ask the subject what factors contributed to the formation of his concepts.

Location. One of the things which the examiner tries to find out is whether the concept was determined by the whole of the blot or by some detail, and if by the latter, whether it was determined by a large detail or by a small detail. And if it was determined by a small detail, was this a usual detail or an unusual detail? And if it was an unusual detail, was it an edge detail or an inside detail? In short, the examiner tries to determine the location of the concept on, or within, the blot area.

Carmen's responses were located as indicated in Table 159. She used the whole blot in 12 of her responses, normal details in 14 of them, small normal details in 2 of them, and she utilized the white space in the remaining 2. Examples of Carmen's use of the whole blot are in her responses of "cat" and "the insides of a person" (Card

TABLE 159. *The Location of Carmen's Responses*

Whole blot	12
Normal detail	14
Small normal detail	2
White space	2
Total	30

2), "skeleton," "bogey man" (Card 3), "bear rug" (Card 4), and so on. Examples of her use of normal detail can be found in her responses of "cliff or precipice with two people on it" (Card 1), "man with mustache" (Card 3), "pair of boots" and "ears of a dog" (Card 4), and so on.

When we contrast this distribution with that which might result from your responses to the Rorschach test (or mine), we find, say the Rorschach experts, our third set of clues to the inner structure of Carmen's, your, and my personalities. The normal subject will give, according to Klopfer and Kelley, about 30 responses. Of these, 20 will be based upon normal details, 7 will be based upon wholes, and the remaining 3 will be based upon small details.

Carmen gave, we saw, 12 concepts in which the entire blot was utilized. This is somewhat more than average and indicates a tendency, say the Rorschachers, toward "an emphasis on the abstract forms of thinking and the higher forms of mental activity." A subject who would base only a small number of his concepts on the whole blot would be considered, in contrast with Carmen, to lack a capacity for higher mental activity. Klopfer and Kelley say that "the intelligent subject will . . . locate half of his responses in the obvious areas of the cards . . . and will place 5 to 15 per cent of his responses in other portions which are not so obvious." According to this, Carmen must be an intelligent subject, for 46 per cent of her responses make use of normal (obvious) details and 7 per cent make use of small (but noticeable) details.

When a subject uses the whole blot, he may do this in several ways. He may respond with a concept showing a superior and elaborate organization; he may give a response making good, but not superior, use of the entire blot; he may give a response suggested by exterior outline, but one involving no extensive elaboration; he may utilize only the crudest features of the blot; or he may give wholly arbitrary responses. The subject can also give responses which tend only toward the use of the whole blot. For example, neglecting some detail either inadvertently or by design, he may not use the entire blot but just most of it. He may rather loosely or poorly organize the various portions of the blot into a combined whole. He may react to only one of the symmetrical halves of the blot, and finally he may select some detail and use this as a basis for building up a response for the whole blot.

When a subject bases too many of his concepts on details in contrast to wholes, Klopfer and Kelley claim that this indicates, if supported by other signs, a "trend toward mental escape from reality." Further, they say that an emphasis on tiny details indicates the presence of obsessional traits, that an emphasis on inside details indicates preoccupation on the part of the subject with his own inner life, and that an emphasis on outside details indicates an attempt to keep from the troubled stirrings of the inner self.

Carmen bases two of her concepts on the white spaces. This represents a normal frequency. When a large number of concepts are based on the white spaces, it is supposed to indicate the presence of oppositional tendencies. This conclusion is reached because the use of the white spaces necessitates the reversal of the usual figure-ground relations. A person who has oppositional tendencies may show these in self-destructive tendencies or in negativistic behavior in general.

The *location* of his responses will reveal, say the Rorschach experts, the subject's mental approach. They will show whether he has a preference for sweeping generalities, a tendency to get lost in unrelated details, the compulsive habits of a perfectionist, or whether he exhibits the arbitrary digressions of an undisciplined mind. We show in Table 160 a considerable number of the variations which, according to Bell, can take place in the location of a subject's concepts.

When a subject bases a large majority of his concepts on the whole blot area, this is taken as evidence that he has a tendency for making sweeping generalities. When he bases a large number of his concepts on details, particularly on small details, and does not integrate these details into a whole blot concept, it is thought that he is exhibiting a tendency to get lost in unrelated details. When a subject is meticulous in pointing out that the whole blot could be a____, except for some detail, or that a normal detail could be a____, except for some lesser detail, it is thought that he is exhibiting the compulsive habits of a perfectionist. And finally, when a subject gives responses that are not well integrated with the blot area or that do not make efficient use of the various concept determinants, it is taken as evidence that he has an undisciplined mind.

TABLE 160. *Location Categories in Rorschach Responses**

1. Whole blot used for interpretation
2. Cut-off whole (a small portion of whole omitted)
3. Confabulatory response: a meaning assigned to the whole on the basis of an interpretation of a detail
4. Whole response in which several details are successfully combined to produce a whole
5. Detail response with a tendency toward a whole interpretation
6. A normal detail of the blot
7. Small normal detail
8. Small infrequently used detail
9. Edge detail
10. Rare small detail
11. Inside detail
12. Oligophrenic detail: choice of a small area of a body where an individual normally gives a whole body
13. White space between blot areas chosen for interpretation
14. Combinations of space details with whole, normal detail, or rare details
15. Interpretation of all the white area of the card

* From Bell, J. E. *Projective Techniques*. New York: Longmans, Green & Co., Inc., 1948.

In connection with this idea of mental approach, much is made of the order in which the locations are used. A subject who proceeds in each blot to give a concept based first on the whole of the blot, then on a normal detail, then on a small detail, then on the white space (or in the exact reverse order) is said to proceed in a rigid manner. If he does this in all but one, two, or three cards, his approach is said to be orderly. But if he fails to use this order in four to seven cards, his approach is loose, and if he does not use any order, or uses it in only one or two cards, his approach is said to be confused.

Determinants. A fourth clue to the structure of personality is to be found, say the Rorschach experts, in the *determinants* of a subjects's concepts. Did Carmen base her concepts on the form or on the color of the blot? Or on both equally? Did she make use of the shading? And if she did, just how did she make use of it? In perspective, surface, or depth? Did she inject movement into her responses? And if she did, was it human movement, animal movement, or inanimate movement?

Inquiry revealed that Carmen used the form of the blot in nine of her responses, human movement in eight of them, shading in five of them, and so on, as indicated in Table 161.

TABLE 161. *Determinants of Carmen's Responses*

Determinant	Number	Determinant	Number
Human movement	8	Form	9
Animal movement	1	Form with color	2
Inanimate movement	2	Color with form	2
Shading, vista	2	Color only	1
Shading, surface	3	Total	30

Examples of Carmen's imputation of human movement can be seen in her response of "bogey man" (Card 3), in her response of "two ladies gossiping together" (Card 7), and in her response of "two people holding hands over a cliff or bucket or object" (Card 10). Examples of her use of form can be seen in her response of "skeleton of a prairie cow" (Card 3), in her response of "profiles" and "man with mustache" (Card 8), and in her response of "pair of boots" (Card 11).

Carmen's injection of human movement into eight of her responses shows, say the Rorschach experts, that she is prompted from within. But her use of form in nine of her responses shows that she keeps these inner impulses under control. When a subject attributes movement to a majority of the blot concepts, his inner impulses are, say the Rorschach experts, running riot; and when he overemphasizes form responses, he is subjecting his inner impulses to overrigid intellectual control.

There are 13 major classes of determinants in the Rorschach test. Each class can be manifested in several different ways. Some of these ways are listed in Table 162, following Bell.

Form. The two chief characteristics of concern in form responses are their definition and their accuracy. It is necessary to be concerned with the form qualities of the concept as imagined by the subject, with the form qualities of the blot itself, and with what are considered the conventional form qualities of the concept. Discrepancies can occur between the individual and conventional

TABLE 162. *Frequently Used Determinants of Rorschach Responses**

1. Form answers:
   a. Good forms
   b. Poor forms
   c. Percent of well-perceived forms in relation to the total number of forms
2. Movement answers:
   a. Human movement
   b. Impending human movement
   c. Animal movement
   d. Impending animal movement
   e. Inanimate movement
   f. Detail involving movement
3. Color responses:
   a. Color responses not involving form
   b. Color naming
   c. Color description
   d. Color symbolism
   e. Color with form used secondarily
   f. Color and form combined
   g. Sum of the color responses
   h. Disturbances in responding to colored cards
   i. Disturbances in reactions to the red color
4. Shading responses (chiaroscuro):
   a. Reactions in which subject responds to specific parts of the shading (e.g., highlights or cast shadows)
   b. Reactions to the total impression of shading
   c. Light-determined responses
   d. Vista responses: shading used to create perspective and differentiated surfaces
   e. Shading as surface texture
   f. Shading involved in projecting a three-dimensional object on a two-dimensional place (e.g., X-Ray, topographical maps)
   g. Shading used as diffusion
   h. Use of black, gray or white as color
   i. Disturbances in reactions to the shading elements in the cards

* From Bell, J. E. *Projective Techniques.* New York: Longmans, Green & Co., Inc., 1948.

concepts or between the form qualities of the individual and the blot itself. These latter discrepancies display themselves in completely arbitrary responses, in the mechanical perseveration of a response from one blot to the next, in the perseveration of a fixed idea from one blot to the next, in confabulation (the attribution to the whole of some concept suggested by a part), in inaccurate outline responses, and in a disregard for obvious form elements in the blots leading, by this neglect, to rather indefinite concepts.

Responses of form are considered mediocre when they are merely of a popular variety, when they are noncommittal, when they seem to evade form, and when they make fairly accurate use of outline but of little else. Form responses above average in accuracy are those in which much elaboration or organization of the blot material occurs, and, of course, the greater the degree of elaboration or organization, or both, the more above average the response is considered to be.

Color. Responses involving color as a determinant can be classified into three general categories: achromatic color responses, combinations of color and form responses, and pure bright color responses. Achromatic color responses involve distinctions between the use or the rejection of achromatic color areas, combination of the achromatic with bright colors, illumination effects, and the photographic (black and white) reproduction of bright colors.

Combination color responses are generally divided into those in which color is predominant but form is a necessary adjunct and those in which form is dominant but color is a necessary adjunct. Each of these two more general classes is subdivided into those responses which seem to represent a "natural" combination, into forced, arbitrary, and loose combinations, and into inaccurate combinations.

Finally, pure, bright color responses are classified as crude, *e.g.*, color naming or color description, and as the use of color in some symbolic way.

In general, color responses are supposed to indicate a readiness to establish healthy emotional relationships with the external world. Form responses are supposed to indicate the state of balance between the intellectual and emotional aspects of personality structure. Movement responses are supposed to indicate the extent to which a person is guided by his internal spontaneous impulses.

Klopfer and Kelley indicate that an optimum relation between form and color responses consists of twice as many responses in which form predominates over color as responses in which color predominates over form and color responses alone. The use of color apart from form is supposed to indicate an impulsive emotionality. The more important form becomes in relation to color, the more the subject's emotion is brought under control. An overemphasis on form in contrast with color, say when more than one-half the form responses have no color determinant, indicates a tendency to repress or control spontaneous reactions.

Shading. Shading, as a determinant, can be used as a surface impression or as a depth impression. If it is used as a surface impression, it is supposed to indicate a tendency for the subject to be cautious in his approach to the external world. If shading is used as a depth impression, it is supposed to indicate an inner stirring, some type of anxiety. Besides these two uses of shading, Klopfer and Kelley indicate that it is important for us to distinguish between a differentiated use of shading and an undifferentiated use of shading. A differentiated use of shading is supposed to indicate caution and a sense of refined control. In contrast, an undifferentiated use of shading is supposed to indicate that the subject's emotional reactions are vague and general.

Movement. The use of movement is supposed to indicate a rich, inner associative life. This movement can be human or humanlike. It can be visualized as human action taking place or as the live posture of some living figure. Other modes of seeing human action are also possible, but those we have listed are those most frequently encountered. Animal action can be visualized, again, in the whole blot or in part of it. It can be seen as the live posture of a living animal, as action apparently occurring in only part of the animal, or as action apparently induced by natural forces. When movement is used more frequently than color, the subject is said to be controlled by his inner, introversive tendencies. When color predominates over movement, the subject is said to be controlled by outer, extrotensive tendencies.

Originality. Finally, we must concern ourselves with the originality of Carmen's responses. Did she give unique responses? Or did she give responses typical of those given by other individuals? The examiner makes no comment on 25 of Carmen's responses. Two of the other five he classes as original, and three as popular. This is not very many, and Klopfer and Kelley state "that the use of less than four popular concepts indicates a lack of conformity on the part of the subject."

INTERPRETATION

To summarize our discussion thus far, we find that we can analyze Rorschach responses in terms of their content, time relationships, location, determinants, and originality. These analyses enable us to gauge, say the Rorschachers, the subject's characteristic mental approach to his problems, the extent to which he possesses introversive vs. extroversive personality habits, the type and degree of control he exercises over his spontaneous impulses, and his degree of emotional adjustment and maturity.

To determine each of the foregoing, it is necessary for the interpreter to concern himself with the quantitative results of the responses, with their configuration, with the distribution of responses for all 10 cards, with a sequence analysis of the scoring list, with a qualitative analysis of all individual responses, with an analysis of the general symbolic character of the content of the responses, and with an analysis of any conspicuous behavior while the subject was responding to the cards.

A basic tenet in Rorschach theory is that human beings are subject to two sets of forces: those arising from within and those impinging upon us from without. It becomes a matter of importance, therefore, for the Rorschach test to assess the relative strengths of these two sets of forces and to determine in what ways and how effectively a subject balances and controls these forces.

The promptings from within are exhibited, say the Rorschachers, in the attribution of movement, particularly human movement. Thus a marked introvert should give a large number of action concepts. This on the theory that to attribute movement requires the exercise of imagination, and imagination comes from one's inner promptings.

A tendency to be responsive to external stimulation is exhibited, say the Rorschachers, in a subject's reactions involving color. On this theory, a marked extrovert should give a large number of color responses. This brings us to the point where we can see that a measure of extroversion-introversion should be contained in the ratio of color and movement responses. When the number of movement responses is divided by the number of color responses, we have a formula in which large values indicate introversion and small values indicate extroversion. Klopfer and Kelley do not accept this formula as the sole measure of introversion-extroversion, but we need not concern ourselves here with their reservations.

Evidence for the type and degree of control which a subject can exercise over his spontaneous impulses is to be found, say Klopfer and Kelley, in responses based on form. There are three types of control we need to consider: outer, inner, and constrictive. Outer control is evidenced by the use of concepts utilizing both form and color but in which form is the dominant determinant. Inner control is evidenced by the use of concepts implying human movement. And finally, constrictive control is evidenced by the use of form alone. The subject who uses form alone is supposed to be showing that he is imposing a rigid intellectual control, amounting almost to repression, of the external stimuli evidenced in color responses and of the internal promptings evidenced in movement responses.

Adjustment and maturity are indicated, say the Rorschachers, by the ratio obtained from dividing the number of human responses (including human details) by the total number of responses. The greater the proportion of human responses, in relation to the total number of responses, the greater the degree of adjustment and maturity, according to the Rorschach expert. Coupled with this measure of adjustment and maturity are several other indices. One is a measure of inferiority. This is supposed to be reflected in the proportion of responses involving wholes. The greater the proportion of concepts involving details, the greater the feelings of inferiority. A second related measure is an index of insecurity. This comes out chiefly, or at least most strikingly, when a subject gives a large number of concepts related to his field of occupational endeavor, for example, when an archaeologist gives a large number of archaeological concepts. This is supposed to indicate that he is clinging to his professional interests as a support for a feeling of personal insecurity. A third index is that indicating the presence of escapist tendencies. This is supposed to be revealed if a subject gives a large proportion of cartoon and mythological concepts. And finally, we might mention the tendency to be overcritical. This is evidenced by a tendency to give parts of animals where most subjects tend to see whole animals. We can conclude this section by noting that indices related directly or indirectly to the measurement of adjustment and maturity are derived primarily from an analysis of the content and of the location of a subject's responses.

RELIABILITY

The unstructured nature of the Rorschach test would seem to make it extremely difficult for us to determine its reliability. And, in fact, some Rorschach experts have taken exactly this stand and blithely ignore the problem altogether. But if the Rorschach test is to be a useful instrument of analysis, it must be made to survive exactly the same standards we impose upon any system of psychological measurement. Therefore it is imperative that we know the degree of reliability which can be attached to Rorschach responses.

The literature reveals only a scattering of information on the reliability of the Rorschach, but that available shows that Rorschach responses possess, in many instances, as satisfactory a degree of reliability as do many of the more classic paper-and-pencil tests. We give in Table 163 a list of the coefficients reported by Hertz,

TABLE 163. *Spearman-Brown Reliability Data for the Rorschach Test**

Variable	Reliability
1. Total number of responses	.89
2. Percentage of whole answers	.84
3. Percentage of normal detail	.75
4. Percentage of rare detail	.86
5. Percentage of oligophrenic detail	.81
6. Percentage of white space detail	.87
7. Percentage of "good" forms	.81
8. Percentage of movement answers	.74
9. Percentage of chiaroscuro answers	.92
10. Percentage of color responses	.81
11. Percentage of animal responses	.83
12. Percentage of human responses	.86
13. Percentage of anatomy responses	.97
14. Percentage of popular responses	.67

* From Hertz, M. R. The reliability of the Rorschach ink-blot test. *J. appl. Psychol.*, 1934, **18**, 461–477.

one of the indefatigable Rorschach workers. These data she secured from the correlations between the responses to the five odd-numbered cards and the responses to the five even-numbered cards. Her subjects were 100 boys and girls in the Cleveland junior high schools.

In addition to these reliability data, Hertz gives the intercorrelations among a number of the separate score variables. These are given in Table 164. The intercorrelations are moderate and, for the most part, lower than the reliability coefficients given in Table

TABLE 164. *Intercorrelations among Several of the Rorschach Variables**

Variable	1	2	3	4	5	6
1. Percentage "good" form............						
2. Percentage original.................	.26					
3. Number of responses................	.00	.39				
4. Percentage animal responses.........	−.01	−.44	−.28			
5. Color...........................	.07	.30	.29	−.31		
6. Whole answers....................	.11	.39	.24	−.25	.39	
7. Movement answers.................	.17	.51	.48	−.29	.18	.42

* From Hertz, M. R. The reliability of the Rorschach ink-blot test. *J. appl. Psychol.*, 1934, **18**, 461–477.

163. This suggests that the several scores do get at different aspects of personality.

VALIDITY

The number of studies on the validity of the Rorschach test is sadly out of proportion to the voluminous literature purporting to show the uses to which the test may be put. This is most unfortunate and demonstrates that the same standards have not been applied as rigidly and as consistently to the Rorschach test as they have been applied to the more conventional type of test. We can report on three studies, however. Two of these yield positive results and the other negative results. Thus the Rorschach test may have value in one type of situation or for one purpose but not in a second type of situation or for a second purpose. In this respect the Rorschach test is no different from any other test we have discussed in this volume.

Munroe. The first study we shall discuss is one reported by Ruth Munroe. She developed a series of diagnostic signs for maladjustment and applied these signs to the records of 348 students at Sarah Lawrence College. Then she compared the adjustment ratings obtained from the application of these diagnostic signs with academic standing one year later. She found a relationship of .49 (coefficient of contingency). This is a definitely significant relationship. The data presented in Table 165 illustrate Munroe's results.

Several of the Rorschach signs which Munroe considers indicative of maladjustment are given in Table 166. Altogether, Munroe used 25 diagnostic signs. In our list we have omitted some of these for the sake of clarity. We can conclude that the Rorschach test, as scored by Munroe for maladjustment, yields an index of some value in predicting future academic standing.

TABLE 165. *Rorschach Adjustment Ratings in Relation to Academic Standing**

Academic standing	Severe problem		Moderate problem		Slight problem		Adequately adjusted		Total	
	N	%	N	%	N	%	N	%	N	%
Superior............	6	7.6	6	7.1	14	21.9	14	18.2	40	11.5
Satisfactory.........	24	30.3	34	49.4	76	70.4	52	67.6	186	53.4
Low average.........	27	34.2	32	38.1	18	16.7	9	11.6	86	24.8
Failing..............	22	27.9	12	14.4	0	0.0	2	2.6	36	10.3
Total............	79	100.0	84	100.0	108	100.0	77	100.0	348	100.0

* From Munroe, R. L. Prediction of the adjustment and academic performance of college students by a modification of the Rorschach method. *Appl. Psychol. Monogr.*, 1945, No. 7.

TABLE 166. *Rorschach Signs of Maladjustment According to Munroe's Inspection Technique**

1. Failure to make a response to one or more cards
2. The use of the whole blot in less than 15 per cent of a subject's responses
3. A vague or bad whole response
4. The use of small or rare details
5. Excessive use of white space
6. A loose succession
7. None or very few popular responses
8. An excessive number, or a poor quality of sex and anatomical responses
9. A limited range of content
10. Very low per cent of responses using form
11. Vague, bad or overexact form responses
12. Poor responses to shading
13. Absence of human movement responses
14. Absence of form color responses
15. Excessive color form responses
16. An extremely high or an extremely low color movement ratio

* From Munroe, R. L. Prediction of the adjustment and academic performance of college students by a modification of the Rorschach method. *Appl. Psychol. Monogr.*, 1945, No. 7.

Eysenck. A test of conformity was devised by Eysenck by a joint adaptation of the Rorschach ink blots and of some of the principles of word association exemplified in the Terman-Miles M-F test. Upon the basis of data compiled by Harrower-Erickson, Eysenck selected four neurotic and five normal response words for each of the Rorschach ink blots. These are given in Table 167. Then he proceeded to show an ink blot to a subject and asked him to rank the responses in order by writing a 1 after the response which seemed most like the ink blot and so on down to 9 after the response that seemed least like the ink blot. This procedure was repeated for each of the ink blots.

In scoring, only the four neurotic answers were considered. Eysenck theorized that the completely consistent neurotic patient would rank the neurotic answers 1st, 2d, 3d, and 4th but that the completely consistent normal person would rank them 6th, 7th, 8th, and 9th. Summing these ranks, we find that the neurotic person would

TABLE 167. *Items in the Ranking Rorschach Test**

Neurotic Answers	*Normal Answers*
Card 1:	
Mud and dirt	An army or navy emblem
An X-ray picture	A bat
A dirty mess	Two people
Part of my body	A pelvis
	Pinchers of a crab
Card 2:	
An insect somebody stepped on	Two scottie dogs
A blood-stained spinal column	Little faces on the sides
A bursting bomb	A white top
Black and red	Two elephants
	Two clowns
Card 3:	
Meat in a butcher's shop	Two birds
Part of my body	Two men
Red and black	A colored butterfly
Spots of blood or paint	Monkeys hanging by their tails
	A red bow-tie
Card 4:	
Lungs and chest	Head of an animal
A nasty mess	A pair of boots
Black smoke and dirt	A man in a fur coat
An X-ray picture	An animal skull
	A big gorilla
Card 5:	
A smashed body	An alligator's head
An X-ray picture	A fan dancer
Lungs and chest	Legs
Black clouds	A bat or butterfly
	A pair of pliers
Card 6:	
An X-ray picture	Two king's heads with crowns
Sex organs	Pagan idol on a pole
Mud and water	A fur rug
A gray smudge	A polished post
	A turtle

Table 167. *Items in the Ranking Rorschach Test* (Continued)

Neurotic Answers	Normal Answers
Card 7:	
Smoke or clouds	Two women talking
Animals or animal heads	Part of my body
Dirty ice and snow	A map
An X-ray picture	Lambs' tails or feathers
	Bookends
Card 8:	
An X-ray picture	Flower or leaves
Pink, blue and orange	A horseshoe crab
Fire and ice, life and death	A colored coat of arms
Parts of my body	Two animals
	Blue flags
Card 9:	
Red, green and orange	Sea horses, or lobsters
Parts of my body	Flowers or underwater vegetation
Smoke, flames or an explosion	Deer or horns of a deer
Clouds with blood	Two people—witches or Santa Clauses
	A candle
Card 10:	
Spilt paint	Two people
An X-ray picture	A Chinese print
Red, blue and green	Spiders, caterpillars, crabs and insects
Parts of my inside	A colored chart or map
	A flower garden or gay tropical fish

* From Eysenck, H. J. *Dimensions of Personality.* London: Routledge and Kegan Paul, Ltd., 1947.

get a score of 10 and that the normal person would get a score of 30. Since there are 10 cards in the Rorschach series, the most neurotic score would be 100 and the most normal score would be 300. Scored

Table 168. *Comparison of High and Low Score Groups on the Ranking Rorschach Test*

Item	Good Rorschach group, per cent	Poor Rorschach group, per cent
N.C.O. status	34	18
Abnormality in parents	20	44
Abnormal sex activity	16	32
Unstable	30	46
Weak, dependent	30	58
Aggressive	12	24
Anxious	26	54
Conversion hysteria	12	56

* From Eysenck, H. J. *Dimensions of Personality.* London: Routledge and Kegan Paul, Ltd., 1947.

in this way, the test is found to have a split-half reliability, corrected by the Spearman-Brown Prophecy Formula, of .84.

Eysenck selected 50 cases with the highest scores and 50 cases with the lowest scores and compared them on a number of personality items. The results are given in Table 168. They show that the test scores are related to a number of items commonly thought to be indicative of a neurotic type of personality. Eysenck also compared a hospitalized (neurotic) group with a nonhospitalized (normal) group and found a significant difference between their respective mean scores.

Kurtz. The third study we wish to report is one on the use of the Rorschach test for the selection of sales managers in the life insurance business. Kurtz, who supervised the study, shows clearly how an investigator can go astray if he does not adhere rigidly to sound principles of statistics and experimental psychology. In this study the Rorschach test was administered by Dr. Helen Margulies Mehr, a psychologist and a Rorschach expert. She administered the test to 80 sales managers in eight life insurance companies. Of these managers, 42 were considered successful and 38 were considered unsuccessful. Established methods of scoring the Rorschach test failed to yield any differentiation whatever between these two groups of managers. Therefore, Dr. Mehr made a special study of the responses made by these two groups of managers and developed a scoring key based upon 16 responses on which these two groups of managers differed from each other. The scoring key assigned a weight of +1 for any response more frequently characteristic of the successful managers and a weight of −1 for any response more frequently characteristic of the unsuccessful managers. If the response did not occur on a particular record, a score of 0 was given. This scoring system gave a theoretical range of scores from +16 to −16. When applied to the records of the 80 managers, it made possible a correct classification of all but one of them as successful or unsuccessful. To many investigators this would seem to be a most striking demonstration of the value of the test as a selective device for sales managers. But let us inquire further into the matter, as did Kurtz, and see why we cannot accept this result as given. Kurtz gives an example which should make the matter clear. He says:

Suppose that eight good managers and one poor manager are of Irish or part Irish ancestry. If we "score" these people on ancestry eight good managers will receive a score of 1 and only one poor manager will receive such a score. This holds regardless of whether there is a real relationship or whether, due to chance, there happen this time to be a few more Irish men in one group than the other.

The real test, continues Kurtz, "is not whether the scoring system will work on the original group but whether it will work on other groups." In the present instance the scoring was extended to 41 additional cases. The new cases were tested by Rorschach experts, who were not informed as to which of the managers were successful and which were unsuccessful, and they sent their analyses to Dr. Kurtz. The results are given in Table 169.

TABLE 169. *A Comparison of Successful and Unsuccessful Managers on the Rorschach Test**

Rorschach scores	20 poor managers	21 good managers
4, 5	3	2
2, 3	4	7
0, 1	4	3
−1, −2	8	8
−3, −4	1	1

* From Kurtz, A. K. A research test of the Rorschach test. *Person. Psychol.*, 1948, **1**, 41–51.

Expressed as a Pearson r, the relationship is negligible, being .02. Lest there be some question as to whether success can be predicted at all, Kurtz reported that a 13-item experience record gives a correlation of .48 for this same group of cases. Table 170 supplies additional details.

Subsequent to this further tryout, Dr. Mehr reanalyzed the records, and, using not only the original 32 signs but also any others

TABLE 170. *A Comparison of Successful and Unsuccessful Managers on an Experience Record**

Experience scores	20 good managers	20 poor managers
60 and up.........	1	0
55–59.............	0	7
50–54.............	3	6
45–49.............	8	6
40–44.............	8	2

* From Kurtz, A. K. A research test of the Rorschach test. *Person. Psychol.*, 1948, **1**, 41–51.

she wished, she made a further classification with the results presented in Table 171. The correlation between these ratings and

TABLE 171. *A Second Comparison of Successful and Unsuccessful Managers on the Rorschach Test**

Rating by Dr. Mehr	20 good managers	20 poor managers
Confident of success..............	5	5
Less confident of success...........	0	3
Borderline......................	2	4
Less confident of failure...........	1	1
Confident of failure..............	12	8

* From Kurtz, A. K. A research test of the Rorschach test. *Person. Psychol.*, 1948, **1**, 41–51.

success is higher (.17), but it is still not significant and still does not compete with the correlation of .48 yielded by the experience record. Kurtz further points out that age alone yields a higher correlation (.31) with success than do the Rorschach test scores.

Kurtz, in this study, shows the utter folly of judging the validity of a scoring key upon the basis of its application to the groups on which it was developed. He also shows that even with tremendous effort the Rorschach test could not, in this instance, be made to yield as valid predictions as two alternate, and more objective, methods.

The point of reviewing this study in detail is to demonstrate the kind of study needed before we can assert that any psychological test yields valid results. This kind of study is almost now nonexistent in the voluminous Rorschach literature. We cannot accept, therefore, many of the claims of its partisan adherents. Admittedly, it is not an easy matter to secure the type of criterion groups needed for such validation studies, but difficult though this may be, it does not make it permissible for us to claim validity in the absence of substantiating data.

The discussion in this section should in no way be taken as implying that small contrasting groups should not be studied nor that hypotheses should not be developed and explored. But once the exploration, development, and setting up of hypotheses are done, their validity must be determined on new and independently selected groups of criterion cases.

13

PROJECTIVE TECHNIQUES: AN IMAGINAL

APPROACH

We saw in the last chapter how Rorschach, and his ardent band of disciples, attempt to derive insights into personality structure by analyzing our responses to a series of meaningless ink blots. We are now to see how Morgan and Murray, and their followers, attempt to gain similar insights by analyzing our responses to a series of ambiguous pictures.

This is done through the medium of the Thematic Apperception Test, a test of a subject's power of imagination. This test consists of a series of 19 pictures and one blank card. These are shown one by one to a subject who is asked to make up a story based on what he sees in each card. These stories become the raw material for our analysis.

CONTENT

Each picture in the Thematic Apperception Test is capable of eliciting a wide variety of interpretations. This is one of the two basic facts which give the test its value. The second "fact" is our tendency to interpret ambiguous situations in directions conforming to our own present wants and to past behavior. One of the pictures in the Thematic Apperception Test is that of a little boy with a violin. In looking at the picture, we can all agree that this is a picture of a small boy with a violin. But we shall differ in our interpretation of what this picture represents. One person will see a boy longing to become a great musician. A second person will see him musing over some piece he has just played. A third person will feel that the boy is frustrated in not being able to play correctly a particularly difficult measure. And a fourth person will see a boy who resents having to practice his lesson because he would rather be outside playing baseball. In these different stories we are to look for our clues to personality.

The pictures in the Thematic Apperception Test are listed in Table 172. Eleven of the pictures are suitable for both men and

TABLE 172. *Pictures in the Thematic Apperception Test**

First series:

1. A young boy is contemplating a violin which rests on a table in front of him.
2. Country scene: in the foreground is a young woman with books in her hand; in the background a man is working in the fields and an older women is looking on.
3. (BM)† On the floor against a couch is the huddled form of a boy with his head bowed on his right arm. Beside him on the floor is a revolver.
3. (GF) A young woman is standing with downcast head, her face covered with her right hand. Her left arm is stretched forward against a wooden door.
4. A middle-aged woman is standing on the threshold of a half-opened door looking into a room.
5. (BM) A short elderly woman stands with her back turned to a tall young man. The latter is looking downward with a perplexed expression.
5. (GF) A young woman sitting on the edge of a sofa looks back over her shoulder at an older man with a pipe in his mouth who seems to be addressing her.
6. (BM) A gray-haired man is looking at a younger man who is sullenly staring into space.
6. (GF) An older women is sitting on a sofa close beside a girl, speaking or reading to her. The girl, who holds a doll in her lap, is looking away.
7. (BM) An adolescent boy looks straight out of the picture. The barrel of a rifle is visible at one side, and in the background is the dim scene of a surgical operation, like a reverie-image.
7. (GF) A young women sits with her chin in her hand looking off into space.
8. (BM) Four men in overalls are lying on the grass taking it easy.
8. (GF) A young woman with a magazine and a purse in her hand looks from behind a tree at another young woman in a party dress running along a beach.
9. A young woman's head against a man's shoulder.

Second series:

10. A road skirting a deep chasm between high cliffs. On the road in the distance are obscure figures. Protruding from the rocky wall on one side is the long head and neck of a dragon.
11. (M) A young man is lying on a couch with his eyes closed. Leaning over him is the gaunt form of an elderly man, his hand stretched out above the face of the reclining figure.
11. (F) The portrait of a young women. A weird old women with a shawl over her head is grimacing in the background.
12. (BG) A rowboat is drawn up on the bank of a woodland stream. There are no human figures in the picture.
12. (MF) A young man is standing with downcast head buried in his arm. Behind him is the figure of a woman lying in bed.
13. (B) A little boy is sitting on the doorstep of a log cabin.
13. (G) A little girl is climbing a winding flight of stairs.

TABLE 172. *Pictures in the Thematic Apperception Test* (Continued)*

14. The silhouette of a man (or woman) against a bright window. The rest of the picture is totally black.
15. A gaunt man with clenched hands is standing among gravestones.
16. A blank card.
17. (BM) A naked man is clinging to a rope. He is in the act of climbing up or down.
17. (GF) A bridge over water. A female figure leans over the railing. In the background are tall buildings and small figures of men.
18. (BM) A man is clutched from behind by three hands. The figures of his antagonists are invisible.
18. (GF) A woman has her hands squeezed around the throat of another woman whom she appears to be pushing backwards across the banister of a stairway.
19. A weird picture of cloud formations overhanging a snowcovered cabin in the country.
20. The dimly illumined figure of a man (or woman) in the dead of night leaning against a lamp post.

* From Murray, H. A. *Thematic Apperception Test Manual.* Cambridge, Mass.: Harvard University Press, 1943.

† Initials indicate whether picture is suitable for boys (B), male adults (M), girls (G), or female adults (F). If no initials, there are no restrictions.

women. Ten are used with men alone, and ten are used with women alone. The pictures in the test are those which Murray and Morgan found most useful in contributing "to the total personality picture." They were selected after the "entire" personalities of a number of subjects had been intensely and thoroughly studied. After this study, Murray and his coworkers rated a series of pictures on their effectiveness in contributing to the over-all personality picture. Pictures with the highest ratings were retained as the elements in the Thematic Apperception Test.

DIRECTIONS

When the pictures are presented to a subject, they are divided into two series of ten pictures each. The subject reacts to each series in two separate one-hour sessions, separated by one or more days. The first series of pictures are more commonplace than the second and are presented to the subject with the following directions:

This is a test of imagination, one form of intelligence. I am going to show you some pictures, one at a time; and your task will be to make up as dramatic a story as you can for each. Tell what has led up to the event shown in the picture, describe what is happening at the moment, what the characters are feeling and thinking; and then give the outcome. Speak your thoughts as they come to your mind. Do you understand? Since you have fifty minutes for ten pictures, you can devote about five minutes to each story. Here is the first picture.

These are the instructions for the second day:

The procedure today is the same as before, only this time you can give freer rein to your imagination. Your first ten stories were excellent, but you confined yourself pretty much to the facts of everyday life. Now I would like to see what you can do when you disregard the commonplace realities and let your imagination have its way, as in a myth, fairy story, or allegory. Here is Picture No. 1.

When the subject come to Card 16, the blank card, the examiner says, "See what you can see on this blank card. Imagine some picture there and describe it to me in detail." Following this description, the examiner says, "Now tell me a story about it."

During each of the two sessions the individual is seated in a chair or is stretched out on a couch, preferably with his back to the examiner. During most of the two sessions the examiner makes no comment. However, after the first picture in the first series, it is desirable, by way of encouraging the subject, to compliment him upon his story and to remind him, if necessary, of the directions. During the remainder of the two sessions he indicates to the subject whether he is ahead of or behind schedule, he encourages him with frequent praise, he calls the subject's attention to any important omission, such as an omitted outcome of a story, he reminds the subject to stick to the major plot of a story (if he is inclined to give many details), and he reminds the subject (once in a while) to give only one story for each picture.

ANALYSIS

The examiner records the subject's stories as nearly verbatim as possible, he has a stenographer take notes, or he sees that the subject's comments are phonographically recorded. At the conclusion of the first session he arranges for the subject to come back for a second appointment, but he does not give the subject any reason to understand that he will have a second set of pictures to interpret. At the conclusion of the second session, either right then or a day or two later, the examiner must query the subject as to the sources of his stories. Did they come from his own experience? From the experiences of friends or relatives? Or did they come from books, magazines, newspapers, radio, and so forth?

In order to interpret the subject's stories, it is necessary that the examiner have a good background in clinical experience, in observing individuals, in interviewing, and in testing. He should also have some knowledge of psychoanalysis, and he must have months of training in the specific technique of interpreting the stories secured in response to the pictures in the Thematic Apperception Test. In this text we can make only superficial examination of the procedures used, and no one should expect to be able from our comments to become an expert user of the Thematic Apperception Test. All we can do is to indicate the types of analysis which are made and thereby give the reader something of the flavor, but not of the substance, of the Thematic Apperception Testing technique.

To make his analysis the examiner must know the sex and age of his subject, whether his parents are living, dead, or separated, the age and sex of his siblings, the subject's vocation, and his marital status. With these facts in hand the examiner begins his analysis of the subject's stories. He breaks each story down into a series of successive events and then looks in each of these events for the force or forces emanating from the "heroes" of the stories and for the force or forces emanating from these heroes' environment. To do this the examiner must find in each story *the hero* or other character with whom the subject identifies himself. He must analyze the motives, trends, and feelings (that is, *the needs*) of this hero or principal character. He must locate the environmental forces that act or *press* upon this hero. And finally, he must compare these needs and presses to determine the *outcome*. Thus the examiner must concern himself with four things in each story: the hero, his needs, his environmental press, and the outcome.

The Hero. Finding the hero or principal character with which the subject identifies himself is not always an easy matter, but the following possibilities should be carefully considered:

1. That the subject identifies himself with the character in whom he shows the greatest interest or whose point of view he adopts
2. That the subject identifies himself with the character whose feelings and motives are most intimately portrayed
3. That the subject identifies himself with the character who most resembles himself in sex, age, status, or role
4. That the subject identifies himself with the character most concerned in the outcome of the story.

Each of these types of identification is fairly straightforward. But since they are not exhaustive of all possibilities, those of a more complex nature must also be considered. Some of these more complex possibilities are indicated below.

1. The subject may shift his identification as the story unfolds.
2. The subject may continually identify himself with two characters, one representing one element in his personality and the other representing a second element.
3. The subject may tell a story that tells a story. In this case there may be a primary and a secondary hero. The subject may identify himself with one or with both of these heroes or with neither of them.
4. The subject may identify himself with a character of the opposite sex. A man with a high feminine component may identify himself with a woman, and a woman with a high masculine component may identify herself with a man.
5. There may be no identification at all. There may be no hero or chief character in the story, or if there is, he may be perceived as a part of the subject's environment.

Needs. To determine motives, trends, and feelings of heroes, the examiner must observe everything the hero or principal character feels, thinks, and does. In particular, he must note everything unusual, uncommon, or unique. Murray states that the Thematic Apperception Test requires no one particular theory of personality, but he makes use of his own conceptual scheme consisting of a catalogue of 28 needs. Included in Murray's list are abasement, achievement, aggression, dominance, nurturance, passivity, sex, and succorance.

In the stories elicited by the pictures, these needs are to be discovered as impulses, wishes, or intentions or are to be found in the overt behavior of the heroes of the stories. When we discover these needs, we need to know their strength. Murray suggests we do this by means of a five-step scale of need intensity. We can, however, use as many or as few steps as we wish. In any event, to determine the intensity of a need we must consider its duration, the frequency of its occurrence, and its importance in the plot of the story. When all needs have been discovered and rated, those that appear unusually strong and unusually weak are listed for further consideration and analysis.

Press. When we have determined needs, we turn our attention to the analysis of the press which operate upon the heroes of our subject's stories. To make this analysis we must observe the details as well as the general nature of all situations in which the heroes find themselves. And we must note, in particular, the uniqueness, frequency, and intensity or the complete absence of any environmental press. Among the press which Murray says we shall most frequently have to consider are affiliation, aggression, dominance, nurturance, and rejection. When the press operating upon our subject's heroes have been determined, we must, as we did in the case of needs, estimate their relative strengths.

Outcomes. We must now compare needs and press and determine how the forces emanating from each hero compare in strength with the forces emanating from his environment. The questions to be considered in this connection, as given by Murray, are as follows:

1. How much force does the hero manifest?
2. What is the strength of the facilitating or beneficial forces of the environment as compared to the opposing or harmful forces?
3. Is the hero's path of achievement difficult or easy?
4. In the face of opposition does he strive with renewed vigor or does he collapse?
5. Does the hero make things happen or do things happen to him?
6. To what extent does he manipulate or overcome the opposing forces and to what extent is he manipulated or overcome by them?
7. Is he coercing or coerced?
8. Is he mostly active or passive?
9. Under what conditions does he succeed? When others help him? Or when he strives alone?
10. Under what conditions does he fail?

When we have considered and have found the answers to the preceding questions, we have to make a list of all major simple and complex outcomes. A simple outcome is any combination of, or interaction between, a need and a press. A complex outcome is any combination of two or more simple outcomes.

INTERPRETATION

We now have before us a list of high and low needs, a list of high and low press, and a list of outcomes. We also have with us two assumptions. One is that the attributes of the hero represent tendencies, traits, or sentiments in the subject's personality, and the second is that the press represent forces in the subject's environment. But we must not take these assumptions as proved facts. We must consider them as leads or as working hypotheses—to be verified or disproved *by other methods of analysis*.

In arriving at our conclusions from Thematic Apperception Test material, Murray suggests that we give careful consideration to the following factors:

The Manner in Which the Test Is Administered. If the test is not properly given, if the subject does not become involved in the stories, or if the stories are short and sketchy, the test is not apt to yield any material of significance. On the average, Murray says, about one-third of the stories will be barren of meaning anyway. So anything which will lower the number of significant stories will prove a serious detriment to the analysis.

The Subject's Judgment. A most important part of the Thematic Apperception Test analysis is that based upon the inquiry into the sources of the subject's stories. Murray suggests that it may not always prove the wisest course for the interpreter to rely solely upon the subject's judgment. Some of the stories which he will attribute to newspapers, books, radio, and so forth may, in reality, represent personal experiences which he may not care to admit. When the source of a story really is a radio serial, it is important, of course, to discover this fact. But it is equally important to know when radio as a source is alleged to cover up a more personal source.

Partial Data. As penetrating as any given Thematic Apperception Test analysis may seem, it gives only a partial picture of personality. One cannot conclude from a Thematic Apperception Test analysis that he really knows a subject in the sense that he would be presumed to know him from an extensive series of depth interviews or from a complete psychoanalysis.

Level of Function. A person can exhibit physical or verbal behavior, or he can have ideas, plans, and fantasies. The conduct of the subject gives the first. The content of the stories gives the second.

Layers in Normal Socialized Personalities. Murray distinguishes between inner, middle, and outer layers of personality. The inner layer, he says, "is composed of repressed unconscious tendencies" which are never or rarely expressed either in thought or action. The middle layer, Murray says "is composed of tendencies which appear in thought in undisguised form, and . . . may . . . also . . . be objectified in action privately and secretly." "Finally," he says, "the outer layer is composed of tendencies which are publicly asserted or acknowledged and [are] openly manifested in behavior." The task of the examiner is to determine to which of these levels each variable noted in the Thematic Apperception Test analysis belongs. It is ordinarily assumed, however, that the great majority of the variables in a Thematic Apperception Test analysis will be found characteristic of the second of the three levels. Overt behavior is not hard to observe and there are many ways of observing it. The first level is the most difficult to observe, and the only way to observe it at present is through a series of depth interviews or through a thorough psychoanalysis.

Crude Analogy. An examiner must guard against the easy and obvious assumption that the variables unusually high in Thematic Apperception Test stories will be extremely strong in the subject's manifest personality and, conversely, that variables unusually weak in Thematic Apperception Test stories will be extremely weak in a subject's manifest personality. This may be true and, if true, should not be overlooked. But many times it will not be true, and the examiner will be led seriously astray if he does not probe beyond superficial similarity. It will not be at all infrequent for an examiner to find that the Thematic Apperception Test analysis shows exactly the opposite of what a subject does or says he does or is going to do. In summary, we might say that if the test did not frequently yield findings at variance with overt and verbal behavior, it would add nothing of significance to our observation of this overt and verbal behavior.

Insight into the Third Level of Personality. Murray and Morgan did not devise the Thematic Apperception Test to get at the outer layer of personality. But they feel that at times it will prove useful in this connection. Murray points out that the stories in the first session, being in response to the more commonplace pictures, can usually be considered more closely related to the outer personality layer than those in the second session. Also, variables or tendencies not restricted by cultural taboos or by sanctions are apt to be related to the outer level of personality.

Sex of Examiner. In Thematic Apperception Test analysis, the sex of the examiner is important. Therefore, it is necessary for the examiner to make allowance for this fact. But in just what manner this allowance is to be effected Murray does not say.

Present-life Situation. The content of Thematic Apperception Test stories will vary with current events, with the status of the subject, with present or momentary emotional states, and so forth. The examiner must be able to isolate from the manifest content of the stories the variables underlying this content. These may appear in one garb for one subject and in another garb for another subject. It is important that the Thematic Apperception Test examiner is not thrown off guard by superficial changes in content—changes which have no effect upon the fundamental mechanisms or dynamics involved.

OBJECTIVITY, RELIABILITY, AND VALIDITY

It is clearly evident that the Thematic Apperception Test technique is not one for the amateur. The technique is not objective. It requires months of training on the part of an examiner. And this training must consist, when it is complete, of a wide background of clinical and, preferably, of psychoanalytic experience. This being the case, there are relatively few psychologists who can be considered fully qualified to administer and to use the Thematic Apperception Test in the manner in which Murray and Morgan feel the test should be used.

Reliability. There have not been many reports on the reliability of the Thematic Apperception Test. Murray, in his *Manual of Directions*, gives no reliability data at all. Tomkins, in his book on the Thematic Apperception Test, summarizes the few data on reliability that are available. These we may briefly list as follows:

1. Sanford had four judges rate ten subjects on their needs and press. The average intercorrelation between the judges' ratings were .57 for needs and .54 for press.

2. Harrison and Rotter, independently of each other, rated the protocols of 70 subjects for emotional maturity and stability. These protocols were based on five pictures. Their ratings intercorrelated .73 or .77 depending upon whether they used a three- or a five-point rating scale.

3. Combs had four judges rate ten protocols. He participated as one of the judges and found that his ratings agreed with the average rating assigned by the other judges to the extent of 60 per cent. He also found that his own reratings, after an interval of six months, agreed with his original ratings to the extent of 69 per cent.

4. Tomkins tested and retested 45 women subjects at various intervals from two to ten months. Fifteen subjects were retested after an interval of two months, 15 more after an interval of six months, and the remaining 15 subjects after an interval of ten months. The stories were rated in terms of Murray's need-press schema and gave the following test-retest correlations:

> After 2 months. 80
> After 6 months. 60
> After 10 months. 50

5. Tomkins collected 400 stories told by one subject over a period of ten months. He divided these stories into two groups of 200 stories each, had each set rated by different raters, and reported a correlation of .91 between the two series of ratings.

We see that there have been two approaches to the reliability problem: the comparison of ratings assigned by different raters and the comparison of test-retest results. The data we have presented show that the reliability of the Thematic Apperception Test varies, as does that of every other test, with its length, with the particular variable being assessed, with the type of rating used, and with the competence and experience of the raters.

It is difficult for us to determine whether some of the test-retest coefficients are low because the Thematic Apperception Test itself is an inherently unreliable instrument or whether the need-press relationships have changed in the interim. In this connection it may help us, however, to recall that the purpose of the Thematic Apperception Test is to reveal the underlying structure of personality. Presumably this underlying structure should represent a stable, significant, and fundamental explanatory principle in human behavior. This being the case, it is a little hard to accept the possibility that such a fundamental and significant explanatory factor can have a reliability as transitory as that indicated by some of the lower test-retest correlations. Murray would undoubtedly disagree with this contention, however, for he has said "that the [Thematic

Apperception Test] responses reflect the fleeting mood as well as the present life situation of the subject. . . . " And for this reason, "we should not expect the repeat reliability of the test to be high. . . . " If we accept this statement, our chief source of reliability data consists of the intercorrelations among the ratings independently assigned by different raters. And so far, these too leave something to be desired.

VALIDITY

Experiments on the validity of the Thematic Apperception Test have, for the most part, been abortive. Attempts have been made to relate the results to those secured by the Rorschach test, but this necessitates the assumption that the Rorschach test itself is a valid measuring instrument. Other attempts have consisted of the blind matchings of results secured from the Thematic Apperception Test with personal-history data, etc. This approach Murray dismisses as nothing more than a parlor trick. Also he claims that much of the personal-history data is needed as a basis for a complete Thematic Apperception Test analysis. And to deny this information to the examiner is to destroy much of the value in the approach. This leaves us with only one avenue of approach to the validity problem, that of comparing the results of a Thematic Apperception Test analysis to those secured from a thoroughgoing psychoanalysis. Murray's own contention is that the two would be found to agree, but few if any data have ever been presented on the point.

We can conclude that the Thematic Apperception Test, like the Rorschach test, represents a unique approach to the measurement of personality. Unlike the Rorschach test, however, it was based upon a more insightful approach as to what was to be accomplished and goes much beyond the crude analogy stage so characteristic of the Rorschach test. The Thematic Apperception Test leaves much to be desired, however, in the way of objectivity, economy, and general usefulness to anyone not extremely well versed in the techniques of psychoanalysis.

14

PERFORMANCE: OBSERVATIONAL

APPROACHES

There is no chapter in this text that does not deal in some way with human performance. But in all the preceding chapters we have started with the performance induced by a specified type of test or by a specific set of directions. And the behavior we have produced by these specific tests, or by these directions, has been of a verbal character. Our subjects have responded with check marks, crosses, or circles, or have told us stories, or have described what they see in ink blots, or have said (on paper) what they would or would not do in certain situations. Or if we have not secured this information from our subjects directly, someone else has supplied the information for us. From the verbal responses induced by our verbal instructions we have tried in various ways to draw implications with respect to the prediction and control of nonverbal performance or behavior.

We come now to a consideration of nonverbal behavior directly and of the ways in which this nonverbal behavior forms a basis for personality measurement. This nonverbal behavior or performance, as we shall call it, may or may not be induced by our special instructions. But it is of a character quite different from that induced in response to any of the measuring techniques we have so far discussed. In nonverbal behavior the subject does something that we can observe—he does not just tell us about it. He gets mad or angry, he laughs or crys, he plays with his toys, he stands up, he sits down, he stamps his feet, he throws things, he prepares a speech, he gives a demonstration, and so forth. We watch him do these things and then draw our inferences from this observed behavior.

We are going to divide our performance-measuring techniques into two categories: observational and experimental. Under the first category we shall discuss the techniques which do not require a rigid delimitation of the subject's responses. We may carefully control the conditions under which these responses can take place, but we do not delimit or circumscribe the responses themselves. Under the second category we shall describe the techniques which require that we carefully delimit the situation *and* the responses also. Both observational and experimental approaches require us to collect and record facts about perceived behavior. And in both approaches we must follow some preconceived, prearranged, or formal plan.

The techniques we plan to discuss in this chapter can be divided into those suitable for the observation of single individuals and those suitable for the observation of groups of individuals. We shall begin our discussion with the former.

OBSERVATION OF SINGLE INDIVIDUALS

Barker, Dembo, and Lewin's study of "Frustration and Regression" provides an excellent demonstration of the application of a technique for the observation of single individuals. And, at the same time, it yields abundant proof of the value of starting our observations with a clear-cut theoretical formulation of the ends or goals to be attained.

Barker, Dembo, and Lewin wished to test the theory that frustration leads a person to behave in an immature manner, in other words, that frustration leads to regression in behavior. Familiar examples of this phenomenon are the crying of the teen-age boy who does not get his expected Christmas bicycle, the temper tantrum of the adolescent when his friend will not do his bidding, and the daydreaming of the young boy who finds no satisfaction in his violin practice.

Creating Frustration. The first problem which Barker, Dembo, and Lewin tackled was that of devising a method to create frustration. The method they evolved consisted of the following steps:

Free Play Period. The observer led a child into a playroom. He demonstrated a set of moderately desirable toys and placed these toys at the child's disposal. The child was allowed to play with these toys for thirty minutes.

Prefrustration Period. Upon a subsequent occasion the child was led into the playroom (enlarged now by the prior removal of an opaque partition) where he found a much more elaborate setup than during his first play period. All the toys from the first period were incorporated in the more elaborate setup. The child was allowed to play in this situation from five to fifteen minutes.

Transition Period. The observer collected all play materials that had been available in the free play situation, distributed them on the cardboard squares where they had first been found, pulled down a transparent partition blocking entrance to the more attractive toys, and said, "Now let's play at this end [of the room]."

Frustration Period. This was the same as the free play situation except for the fact that the child now had knowledge of the more attractive toys. He could see them, but he could not gain access to them. This period lasted for thirty minutes.

Postfrustration Period. When the observer had concluded his observations for the frustration period, he raised the partition and allowed the child to play with the more elaborate toys. This period continued as long as the child cared to play. This period was permitted so that no undesirable effects of the frustrating experience would remain to affect the child's behavior or personality after the conclusion of the observations.

Observational Techniques. During each of the periods we have described an observer was present at a small table in a corner of the playroom. After leading the child into the room and doing what was necessary to "set the stage," the observer sat at the table "to do his lessons." While "doing his lessons," he made notes concerning the child's behavior. He participated as little as possible in the child's play activity, but he gave brief answers to any questions which the child put to him.

In addition to the observer we have already mentioned, a second observer was stationed behind a one-way vision screen. This second observer made a running account of the child's behavior and recorded his observations on the tape of a specially constructed and constant-speed polygraph. The tape on this polygraph was set to move at a speed of one inch every thirty seconds so that the time of all observations could be accurately determined. There was a switch underneath the first observer's table so that he could activate one of the pens of the polygraph. This was used to indicate the beginning and end of any event in which he was particularly interested.

Barker, Dembo, and Lewin list the following advantages of having two observers:

1. When the first observer was actively occupied with the child or toys, the second observer's record was available.
2. The behavior of the first observer could be recorded by the second observer.
3. The presence of two observers made it possible for each one to concentrate on different aspects of behavior. This made possible the collection of more and also better and more careful observations. The first observer emphasized the activities of the child while the second observer emphasized the conversation and general meaning of what was happening.
4. The availability of two observers permitted their roles to be interchanged. This minimized the effects caused by the biases, attitudes, and personality characteristics of each observer.

Measuring Regression. The second problem which Barker, Dembo, and Lewin tackled was that of devising a method for the measurement of regression. The records available for analysis consisted of the running accounts of the two observers. These were combined into one integrated account, and this account was subjected to study and analysis. The first step in this analysis was that of dividing up the complete running account into meaningful "units of action." This meant that each record had to be examined for a complete or fairly complete unit of play and divided into as many units of action as there appeared to be meaningful and relatively complete play sequences. An example of such a unit is as follows:

The child picks up the teddy bear and pulls the truck and trailer. Hauls the doll, the phone, and the teapot. "Teddy bear, teddy bear, you stay right here." She shows off, talks, and looks at observer. Pushes truck and trailer into middle of the room, makes a noise, "rrrr." "Oh, teddy! You are going to sleep." The load falls off the truck and trailer. Reloads teddy bear and doll, whispering.

Barker, Dembo, and Lewin classified these units of action into occupation with accessible goals and occupation with inaccessible goals. In the first instance, they made note of the actions which the child actually performed, and in the second instance, they made note of his attempts to get at the inaccessible toys.

Under Category 1, occupation with accessible goals, Barker, Dembo, and Lewin distinguished five types of behavior:

1. Playing with accessible toys
2. Diversions with non-toy objects: activities with experimenter, activities at window, and so forth

3. Island behavior: playing with objects not intended to be part of the experimental set-up, such as stray pins found on the floor
4. Looking and wandering about
5. Disturbances and activities created by outside noise, and so forth

Under Category 2, occupation with inaccessible toys, Barker, Dembo, and Lewin noted the following types of activity.

1. Physical approaches to the inaccessible regions, kicking the floor, and so forth
2. Social attempts by means of threats, pleadings, requests, coaxing, and so forth
3. Passive directed actions such as looking at or talking about inaccessible toys

Barker, Dembo, and Lewin now wished to evaluate these play units from the standpoint of their constructiveness. They desired to do this because they felt that constructiveness of play could be taken as a sensitive indicator of regressive behavior. They felt this in view of their premises that a child's entire mind, personality, and behavior are involved or reflected in his free play activity and that fantasy and realistic judgment are closely interwoven in any constructive action. Barker, Dembo, and Lewin describe their evaluation procedure as follows:

The play units of the first six children were transcribed seriately upon cards which were grouped according to the toy or group of toys involved. Three persons working together in conference arranged the play units for each toy in order of their increasing constructiveness. No attempt at independent ranking was made. The resulting order represented the consensus of opinion of the raters after discussion, disagreement, and compromise. It became evident that irrespective of *a priori* theories of "constructiveness," it was possible to agree upon the relative ranking of different play with the same toys.

The play units were briefly characterized and the characterizations set down in tabular form. . . . Each rank order was assigned a numerical weight which in the final scale ranged from 2 to 8. . . . The records of the six children were then scored by assigning a numerical value to each consecutive play unit in the record in accordance with the rating given in the scale, weighted for the duration of the unit by multiplying by the time. The mean constructiveness of each child's play was determined by summing these values for the whole record and dividing by the total duration of play. . . .

Using the constructiveness scale as thus devised, one of the raters scored the remaining records. The items of the original scale covered the great majority of the units which occurred. However, it was inevitable that a number of unrated units should occur in the other records. When this happened, the three raters considered the new unit and agreed upon its placement in the scale.

The observers made their ratings on the assumption that a constructiveness of play continuum would extend from primitive, simple, little-structured activity to elaborate, imaginative, and highly developed play. Seven levels on this scale were ultimately differentiated. They are as follows:

Constructiveness 2. Toys examined superficially. (*a*) Sits on floor and takes truck and trailer in hand, 10 seconds; (*b*) Shakes iron once, teddy bear once, holds truck in hand, holds truck fingering it, 20 seconds.

Constructiveness 3. The truck is moved to a definite place or from one place to another. (*a*) Phone, truck, and trailer, manipulated and carried to window sill, 25 seconds; (*b*) Bends over to truck and trailer, pushes back and forth, 15 seconds.

Constructiveness 4. This is a somewhat more complicated manipulation of the truck. (*a*) Truck and trailer backed under chair, 15 seconds; (*b*) Stands up. Picks up truck and trailer, detaches. Takes truck in hand, examines closely. 70 seconds.

Constructiveness 5. This is a definitely more complicated and elaborated manipulation of the truck. (*a*) Truck and trailer unloaded, detached; pulled in circles, reattached, detached, reattached; pulled in circles. 45 seconds. (*b*) takes doll, puts on truck and trailer, "He doesn't sit up very well." "I lay the teddy down." They are both lying down on trailer as trailer is pushed back and forth.

Constructiveness 6. The truck is used as a means to haul other things. (*a*) Takes truck and trailer. "More things are going to be hauled." Puts cup, saucer, teapot on trailer. Talks to self. "Ride along, mister." To square 3. 60 seconds. (*b*) "This is a fire truck." To middle of room. Around in middle. "You can load things in it. Mr. Duck! I'll haul Mr. Duck." 45 seconds.

Constructiveness 7. The meaning of the play is an extensive "trip" or another elaborated story in which the handling of the truck is merely a part of a larger setting. (*a*) "Here's a car-truck, and it's going out fishing, so we have to take the trailer off. First, we have to go to the gas station. Toot! Toot! Now, he's going to the gas station. Ding, ding, ding." Gets gas. Now back for the trailer and the fish pole; child has truck and takes the motor boat. Attaches it to the truck and trailer. "Hmmmmmmm! Here he goes." Behind square 2 to 1. "Quack! Quack! Mr. Ducky come," (places on truck and trailer). Goes to 3. "Here's the sailboat." 225 seconds. (*b*) "I want the teddy bear to sleep. Where will be the bed for the teddy bear?" Chooses the truck and trailer. "Now you go to sleep. We are going to Minneapolis." Puts teddy on trailer. "You can't go, Mr. Dolly, Teddy bear goes." Subject lies down on the floor and looks at teddy bear on trailer. "Toot, toot." Pushes truck and trailer to barrier, then pulls back. Plays with truck and trailer and teddy. "Teddy bear, you will sit in the back." Pushes truck to table. "We're going to Chicago." Gets crayon. "I want some crayon to go." 175 seconds.

Constructiveness 8. Play showing more than usual originality is classified here. (*a*) To square 1. Truck and trailer reattached. "I'll bring them here." Detaches truck, has it coast down trailer as in incline, reattaches. 30 seconds. (*b*) To truck and trailer at square 1. Detaches trailer, uses it as incline against ironing board. Runs truck up, carries it up further and further, and lets it go. Looks to experimenter for approval, smiling, "Did you see it? Now watch it." Pushes truck across floor, big push. Hits E. "See how fast it goes!" "Chugs" it over to observer's window, looks underneath, "Chugs" to table, to barrier. 205 seconds.

Reliability. Barker, Dembo, and Lewin determined the reliability of their constructiveness ratings in two ways. One way required the dividing of the thirty-minute observation period into three periods of ten minutes each. Then a constructiveness score was assigned for each one of the three ten-minute intervals, and the intercorrelations presented in Table 173 were computed.

TABLE 173. *Reliability Data for Barker, Dembo, and Lewin's Constructiveness Ratings**

First and second periods............ .72
Second and third periods........... .48
First and third periods............. .39

* From Barker, R., Dembo, T., and Lewin, K. Frustration and regression. An experiment with young children. *Univ. Ia. Stud. Child Welf.* 1941, **18**, No. 1.

These correlations are not remarkably high, but Barker, Dembo, and Lewin concluded that they were satisfactory. The second method required that units of play be classified as to time involved. Then those that lasted from 1 to 15 seconds, from 31 to 45 seconds, from 61 to 90 seconds, and from 121 to 180 seconds were selected as one series. Those that lasted from 16 to 30 seconds, from 46 to 60 seconds, from 91 to 120 seconds, and 181 seconds or more were put into a second series. Then the correlation between the constructiveness indices for each of these two series was computed. It was found to be .79. Barker, Dembo, and Lewin entered this value in the Spearman-Brown Prophecy Formula and found a value of .88 for the reliability of the entire series of ratings.

Barker, Dembo, and Lewin are careful to point out that constructiveness of play could easily have varied from one of the above periods to another and that this should not be taken as proof that the ratings were unreliable. They also point out, however, that they were concerned with assigning a constructiveness level to each child so that they could use this constructiveness score as an indicator to determine regression. This being the case, it became appropriate for them to determine the self-reliability of the constructiveness score for an entire observational period.

Validity. Barker, Dembo, and Lewin's constructiveness scale possesses validity by definition only. They developed their scale, as Landis did his, upon the basis of the empirical distinctions their data afforded. Therefore, they could not check its validity by correlating the constructiveness ratings with results secured by other methods of measuring constructiveness of play, for no other measures were available.

While our primary interest is in Barker, Dembo, and Lewin's methodology, we cannot leave their experiment without some comment as to their findings. These are that frustration decreases the average constructiveness of play with accessible toys and that the amount of regression depends upon the strength of the frustration involved.

We can see in this experiment definite value in starting with a theoretical formulation of a problem. This framework was responsible for the design of the experiment, and this provided for the collection of data appropriate to testing the hypothesis in question. Barker, Dembo, and Lewin were well aware of the mistakes to be avoided in making observations. Therefore, they provided for two observers. They also made earnest attempts to see that all assessments, observations, evaluations, and ratings possessed a sufficient degree of objectivity, reliability, and validity to give their conclusions substantial meaning.

OBSERVATIONS OF GROUPS OF INDIVIDUALS

We can now turn our attention to the observation of groups of individuals. The outstanding example of the use of group observation for the prediction of individual behavior is that exemplified in the program of the Assessment Staff of the Office of Strategic Services.

The Office of Strategic Services was established during World War II by the President of the United States and by Congress. Its purposes were to set up and maintain research units in the United States and overseas, to establish and maintain a network of agents for gathering information concerning the nation's enemies, and to conduct destructive operations behind enemy lines. The Assessment Staff was charged with the responsibility of selecting the personnel who were to be instrumental in helping the Office of Strategic Services achieve these objectives. This meant that the Assessment Staff had to develop a series of procedures which would reveal the potentialities of the candidates for assignment to positions in the Office of Strategic Services. As in all other selection programs, the basic purpose was to increase the number of successes and to decrease the number of failures. The procedures developed by the OSS Assessment Staff are described in a volume called *Assessment of Men*. We shall review this work here, even though it leaves much to be desired in the way of making a really significant contribution to the prediction of individual behavior.

The authors of *Assessment of Men* describe their work as a "multiform organismic approach." They say it is "multiform because it consists of a rather large number of procedures based on different principles," and that it is "organismic because it utilizes the data obtained through these multiform procedures . . . to arrive at a picture of personality as a whole." The authors contrast their multiform organismic approach with what they call the elementalistic approach. This latter approach "calls," they say, "for . . . quantitative measurements of partial isolated processes," while "the organismic approach" requires estimates "of total integrated processes." For the organicist, "personality is not a series of perceptible facts, but . . . a *hypothetical formulation*, the aim of which is to *explain* and to *predict* the perceptible facts." Consequently, the method which the organicist supports "is that of predicting the future by thinking inductively from an observed set of facts to a conception (a hypothetical formulation of the personality)" and then "to think deductively from this conception to the facts which should be expected." Thus, "organismic assessment is based on the hypothesis that a trained psychologist or psychiatrist . . . is . . . capable of improving to a significant degree the accuracy of mechanical predictions derived from test scores alone."

Guided by Henry A. Murray's contagious and enthusiastic gestaltism, the OSS Assessment Staff developed a most elaborate set of assessment procedures. These we shall set forth in some detail, but we must point out, if indeed it will not become self-evident, that the great majority of these procedures were novel, new, and untried. The object in most of them was to attempt a deeper and more penetrating analysis of personality than seemed possible with the traditional types of measuring technique.

Assessment Procedures. Before we describe the assessment procedures themselves, we shall find it profitable to review the steps which the OSS Assessment Staff itself says should be followed in their development. These steps are to

1. Make a preparatory analysis of all jobs for which candidates are to be assessed.
2. List all the personality determinants of success and failure in each job.
3. Select the variables to be measured.
4. Construct a rating scale for each of the personality variables to be assessed.
5. Design a program of assessment procedures which will reveal the strength of the selected variables.
       a. Plant the assessment procedures in a social matrix.
       b. Select several different types of procedures and several procedures of the same type for estimating the strength of each variable.
       c. Include situational tests.
6. Formulate the personality of each assessee before making specific ratings, predictions, and recommendations. Acquire a concept of the individual as a whole before assessing each variable.
7. Write a personality sketch of each assessee.
8. Hold staff conferences for the purpose of reviewing and correcting the personality sketch and of deciding upon ratings and recommendations of each assessee.
9. Construct experimental designs as frames for assessment procedures so that all data necessary for the solution of strategic problems will be systematically obtained and recorded. Set up situations that will reflect to what degree the assessee possesses each of the several variables.

It becomes our duty to report, in evaluating this ambitious study, that the OSS Assessment Staff did not arrange its procedures to meet its own requirements. For example, no preparatory job analyses were made. This for the reason that great secrecy surrounded all field operations in the Office of Strategic Services, and apparently the nature of the duties for the jobs for which candidates were to be recruited could not be made available to the Assessment Staff.

Job analyses are frequently overrated as to the amount of help they can yield in a selection-research program. Nevertheless, the OSS Assessment Staff indicates that such analyses are basic to an assessment program. This being the case, its proper course of action would have been to state to the proper executive and administrative officers that it could not proceed unless the necessary information were supplied. But instead of doing this, the OSS Assessment Staff disregarded its own first principle and proceeded to its second, the listing of all personality determinants of success and failure for each type of job for which candidates were to be assessed.

The OSS Assessment Staff states that such personality determinants will differ from job to job. Therefore they should be separately determined for each job. But not knowing what jobs were involved and not knowing whether they differed from each other, the

OSS Assessment Staff proceeded to disregard its second principle and prepared a standard list of personality traits. It implies that this list of traits is important in determining success or failure on jobs for which the duties and requirements were almost completely unknown. The variables which the OSS Assessment Staff chose to assess are as follows:

1. Motivation for assignment
2. Energy and initiative
3. Effective intelligence
4. Emotional stability
5. Social relations
6. Leadership
7. Security

Like the fortuneteller in telling a fortune, the OSS Assessment Staff picked out good traits. These are socially acceptable and are popularly supposed to be important for almost any job of consequence. This does not prove, however, that they are important. Having selected the personality variables to be assessed, a rating scale for each trait was needed. This turned out to be one scale, and it was used for all traits. It provided for six degrees of variation: very superior, superior, high average, low average, inferior, and very inferior. We have already described this scale in some detail in Chap. 10.

We need not go into great detail in describing the OSS Assessment procedures, but we shall give a list of them, with brief explanatory comments.

1. *Sentence completion test.* This consisted of the beginnings of 100 sentences. The task set for the candidate was that of completing these sentences in as rapid a manner as he could. The areas covered by the sentences were "(a) family, (b) the past, (c) drives, (d) inner states, (e) goals, (f) likes and dislikes, (g) energy, (h) reaction to frustration and failure, (i) time perspective, (j) optimism-pessimism, (k) reaction to others, and (l) reactions of others."

2. *Health questionnaire.* Typical type.

3. *Work conditions survey.* A list of 43 conditions which can exist in a job. Candidate was required to rate each condition on a 6-point scale, indicating how acceptable or unacceptable it would be to him.

4. *Vocabulary test.* Fifty multiple-choice items taken from the American Council on Education Psychological Examination, the Atwood-Wells Wide Range Vocabulary Test, and the CAVD (The Institute of Educational Research Intelligence Scale).

5. *Personal history form.* Typical type.

6. *Projective questionnaire.* Twelve questions such as "What was the greatest lack in your childhood?" "What things or situations are you most afraid of?" and so forth.

7. *Belongings test.* Thirty-six questions concerning the character of a man. The answers to these questions were to be inferred from the nature of 26 items left in the man's bedroom which the candidate was given four minutes to examine.

8. *Terrain test.* A test of the extent to which the candidate was able to reproduce from memory the various points depicted on a map of the surrounding country and the location of the buildings and of his ability to infer the history of the farm from his observations. The time allowed for the observations and for study of the map extended from one day to the next, but the candidate had to fit this as best he could into a crowded schedule.

9. *The brook test.* Four to seven candidates, as a group, were instructed to transport certain objects across a brook. This required their utilization of boards and ropes to build a bridge or of pulleys, trees, and ropes to form a cable or swing. The object was to test leadership and methods of procedure, neither of which items were covered by specific instructions.

10. *The wall problem.* Four to seven candidates, as a group, were led to a wall 10 feet high and 15 feet long. They were told that the only way to escape (from the Japanese) past this barrier was over the top (they could not go or look around it). Furthermore there was an additional wall behind the first, and between the two walls there was a 200-foot canyon. Their task, in addition to getting themselves past the two barriers, was to transport a heavy log (their king-size bazooka) over with them. Scattered about and available for use (if the candidates so chose) were one board and two two-by-fours. The board was a little longer than the log, and the two-by-fours were 2 feet and 3 feet in length.

11. *Construction test.* The task set for the candidate was that of directing two workmen in the construction of a giant Tinker Toy cube. The two workmen were to do all that the candidate specifically directed them to do but, unknown to the candidate, were to obstruct progress in every way possible. Ten minutes was allowed.

12. *Postconstruction interview.* Intended to be therapeutic because of the stress engendered by the construction test, which, incidentally, no candidate was ever able to complete.

13. *The interview.* A typical type of clinical interview.

14. *The OWI test.* The candidate was told he was to have charge of propaganda activities in Korea to win Koreans over to our side. In twenty minutes he was to tell "what information he would want to have" in order to carry on a successful campaign. The object was to find out if the candidate was sensitive to items of Korean culture.

15. *Map memory test.* The candidate was given eight minutes to study a map, and then had to answer 30 multiple-choice questions concerning it.

16. *Mechanical comprehension test.* The Bennett Mechanical Comprehension Test.

17. *Manchuria test.* The candidate was instructed to prepare (*a*) a leaflet and (*b*) a two-minute 200-word spot radio broadcast designed to lower the morale of the workers and guards on the South Manchuria Railway.

18. *Discussion.* Candidates, as a group, were instructed to discuss for forty minutes the major postwar problems facing the United States and, if time permitted, the lines along which these problems should be solved.

19. *Interrogation test.* The candidate was given twelve minutes to interview a "tail gunner" recently escaped from a Japanese prison camp. He was to find out (*a*) the location of the camp, (*b*) how prisoners were treated, (*c*) the size of the camp, and (*d*) any other intelligence deserving consideration.

20. *Stress interview.* The candidate was allowed twelve minutes to invent a cover story for the "fact" that he had been discovered going through some secret papers in a government office (of which he was not an employee) in Washington. He was then interrogated in rapid-fire, third-degree fashion for ten minutes, was told that he had not been telling the truth and that he had failed the test, and was then dismissed.

21. *Poststress interview.* To some extent therapeutic, but it also consisted of an attempt to have the candidate break the security regulations under which he had been placed at the beginning of the three-day testing period.

22. *Six-2 test.* The candidate was given a map and four documents: (*a*) a report on the interrogation of Chinese refugees, (*b*) an English translation of a Japanese captain's report, (*c*) an American lieutenant's report on conditions in occupied territory, and (*d*) a translation of a Chinese military document. The candidate was given thirty-five minutes to make a list of all items of information having relevance for enemy action in a designated area and to classify these items of information with respect to their probable truth or falsity. He was then given ten minutes to prepare a 50-word dispatch for transmission to headquarters.

23. *Teaching test.* The task set was that of explaining the construction and use of a time-pencil: a device similar to a delayed-rection fuse used in demolition work. The candidate was given a typed 400-word description of the device, assembled and unassembled samples, and diagrams, He was to prepare a talk lasting not more than fifteen minutes which would make clear both the construction and the use of the time-pencil.

24. *Assigned leadership.* Candidates, in groups of five or more, one of whom had been designated as a leader, were instructed to solve five field problems. The nature of these problems can be illustrated by the instructions given for one of them, the mined road, to the leader of one of the candidate groups.

"Joe, you're the leader in this situation. You're leading this group back from a mission in enemy-occupied territory. You and your men have blown up a bridge about a mile away in this direction (points behind them). According to prearranged plans, you must meet a guerilla truck about a mile away from here in this direction at a time which leaves you only ten minutes to spend getting across this road. You have discovered that this road has been mined with a new type of sensitive Jap mine which you won't be able to neutralize or dig up. The limits of the problem are this: the road is assumed to be between these white lines (distance about 12 feet), and you can work up and down the road as far as the white lines extend. The explosion at the bridge has aroused the enemy, but so far they don't know in which direction you have gone. Your problem is obvious: to get across and leave as little trace of your escape route as possible."

There were scattered about for use by the group, if it chose to use them, two logs (12 and 14 feet), some stones, a few 4-foot two-by-fours, and two lengths of rope.

25. *Names and Identifications.* This test consisted of two sets of 12 slides. Each slide in the first set contained (*a*) a man's photograph, (*b*) his name, (*c*) age, (*d*) occupation, and (*e*) residence, city, and state. The second set had only the photographs. The slides were shown in sets of four, each slide being exposed for twenty seconds. The corresponding slides in the second set were then exposed for thirty seconds, and the candidate was to reproduce correctly for each man all data contained in the first slide.

26. *Movie observation test.* This consisted of two motion-picture sequences lasting about two and one-half minutes each. The task of the candidate was to observe the actions of two men, after they had been identified, and then later to answer a set of questions about their actions.

27. *Code aptitude test.* The Signal Corps Code Aptitude Test. It consists of 78 pairs of patterns of code sounds. The task of the candidate was to indicate whether these patterns are the same or different.

28. *Obstacle Course.* This included such tasks as rings, hand-over-hand progression on a horizontal rope, scaling a hedge by means of variously inclined boards, scaling a smooth wall, getting across narrow ($3\frac{1}{2}$ inch) and high (8 or 10 feet) catwalks, and the Army's Running Time Course.

29. *Improvisations.* A Moreno-type psychodramatic test. Each candidate could choose a role he wished to play from any one of nine previously prepared manuscripts. Then with another candidate or staff member he had to act out the situation portrayed in the manuscript. One of the situations was as follows:

Mr. F of this organization has been working as an administrative assistant for about two months. He feels that he has been doing a good job. His superior, Mr. G, however, is so dissatisfied with the work of his assistant that he decides to call him into his office. The scene to be enacted is the conversation between Mr. F and Mr. G.

30. *Debate.* An informal panel discussion of such questions as "What are we fighting for?" and "What shall we do with Germany (or Japan) after the war?" Candidates were divided into opposing groups, according to whether leniency or severity was favored, and were given twenty minutes to select a chairman and to prepare arguments. Debate was carried on in an informal manner. Drinking was encouraged.

31. *Sociometric questionnaire.* The candidate was asked to answer a series of questions concerning other candidates. He was, for example, asked to list by number those candidates whom he would recommend as supervisors of a group dealing with the problems of planning and organization. Each candidate could name as many or as few other candidates as he wished. There were 11 questions.

32. *Judgment of others.* The candidate was asked to write personality or character sketches of five of the other candidates.

33. *Murder mystery.* The candidate was given a copy of the mythical "Fairfield Chronicle," detailing the discovery of the dead body of a woman. The candidate was asked to decide whether the presumption of suicide, as given in the paper, was correct. If the candidate decided it was not and if he felt that foul play had been

involved, he had to decide who committed the murder. As help, he could question certain designated staff members who presumably knew some of the gossip in connection with the case. When candidates had prepared their solution, they were presented in a "court" session called for the purpose.

34. *Athletic events.* Broad jump, high jump, and shot-put.

35. *Baseball game.* A frivolous competition between staff and candidates on opposing teams.

Analysis. It is difficult to describe the methods of analysis used by the OSS Assessment Staff in assessing each of the personality variables by means of the foregoing tests. Indeed the authors of *Assessment of Men* state that they are not entirely sure themselves as to the exact nature of the mental processes involved in making any given assessment. The nearest we can come to giving some insight into these processes, whatever they may have been, is to show how the variable "social relations" was evaluated.

First, let us note that "social relations" encompasses in its definition the ability to get along well with other people, good will, team play, tact, freedom from disturbing prejudices and annoying traits, and so forth. It can be assessed, according to the OSS Assessment Staff, by interview, by informal observation, by individual test situations (construction and improvisations, for example), by group task situations, by projective tests, and by sociometric questionnaire.

The procedures followed by the OSS Assessment Staff carry with them the implicit assumption that each test or situation is useful as a basis for diagnosing the strength of several different traits. For example, in the brook test it was felt that a candidate who offered a suggestion had "energy and initiative"; if his suggestion was relevant, he had "effective intelligence"; if the candidate accepted, in a good-natured manner, the rejection of his suggestion, he had good "social relations"; and if his suggestion was adopted and if it worked, he had "leadership ability." Thus the strength of each personality variable was to be assessed upon the basis of several different tests and situations, and each test and situation was to contribute to the analysis of several different personality variables.

The steps in making each assessment were as follows: Following each situation the observers, who were staff members, would make their ratings independently of each other. They would then meet in conference and decide upon one joint rating to be submitted for later consideration. The staff would meet in a postimprovisations conference, discuss the performance of the candidates during improvisation, and come to some joint decision concerning the ratings to be assigned. A personality sketch was written, in part by the interviewer and in part by the situationist, *i.e.*, the staff member who observed the candidate in the various test situations. A staff conference was held. At this conference the sketch just mentioned would be read, discussed, amended, and corrected. Then a decision would be made as to whether the candidate was acceptable or unacceptable. Following this decision the staff proceeded, in conference, to give final ratings on all personality variables.

Situational Tests. Most of the tests used by the OSS Assessment Staff were situational in nature. We shall do well, therefore, to acquaint ourselves with the specialized requirements for such testing. As formulated by the OSS Assessment Staff, these requirements are as follows:

1. *Each task should have a number of solutions.* This is exemplified in the brook test which could be solved (*a*) by building a bridge, (*b*) by using a rope and pulley, or (*c*) by lassoing a tree and constructing a swing. The facility with which a solution is selected and acted upon can then be observed.

2. *The task should not require specialized abilities.* This requirement undoubtedly stems from the organicist's philosophy that he is interested in personality as a whole and thus wants to tap those aspects of the components of personality which tend to color or influence the whole of personality rather than just one aspect of it.

3. *Each task should be designed to reveal kinds of behavior which cannot be registered mechanically.* This requirement does not seem necessary. It would be expensive, of course, but there is no intrinsic reason preventing the photographing and recording of all behavior that any observer can see or hear. In fact it might have proved a valuable thing for the OSS Assessment Staff to have photographed and to have recorded all situations in which candidates were observed. This would have made it possible for other observers to attempt an evaluation of the behavior and through this experience to provide clues as to their methods of analysis.

4. *Each task should force the candidate to reveal a dominant disposition of his personality.* This requirement is obviously rooted in the philosophy of the organicist's approach in desiring to assess the whole of personality rather than some single component of it.

5. *Each task should, if possible, require group interaction.* The OSS Assessment Staff asserts that such tasks are more productive than tasks which do not require such interaction. This assertion is rather hard to reconcile with another to the effect that the interview is the most revealing single test or situation that has been tried.

6. *The task should require the coordination of numerous components of personality.* Again, a requirement rooted deep in the philosophy of the organicist's approach.

7. Each task should be modified to fit the experience and abilities of the candidate. While this at first might seem a desirable requirement, its constant application would defeat the experimental nature of the test situation. After all, one of the main requirements for making predictions is that we submit all candidates to the same tests or situations and see how they react differentially. Only if we do this can we be sure of knowing whether one candidate is better or worse than or equal to some other candidate.

8. Candidates should discuss performance after each situation. This seems a desirable and reasonable requirement. Emotional catharsis is needed after some of the more stressful situations to which the candidate is subjected.

9. The members of the staff should have time to confer with each other concerning the results of the assessment. Obviously!

The type of data which a situational test makes available for analysis can best be illustrated by the protocol secured in testing a candidate in the construction test. This protocol is given in Table 174 and was secured in response to the following directions:

We have a construction problem for you now. We want you to build a structure using the equipment lying around here. Let's see. (The staff member appears to ponder which of two or three models of different design to use.) I guess we'll give you this model to copy. (Staff member picks up the model which is always used from among the others and shows it to the candidate.) You see there are short 5-foot and long 7-foot poles lying on the ground. (Staff member points out one of each size.) The sides of the frame which you are to build are made of 5-foot poles, and the diagonals of 7-foot poles. (Staff member demonstrates this on the model.) Do you understand?

Now the corners where the poles come together are made like this. You take a half block and put it through a full block. Then you cinch it with a peg, like this. (Staff member demonstrates all this.) Then when you put the corner down on the ground, you can put the 5-foot poles in here, here, and here, and the 7-foot diagonals here and here. Do you understand?

Now (Staff member picks up the corner and points to the peg) you will notice there are holes for pegs like this at each socket, and similar holes in the end of each pole. Be sure, whenever you put a pole into a socket, to cinch it with a peg, because unless that is done all over the structure it will not be stable. (Staff member then throws the sample corner to the ground.) Is this all clear?

This is a construction problem but even more important than that, it is a test of leadership. I say that because it is impossible for one man working alone to complete this task in the ten minutes allotted to do it. Therefore we are going to give you two helpers who work here on the estate. You are to be the supervisor, their boss. You are to guide them in their work, but as foreman, you will follow more or less of a hands-off policy. Let them do the manual labor. You can assume that they have never done such work before and know nothing about it. Any questions? (Final pause to amplify any details not understood by the candidate.)

All right. It is now ten o'clock. You have just ten minutes in which to do the job. I'll call your two helpers.

TABLE 174. *Sample Protocol for the Construction Test* *

STAFF MEMBER (calling toward the barn).—Can you come out here and help this man for a few minutes?

BUSTER AND KIPPY.—Sure, we'll be right out.

STAFF MEMBER.—O.K. Slim, these are your men. They will be your helpers. You have ten minutes.

SLIM.—Do you men know anything about building this thing?

BUSTER.—Well, I dunno, I've seen people working here. What is it you want done?

SLIM.—Well, we have got to build a cube like this and we only have a short time in which to do it, so I'll ask you men to pay attention to what I have to say. I'll tell you what to do and you will do it. O.K.?

BUSTER.—Sure, sure, anything you say, Boss.

SLIM.—Fine. Now we are going to build a cube like this with 5-foot poles for the uprights and 7-foot poles for the diagonals, and use the blocks for the corners. So first we must build the corners by putting a half block and a whole block together like this and cinching them with a peg. Do you see how it is done?

BUSTER.—Sure, sure.

SLIM.—Well, let's get going.

BUSTER.—Well, what is it you want done, exactly? What do I do first?

SLIM.—Well, first put some corners together—let's see, we need four on the bottom and four topside—yes, we need eight corners. You make four of these corners and be sure that you pin them like this one.

BUSTER.—You mean we both make eight corners or just one of us?

SLIM.—You each make four of them.

BUSTER.—Well, if we do that, we will have more than eight because you already have one made there. Do you want eight altogether or nine altogether?

SLIM.—Well, it doesn't matter. You each make four of these and hurry.

BUSTER.—O.K., O.K.

KIPPY.—What cha in, the Navy? You look like one of them curly-headed boys all the girls are after. What cha in, the Navy?

SLIM.—Er, no. I am not in the Navy. I'm not in anything.

KIPPY.—Well, you were just talking about "topside" so I thought maybe you were in the Navy. What's the matter with you—you look healthy enough. Are you a draft dodger?

SLIM.—No, I was deferred for essential work—but that makes no difference. Let's get the work done. Now we have the corners done, let's put them together with the poles.

KIPPY.—The more I think of it, the more I think you are in the Army. You run this job just like the Army—you know, the right way, the wrong way, and the Army way. I'll bet you are some second lieutenant from Fort Benning.

SLIM.—That has nothing to do with this job. Let's have less talk and more work.

KIPPY.—Well, I just thought we could talk while we work—it's more pleasant.

SLIM.—Well, we can work first and talk afterward. Now connect those two corners with a 5-foot pole.

BUSTER.—Don't you think we ought to clear a place where we can work?

SLIM.—That's a good idea. Sure, go ahead.

BUSTER.—What kind of work did you do before you came here? Never did any building, I bet. Jeez, I've seen a lot of guys, but no one as dumb as you.

SLIM.—Well, that may be, but you don't seem to be doing much to help me.

BUSTER.—What—what's that? Who are you talking to, me? Me not being helpful—why,

---

* From *Assessment of Men*. New York: Rinehart & Company, Inc., 1948.

TABLE 174. *Sample Protocol for the Construction Test (Continued)*

I've done everything you have asked me, haven't I? Now, haven't I? Everything you asked me. Why, I've been about as helpful as anyone could be around here.

SLIM.—Well, you haven't killed yourself working and we haven't much time, so let's get going.

BUSTER.—Well, I like that. I come out here and do everything you ask me to do. You don't give very good directions. I don't think you know what you are doing anyway. No one else ever complained about me not working. Now I want an apology for what you said about me.

SLIM.—O.K., O.K., let's forget it. I'll apologize. Let's get going. We haven't much time. You build a square here and you build one over there.

BUSTER.—Who you talking to—him or me?

KIPPY.—That's right—how do you expect us to know which one you mean? Why don't you give us a number or something—call one of us "number one" and the other "number two."?

SLIM.—O.K. You are "one" and he is "two."

BUSTER.—Now wait a minute. Just a minute. How do you expect to get along with people if you treat them like that? First we come out here and you don't ask us our names. You call us "you." Then we tell you about it, you give us numbers. How would you like that? How would you like to be called a number? You treat us just like another 5-foot pole and then you expect us to break our necks working for you. I can see you never worked much with people.

SLIM.—I'm sorry, but we do not have much time and I thought—

KIPPY.—Yes, you thought. Jeez, it doesn't seem to me that you ever did much thinking about anything. First you don't ask our names as any stupid guy would who was courteous. Then you don't know what you did before you came here or whether you are in the Army, Navy or not, and it's darn sure you don't know anything about building this thing or directing workers. Cripes, man, you stand around here like a ninny arguing when we should be working. What the hell is the matter with you, anyway?

SLIM.—I'm sorry—what are your names?

BUSTER.—I'm Buster.

KIPPY.—Mine's Kippy. What is yours?

SLIM.—You can call me Slim.

BUSTER.—Well, is that your name or isn't it?

SLIM.—Yes, that is my name.

KIPPY.—It's not a very good name—Dumbhead would be better.

BUSTER.—Where do you come from, Slim?

SLIM.—Cincinnati.

BUSTER.—That's out in Ohio, isn't it?

SLIM.—Yes.

BUSTER.—What's the river it's on?

SLIM.—Uh—Why the Ohio.

BUSTER.—You don't sound very sure. I almost wonder if you do come from there. I'd think any Cincinnatian would remember the name of the river.

SLIM.—I'm from Cincinnati, all right. I lived there for eight years.

BUSTER.—Down by the river? In the tenement district?

SLIM.—No, in a residential region up to the north?

BUSTER.—What street?

SLIM.—Why, 1490 Kingsbury Street. What does that have to do with the present problem?

BUSTER.—The reason I asked was you don't seem to be very well dressed, and I thought

TABLE 174. *Sample Protocol for the Construction Test (Continued)*

probably you hadn't made much of a success of your business and couldn't live in a nice part of town.

SLIM.—Be that as it may—we've got to get back to work. You aren't doing anything except talking and the time is passing rapidly.

BUSTER.—Well, what kind of a boss are you anyway? You haven't told me anything to do. You stand there and say "get to work, get to work," but you don't say what I should do. Another thing, Kippy's just sitting over there trying to make that pole stick into the dirt and you don't make him work. You might at least treat us both the same. Why don't you act like a boss? Why don't you say, "Come here, Kippy, you good-for-nothing, and justify your existence. Get some work done."?

SLIM.—Come on over, Kippy; he's right. We all have to work together. You haven't been doing your part. Don't you want to help?

KIPPY.—Sure I do, but you haven't told me anything to do.

SLIM.—I certainly did. I said to make some corners and you just went over there and sat down.

KIPPY.—If that's the way you're going to talk to me—yelling and hollering and losing your temper—just because you can't give orders a fellow can understand, I don't have to work for you. You've got to be decent.

SLIM.—Well, O.K. I'll show you exactly. I want you to help me make four corners for the bottom of this using a whole block and a half block pegged together with a peg like this.

KIPPY.—Well, why didn't you say so long ago? You sure wasted a lot of time.

BUSTER.—We've got to work faster.

SLIM.—That's right, Buster.

BUSTER.—I suppose you know you're not very observant.

SLIM.—What do you mean?

BUSTER.—See those four holes in the ground? They're just 5 feet apart in a square, aren't they? What does that bring to your mind? Could it be the place to lay the corners down on the ground to make them firm? You have your corners standing up on the rolling edges and that isn't very stable.

SLIM.—It looks all right to me, if the four poles were put into the corners.

BUSTER.—O.K., if you want to sacrifice stability for mobility, it's up to you. But you might at least accept a suggestion in the spirit in which it's given. "I'm the boss," you say, "I'm better than those other guys. If I'm in charge I'm not going to listen to them. Even if they are right, I won't admit it, because I'm going to show them who's in control around here."

SLIM.—Well, we'll try it your way, but I don't think it's necessary.

BUSTER.—Slim isn't your real nickname, is it? It couldn't be with that shining head of yours. What do they call you, Baldy or Curly? Did you ever think of wearing a toupee? It would keep you from getting your scalp sunburned.

SLIM.—I don't see what difference it makes. Come on, both of you, and put an upright in each corner.

KIPPY.—He's sensitive about being bald.

BUSTER.—Yeah. . . . Well, Captain, we don't seem to be getting much done here, do we?

SLIM.—Well, if you guys would get to work we would.

BUSTER.—Well, it seems to me it's sorta late now. Why don't you be a man and admit that you can't do this job. After all, it's only a toy and sort of foolish for a grown man. It's nothing to be ashamed of that you can't build it. It's just not in your line.

SLIM.—Well, I'd like to do as much of this as possible. Will you help me?

TABLE 174. *Sample Protocol for the Construction Test (Continued)*

BUSTER.—Sure, sure, we'll help you, but it doesn't seem to be much use. What do you want us to do now?

SLIM.—Well, one of you build a square over there just like this one while the other one puts in the uprights and diagonals on this one.

KIPPY.—May I ask a question?

SLIM.—Sure, go ahead.

KIPPY.—Why build one over there? What are you going to do with it then?

SLIM.—Well, we'll put it on top—the top of this cube is like the bottom.

KIPPY.—Well, if that isn't the most stupid thing I ever heard of. Since when do you build the roof of a house and lift it to the top? Why not build it right on the top? Listen, when you build a house you build the foundation, then the walls, and then the roof. Isn't that right?

SLIM.—Well, that is usually the way it's done, but I think we can do this job this way. In fact, I don't think it matters much which way we do it. Either way is O.K., I guess.

BUSTER.—You guess, you guess. What kind of a man are you anyway? Why in hell don't you make up your mind and stick to it? Be decisive—didn't they tell you that in OCS—be decisive—even if you are wrong, be decisive, give an order. What are you?—man or mouse?

KIPPY.—Oh, it's no use talking, Buster, when he doesn't have a bar on his shoulder he doesn't know what to do. Listen, Mac, you're not on Company Street now. You haven't a sergeant to do your work for you. You're all alone and you look pretty silly. Why, you can't even put together a child's toy.

SLIM.—Now, listen to me, you guys, are you going to work for me or aren't you?

BUSTER.—Sure, we want to work for you. We really don't care. We'd as soon work for you as for anyone else. We get paid all the same. The trouble is we can't find out what you want done. What exactly do you want?

SLIM.—Just let's get this thing finished. We haven't much more time. Hey there, you, be careful, you knocked that pole out deliberately.

KIPPY.—Who, me? Now listen to me, you good for nothing young squirt. If this darned thing had been built right from the beginning the poles wouldn't come out. Weren't you told that you have to pin these things? Why, none of it is pinned; look at that, and that, and that! (Kicks the poles which were not pinned out of position and part of the structure collapses.)

SLIM.—Hey—you don't have to knock it all down.

BUSTER.—Well, it wasn't built right. What good was it without pins?

SLIM.—I told you guys to pin it.

KIPPY.—I pinned every one you told me about. How did I know you wanted the others pinned? Jeez, they send a boy out here to do a man's job and when he can't do it he starts blaming his helpers. Who is responsible for this—you or me? Cripes, they must really be scraping the bottom of the barrel now.

STAFF MEMBER (walking in from the sidelines).—All right, Slim. That is all the time we have. The men will take this down.

BUSTER.—Take what down? There's nothing to take down. Never saw anyone get so little done.

Reliability, Objectivity, and Validity. Let us now examine the value of the OSS assessment procedures in terms of their reliability, objectivity, and validity.

Reliability. We usually define reliability as some type of self-consistency, and usually as the type that obtains between two equivalent tests of the same psychological function. Very few tests in the OSS Assessment program allowed a determination of reliability in the usual way.

For most of the tests reliability was determined from the intercorrelations found to obtain between the assessments of the same variable in different situations. For example, "energy and initiative" was assessed by interview, by the brook test, by the construction test, by assigned leadership, by the obstacle course, by discussion, and by debate. The median intercorrelation between assessed "energy and initiative" in all of these tests was .37. A complete summary for all variables is given in column 1 of Table 175.

TABLE 175. *Reliability Data for the OSS Assessment Variables**

Trait	Average intra-trait correlation	Average inter-trait correlation
Physical ability...............	.52	.10
Propaganda skills..............	.47	.30
Leadership....................	.41	.45
Energy and initiative...........	.37	
Emotional stability.............	.30	.31
Social relations................	.30	.31
Effective intelligence...........	.29	.32
Observation and report.........	.26	.27
Security......................	.19	.30

* From *Assessment of Men*. New York: Rinehart & Company, Inc., 1948.

These values are certainly not very high. They are also far below minimum acceptable standards for use in individual prediction. In their defense, however, it may be said that the values given fail to take into account the fact that the final assessment of each personality variable was based on a number of situations. Thus "energy and initiative" was assessed upon the basis of seven tests. Therefore if the total test of "energy and initiative" is considered 7 times as long as each component part of the test, the reliability of the final assessment of "energy and initiative" may be considerably greater than that indicated.

This allowance cannot wholly mitigate our concern, however. Column 2 of Table 175 shows the average intercorrelations of the assessments for each variable. Thus the assessment of "emotional stability" correlates, on the average, .31 with the assessments on all other variables. This correlation, be it noted, is even a little higher than the intercorrelation of the various assessments of "emotional stability" among themselves. In view of the fact that various assessments of "emotional stability" do not correlate any higher with each other than an over-all assessment of "emotional stability" correlates with other personality variables, it is difficult to see how these other variables have, in fact, proved to be such. Are they not, too, just additional manifestations of the trait "emotional stability?"

In only two instances are the intercorrelations among the assessments for one variable higher than those among the assessments for all variables. These two variables are physical ability and propaganda skills. In the first instance the average intracorrelation for various assessments of physical ability is .52, and the average intercorrelation of physical ability with all other traits is only .10. In the second instance, propaganda skills, the difference is not nearly so marked. The intracorrelation is .47, and the intercorrelation is .30. In all other cases the intra and intercorrelations are practically identical. In view of this fact, we cannot refrain from concluding that the OSS Assessment Staff was unsuccessful in making assessments with a very satisfactory degree of reliability.

We can examine reliability not only from the standpoint of the final assessment for each personality variable but also from the standpoint of the relative value of each method of assessment. That is, in assessing "social relations," is the interview more or less reliable than the construction test, and so forth? Because of the low reliabilities reported and because of the fact that these reliabilities do not differ greatly from the intercorrelations between the personality variables, it might seem that we cannot answer the questions which we have just posed. In a strict sense this is true, but we can at least determine the relative influence which each test or situation has upon the final rating for each variable. We can determine the extent to which the assessment made in each situation correlates with the final rating assigned on each variable. For example, Table 176 shows that "energy and initiative," as assessed by interview, correlates .78 with the final rating (based on interview, brook, construction, assigned leadership, obstacle, discussion, and debate). This correlation is spurious because the interview itself, along with other tests, is included as a basis for the final rating. The OSS Assessment Staff does not present the nonspurious correlation, however (that is, the correlation between the interview assessment and the final rating with the interview excluded), so we must do the best we can with the data which it presents.

The OSS Assessment Staff reports that the interview correlates higher with the final ratings on all variables than does any other test or situation. Therefore the interview turns out to be the most important single factor in assessment. This can be gratifying, or it can be disturbing—gratifying if the data are taken as demonstrating that the time-honored, much-maligned technique of interviewing

TABLE 176. *The Relation of Individual Energy and Initiative Ratings to Final Energy and Initiative Ratings**

Interview	.78
Brook	.67
Construction	.56
Assigned leadership	.77
Obstacle	.41
Discussion	.55
Debate	.54

* From *Assessment of Men*. New York: Rinehart & Company, Inc., 1948.

does have value after all, disturbing if the data are taken as demonstrating that no other test or situation tried is as good as the interview, which itself is not very reliable anyway.

The authors of *Assessment of Men* state that the interview was one of their most valuable techniques of assessment. This can only mean that they relied on it because the other tests and situations failed to give the data sought. Practically all judgments and evaluations were modified, if modified at all, in the direction indicated by the interview. The fact that this occurred, however, cannot be taken as evidence that the interview is effective as a basis for making predictions.

Objectivity. From the standpoint of objectivity we have little comment to offer. Objectivity ordinarily implies that the result of any evaluation is independent of the observer who makes the evaluation. In the OSS Assessment program the only tests which meet this requirement are those of the usual paper-and-pencil variety. All the rest suffer seriously from the lack of objectivity in their scoring. The low intercorrelations discussed in connection with reliability may be due in part to lack of objectivity. The observer in one situation frequently was not the observer in a second situation. Therefore it is difficult to separate the relative influence of the lack of reliability intrinsic to the situation from that due to lack of objectivity when assessment was made by different observers. The OSS Assessment Staff properly objects to many paper-and-pencil tests, but they possess a much greater degree of objectivity than the situational tests which it used.

Validity. An attempt was made to evaluate the effectiveness of the assessments or of their predictive value by relating them to overseas staff appraisals, theater-commander appraisals, reassignment-area appraisals, and returnee appraisals. The number of candidates for whom one or more of these types of appraisals were secured were pitifully small, and the validities secured were amazingly low. The coefficients which the OSS Assessment Staff reports are given in Table 177.

TABLE 177. *Validity Data for the OSS Assessment of Over-all Success**
1. Overseas appraisal.................... .37
2. Returnee appraisal.................... .19
3. Theater commander appraisal.......... .23
4. Reassignment appraisal................ .08

* From *Assessment of Men*. New York: Rinehart & Company, Inc., 1948.

Validities for specific traits were obtained only for the overseas staff appraisals. These are given in Table 178.

TABLE 178. *Validity Data for Specific Trait Ratings in the OSS Assessment Program**
1. Motivation................... .12
2. Effective intelligence.......... .32
3. Emotional stability............ .08
4. Social relations............... .06
5. Leadership................... .16

* From *Assessment of Men*. New York: Rinehart & Company, Inc., 1948.

The most valid of the predictors proved to be ratings of effective intelligence. This suggests that a standardized intelligence test might have been used, and the chances are that it might have given higher validity.

The overseas staff appraisal consisted of a threefold classification: outstanding, average, and unsatisfactory. Placement in one or the other of these categories was upon the basis of information secured by a staff member. He rated each candidate on his over-all performance and then made an estimate of how reliable he thought his rating to be. To determine this reliability, the staff member was asked to consider the number of people who gave him pertinent information concerning the assessee, how much agreement there was among them, how well each informant knew the assessee, and how dependable each informant seemed to be.

We shall have to agree with the OSS Assessment Staff's indictment of its own work. In its own words, "None of the statistical computations demonstrates that the system of assessment was of great value." Most of the procedures followed by the OSS Assessment Staff violate time-honored and proved techniques of rating. Opportunity for independent judgments by independently working observers was all but made completely impossible. The procedures followed allowed the ratings to be influenced to too great an extent by the chairman of the staff discussions and conferences. And the procedure required the submission of a general rating and full knowledge of it before any of the more specific ratings could be made. Comments of the OSS Staff to the contrary, this last procedure is highly questionable. If ratings are to be made on specific traits, they should be made first. If generality is found in them thereafter, well and good, but it should not be put into the ratings ahead of time. This is just what the OSS Assessment procedure did.

15

PERFORMANCE: EXPERIMENTAL

APPROACHES

In the analysis of personality relatively little has been done with experimental techniques in contrast with what has been done with inventory, questionnaire, and related techniques. It may be that the area encompassed in personality research is not amenable to treatment by experimental methods, or it may be that those interested in personality measurement have not been, primarily, experimental psychologists. There is considerable truth in both of these premises, but we ought to be sure that sufficient and adequate experimentation is undertaken in the field of personality measurement before we become tempted to conclude that its problems are not amenable to experimental attack.

EYSENCK

We shall first find it profitable to review several of the studies which Eysenck reports in his volume *Dimensions of Personality*. In this volume, Dr. Eysenck reports several attempts to determine by experimental means some of the differences between clinically diagnosed neurotics and nonneurotics and between clinically diagnosed introverts and extroverts. According to Eysenck, there is no correlation between neuroticism and introversion, as some of the data reported in connection with the Bernreuter Personality Inventory would seem to indicate. Eysenck came to this conclusion as a result of some factor analyses. Whether Eysenck's contention is correct or not need not deter us from examining his experimental studies. In each of these studies his subjects were selected upon the basis of clinical judgment and not upon the basis of his factorial studies. We shall discuss Eysenck and his collaborators' experimentation on autonomic activity, dark vision, exercise response, reversal of perspective, level of aspiration, personal tempo, perseveration, persistence, suggestibility, and narcosis. In each of the following sections, the hypotheses to be examined are that clinically diagnosed neurotics differ from clinically diagnosed nonneurotics and/or that clinically diagnosed introverts (dysthymics) differ from clinically diagnosed extroverts (hysterics).

Autonomic Activity. Eysenck and Yap measured the amount of salivary secretion under various conditions "such as reading, rest, mental work, food imagery, and whilst doing a test involving hand-eye coordination." The method used to measure salivary secretion was that developed by Lashley and further standardized by Richter and Wada. In this method "a disc is held over the opening of Stenson's duct by suction and the saliva issuing from the parotic gland drained off through a rubber tube to a measuring device . . . enabling the experimenter to measure secretion per unit of time in cubic centimeters." Eysenck and Yap tested 24 introverts (dysthymics) and 52 extroverts (hysterics) and found that "in each of . . . eleven experimental periods, the dysthymic [introvert] group [showed] less salivation than the hysteric [extrovert] group." Introverts (dysthymics) secreted 41 percent more saliva than the extroverts (hysterics).

Dark Vision. The apparatus used to test night visual capacity was the Livingston rotating hexagon. Eysenck reports that this is:

. . . a hexagonal structure which can be rotated so as to present different panels to the subject tested; there are altogether 96 letters and objects on its six sides. The letters are placed in various positions, and the objects are outlines of aircraft, ships, parallel lines, etc. . . . Preparation for the test includes 30 minutes dark adaptation, with dark goggles, admitting only 3 per cent light, followed by 10 minutes in the dark room during which the details of the test are carefully explained. The subject [records] his interpretation of the objects and letters in the dark by means of special Braille cards.

Eysenck indicates that this Hexagon test " . . . measures both photopic and scotopic vision . . . at various levels of illumination . . . ranging from .00015 square foot candles to .0012 square foot candles." At each level of illumination six letters and two objects are exposed, and one minute is allowed for the recording of answers. Eysenck tested 96 neurotic patients and compared their responses with those of over 6,000 RAF personnel. On a scale with a range from 0 to 32, the neurotics secured an average score of 7.1 and the RAF personnel an average score of 19.3. These groups are clearly differentiated in terms of mean scores and also, as shown in Fig. 13, in terms of the shapes of their respective distributions.

Poor night vision clearly differentiates neurotic individuals from normal subjects and also, Eysenck found, distinguishes the more seriously ill neurotic patients from the less seriously ill neurotic

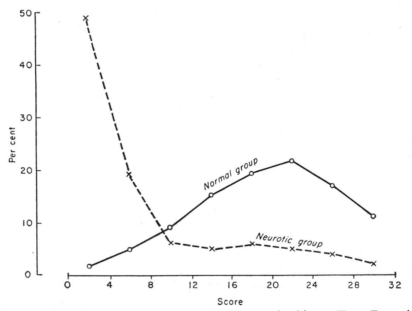

Fig. 13. Dark vision test scores for neurotic and normal subjects. (From Eysenck, H. J. *Dimensions of Personality*. London: Routledge and Kegan Paul, Ltd., 1947.)

patients. To demonstrate this fact he compared 50 patients with poor night vision (scores of 4 or less) with 13 men with good night vision (scores of 19 or more) on a number of items. The items found to show significant differences between these two groups are presented in Table 179.

Exercise Response. Exercise affects oxygen uptake, pulse, and lactate consumption. According to Eysenck:

Oxygen uptake was measured in cubic centimeters per minute . . . by means of a Douglas bag. Pulse rate was measured by the following formula: [(pulse rate first four minutes after cessation of exercise) + (mean of 8th, 9th, and 10th minutes) − 5(resting pulse)]. Lactate rise [was measured] by comparing lactate content of a sample of venous blood removed before and another removed 10 minutes after standard exercise.

Eysenck states that the average intercorrelation of these responses is .56. Oxygen consumption and pulse rate correlate .63; oxygen consumption and lactate output correlate .49; and pulse rate and lactate output correlate .56. All three indices reflect some one underlying common factor.

TABLE 179. *Comparison of Patients with Good and Poor Night Vision**

Item	Good group	Poor group	Critical ratio
Considerable unemployment..............	0.0	28.0	4.41
Poor work history.......................	0.0	10.0	2.36
Discharged from the army................	15.4	46.0	2.44
Poor education..........................	7.7	30.0	2.29
Good mental health before illness..........	61.5	16.0	3.04
Previous mental illness...................	0.0	16.0	3.08
Well organized personality................	76.9	30.0	3.40
Very anxious and highly strung............	0.0	22.0	3.76
Obsessional traits.......................	0.0	14.0	2.85
Cyclothymic personality..................	7.7	52.0	3.67

* From Eysenck, H. J. *Dimensions of Personality*. London: Routledge and Kegan Paul, Ltd., 1947.

The task used to evoke exercise was that of pedaling on a bicycle ergometer at 42 revolutions per minute. The friction of the brake was set equivalent to a weight of 9 pounds, so in a five-minute work period each subject was required to do 6,750 foot-pounds of work. Then 20 controls and 30 hospital patients, equated for weight and age, were tested. The scores for the three responses were normalized and then added (to give equal weight to each component) to give one combined index of exercise response. On this combined index 10 extroverts (hysterics) secured a mean score of 7.8, and 10 introverts (dysthymics) secured a mean score of 5.8. The 20 normal controls secured a mean score of 4.3. Both of the hospitalized groups differ significantly from the normal controls as well as from each other. Therefore we may conclude, with Eysenck, that neurotics show poorer exercise response than normals and that extroverts show poorer exercise response than introverts.

Reversal of Perspective. In looking at ambiguous figures such as the Maltese cross and face-vase, do introverts differ from extroverts in the number of reversals which occur? Petrie gave these tests to 34 extroverts (hysterics) and to 38 introverts (dysthymics) in an effort to find out. Each of the tests was given twice: once when each subject was told to be passive and a second time when each subject was told to secure as many reversals as possible. No significant differences were found.

Level of Aspiration. This concept denotes an expected level of achievement. A person who decides that he is going "to make" Phi Beta Kappa has a higher level of aspiration than the student who decides he is going to be satisfied with a gentleman's C average. Thus, level of aspiration refers to expected achievement.

The tests which Eysenck used to measure aspiration level were the Triple-Tester and a punch test. The Triple-Tester was constructed by Dr. Craik of Cambridge and

. . . consists of a brass drum carrying an Ivorine cover, rotating towards the subject. This Ivorine cover is marked out as a helical "road" with holes punched in it. A "vehicle" in the form of a bronze ball moved sideways on a rack is steered along this road by a steering wheel. The purpose is to keep the ball on the line of holes; each "hit" is scored on an electric counter. The steering wheel operates the rack through an integrating gear instead of directly. Instantaneous deflection of the vehicle from its path is impossible with this method of transmission, and the subject is forced to anticipate the necessary moves. The more he anticipates, the smoother will be the path which he describes whereas rapid movements made at the last moment will result in violent oscillations or wobbling of the vehicle which requires correction and leads to still worse scores.

The punch test is nothing more than a Hollerith key punch used as a basis for a code-substitution test. This is accomplished by

. . . putting before the subject a chart giving equivalent letters for the number appearing on the keys of the punch, and exposing automatically a certain letter whenever the punch is depressed. Thus the subject would look at the letter exposed, read off the corresponding number from the card, depress the key bearing the correct number, thus exposing the next letter.

After preliminary explanation and trial and after having been told the maximum possible scores, the subject was asked to estimate what score he would get on each of these two tests. Then he performed the task, and was asked what score he thought he got. He was told what score he got and was asked to estimate what score he would get on the next trial. This sequence of estimate, performance, and judgment of performance was repeated 10 times on each test, and leads us to a consideration of the following score variables.

Goal-discrepancy Score. This is the difference between actual performance on a given trial and the expected performance on the next trial. The difference is said to be positive when the expected level of performance is above actual performance and it is said to be negative when the expected level of performance is below actual performance.

Attainment-discrepancy Score. This is the difference between the performance level attained and the expected performance level for this same trial. If performance turns out to be higher than the expected performance, the attainment-discrepancy score is positive, but if not, it is negative.

Judgment-discrepancy Score. This is the difference between actual performance on a trial and the subject's judgment of what performance level was attained. If judgment is higher than performance, the difference is assigned a positive sign, but if performance is higher than judgment, the difference is assigned a negative sign.

Affective-discrepancy Score. This is the difference obtained when the judgment-discrepancy score is subtracted from the goal-discrepancy score. Thus we start with the difference between the expected level of achievement and the last previous performance and subtract from this the difference between actual performance on the last trial and his judgment as to what his performance actually was. This process presumably objectifies the original goal-discrepancy score by ridding it of the error caused by inability to estimate what past performance actually was. A person with a high affectivity score, even more than a person with a high goal-discrepancy score is (supposedly) unable to keep his level of aspiration in close contact with reality, that is, with actual performance.

Index of Flexibility. This "is the simple sum of all shifts in the level of aspiration during the test." It was computed without regard to the direction of the change.

Index of Responsiveness. This consisted of a simple count of the number of times that the level of aspiration was raised after success and was lowered after failure. A successful trial was, of course, one in which performance equaled or exceeded expected performance, and a failure was a trial in which performance fell below that expected.

Fifty introverts (dysthymics) were equated to 50 extroverts (hysterics) on age, intelligence, and ability on the test. They were then compared with each other with respect to their average aspiration, performance, and judgment scores. When compared with actual performance, the aspiration scores of extroverts (hysterics) were found to be higher than those of introverts (dysthymics), and the judgment scores of extroverts (hysterics) were lower than those of introverts (dysthymics). The differences are statistically significant and are clearly demonstrated in Fig. 14. In comparing the responsiveness scores, Eysenck also found that extroverts (hysterics) are more rigid and less modifiable through experience than introverts (dysthymics). And, as might be expected, they show less flexibility.

On the punch test Himmelweit tested 69 extroverts (hysterics) and 58 introverts (dysthymics). He found that extroverts (hysterics) have higher goal-discrepancy scores, higher affective discrepancy scores, and are more rigid than introverts (dysthymics).

We may cite here a good example of what Hull might call the hypothetico-deductive approach in psychological research. Certain experimental results, those just discussed, led to the hypothesis that high affectivity scores are correlated with, or are symptomatic of, a poorly organized personality. If this hypothesis is correct, Eysenck reasoned that any condition which would "increase the affective relation of the patient to the task" should cause the differences between introverts (dysthymics) and extroverts (hysterics) to be augmented over those already reported. Therefore he had Himmelweit offer 22 extroverts (hysterics) and 20 introverts (dysthymics) 50 cigarettes or 5 shillings if they would, upon a second testing a week after the first test, beat their own previous score by 30 points on the Triple-Tester. Eysenck reports:

> The average scores on the actual test rose very significantly from the first to the second testing for the extroverts (hysterics), but failed to show a significant rise for the introverts (dysthymics). The affective discrepancy was larger on the second testing for the extroverts (hysterics), smaller for the introverts (dysthymics). Lastly, the judgment discrepancy on the second testing was considerably lower for the extroverts (hysterics), and considerably higher for the introverts (dysthymics). In other words, the extroverts (hysterics) under conditions of special motivation tended to underrate their performance even more than usual, while under these conditions the introverts (dysthymics) overrated their performance even more. [Further] the rigidity of the hysterics did not change to any extent from first to second testing, the dysthymics became considerably more rigid.

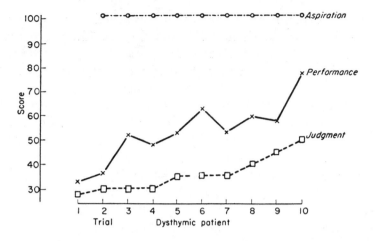

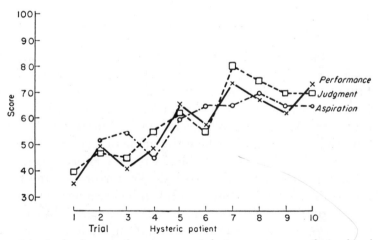

Fig. 14. Aspiration, performance, and judgment scores of dysthymic and hysteric patients. (From Eysenck, H. J. *Dimensions of Personality*. London: Routledge and Kegan Paul, Ltd., 1947.)

An experiment was performed. It led to a certain hypothesis. A second experiment was performed to test the validity of the deductions of the hypothesis, and, in this case, these deductions appeared to be verified. Thus, the hypothetico-deductive method means nothing more than the setting up of a hypothesis, the deducing of certain consequences which should follow from it, and the setting up of experiments to test the validity of such deductions. By inference from the experiment, a conclusion is reached as to whether or not the original hypothesis is valid. Strictly, according to the rules of logic, one cannot judge the correctness of an antecedent from the truth or falsity of its consequent, but if a hypothesis leads to too many false consequences, it certainly becomes suspect.

Personal Tempo. Petrie tested a total of 75 introverts (dysthymics) and extroverts (hysterics) on a number of tests of word fluency but found no significant differences among them. The nature of the eight tasks which Petrie set for her subjects was to give as many responses as possible when asked to write:

1. Round things
2. Birds
3. Things which might be at a certain point on the picture of a tree
4. Things which might be at a certain point on the picture of a street corner
5. Number of concepts for a colored Rorschach ink blot
6. Things to eat
7. Flowers
8. Number of concepts for a black and white Rorschach ink blot

Perseveration. Eysenck lists five types of perseveration. These are sensory, associative, creative, motor, and *Umstellbarkeit*. The first is that evidenced by the rate at which a color wheel with black and white stripes must be rotated in order to make the flicker sensation disappear. Associative perseveration is illustrated in the task of naming the color of ink in which the name of a color is printed on a background of still a different color. Creative effort perseveration is that tested by use of a device, such as the mirror-drawing test, for which an established habit must be broken before a new one can take its place. Motor perseveration is usually measured by having a subject do two opposite things in alternation, such as writing zzzz for thirty seconds then ssss for thirty seconds, then zszszszs for sixty seconds, and so forth. *Umstellbarkeit* means change from one activity to another. We shall not take time to discuss the results secured with these tests, since none yielded anything of significance between certain subject groups, as between introverts and extroverts or between neurotics and normals.

Persistence. A simple test of persistence consists in asking a subject to sit on one chair and to hold his leg extended over another chair with the heel of his shoe about an inch above the second chair. The subject is asked to keep his leg in this position as long as possible, and then he is timed until the heel of his shoe touches the chair. Introverts (dysthymics) touched the chair in an average of fourteen seconds while extroverts (hysterics) touched the chair in an average of thirty-one seconds. Extroverts can persist in their muscular pose over twice as long as introverts.

Suggestibility. Eysenck distinguishes between what he calls primary, secondary, and prestige suggestibility. Primary suggestibility he defines as some overt behavioral act resulting from a verbal suggestion; secondary suggestibility he defines as some sensory perception aroused as a result of suggestion; and prestige suggestibility he defines as a change in opinion or attitude due to knowledge of the opinions of other people (say of the majority or of prominent individuals).

Three tests of primary suggestibility are the Chevreul pendulum test, Hull's body-sway test, and Eysenck and Furneau's press-release test. In the first of these tests, the Chevreul pendulum test, the subject is given a string with a small weight attached. He is instructed to hold this weighted string over a particular spot marked on a table (in front of him), but while he is attempting to do this, the experimenter keeps telling him that the string will start oscillating along a line and will not stay over the point marked out. The extent to which swing is imparted to the string becomes the measure of the subject's suggestibility.

In the body-sway test the subject is asked to close his eyes and to stand relaxed and quite still. While the subject is attempting this, the experimenter keeps telling him that he is falling forward, and the amount of sway which occurs is taken as the measure of suggestibility.

Finally, in the press-release test the subject is asked to lie on a couch and to hold a rubber bulb. In one part of the test he is told to hold the bulb just as he is holding it now, but suggestions are repeatedly made to the effect that he is squeezing the bulb. In a second part of the test the subject is told to squeeze the bulb as tightly as he can, and then suggestions are repeatedly made to the effect that he is relaxing his grip. Suggestibility is measured by change in pressure. In the first part of the test an increase in pressure is taken as being indicative of suggestibility, while in the second part of the test diminution in pressure is taken as being indicative of suggestibility.

Tests of secondary suggestibility are Binet's progressive lines and progressive weights tests and Whipple's picture tests. In Binet's progressive lines and progressive weights tests a series of approximately 15 lines or 15 weights is presented to the subject. The first five lines (or the first five weights) differ progressively in that each succeeding stimulus is longer or shorter (heavier or lighter) than the preceding one. The point is to set up in the subject an expectation of a continual increase (or decrease) in length or weight. Then when this expectation is presumably established, the subject is presented successively with, let us say, 10 additional stimuli. These are all objectively equal (in length or weight), so the measure of suggestibility is the number of these objectively equal stimuli that are said by the subject to be longer (or shorter) or heavier (or lighter) than the last of the changing stimuli.

In Whipple's picture test a picture is shown and then a number of memory-type questions are asked. Inserted among these questions, however, are several ringers, such as "What was the color of the tie which the man was wearing?" In fact, the man was not wearing a tie. The measure of suggestibility is the number of such questions to which an answer is given.

Finally, a test of prestige suggestibility can be arranged by giving a subject a chance to express his opinions on a variety of controversial topics, then informing him of majority opinion, of the opinion of experts, or of that of prominent people, and asking him then to reexpress his own opinions. The degree to which he departs from his own original opinion toward that of the majority, that of the experts, and so forth, is used as a measure of suggestibility.

We have described these various measures of suggestibility to show that the term has numerous meanings and that we must be careful in using the concept to denote the particular type of suggestibility we have in mind. The easiest way to do this is, of course, to describe the experimental procedures used to induce the suggestibility which is the object of study.

We can now turn to Eysenck's experimentation showing that a certain type of suggestibility is related to neuroticism. This type is primary suggestibility, and was measured by means of the body-sway test. In preparation for this test a subject is asked to stand in a certain place, and a string is run from his collar to a device that will indicate the amount of body sway that will occur. Before the test itself begins, he is observed for a period of thirty seconds, and during this time the extent of his "natural" body sway is noted. Then following this thirty-second preliminary period, the subject is told that a record is to be played. The experimenter says:

I want you to listen carefully to what the record says, while you go on just standing there, quite still and relaxed, with your eyes closed. Listen carefully, and just keep on standing as you are standing now. I am putting the record on now.
[The record continues:]
"Now just keep standing there, please, quite still and relaxed, with your eyes closed, and think of nothing in particular. Just keep standing quite still and relaxed and listen to me. Now I want you to imagine that you are falling forward, you *are* falling, falling forward, falling forward all the time. Falling, falling forward, you are falling forward now. You are falling, falling forward, falling forward all the time. . . . "
[This continues for two and one-half minutes.]

The maximum amount of sway is taken as a measure of suggestibility. For example, if the subject sways forward three inches and backward one inch, the suggestibility score is 3. If he sways backward six inches and forward four inches, his suggestibility score is 6. If the subject falls or has to be caught by the experimenter to prevent his falling, the suggestibility score is arbitrarily set at 12.

TABLE 180. *Body Sway in Relation to Neuroticism**

Neurotic classification	Men		Women	
	Number	Mean	Number	Mean
Normal	60	1.02	60	1.11
I	54	2.53	13	1.38
II	132	3.10	54	1.91
III	247	3.92	90	2.74
IV	244	4.17	100	3.40
V	154	5.50	54	3.61
VI	69	5.55	19	6.72

* From Eysenck, H. J. *Dimensions of Personality*. London: Routledge and Kegan Paul, Ltd., 1947.

Table 180 shows the mean absolute amounts of body sway for each of six groups of neurotic men and for each of six groups of neurotic women. These figures demonstrate a definite and significant relation between neuroticism and primary suggestibility.

Narcosis. Upon the basis of the body-sway test, two contrasting groups of subjects were selected. One called "the suggestibles" were those who swayed three or more inches, and the other called the "nonsuggestibles" were those who swayed less than two inches. Ten of the suggestibles and ten of the nonsuggestibles were given an intravenous injection of sodium amytal "till they could no longer count backwards without making gross mistakes." They were then given the Press-Release test. All suggestible patients became more suggestible, but none of the nonsuggestible patients became suggestible. Thus sodium amytal can make a suggestible person more suggestible, but it apparently cannot turn a nonsuggestible person into a suggestible one. A control experiment on ten suggestible patients first tested in a normal state and then after an injection of a neutral saline solution showed that the increase in suggestibility cannot be accounted for in terms of the injection alone. It is due to the sodium amytal.

A similar experiment involving the inhalation of nitrous oxide gave similar results. Not a single nonsuggestible patient, out of ten, became suggestible under the influence of nitrous oxide. But all but one, out of ten, of the suggestible patients became even more suggestible under its influence.

We turn now to a consideration of three studies reported in the Terman Commemorative Volume *Studies in Personality*. These studies were conducted by Roger G. Barker, L. P. Herrington, and Robert R. Sears. We shall learn from these studies methods of defining a psychological variable and of determining some of its correlates. In Barker's study, we shall find a definition of vicarious trial-and-error behavior, and we shall learn how this behavior is influenced by conflict—on the one hand, by a conflict between two desirable goals and on the other hand, by a conflict between two undesirable goals. In the second study, that conducted by L. P. Herrington, we shall discover a statistical way of defining a psychological trait of variability, and we shall find that this trait has predictive value with respect to the total amount of activity in which a subject engages. Finally, in contrast with Herrington's study, we shall review the study on motility conducted by Sears. In this study, motility was the variable defined, subjects were led into situations of success or failure, and the effect of this success or failure on the amount of motility was noted. The chief result which

Sears reports is an increase in variability. We have here two opposing but complementary approaches. Herrington starts out with the trait of variability and finds that it is predictive of activity, whereas Sears starts out with activity and finds that it is predictive of variability.

BARKER

The experimental situation which Barker designed made it possible for him to present in pairs the names of two liquids. He asked each of his subjects to turn an upright (vertical) lever from the center of the table (at a position intermediate to the two cards on which the names of the liquids were exposed) toward the name of the liquid he would prefer to drink. In one trial the subject actually had to drink the preferred liquid (6 cubic centimeters), but in an alternate trial he merely had to indicate his preference and did not have to drink the liquid.

Prior to the experiment proper, each subject had been asked to taste each of the seven liquids involved. These were pineapple juice, orange juice, tomato juice, water, lemon juice, salt water, and vinegar. These liquids were ranked individually for each subject so that his order of preference was known.

Nineteen boys, aged 9 to 11 years, were tested. Nine of them were given the "real" sequence first, followed by the "hypothetical" sequence, while the other ten were given the "hypothetical" sequence first, followed by the "real" sequence. When the order of preference had been determined for a subject, he was presented with a list (serially and successively presented) of all possible pairs of stimuli. Since seven liquids were involved, this meant that there were 21 possibilities. Two series were run, one in which the subject had to taste the liquid and the other in which he merely had to indicate his preference. A total of 42 choices was required.

The lever which the subject had to operate to indicate his choice was arranged so that its movements were recorded on an automatically moving tape. The times of exposure of the cards were also recorded so that the time between the exposure of the contrasting stimuli and the occurrence of the response could be determined. To make the consummation of the response a definite affair, the lever was constructed so that it would have to be turned through an arc of 5 inches, and would then cause a buzzer to ring. The ringing of the buzzer indicated that a choice had been made. Prior to this ringing, the lever could be turned as much as the subject desired (short of 5 inches) and in either direction. No amount of turning counted unless the buzzer was sounded. Once the buzzer sounded, however, the trial was concluded, and the choice was considered made.

Two measures of the resolution of conflict were obtained, namely, the total time, in seconds, before the buzzer sounded and the number of wavers which occurred before the choice was made. A waver was defined as "a shifting of the lever followed by a return to the original position" without the buzzer's having sounded. The wavers were arbitrarily classified into small, medium, and large and were given weights of 1, 2, and 3 in this order. A subject's vicarious trial-and-error score consisted of "the sum of his wavers as thus weighted for the extent of displacement." Barker computed the mean time required and the mean vicarious trial-and-error score for conflicts between liquids separated one step, two steps, three steps, and so on, up to six steps in the preference series. The data obtained show clearly that the greater the conflict the greater the time required for its resolution and that this additional time is required by the increased amount of vicarious trial and error before the choice is made.

The data we have just discussed take into consideration the difficulty of the conflict only in terms of the number of steps between the two stimuli offered in comparison. We can now consider, with Barker, whether the relations just discussed will hold if the desirable goals, say orange juice and pineapple juice, are considered apart from conflicts between undesirable choices, for example, between salt water and vinegar. Barker found that it takes a longer and much more vicarious trial and error for the resolution of an undesirable conflict than it does for the resolution of a desirable conflict.

HERRINGTON

Barker's study shows the way we can use experimental data in relation to personality theory. Now let us examine Herrington's study which shows us how to relate psychological with physiological measures. The principal purpose envisaged by Herrington was that of discovering what relationship, if any, existed between activity level (a psychological concept) and various physiological measures such as "basal metabolic rate, total metabolism, pulse, respiration, and blood pressure." On both the psychological and physiological levels, Herrington was concerned primarily with mean scores and with individual variability. Eleven male medical students, aged 19 to 24, were the subjects for this study.

TABLE 181. *Means and Standard Deviations for Four Physiological Functions under Basal Conditions**

Sub-ject	Basal calories per hour		Basal basal rate, percent-age Dubois		Systolic blood pressure, milli-meters of mercury		Respiration per minute		Pulse per minute	
	Mean	SD	Mean	SD	Mean	SD	Mean	SD	Mean	SD
1	75.8	4.15	104.1	5.70	110.4	6.93	17.6	2.82	70.1	5.53
2	72.5	3.95	100.2	5.45	113.4	5.06	10.8	1.50	64.7	2.57
3	61.5	3.28	94.2	5.05	99.5	4.28	15.6	0.93	68.8	4.30
4	62.4	3.84	89.4	5.50	103.6	6.78	7.2	1.33	53.8	4.31
5	74.9	3.56	94.5	4.50	104.8	4.77	9.2	1.68	65.2	3.43
6	73.7	4.45	97.4	5.80	108.9	3.57	10.1	2.69	65.3	4.95
7	69.0	3.59	102.6	5.35	103.2	4.34	14.5	2.23	64.1	4.64
8	61.0	4.49	96.3	7.10	96.8	6.07	10.0	1.40	58.2	2.80
9	64.0	5.46	90.8	7.75	96.2	3.74	8.7	1.84	52.8	3.39
10	70.2	3.16	96.6	4.35	116.4	5.31	12.1	1.03	53.3	4.44
11	61.9	3.35	90.5	4.90	102.8	3.83	10.1	.91	50.7	2.94

* From McNemar, Q. and Merrill, M. A. (Eds.) *Studies in Personality.* New York: McGraw-Hill Book Company, Inc., 1942.

Table 181 shows the means and the standard deviations of the distributions for 45 daily observations (secured over a period of ninety days) of the physiological functions for the 11 subjects of the experiment. These data are of particular interest because of Herrington's claim that they are the most accurate determinations of these functions ever reported.

Herrington claims that there are at least two contributory causes of the variability in these physiological measures. The first is due to error and to uncontrolled factors, and our only interest in these is to eliminate them as far as possible. Over and above the portion of the variability due to error and to uncontrolled factors, however, Herrington believes that there is a proportion that is "basically biological and is a reflection of the delicacy with which a given function is regulated." This being the case, it becomes important, says Herrington, to determine the relationship between the mean intensity of a physiological function and its variability, this latter being "heavily weighted with intraorganic factors of homeostatic significance." The correlations which Herrington reports are given in Table 182. The standard errors are large, so Herrington is forced to conclude that there has been demonstrated no significant relation

TABLE 182. *Intercorrelations between the Means and Standard Deviations for Each of Four Physiological Functions**

Function	r	σ_r
Basal metabolic rate.............	.10	.30
Systolic blood pressure..........	.13	.30
Respiration rate................	.30	.27
Pulse rate.....................	.42	.25

* From McNemar, Q., and Merrill, M. A. (Eds.) *Studies in Personality.* New York: McGraw-Hill Book Company, Inc., 1942.

between the variability and intensity of these four physiological functions. He goes further. He concludes that variability is sufficiently independent of mean intensity to constitute, itself, some measure of a "general factor of intraorganic control." This being the case, he considers each of the four standard deviations as but an estimate of this general factor and combines them, giving equal weight to each, into a composite index of this general factor. Now our question is "Does this index have utility as a predictor of general activity?"

To get the answer to this question, Herrington had each of the 11 subjects rated on activity by three raters. One rater was a junior member of the laboratory staff, one was a faculty member who had all the students in class and in laboratory, and a third rater was a student in the medical class concerned. Each of these raters was provided with the following instructions:

In the course of the next 90 days please observe the following 11 men for the purpose of rating them individually on general activity and drive. We cannot define this trait precisely but you are asked to consider (1) physical vigor as suggested by athletic pursuits, speed of movement, and typical postures at work or when idle, (2) excitable speech and pressure for expression in group situations, (3) energy and enthusiasm in meeting class work requirements. At the end of the period each man will be compared with every other member of the group, in turn, and judged as *more* or *less* active in terms *of the general* impression you gain from considering at frequent intervals the criteria listed above. Since the period of observation will be relatively long, it is probable that you will often see all or several of these men together, in class, gymnasium, laboratory, lunch room, or at social gatherings. We believe the final judgment will be improved if you make trial ratings in these face-to-face situations without preserving the results.

The composite activity ratings resulting from these instructions were found to correlate with the physiological measure of control to the extent of .51. This indicates, according to Herrington, "that the rated activity and objective measures of physiological variability are related to some degree." The activity ratings are more highly related to the mean intensity levels, however, as the data in Table 183 demonstrate.

TABLE 183. *The Relation of Activity to 4 Physiological Functions**

Physiological function	Activity	Pulse	Respiration	Systolic blood pressure
Variability:				
Pulse.....................	.33			
Respiration................	.39	.57		
Systolic blood pressure.......	.56	.23	.05	
Basal metabolic rate..........	− .08	− .19	.26	− .02
Intensity level:				
Pulse.....................	.81			
Respiration................	.44	.66		
Systolic blood pressure.......	.24	.23	.20	
Basal metabolic rate..........	.45	.73	.75	.49

* From McNemar, Q., and Merrill, M. A. (Eds.) *Studies in Personality*. New York: McGraw-Hill Book Company, Inc., 1942.

In relation to activity, from the standpoint of physiological variability, systolic blood pressure appears to be most predictive, and from the standpoint of mean intensity level, pulse rate appears to be most predictive. The first, that is, systolic blood pressure, correlates with activity level to the extent of .56; while the second, that is, pulse rate, correlates with activity to the extent of .81. The two physiological measures, systolic blood pressure (variability) and pulse rate (intensity), correlate with each other in the neighborhood of .10, so when combined, they produce a multiple correlation with rated activity of .91. If this correlation is accepted as valid, it indicates, according to Herrington

. . . that the popular impression of activity in the individual is very closely related to the balance of autonomic influences acting through the vagus and cardiac accelerator nerves upon resting cardiac rates and to the lability of blood pressure control, which, in turn, not only is affected by the above mentioned factors, but also reflects the general action of the vasomotor centers of the circulation.

It seems clear from Herrington's data that there is a fundamental relation between activity and certain physiological functions. We can best summarize the significance of Herrington's study by quoting his own conclusions.

Pressure of activity, in a broad psychosomatic sense, is an important aspect of personality. In groups in which variations in intelligence and educational background are controlled, it is possible to evaluate the trait by rating methods in a manner that yields considerable objective evidence of validity. A partial physiological background for the trait is strongly suggested by the association between it and several characteristics of circulatory regulation. There is no reason to believe that this association is a direct one. It appears more probable that the physiological signs appearing as correlates are superficial indicators of much more general properties of the autonomic nervous system.

SEARS

We turn now to a consideration of an experiment conducted by Robert R. Sears. This experiment had as its chief purpose the determination of the effect of success and failure on motility or activity. This motility or activity is measured in a different way, however, than it was in Herrington's study.

As soon as a subject arrived at the laboratory, he was met by Dr. Sears or by an assistant and was conducted to an experimental room. If he was met by Dr. Sears, Dr. Sears said he was not quite ready. If he was met by Dr. Sears's assistant, the assistant told the subject that Dr. Sears was not quite ready or was a little late but would be available shortly. The subject was then left alone for six minutes, but his behavior during this six-minute period was carefully observed. The observer, behind a one-way vision screen and wearing a pair of earphones that gave a click every five seconds, made 70 observations. These observations consisted of notes on the degree and direction of the activity of the subject. Three levels of activity were distinguished: apparently autistic thinking, standing or sitting without focus of attention on either the body or the environment, daydreaming, orientation toward objects in the environment perceptually but without actual manipulation of anything, and overt movement such as walking, manipulation of the environment, object-directed behavior.

The reliability of the observations, as measured by agreement between two observers, was quite high. The experiment proper was not conducted until the observers had had sufficient practice, and were found to disagree with each other on no more than 3 of the 70 judgments in the various observation periods.

Upon the basis of the activity or motility ratings secured in the preliminary observation period, the 24 subjects were divided into two equated groups of 12 subjects each. The members of one of these groups were then put through a card-sorting test in which they experienced success, and the members of the other group were put through the same card-sorting test but conditions were so arranged that they experienced failure. Subsequent to these experiences, that is, success or failure, the groups were again observed on motility.

Immediately following the preobservational period the subjects were asked to participate in a card-sorting experiment. After the first or second trial the attention of the subject was drawn to a large chart on the wall, purporting to give the results for some Ohio high-school students. The chart was purely fictitious but was designed so that anyone in the experimental group paying close attention to it and comparing the scores on it with his own true scores could not help but consider himself a failure. To create a feeling of success the second group of subjects were given fictitious time scores. These scores showed the subject that he was superior to about 85 per cent of the Ohio high-school students.

Following the card sorting a six-minute observation period was allowed, and then a second experiment, irrelevant to this report, was performed. On the second day the subject was again asked to sort cards and was again made to experience success or failure. A six-minute observation period followed. Following this a task in which the subject was made to feel successful was given, and then there was a final six-minute observation period.

To make it seem plausible to the subject that there should be so many periods (four altogether) during which the experimenter could not be in the room, various excuses were offered. For the first period it was that Dr. Sears was a little late or that he was not quite ready. For the second period he had to leave the room to get some material for the next part of the experiment. For the third period Dr. Sears received a long-distance telephone call, and for the last period he had to go to the cashier to get money to pay the subject.

The data show a clear-cut change in autism as a result of the experience of success or failure. In the preliminary observation period, the success group exhibited this kind of behavior with greater frequency than did the failure group, but on the two experimental days, the relation was clearly reversed, and there is no question of the significance of the difference.

In choice of activity there was also found to be a significant difference between the success and failure groups. In the preliminary period, the success group paid more frequent attention to the cards, but after success or failure had been experienced, it was the failure group that paid more frequent attention to the cards. Sears points out that this "card oriented activity was a variety of persistent non-adjustive behavior that almost guaranteed a perpetuation of the feelings of failure."

The success and failure groups also differed from each other in the amount of time they spent looking at the Ohio chart and in the number of times they forgot to give an estimate for their scores on the next succeeding trial in the card-sorting experiment. The success group looked at the chart more frequently, and the failure group forgot to give their estimates more frequently. Sears points out that both these phenomena are in line with Thorndike's law of effect. Success has stamped *in* an activity (that of looking at the chart) and failure has tended to stamp *out* an activity (that of giving an estimate as to the next succeeding score). Sears concludes:

These data reveal three characteristics of the reactions to failure that are deserving of further consideration. First, although there was no evidence of a decrease in object-manipulative activity, the general motility level was less for the failure than for the success subjects. The frequency of day-dreaming and autistic thinking was sharply increased, and the social responsiveness was reduced. These changes inevitably serve to modify the effectiveness of a person's relation to his environment. He is less sensitive to changes, less likely to perceive new instigators. He is not so adjustive or so modifiable as he would be if the failure had not occurred. All this reduces the possibility of his having new experiences or of initiating new ways of behaving. He avoids his environment.

Second, in direct relation to this, failure leads to a dogged but ineffectual continuation of the task at which failure occurred. What interaction with the environment there is is in the direction of the old activity. But the old activity is half avoided, the card sorting is unfinished in order to avoid the danger of failing; this effectively precludes success, and therefore the person fails anyway. This persistent nonadjusting behavior . . . necessarily prevents the development of adjustive responses. There is no seeking for new tasks or new methods to circumvent the failure. Worse, this failure-induced behavior alienates the environment. Nonresponsive persons are neither pleasant companions nor cooperative instruments in activities that require mutual assistance. . . .

Finally, the process of decontextualization that failure subjects exhibits serves in still another way to reduce their adjust-effectiveness. This process splits off the activity from its social frame of reference, reduces its contact with reality, and hence decreases the opportunities for the person to check up on the task's importance by reference to reality. In a sense, decontextualization as a response to failure might be said to reduce the influence of the reality principle, to make reality testing more difficult.

We have now demonstrated through our accounts of the experiments conducted by Eysenck, Barker, Herrington, and Sears that the measurement of personality variables can be attacked through experimental means. The treatments involved are much more time-consuming and expensive than most of the other techniques we have discussed. But they are, of course, much more subject to control. In our present state of knowledge, we are forced to pay a high price either way we turn. If we want quick and easy techniques of personality measurement, we find that we pay heavily in our loss of control over the situation in which the subject's responses are to be made. But when we set up situations so as not to lose this control, we find our techniques so cumbersome, expensive, and time-consuming that we can apply them, at best, only to a few individuals. It is to be hoped that whatever direction personality testing may eventually take, the techniques will possess both maneuverability and control. In fact, personality testing must proceed in this direction if we are ever to realize the values which we assume such measurements to possess.

16

EVALUATION AND SUMMARY

We have by no means exhausted the field of personality measurement. But the methods we have treated are important and should be thoroughly understood. Once they are understood, the basic principles can be applied to the understanding of any personality test now in existence.

There has been a tendency among the writers of textbooks on personality to try to give some comment on a great variety of personality tests. The theory is that the student must know the stock available—take inventory, so to speak—before he can delve very deeply into any one of them. The reader has discovered that the treatment in this volume has followed a different pattern. We have concerned ourselves with only a few tests and have tried to go into their development in some detail. We have done this so the reader can gain some fundamental insight into the methodology of personality-test construction—an insight that he cannot get from a "cookbook" coverage of the subject. This treatment has enabled us to discover that there are only a few basic techniques involved in all personality-test construction and that superficialities, for the most part, are what give rise to the multitudinous supply of personality tests commercially available.

If a student will take the trouble to digest the contents of this text in a thoroughgoing manner, he will secure an appreciation of some of the traditional or classical types of test that current emphasis in the field fails to give. Whether the fault lies in the instructor or student the author does not pretend to know. But he is continually appalled at the lack of knowledge on the part of many otherwise competent psychologists of some of the basic methodologies which have been employed in personality-test construction.

In our treatment of the subject we have, perhaps, been overneat in the suggestion of a basic dichotomy within each of the areas we have chosen to discuss. Our treatment seems to indicate that there are just two opposing methods of measuring attitudes, that there are just two opposing methods of measuring interests, that there are just two opposing methods of measuring adjustment, and so on. This suggests a pattern which does not in fact exist. There are multiple methods of measurement in each of the areas with which we concerned ourselves. But we selected, in each instance, two methods to point up some important contrast, to highlight different emphases, to illustrate diverging principles, and so forth. It was our feeling that such contrasts would add interest to our story and would help the student fix more clearly in his mind the fundamental methodologies involved.

METHODS OF MEASUREMENT

Let us attempt a review of these methodologies and see if we can arrive at some evaluation of their relative degrees of effectiveness in contributing to our better description, control, and prediction of human behavior. First, let us make a list of the methodologies we have discussed. They are as follows:

An empirical approach	A rational approach
An a priori approach	An a posteriori approach
A unidimensional approach	A multidimensional approach
A diagnostic approach	A prognostic approach
A nonanalytical approach	An analytical approach
A perceptual approach	An imaginal approach
An observational approach	An experimental approach

This list shows that we have studied 14 methods of personality measurement. This seems like a sizable number—and it is—but let this fact not blind us to the equally important fact that there are other methods of measurement (interviewing, for example) that we did not treat in this volume. Now let us fix clearly in our minds the basic idea in each of the 14 methods of personality measurement we have studied.

Empirical Approach. An empirical approach is one which makes use of the data derived from experience. In some way the uniformities or dissimilarities derived from experience are harnessed for use in the derivation of implications relative to personality structure. The positive advantage of the method is that the implications are embedded in a solid structure of fact. Therefore, the method works. This does not mean that our predictions can be 100 per cent accurate or that our understanding is complete. The example we chose to illustrate this method was the Strong Vocational Interest Test. This does not mean that other methods of personality measurement are not also empirical. But we can safely say that the Strong Vocational Interest Test is the outstanding example of such an approach. Our discussion of the development of the Strong Vocational Interest Test makes it apparent that the empirical approach is a long, laborious, and tedious one. But the practical value which thousands of students have derived from it shows that the method pays handsome dividends.

Rational Approach. A rational approach is one which starts with theory and proceeds toward a predetermined objective without reference to experience or to data derived from it. The purpose is to be able to follow out systematically some particular line of reasoning to see if this particular line of reasoning will lead to productive results so far as the measurement of personality is concerned. A final test of the method can come only by reference to empirical data, but during the course of test construction, theory serves as the basic and, perhaps, only guide. Our example of this method was found in the Kuder Preference Records. Kuder's objective was to develop several scales of measurement that would operate independently of each other. This on the theory that a relatively small number of such scales would suffice to tap all the major subareas of the general area in which he, Kuder, was interested. The purpose of pursuing such a rational objective lies in the supposition that the goal, once accomplished, would make for a much more economical technique of measurement. It might not be more economical in time but would be more economical in the light of the presumed fact that more useful information, and a greater amount of it, would be secured.

We saw in Chap. 3 that the attainment of a rational objective, even though explicitly set forth, is not necessarily an easy matter. Kuder did not find it easy to develop his independent scales. But these difficulties, while wearying, exasperating, and perhaps heartbreaking, are not fundamentally important. They are mere impedimenta along the road we choose to travel. Of great importance in the rational approach, however, is the fact that the attainment of our original objective tells us very little about the value of the method as an aid to us in describing, understanding, predicting, and controlling human behavior. We have this to learn after we have accomplished our rational objective. Thus Kuder had to secure occupational data subsequent to the development of his Preference Records to show that the information they provide is useful in vocational guidance. In the empirical approach used by Strong this final step was not necessary because the securing of such data was propaedeutic to the development of the scales. Ergo, it was available when they were complete. Kuder would argue, as we pointed out in Chap. 3, that once the occupational data for his scales are as complete as those for the Strong Vocational Interest Test, his Preference Records will provide a more effective coverage of the areas involved. We cannot properly pass judgment on this contention at present, however, because the occupational data provided by Kuder are far less complete and clear-cut than those provided by Strong for his Vocational Interest Test.

A Priori Approach. An a priori approach is one in which the measuring scale is prepared in advance and is completely ready before it is given to the group or groups which the investigator is primarily interested in studying. Their responses have played no part in the basic construction of the scale. This allows the measuring technique to transcend the particular group under study and gives it a type of universal applicability. For this reason, it possesses a certain degree of utility not found in certain contrasting techniques. It possesses inherent disadvantages, however, as well as advantages. One of the major disadvantages is that the scale-construction process, being divorced from the groups to be studied, may not be found appropriate. The continuum involved may be too long or too short or misplaced. The words in such a scale may be too difficult or too easy, and so forth. Another disadvantage is the requirement that the scale be built ahead of the time it is to be used, and if the variable under consideration is a transitory affair, such as our attitude toward the North Koreans on such and such a date, we may not have our scale ready in time to use it.

In general, however, the advantages of this technique have more than outweighed the disadvantages, so the method has had widespread use. Among the advantages that give the method its popularity and utility are the standardized stimulus situations that can be set up, the uniform scoring standards, and the objective nature of the comparisons it makes possible.

A Posteriori Approach. An a posteriori approach is one in which the measuring scale is prepared after the responses to the group to be studied have been secured. It is in fact directly dependent upon these responses. This gives the method the unique advantage of being adaptable to the group being measured. It cannot help but be appropriate since it is designed upon the basis of the data that the group itself supplied. But this same advantage leads to the method's principal disadvantage: that the scale must be developed anew for each group measured. And when this is necessary, we have no assurance that we can maintain a proper degree of comparability among, or the same standards for, these different groups.

This technique is advantageous, however, when we do not have time to follow through on a thoroughgoing a priori approach. To hark back to our previous example of attitude toward the North Koreans on such and such a date, the a posteriori approach is about the only one that can be readied in time to meet the situation.

Unidimensional Approach. A unidimensional approach is one that provides an index that can vary back and forth on just one linear variable. All it shows, therefore, is more or less of whatever variable is being measured. The primary advantage of the method is the clear understanding on our part of just what it is we are measuring. This advantage accrues, however, only when we have succeeded in confining our measurement to the intended linear variable. Frequently we fool ourselves into thinking we have this when in reality we have not. But on the assumption that we can achieve or approximate the ideal under consideration, we can predict more precisely any of the concomitant behavior variables tapped by, or related to, our one linear measure. We can determine its precise importance in contrast to that of other linear measures related to the same concomitant variables.

The examples we gave in Chap. 6 are not ideal examples for a demonstration of a unidimensional approach. The tests discussed were designed by their authors, however, with the unidimensional approach in mind, so the methodologies of test construction which they followed show some of the ways in which psychologists have tried to develop unidimensional personality-measuring instruments.

One of the major disadvantages of the unidimensional approach is the paucity of information it provides. All we get is one score, one rating, or one grade. This one datum may be of the utmost importance, but we have no difficulty in thinking of other data which, if we had them, would be of equal and, perhaps, of even greater importance. Therefore, even if we had a perfect unidimensional index of every important personality trait, it is conceivable that it would take us so long to get the information we needed for each subject that our measuring techniques would not serve any particularly practical purpose.

We shall undoubtedly continue to attempt the derivation of unidimensional methods of personality measurement for some time to come, however, for there still is no agreed-upon list of personality traits important for the basic understanding of human behavior. This means that the field is wide-open for an attempt on the measurement of any of the innumerable aspects of personality. Only when many more attempts have been made shall we be able to begin a synthesis to give some basic structure which all psychologists can rely upon as a foundation for the understanding of human personality.

Multidimensional Approach. A multidimensional approach to the measurement of personality can imply any one of several things. It can mean the simultaneous use of two or more of the unidimensional approaches to the measurement of personality. We can measure, let us say, several different attitudes by means of the simultaneous application of several of the Thurstone attitude scales. Or we can measure several different personality traits by the simultaneous application of several of the tests we discussed in our chapter on unidimensional approaches to the measurement of personality. Or a multidimensional approach can indicate an approach such as that exemplified in the Guilford-Martin Inventories, namely, the simultaneous measurement of independent traits. This variation of the approach requires the utilization of many more items than are needed for the measurement of any one of the traits, but the provision for measuring the individual traits could not have been made unless all the items were considered in relation to and in contrast with each other. In other words, independence of two or more traits cannot be established if all the traits involved are not measured simultaneously.

Lastly, a multidimensional approach may denote the use of one set of items scored in different ways to give rise to measures on several different personality traits. The outstanding example of this approach is, of course, the Bernreuter Personality Inventory. This variation assumes, as we pointed out in Chap. 6, that one item can have significance for more than one personality trait. This position can be granted, or we can argue that if such is apparently the case, the seemingly disparate personality traits may be one and the same variable parading under two different names. In the light of our present knowledge, there seems to be no reason to deny the assumption that an item can have differential degrees of significance for substantively different personality traits.

One of the major advantages of the multidimensional approach is its economy. It gives us data on several personality variables in just about the same amount of time as we can get data on just one unidimensional personality trait. And we presume, of course, that the greater the number of measured variables, the greater can be our understanding, prediction, and control of human behavior. This economy will vary with each particular variant of the multidimensional approach. If the multidimensional variables are independent of each other, we can cover more adequately a given segment of personality structure than if the variables show substantial intercorrelations. There is nothing sacred about uncorrelated variables, however, and there is no reason for us to suppose that human behavior or personality is such that it can best be described in terms of uncorrelated variables. Most of our measures of personality provide such gross measurements, however, that it is economical for us to utilize uncorrelated variables as a first approximation to the true nature of the personality dimensions in question. When our knowledge becomes more precise, we may find it profitable to abandon our present-day emphasis upon the economic utility of uncorrelated measures of personality.

When the multidimensional approach in question is that exemplified in the Bernreuter Personality Inventory, we run into a technical disadvantage to which too little attention has been given. This is the relation between the scoring weights and the total scores on each scale. Many investigators have gone to much trouble to determine interscale correlations by administering tests to various groups of subjects and correlating the total scores. They have done this quite unaware of the fact that these total scores are a function of the item weights and that the intercorrelation between total scores is predetermined by them. To illustrate this fact in a concrete manner, suppose we had gone through two separate item-analysis procedures and had arrived at two sets of item weights. But let us suppose that the weights in one of these sets completely duplicated those in the other set. Their intercorrelation would be 1.00. Now, would we need to give this test to new groups of subjects and get their total scores on two variables to find that the intercorrelation between them is 1.00? Obviously not! But suppose the item-weight intercorrelations were .90, .80, or .50. Do not these values also determine pretty largely the intercorrelations we shall secure between total scores? The author does not pretend to know whether the intercorrelations between the total score intercorrelation and the item-weight intercorrelation is a strictly linear one, but it does not seem unreasonable for us to assume that the relationship is pretty direct. This being the case, once we have established our item weights for our different scales, we have preestablished the intercorrelations between the total scores on these same variables. The scores on such a test cannot be used to establish anew the fundamental interrelationships involved. This fact, ignored by many investigators, calls into question much of the published interscale correlational data for tests such as the Bernreuter Personality Inventory and the Strong Vocational Interest Test. In fairness to Dr. Strong, we must point out that he has been aware of this problem and that he has presented his views on the subject in his book *Vocational Interests of Men and Women*. The reader will find it worth while to familiarize himself with Strong's treatment of this subject.

One of the difficulties in the variant of the multidimensional approach exemplified by the Guilford-Martin Inventories is that of maintaining independence between the supposedly uncorrelated variables. In a standardization group, an investigator can keep at the problem until all correlations are at or are near zero. However, when he applies his test to a new group of cases, he is very apt to find a substantial increase in the interscale correlations. This has caused some surprise, particularly when the items basic to the different variables were not in any way common to each other. These investigators have failed to realize, however, that even though the items were not the same, the subjects were. Therefore, whatever errors the subject made in answer to one set of items are undoubtedly of the same kind he made in response to the other set of items. This communality of errors, even when nothing else is involved, is sufficient to introduce substantial interscale correlations. The juggling that an experimenter does on his standardization group merely attunes his instrument to the sampling errors of that group. As soon as he applies his test to a new group, he loses this basic attunement, and with this he loses his zero intercorrelations.

With all its faults, hazards, and difficulties we can conclude that the multidimensional approach to the measurement of personality has much to offer. It gives us a deeper insight, we believe, into the basic structure of personality. And it gives us multiple landmarks by which to plot the course of human behavior. Admittedly, our plotting is not very accurate, but it is something better than chance and would appear to hold out for us somewhat more hope than the continued exclusive use of the unidimensional approach.

Diagnostic Approach. A diagnostic approach to the measurement of personality emphasizes the present. We want to know something about our subject now, and we probably want to do something about it when we get our information. A student is failing in his studies, so we give him, among other things, an adjustment inventory to see if his trouble lies in his emotional life. If we find that his study habits are above reproach and that his home adjustment is poor, we infer that lack of home adjustment may be the seat of the student's difficulty. And if our further investigation confirms this belief, we bring this to the attention of the student or, in other ways, try to do something about improving his home adjustment. We can see, therefore, that the utility of a diagnostic approach to the measurement of personality lies in the possibility that we can make immediate practical application of the results. Our predict on is that something is now in need of correction or is not now in need of correction, and our further action or lack of action follows accordingly.

No matter what our approach to the measurement of personality, we want the maximum possible degree of objectivity, reliability, and validity. But we probably need greater objectivity, greater reliability, and greater validity for the diagnostic approach than we do for any of the other approaches we have mentioned. This is because the principal use of the diagnostic approach is in its application to the individual. And for such individual application, we need more objective, more reliable, and more valid measures than when we wish to apply our implications to group behavior. The reader may object at this point and claim that we want all of our personality measures to be applicable to individuals as well as to a group. This is true, but the fact remains that all approaches except the diagnostic do have value with reference to groups as well as with reference to individuals. The diagnostic approach does not have this twofold applicability, at least not to as great an extent as the other techniques of personality measurement.

Prognostic Approach. A prognostic approach to the measurement of personality emphasizes some future outcome. We get our measure now, but our interest is in the prediction of some future event. Sometimes this future is only a little way off, but at other times it is a long way off. In either case, we are trying to get advance information. Sometimes we might wish to apply the knowledge gained so that the anticipated future course of action or the series of events can be changed, but most frequently we are merely interested in observing what happens in the future so we can assay the relative contributions of psychological and other factors to the outcomes which we observe. We chose to illustrate the prognostic approach by discussing marital-happiness prediction scales and the prediction of success in selling life insurance. These examples illustrate the importance, nay, the necessity, of a clear-cut definition and understanding of that which is to be predicted and of our deciding ahead of time how the various outcomes are to be measured. Once these problems are settled, we can proceed to the measurement of our predictors and from these derive the basis for the predictions which we desire to make.

Nonanalytical Approach. A nonanalytical approach to the measurement of personality is one which provides an index on any defined variable but which does not contain or provide any of the supporting reasons, or the particular bases, from which the index value was derived. We pointed out in Chap. 10 that such an index is frequently all we need and so can serve as a useful datum in personality measurement. But the occasions when such an approach is permissible are gradually being reduced. Therefore, over the years to come, we shall use nonanalytical methods of measurement less and less frequently.

Analytical Approach. An analytical approach to the measurement of personality is one which provides supporting reasons or makes evident the bases for the indices derived from it. Any method of measurement which requires that the indices be based upon several or upon many specific items of behavior or responses can qualify as an analytical approach to the measurement of personality. Some techniques of measurement provide more insight than others, but this is not the crucial point in this discussion. The principal objectives of the analytical approach are, of course, increases in the degrees of objectivity, reliability, and validity which characterize the resultant indices. But in addition to these, it permits an examination of the responses or items leading to the over-all indices. In this way it is thought some insight will be gained. And this insight would not have come about with the use of a nonanalytical approach. Analytical approaches, too, are usually more objective, more reliable, and more valid than nonanalytical approaches. Also, the approach permits more careful analyses designed to improve objectivity, reliability, and validity.

Perceptual Approach. A perceptual approach is one that attempts to derive implications relative to personality from our various sense perceptions. These perceptions can be visual or auditory, or they can be in any of the other sense modalities. So far, the method has been exploited only in the visual field. The theory is that the various things we see or hear may provide clues to personality structure. They do this, if they do it at all, because different individuals see different things in the same objective and external stimulus. And it is thought that the fact that our personality structures differ is one of the reasons for our seeing these different things. This approach holds much appeal because it seems possible that the personality nuances involved in differing perceptions to the same visual stimulus would not be apparent to the naïve subject. And being naïve to the nuances involved, the subject would not be able to slant his responses to achieve any desired outcome in the way he could in most of the other approaches we have discussed.

This theory can be questioned. The presumably naïve subject can read about the Rorschach Ink Blot Test just as easily as he can read something about the Terman-Miles M-F test, and as soon as he does so, he is no longer naïve with respect to the interpretation which will be put upon his responses. The naïveté comes directly from the Rorschach cult itself in its crude and shallow analogies. If the Rorschach test has merit, very little of this merit has been demonstrated. And it has not been demonstrated because most Rorschachers back away from a rigid validation procedure. The test is not amenable to such treatment, they say. But there is no reason why the implications drawn from the Rorschach responses should not be subject to the same rigid validation procedures that we require of any other technique of personality measurement.

Imaginal Approach. An imaginal approach to the measurement of personality makes use of our imaginal concepts in the same way as a perceptual approach makes use of our percepts for the derivation of insights into our personality. The chief difficulty with the method which we chose to illustrate, the Thematic Apperception Test, is its lack of objectivity. This permits or leads to low degrees of reliability and, of course, makes validation difficult. There is apparently something more to the Thematic Apperception Test than there is to the Rorschach Ink Blot Test, and we see in it considerably more sophistication than we see in the Rorschach camp. The method requires such highly and intensively trained examiners, however, that the technique is likely not to be applied widely. Of course, if we had somewhat greater demonstration of its practical utility in contrast with the utility of other methods of personality measurement, this would provide a degree of motivation for a sufficient number of psychologists to learn the technique and thus would give it more extensive application than it now enjoys. We must realize, however, that of all the techniques of measurement discussed in this volume, the validation of the Thematic Apperception Test presents the most difficult problem. It presents a difficult problem because, as we pointed out in Chap. 13, the only adequate method of validation is against the findings of a complete psychoanalysis. This takes much time, and probably no one is going to want to spend the necessary amount of time required just to provide validation data for the Thematic Apperception Test. And, of course, we might question the validity of the psychoanalytic findings also. Psychoanalysis, at best, is a highly subjective procedure and is one which permits any one of many rationalizations to appear as a plausible explanation of a person's behavior. We have had ample evidence that psychoanalysts do not agree among themselves on the implications of any given series of events or episodes of behavior.

Observational Approach. By an observational approach we mean one that utilizes performance as a basis for the derivation of inferences with respect to personality. The performance which serves as a basis for the inference is not controlled, however, or forced into any particular channel. As far as the subject is concerned, the behavior or performance is spontaneous or, at least so far as he is aware, subject to his own control. There may be forces operating upon him which will cause him to exhibit one type of performance rather than another, but these forces arise from the situation in which the performance takes place rather than from any manipulation imposed by the investigator. Thus, in Barker, Lewin, and Dembo's study, the child played in one situation or in another. The investigators did not ask the child to exhibit one type of behavior rather than another. Nor did they subject the child to any manipulation. The child was free to do what he wished. Barker, Lewin, and Dembo merely recorded what happened. We found in this study that careful observation can lead to significant inferences for personality. Those made by Barker, Lewin, and Dembo were demonstrably reliable and were presumably valid. But the technique is cumbersome for general use, and cannot readily be applied to a large number of individuals in any rigidly systematic manner. Therefore, the observational technique is one best used to test a theory, to set up a hypothesis, and so forth. It cannot be picked up and carried around like a Kuder Preference Record and applied to one or to many individuals as the situation may require. It is possible, however, that ultimately the implications derivable from carefully controlled observational approaches can be incorporated into one of the other approaches that can be applied more readily to many individuals.

Experimental Approach. The last approach we discussed in this volume was the experimental approach. This requires that the investigator set up a situation requiring the subject to go through a specified set of procedures. Then observations are made before, during, and after, and are compared with each other to give rise to inferences regarding personality. Sears's study on motility and Eysenck's studies on level of aspiration fall clearly into this category. The experimental method is undoubtedly the best approach we have discussed but, like the observational approach, is extremely limited in general applicability to a large number of individuals.

Imagine how cumbersome and time-consuming it would be, for example, to run 1,000 subjects through the procedures involved in Sears's motility study. Therefore, the experimental method, like the observational method, will continue to exhibit its greatest utility in the exploration, setting up and derivation, and testing of hypotheses. Those that seem worthy of being applied, in a measuring sense, to many individuals will have to be incorporated somehow in one of the other approaches. It is too bad that the approach having in it the best of all possible controls cannot be easily applied to many subjects. It seems, however, to represent one extreme of a continuum. For when we seek methods of wide and easy applicability to many subjects, we find almost no control in the sense implied by the experimental approach.

It is possible that we should be more patient and do a lot more work of a rigid experimental nature before we continue with some of the other approaches. But we are impatient and anxious to find ways of getting at the personalities of a lot of people, not of just a few. So we shall probably continue our varying approaches, sometimes advancing on this front and sometimes advancing on that. But we must admit we are still a long way from having in our possession the kind of personality-measuring instrument that can give us information comparable in reliability and validity to that now provided by the better mental-alertness, intelligence, and achievement tests.

PERSONALITY VARIABLES

We have discussed in this volume only seven measurement rubrics. These are interest, attitude, personality, adjustment, rating, projection, and performance. And under each of these rubrics we have examined one or more test-construction methodologies. It may seem, therefore, that our coverage of the vast complex field of personality measurement has not been very extensive. However, under these seven measurement rubrics we have discussed over 250 identifiable personality traits. So our coverage of the complex field of personality measurement has not been so limited as it might at first have seemed.

Unfortunately, the methods of measurement are not comparable to each other, so we must doubt the value of certain of the techniques while accepting the value of others. Another disturbing thing is the lack of correlation between two different instruments designed to measure the same trait. We have not commented on this to any great extent in the previous chapters, but there is abundant evidence in the literature to suggest that for a guide to the comparability of any two measures, we ought to rely more upon the technique of measurement employed than upon the trait names used to identify the scales.

The fact that we have touched upon more than 250 identifiable personality traits raises the question as to how many traits there really are. The answer to this depends upon one's point of view. If we are going to be extremely fastidious, the answer probably is an infinite number. But to give such an answer gets us nowhere. Therefore, Allport and Odbert, and more recently, Cattell, have attacked this problem and have tried to identify traits of some presumed psychological importance. We shall not discuss their studies, however, as the interested reader can go directly to them.

But no matter what the exact answer, if we have to deal with hundreds of traits to understand the human personality, we shall find our task a long, hard, and burdensome one. It is understandable, therefore, that much effort is being devoted to a search for some small and convenient number of traits of major importance which can serve as outstanding landmarks for our describing, understanding, predicting, and controlling human behavior. It may be a false hope, but the fact that we can describe any point in space in terms of only three dimensions (north-south, east-west, and up-down) gives us the model we seek in the field of personality. We shall not mind settling for 10 or 15 variables, but to have to deal with 250 or more makes the problem exceedingly complex.

The purpose of this text was to explain several of the major methodologies used in personality-test construction. If the student thoroughly understands these methodologies, he will be in a position to appreciate the differences in findings reported by different investigators. He will be able to see why certain results should be given credence and why others should be discounted. And it may be that some student, after familiarizing himself with the methodologies we have discussed, will be able to derive new methodologies and will be able to accomplish, more effectively, those objectives set forth at the beginning of this volume.

REFERENCES

It would be pointless for us to give here all references on personality measurement. Therefore, the following list is restricted to the sources found most useful in the preparation of this volume. However, a few which expand, emphasize, or disagree with some point made in the text are also included.

ADAMS, C. R. A new measure of personality. *J. appl. Psychol.*, 1941, **25**, 141–151.

ADAMS, C. R. *Manual of Directions for Using and Interpreting the Personal Audit.* Chicago: Science Research Associates, 1945. Pp. 16.

ALLPORT, G. W. A test for ascendance-submission. *J. abnorm. soc. Psychol.*, 1928, **23**, 118–136.

ALLPORT, G. W. *Personality: A Psychological Interpretation.* New York: Henry Holt and Company, Inc., 1928. Pp. 588.

ALLPORT, G. W. The neurotic personality and traits of self-expression. *J. soc. Psychol.*, 1930, **1**, 524–527.

ANASTASI, A., and FOLEY, J. P., JR. *Differential Psychology.* New York: The Macmillan Company, 1949. Pp. xv + 894.

BALL, R. J. The general emotionality of the prisoner. *J. appl. Psychol.*, 1931, **15**, 436–461.

BALLIN, M. R., and FARNSWORTH, P. R. A graphic rating method for determining the scale values of statements in measuring social attitudes. *J. soc. Psychol.*, 1941, **13**, 323–327.

BARKER, R., DEMBO, T., and LEWIN, K. Frustration and regression: An experiment with young children. *Univ. Ia. Stud. Child Welf.*, 1941, **18**, No. 1.

BELL, H. M. *The Theory and Practice of Personal Counseling.* Stanford University, Calif.: Stanford University Press, 1939. Pp. v + 167.

BELL, J. E. *Projective Techniques.* New York: Longmans, Green & Co., Inc., 1948. Pp. xvi + 533.

BERNREUTER, R. G. The measurement of self-sufficiency. *J. abnorm. soc. Psychol.*, 1933, **28**, 291–300.

BERNREUTER, R. G. The theory and construction of the personality inventory. *J. soc. Psychol.*, 1933, **4**, 387–405.

BERNREUTER, R. G. The validity of the personality inventory. *Person. J.*, 1933, **11**, 383–386.

BERNREUTER, R. G. The imbrication of tests of introversion-extroversion and neurotic tendency. *J. soc. Psychol.*, 1934, **5**, 184–201.

BEYLE, H. C. A scale for the measurement of attitude toward candidates for elective governmental office. *Amer. pol. Sci. Rev.*, 1932, **26**, 527–544.

BRAY, C. W. *Psychology and Military Efficiency.* Princeton, N. J.: Princeton University Press, 1948. Pp. xviii + 242.

Bridges, E. L. *Uttermost Part of the Earth.* New York: E. P. Dutton & Co., Inc., 1929. Pp. 558.

Broom, M. E. A critical study of a test of extroversion-introversion traits. *J. juv. Res.*, 1929, **13**, 104–123.

Broom, H. E. A study of a test of ascendance-submission. *J. appl. Psychol.*, 1939, **14**, 405–413.

Brotemarkle, R. A. What the Bernreuter Personality Inventory does not measure. *J. appl. Psychol.*, 1933, **17**, 559–563.

Burgess, E. W., and Cottrell, L. S., Jr. *Predicting Success or Failure in Marriage.* New York: Prentice-Hall, Inc., 1939. Pp. xxiii + 472.

Cady, V. M. The estimation of juvenile incorrigibility. *Juv. Delinqu. Monogr.*, 1923. No. 2.

Cantril, H., and Allport, G. W. Recent applications of the Study of Values. *J. abnorm. soc. Psychol.*, 1933, **28**, 259–273.

Carlson, H. B. Attitudes of undergraduate students. *J. soc. Psychol.*, 1934, **5**, 202–213.

Churchman, C. W., Ackoff, R. L., and Wax, M. *Measurement of Consumer Interest.* Philadelphia: University of Pennsylvania Press, 1947. Pp. vi + 214.

Cox, C. M. *The Early Mental Traits of Three Hundred Geniuses.* (Volume II of Genetic Studies of Genius, edited by Lewis M. Terman.) Stanford University, Calif.: Stanford University Press, 1926. Pp. xxiii + 842.

Darley, J. G. Changes in measured attitudes and adjustments. *J. soc. Psychol.*, 1938, **9**, 189–199.

Darley, J. G., and McNamara, W. J. Factor analysis in the establishment of new personality tests. *J. educ. Psychol.*, 1940, **31**, 321–334.

Darley, J. G., and McNamara, W. J. *Manual of Directions. Minnesota Personality Scale.* New York: The Psychological Corporation, 1941. Pp. 4.

Davis, A., and Havighurst, R. J. Social class and color differences in child rearing. *Amer. sociol. Rev.*, 1946, **11**, 698–700.

Duffy, E., and Crissy, W. J. E. Evaluative attitudes as related to vocational interests and academic achievement. *J. abnorm. soc. Psychol.*, 1940, **35**, 226–245.

Edwards, A. L., and Kenney, K. C. A comparison of the Thurstone and Likert techniques of attitude scale construction. *J. appl. Psychol.*, 1946, **30**, 72–83.

Edwards, A. L., and Kirkpatrick, F. P. A technique for the construction of attitude scales. *J. appl. Psychol.*, 1948, **32**, 374–384.

Eysenck, H. J. *Dimensions of Personality.* London: Routledge and Kegan Paul, Ltd., 1947. Pp. xi + 308.

Farnsworth, P. R. Shifts in the values of opinion items. *J. Psychol.*, 1943, **16**, 125–128.

Farnsworth, P. R. Attitude scale construction and the method of equal appearing intervals. *J. Psychol.*, 1945, **20**, 245–248.

Farnsworth, P. R. Further data on the obtaining of Thurstone scale values. *J. Psychol.*, 1945, **19**, 69–73.

Farnsworth, P. R., and Ferguson, L. W. The growth of a suicidal tendency as indicated by score changes in Bernreuter's Personality Inventory. *Sociometry*, 1938, **1**, 339–341.

FERGUSON, L. W. The influence of individual attitudes on the construction of an attitude scale. *J. soc. Psychol.*, 1935, **6**, 115–117.

FERGUSON, L. W. Primary social attitudes. *J. Psychol.*, 1939, **8**, 217–223.

FERGUSON, L. W. The evaluative attitudes of Jonathan Swift. *Psychol. Rec.*, 1939, **3**, 26–44.

FERGUSON, L. W. The measurement of primary social attitudes. *J. Psychol.*, 1940, **10**, 199–205.

FERGUSON, L. W. The stability of the primary social attitudes. I: Religionism and II: Humanitarianism. *J. Psychol.*, 1941, **12**, 283–288.

FERGUSON, L. W. A study of the Likert technique of attitude scale construction. *J. soc. Psychol.*, 1941, **13**, 51–57.

FERGUSON, L. W. The cultural genesis of masculinity-femininity. *Psychol. Bull.*, 1941, **38**, 584–585.

FERGUSON, L. W. The isolation and measurement of nationalism. *J. soc. Psychol.*, 1942, **16**, 215–228.

FERGUSON, L. W. An analysis of the generality of suggestibility to group opinion. *Character and Pers.*, 1944, **12**, 237–243.

FERGUSON, L. W. A revision of the primary social attitude scales. *J. Psychol.*, 1944, **17**, 229–241.

FERGUSON, L. W. The sociological validity of primary social attitude scale No. I: Religionism. *J. soc. Psychol.*, 1946, **23**, 197–204.

FERGUSON, L. W. The development of a method of appraisal. *Personnel*, 1947, **24**, 127–136.

FERGUSON, L. W. A brief description of a reliable criterion of job performance. *J. Psychol.*, 1948, **25**, 389–399.

FERGUSON, L. W. The value of acquaintance ratings in criterion research. *Person. Psychol.*, 1949, **2**, 93–102.

FERGUSON, L. W. The L.O.M.A. Merit Rating Scales. *Person. Psychol.*, 1950, **3**, 193–216.

FERGUSON, L. W. (Ed.) *Clerical Salary Administration*. New York: Life Office Management Association, 1948. Pp. xv + 220.

FERGUSON, L. W., HUMPHREYS, L. G., and STRONG, F. W. A factorial analysis of interests and values. *J. educ. Psychol.*, 1941, **32**, 197–204.

FERGUSON, L. W., and LAWRENCE, R. R. An appraisal of the validity of the factor loadings employed in the construction of the primary social attitude scales. *Psychometrika*, 1942, **7**, 135–138.

FLANAGAN, J. C. *Factor Analysis in the Study of Personality*. Stanford University, Calif.: Stanford University Press, 1935. Pp. x + 103.

FREEMAN, G. L. *The Energetics of Human Behavior*. Ithaca, N.Y.: Cornell University Press, 1948. Pp. vii + 344.

FREYD, M. Introverts and extroverts. *Psychol. Monogr.*, 1924, **31**, 75–87.

GUILFORD, J. P. *Psychometric Methods*. New York: McGraw-Hill Book Company, Inc., 1936. Pp. xvi + 566.

GUILFORD, J. P. *Manual of Directions*. (Rev. Ed.) *An Inventory of Factors STDCR*. Beverly Hills, Calif.: Sheridan Supply Company, undated. Pp. 2.

GUILFORD, J. P. *Manual of Directions and Norms. The Guilford-Martin Inventory of Factors GAMIN.* Beverly Hills, Calif.: Sheridan Supply Company, undated. Pp. 2.

GUILFORD, J. P. *Manual of Directions and Norms. The Guilford-Martin Personnel Inventory.* Beverly Hills, Calif.: Sheridan Supply Company, undated. Pp. 2.

GUILFORD, J. P. *Fundamental Statistics in Psychology and Education.* New York: McGraw-Hill Book Company, Inc., 1942. Pp. xi + 333.

GUILFORD, J. P., and GUILFORD, R. B. An analysis of the factors in a typical test of introversion-extroversion. *J. abnorm. soc. Psychol.,* 1934, **28,** 377–399.

GUILFORD, J. P., and GUILFORD, R. B. Personality factors S, E, and M, and their measurement. *J. Psychol.,* 1936, **2,** 109–127.

GUILFORD, J. P., and GUILFORD, R. B. Personality factors D, R, T and A. *J. abnorm. soc. Psychol.,* 1939, **34,** 21–36.

GUILFORD, J. P., and GUILFORD, R. B. Personality factors N and GD. *J. abnorm. soc. Psychol.,* 1939, **34,** 239–248.

GUTTMAN, L. The Cornell technique for scale and intensity analysis. In Churchman, C. W., Ackoff, R. L., and Wax, M. *Measurement of Consumer Interest.* Philadelphia: University of Pennsylvania Press, 1947. Pp. vi + 214.

HANNA, J. V. Clinical procedure as a method of validating a measure of psychoneurotic tendency. *J. abnorm. soc. Psychol.,* 1934, **28,** 435–445.

HARTSHORNE, H., and MAY, M. A. *Studies in Deceit.* New York: The Macmillan Company, 1928. Pp. xxi + 414.

HARVEY, O. L. Concerning the Thurstone "Personality Schedule." *J. soc. Psychol.,* 1932, **3,** 240–251.

HATHAWAY, S. R. *Supplementary Manual for the Minnesota Multiphasic Personality Inventory.* New York: The Psychological Corporation, 1946. Pp. 8.

HATHAWAY, S. R., and McKINLEY, J. C. A multiphasic personality schedule: I. Construction of the schedule. *J. Psychol.,* 1940, **10,** 249–254.

HATHAWAY, S. R., and McKINLEY, J. C. A multiphasic personality schedule: III. The measurement of symptomatic depression. *J. Psychol.,* 1942, **14,** 73–84.

HATHAWAY, S. R., and McKINLEY, J. C. *Manual for the Minnesota Multiphasic Personality Inventory.* New York: The Psychological Corporation, 1943. Pp. 16.

HERTZ, M. R. The reliability of the Rorschach ink-blot test. *J. appl. Psychol.,* 1934, **18,** 461–477.

HINCKLEY, E. D. The influence of individual opinion on construction of an attitude scale. *J. soc. Psychol.,* 1932, **3,** 283–295.

HOITSMA, R. K. The reliability and relationships of the Colgate Mental Hygiene Test. *J. appl. Psychol.,* 1925, **9,** 293–303.

HOUSE, S. D. A mental hygiene inventory. *Arch. Psychol.,* 1926, **14,** 1–112.

HULL, C. L. *Aptitude Testing.* Yonkers, N.Y.: World Book Company, 1928. Pp. 536.

HUNT, J. McV. An instance of the social origin of conflict resulting in psychoses. *Amer. J. Orthopsychiat.,* 1938, **8,** 158–164.

JOHNSON, B. Emotional instability in children. *Ungraded,* 1920, **5,** 73–79.

KINSEY, A. C., POMEROY, W. B., and MARTIN, C. E. *Sexual Behavior in the Human Male.* Philadelphia: W. B. Saunders Company, 1948. Pp. xv + 804.

KLOPFER, B., and KELLEY, D. McG. *The Rorschach Technique.* Yonkers, N.Y.: World Book Company, 1946. Pp. xv + 475.

KLUCKHOHN, C., and LEIGHTON, D. *The Navaho.* Cambridge, Mass.: Harvard University Press, 1947. Pp. xx + 258.

KLUCKHOHN, C., and MURRAY, H. A. (Eds.) *Personality in Nature, Society and Culture.* New York: Alfred A. Knopf, Inc., 1949. Pp. xxxi + 561.

KRIEDT, P. H., and CLARK, K. E. "Item analysis" versus "scale analysis." *J. appl. Psychol.*, 1949, **33**, 114–121.

KUDER, G. F. *Revised Manual for the Kuder Preference Record.* Chicago: Science Reserve Associates, 1946. Pp. 31.

KUDER, G. F. *Examiner Manual for the Kuder Preference Record—Personal.* Chicago: Science Reserve Associates, 1948. Pp. 4.

KURTZ, A. K. *How Well Does the Aptitude Index Work?* Hartford, Conn.: Life Insurance Agency Management Association, 1941. Pp. 74.

KURTZ, A. K. A research test of the Rorschach test. *Person. Psychol.*, 1948, **1**, 41–51.

LAIRD, D. A. Detecting abnormal behavior. *J. abnorm. soc. Psychol.*, 1925, **20**, 128–141.

LANDIS, C. *Sex in Development.* New York: Paul B. Hoeber, Inc., 1940. Pp. xx + 329.

LANDIS, C., and KATZ, S. E. The validity of certain questions which purport to measure neurotic tendencies. *J. appl. Psychol.*, 1934, **18**, 343–356.

LEIGHTON, A. H. *Human Relations in a Changing World.* New York: E. P. Dutton & Co., Inc., 1949. Pp. 354.

LEIGHTON, D., and KLUCKHOHN, C. *Children of the People.* Cambridge, Mass.: Harvard University Press, 1947. Pp. xvi + 277.

LEVY, D. M. Psychosomatic studies of some aspects of maternal behavior. *Psychosom. Med.*, 1942, **4**, 223–227.

LIKERT, R. A technique for the measurement of attitudes. *Arch. Psychol.*, 1932. No. 140. Pp. 55.

LIKERT, R., ROSLOW, S., and MURPHY, G. A simple and reliable method of scoring the Thurstone attitude scales. *J. soc. Psychol.*, 1934, **5**, 228–238.

LORGE, I. The Thurstone attitude scales: I. Reliability and consistency of rejection and acceptance. *J. soc. Psychol.*, 1939, **10**, 187–198.

LOVELL, C. A study of the factor structure of thirteen personality variables. *Educ. psychol. Measmt.*, 1945, **5**, 335–350.

MARRIOTT, A. *Maria: The Potter of San Ildefonso.* Norman, Okla.: University of Oklahoma Press, 1948. Pp. xxi + 294.

MARTIN, H. G. Locating the troublemaker with the Guilford-Martin Personnel Inventory. *J. appl. Psychol.*, 1944, **28**, 461–467.

MARTIN, H. G. The construction of the Guilford-Martin Inventory of Factors GAMIN. *J. appl. Psychol.*, 1945, **29**, 298–300.

MATHEWS, E. A study of emotional stability in children. *J. Delinqu.*, 1923, **8**, No. 1.

McKINLEY, J. C., and HATHAWAY, S. R. A multiphasic personality schedule: II. A differential study of hypochondriasis. *J. Psychol.*, 1940, **10**, 255–268.

McKINLEY, J. C., and HATHAWAY, S. R. A multiphasic personality schedule: IV. Psychasthenia. *J. appl. Psychol.*, 1942, **26**, 614–624.

McKINLEY, J. C., and HATHAWAY, S. R. The MMPI: V. Hysteria, hypomania, and psychopathic deviate. *J. appl. Psychol.*, 1944, **28**, 153–174.

McNemar, Q. *Psychological Statistics*. New York: John Wiley & Sons, Inc., 1949. Pp. vii + 364.

McNemar, Q., and Merrill, M. A. (Eds.) *Studies in Personality*. New York: McGraw-Hill Book Company, Inc., 1942. Pp. x + 333.

Mead, M. (Ed.) *Cooperation and Competition among Primitive Peoples*. New York: McGraw-Hill Book Company, Inc., 1937. Pp. xii + 531.

Meehl, P. E., and Hathaway, S. R. The K factor as a suppressor variable in the Minnesota Multiphasic Personality Inventory. *J. appl. Psychol.*, 1946, **30**, 525–564.

Merrill, M. A. *Problems of Child Delinquency*. Boston: Houghton Mifflin Company, 1947. Pp. xxiii + 403.

Moore, H., and Steele, I. Personality tests. *J. abnorm. soc. Psychol.*, 1934, **29**, 45–52.

Mosier, C. I. A factor analysis of certain neurotic tendencies. *Psychometrika*, 1937, **2**, 263–287.

Mosier, C. I. On the validity of neurotic questionnaires. *J. soc. Psychol.*, 1938, **9**, 3–16.

Mosier, M. F., and Kuder, G. F. Personal preference differences among occupational groups. *J. appl. Psychol.*, 1949, **33**, 231–239.

Murphy, G. *Personality*. New York: Harper & Brothers, 1947. Pp. xii + 999.

Murray, H. A. *Thematic Apperception Test Manual*. Cambridge, Mass.: Harvard University Press, 1943. Pp. 20.

Neprash, J. A. The reliability of questions in the Thurstone Personality Schedule. *J. soc. Psychol.*, 1936, **2**, 239–244.

OSS Assessment Staff. *Assessment of Men*. New York: Rinehart & Company, Inc., 1948. Pp. xv + 541.

Oliver, R. A. C. The traits of extroverts and introverts. *J. soc. Psychol.*, 1930, **1**, 345–366.

Papurt, M. J. A study of the Woodworth psychoneurotic inventory with suggested revision. *J. abnorm. soc. Psychol.*, 1930, **25**, 335–352.

Pintner, R., and Forlano, G. The influence of attitude upon scaling of attitude items. *J. soc. Psychol.*, 1937, **8**, 39–43.

Remmers, H. H. (Ed.) *Studies in Higher Education XXVI. Studies in Attitudes*. Lafayette, Ind.: Purdue University, 1934. Pp. 112.

Remmers, H. H. (Ed.) *Studies in Higher Education XXXI. Further Studies in Attitudes, Series II*. Lafayette, Ind.: Purdue University, 1936. Pp. 298.

Remmers, H. H. (Ed.) *Studies in Higher Education XXXIV. Further Studies in Attitudes, Series III*. Lafayette, Ind.: Purdue University, 1938. Pp. 151.

Rundquist, E. A., and Sletto, R. F. *Personality in the Depression*. Minneapolis: University of Minnesota Press, 1936. Pp. xxii + 398.

Sarbin, T. R., and Berdie, R. F. Relation of measured interests to the Allport-Vernon Study of Values. *J. appl. Psychol.*, 1940, **24**, 287–296.

Schaefer, B. R. The validity and utility of the Allport-Vernon Study of Values test. *J. abnorm. soc. Psychol.*, 1936, **30**, 419–422.

Schultz, R. S., and Roslow, S. Restandardization of the A-S Reaction Study as a personnel form. *J. appl. Psychol.*, 1938, **22**, 554–557.

SEASHORE, R. H., and HEVNER, K. A time saving device for the construction of attitude scales. *J. soc. Psychol.*, 1933, **4**, 366–372.

SIMPSON, R. M. A psychoneurotic inventory of penitentiary inmates. *J. soc. Psychol.*, 1934, **5**, 56–64.

SISSON, E. D. Forced choice—the new Army rating. *Person. Psychol.*, 1948, **1**, 365–381.

SMITH, H. N. A study of the neurotic tendencies shown in dementia praecox and manic depressive insanity. *J. soc. Psychol.*, 1933, **4**, 116–128.

SPRANGER, E. *Types of Men (Lebensformen)* Halle: Niemeyer, 1928. Pp. 402.

STAGNER, R. The intercorrelations of some standardized personality tests. *J. appl. Psychol.*, 1932, **16**, 453–464.

STAGNER, R. Validity and reliability of the Bernreuter Personality Inventory. *J. abnorm. soc. Psychol.*, 1934, **28**, 413–418.

STAGNER, R. *Psychology of Personality*. (Rev. Ed.) New York: McGraw-Hill Book Company, 1948. Pp. xiii + 485.

STONE, C. L. The personality factor in vocational guidance. *J. abnorm. soc. Psychol.*, 1933, **28**, 274–275.

STRONG, E. K., JR. *Vocational Interests of Men and Women*. Stanford University, Calif.: Stanford University Press, 1943. Pp. xxix + 746.

SYMONDS, P. M. *Diagnosing Personality and Conduct*. New York: Appleton-Century-Crofts, Inc., 1931. Pp. xvi + 602.

TERMAN, L. M. *Psychological Factors in Marital Happiness*. New York: McGraw-Hill Book Company, Inc., 1938. Pp. xiv + 474.

TERMAN, L. M., and MILES, C. C. *Sex and Personality*. New York: McGraw-Hill Book Company, Inc., 1936. Pp. xi + 600.

THOMSON, G. H. *The Factorial Analysis of Human Ability*. Boston: Houghton Mifflin Company, 1939. Pp. xv + 326.

THURSTONE, L. L. The method of paired comparisons for social values. *J. abnorm. soc. Psychol.*, 1927, **21**, 384–400.

THURSTONE, L. L. Equally often noticed differences. *J. educ. Psychol.*, 1927, **18**, 289–293.

THURSTONE, L. L. A law of comparative judgment. *Psychol. Rev.*, 1927, **34**, 273–286.

THURSTONE, L. L. An experimental study of nationality preferences. *J. gen. Psychol.*, 1928, **1**, 405–424.

THURSTONE, L. L. The measurement of social attitudes. *J. abnorm. soc. Psychol.*, 1931, **26**, 249–269.

THURSTONE, L. L. The vectors of mind. *Psychol. Rev.*, 1934, **41**, 1–32.

THURSTONE, L. L. *Multiple-Factor Analysis*. Chicago: University of Chicago Press, 1947. Pp. xix + 535.

THURSTONE, L. L., and CHAVE, E. J. *The Measurement of Attitude*. Chicago: University of Chicago Press, 1929. Pp. xii + 97.

THURSTONE, L. L., and THURSTONE, T. G. A neurotic inventory. *J. soc. Psychol.*, 1930, **1**, 3–30.

TOMKINS, S. S. *The Thematic Apperception Test*. New York: Grune & Stratton, Inc., 1947. Pp. xi + 297.

UHRBROCK, R. S. Attitudes of 4430 employees. *J. soc. Psychol.*, 1934, **5**, 365–377.

Vernon, P. E., and Allport, G. W. A test for personal values. *J. abnorm. soc. Psychol.*, 1931, **26**, 231–248.

Wang, C. K. A. The internal consistency of the Allports' Ascendance-Submission test. *J. abnorm. soc. Psychol.*, 1931, **26**, 154–161.

Wang, C. K. A. Suggested criteria for writing attitude statements. *J. soc. Psychol.*, 1932, **3**, 367–373.

Whitely, P. L. A study of the Allport-Vernon test for personal values. *J. abnorm. soc. Psychol.*, 1933, **28**, 6–13.

Whitman, R. H. A short scale for measuring introversion-extroversion. *J. appl. Psychol.*, 1929, **13**, 499–504

Williams, H. M., Kephart, N. C., and Houtchens, H. M. The reliability of the psychoneurotic inventory with delinquent boys. *J. abnorm. soc. Psychol.*, 1936, **31**, 271–275.

Williamson, E. G., and Darley, J. G. The measurement of social attitudes of college students: I. Standardization of tests and results of a survey. *J. soc. Psychol.*, 1937, **8**, 219–229.

Williamson, E. G., and Darley, J. G. The measurement of social attitudes of college students: II. Validation of two attitude tests. *J. soc. Psychol.*, 1937, **8**, 231–242.

Willoughby, R. R. Some properties of the Thurstone Personality Schedule and a suggested revision. *J. soc. Psychol.*, 1932, **3**, 401–424.

Woodworth, R. S. Personal data sheet. In Franz, S. I. *Handbook of Mental Examination Method*. New York: The Macmillan Company, 1920. Pp. 170.

INDEX

A

Ability and interest, 31–32
Academic success, 53–54
  predicted from occupational scales, 53
  and Rorschach test responses, 352–353
Accountants differentiated from other groups, 63
Achievement level, 400–404
Activity, autonomic, 397
  general, 200
Activity drive, 207
Activity level, 410–417
Activity ratings, 410–417
Adams, C. R., 184–191
Adjustment, diagnostic approaches to, 227–243
  general, measurement of, 349–350
  marital (*see* Marital adjustment)
  prognostic approaches to, 244–287
  and Rorschach test responses, 349–350, 352–355
  social, measurement of, 192–198, 228–233
Adjustment inventory, 228–233
  content of, 229
  criterion groups for, 231–233
  development of, 229–230
  item analysis of, 230
  mean scores of students on, 233
  number of items in, 230
  and other personality tests, 232
  reliability of, 231
  scoring of, 230
  traits measured by, 230
  validity of, 231–233

Affective discrepancy, measurement of, 401
Age, and intercourse, 275
  and interest, 42–43
  and interest maturity, 42–43
  and marital happiness, 268
  and masculinity-femininity, 46
  and psychosexual development, 297–302
  and success, 358
Agreeableness, measurement of, 199–200, 208–209
Allison Division of General Motors, rating scale used by, 289
Allport, F. H., 153–156
Allport, G. W., 15, 153–156, 212–217
Allport-Vernon Study of Values (*see* Study of Values)
Ambiguity, criterion of, 96
Analysis, statistical, 26–27
Aptitude and interest, 31–32
Aptitude Index, 8, 280–286
  development of, 283–285
  scoring of, 284
  validity of, 285–286
Architect interest scale, norms for, 36
Artists differentiated from other groups, 62
Ascendance-submission (A-S), 153–156, 173–178, 200, 207–208
A-S Reaction Study, 153–156
  development of, 154–155
  directions for, 154
  rating of subjects for, 154–155
  reliability of, 155
  validity of, 155–156
Aspiration level, measurement of, 400–404
Assessment procedures, 378–384
Attainment discrepancy score, 401